Intelligence and Cognition: Contemporary Frames of Reference

edited by:

Sidney H. Irvine
Stephen E. Newstead

Plymouth Polytechnic
Plymouth
Devon
U.K.

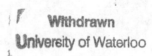

1987 **Martinus Nijhoff Publishers**
Dordrecht / Boston / Lancaster
Published in cooperation with NATO Scientific Affairs Division

Post-Conference Proceedings of the NATO Advanced Study Institute on "Human Assessment: Cognition and Motivation", Athens, Greece, December 10–24, 1984

Library of Congress Cataloging in Publication Data

NATO Advanced Study Institute on "Human Assessment,
   Cognition and Motivation" (1984 : Athens, Greece)
   Intelligence and cognition.

   (NATO ASI series. Series D, Behavioural and social
sciences ; no. 38)
   "Post-conference proceedings of the NATO Advanced
Study Institute on 'Human Assessment: Cognition and
Motivation,' Athens, Greece, December 10–24, 1984"––
T.p. verso.
   "Published in cooperation with NATO Scientific
Affairs Division."
   Includes index.
   1. Intellect––Congresses. 2. Cognition––Congresses.
I. Irvine, S. H. II. Newstead, Stephen E. III. Title.
IV. Series.
BF431.N3765 1984   153.9   87–11011

ISBN 90-247-3522-X (this volume)
ISBN 90-247-2688-3 (series)

Distributors for the United States and Canada: Kluwer Academic Publishers, P.O. Box 358, Accord-Station, Hingham, MA 02018-0358, USA

Distributors for the UK and Ireland: Kluwer Academic Publishers, MTP Press Ltd, Falcon House, Queen Square, Lancaster LA1 1RN, UK

Distributors for all other countries: Kluwer Academic Publishers Group, Distribution Center, P.O. Box 322, 3300 AH Dordrecht, The Netherlands

For Norman Frederiksen

PREFACE

In December, 1984 a NATO-sponsored Advanced Study Institute entitled "Human Asessment:Cognition and Motivation" took place in Athens. It succeeded in attracting a great many of the most eminent scholars and researchers in this area, both as lecturers and participants. The contributors to this book are mostly members of staff who taught at the Institute. The chapters they have written are designed to provide an introduction to the principal issues that arise in the study of the assessment of intelligence and cognition. Since most of the protagonists are represented in this book the student is provided with an excellent overview.

Many different people are responsible for preparation of a book such as this. We would like to express particular thanks to Siobhan Breslin and Julie Coleman, who typed the text despite an unfriendly and unreliable word-processing system. Thanks are also due to Steve Gill who helped with the preparation of the figures. Finally, as a mark of respect for his achievements and leadership in the field of mental measurement, we dedicate this volume to Norman Frederiksen.

Sidney H. Irvine
Stephen E. Newstead
Plymouth, September 1985.

CONTENTS

List of contributors to this volume:

David L. Alderton: Department of Psychology, University of California, Santa Barbara, CA 93106, USA

John W. Berry: Psychology Department, Queen's University, Kingston, Ontario, Canada. K7L 3N6.

John B. Carroll: The L.L. Thurstone Psychometric Laboratory, University of North Carolina, Chapel Hill, NC 27514, USA.

Hans J. Eysenck: Department of Psychology, Institute of Psychiatry, De Crespigny Park, London, SE5 8AF, UK.

Earl Hunt: Department of Psychology, University of Washington, Seattle, Washington 98195, USA.

Michael Hyland: Department of Psychology, Plymouth Polytechnic, Drake Circus, Plymouth, PL4 8AA, UK.

Sidney H. Irvine: Department of Psychology, Plymouth Polytechnic, Drake Circus, Plymouth, PL4 8AA, UK.

L. Z. Klich: Centre for Behavioural Studies, University of New England, Armidale, New South Wales 2351, Australia.

David F. Lohman: College of Education, Division of Psychological and Quantitative foundations, University of Iowa, Iowa City, Iowa 52242, U.S.A.

Stephen E. Newstead: Department of Psychology, Plymouth Polytechnic, Drake Circus, Plymouth, PL4 8AA, UK.

James W. Pellegrino: Department of Psychology, University of California, Santa Barbara, CA 93106, USA.

J. W. Regian, Department of Psychology, University of California, Santa Barbara, CA 93106, USA.

Robert J. Sternberg: Department of Psychology, Yale University, PO Box 11a, Connecticut, USA.

Philip E. Vernon: University of Calgary, 2500 University Drive N.W., Calgary, Canada. T2N 1N4.

John M. Verster: National Institute for Personnel Research, Box 32410, Braamfontein, Johannesburg, South Africa 2017.

CHAPTER 1

FUNCTIONS AND CONSTANTS IN MENTAL MEASUREMENT:

A TAXONOMIC APPROACH

S.H. IRVINE

Plymouth Polytechnic, U.K.

INTRODUCTION

Psychologists in the field of individual differences seldom agree on precisely what abilities they can measure, or indeed how to measure those abilities that they give accepted names to. The best example of this is "intelligence", because there have been many theories of intelligence, as Figure 1 shows. This climate of uncertainty has become a constant in mental measurement because the theories and practices behind the assessment of human skills, achievements, aptitudes and capacities, are imperfect. If they had been perfect, debate since Spearman published his great work "The Abilities of Man" in 1926 would not be focussed on what abilities can be measured, by what methods, and in what contexts. These preoccupations still exercise us sixty years on, in this book as in others before it.

The material in this collection constructs a modern frame of reference for ability measurement. What distinguishes it from others is its balance between history and innovation, theory and empiricism, experimental and correlational approaches. Taken together, the chapters constitute a complete, scholarly description of the science of mental measurement as it approaches the end of the century. What this opening tries to give the reader is a key to the understanding of the chapters that follow. In the process human abilities are implicitly defined not in any operational sense, but in a fashion that makes good science possible, and better theory a reasonable expectation.

The first step on the path to understanding what is going on in individual differences is the realisation that there is not one correct theory of the nature and nurture of abilities, but many. Major theories of ability have been proposed regularly since Spearman. Verster's chapter provides details of their strengths as well as their faults; and the exposition of both leads to a realisation of their role in the development of current thinking. Sternberg, in his chapter, suggests that they were far more alike than their proponents and critics thought. This idea is worth

1925	Spearman	Single General Factor
1940	Thurstone	Primary Mental Abilities Each Distinctive
1950	Thomson	Group Factor, Associationist
1920-60	Burt-Vernon	Hierarchical, General Plus Group
1960-	Guilford	Multiple-Orthogonal
1970-	Cattell	Two-Factors, Qualitatively Distinct
1976	Carroll	Distributive-Memory Factors
1977	Sternberg*	Componential Theory

*Note: Sternberg's (1977) Componential theory of intellect must be included, although it is non-factorial as a rival to current-formulations, since it is based on correlations

Figure 1   Structures of Intellect based on Test
Intercorrelations and Factors

pursuing, and Figure 1 gives a clue to the nature of their unity. As we shall see, their dependence on the correlation coefficient, and its unstated assumptions, gives them a coherence that requires some understanding.

THE TAXONOMY

If an applied psychologist is at the mercy of imperfect theory, and this is used in research within and across cultures, how can empiricism produce other than poor science? It is a fair question, and not one to which there is no ready answer. One way to avoid gross errors is to stay within the logical limits of the data. But for that one must first know how to go about evaluating the results from the different schools of individual differences measurement that have grown up since the turn of the century.

In this section, a taxonomy is suggested for the understanding and evaluation of the empirical data produced by research into the measurement of cognitive abilities. A taxonomy of data types is produced from a rationale that has emerged from cross-cultural psychology (Irvine and Berry, in press). The subsequent framework is itself a definition of abilities that Miles (1957) would describe as "a key to understanding". The other definition of abilities that comes from this book is an ostensive one, in that the reports and reviews of research point out what is now being measured. All of the contributors try to avoid one of the most common faults of those who measure mental functions, that of producing stipulative definitions. These arise out of labelling test scores as measures of this or that ability without taking into account the strict controls necessitated by a theory of knowledge. An understanding of the limitations of empirical research as we now know it will hopefully lead to the creation of instruments that provide systematic operational definitions of the abilities of man.

The first step on the road to understanding what test scores contribute to science is a specialised theory of knowledge. Although such an approach may seem strange at first, knowledge of the logical constraints of the various conventional approaches to collecting cognitive data is crucial. The taxonomy draws attention, first, to three paradigms, or patterns of enquiry that are distinct in their assumptions about the nature and measurement of abilities. In the first column of Figure 2 these are labelled psychometric, Piagetian, and cognitive information-processing. How they differ in their assumptions, in their ways of collecting data and in their conclusions, is important. If one confuses one paradigm with any other, then the errors that result are self-inflicted. Why they are more than flags of convenience is explained in the next three sections.

Psychometric measurement

Sixty years ago, the abilities of man were the theme of Spearman's (1926) book on the nature and measurement of intelligence. In that work, the constants in modern psychometrics were expressed mathematically. Every work thereafter has had to come to terms with the assumptions behind its tools and technology, and, above all, its model of man's abilities. Spearmans' theory was energy-focussed, not an unusual approach for an engineer turned psychologist, perhaps. Mental events could be construed as expressions of energy, just as the universe could be thought of in the same terms. Spearman's empirical base for his model was necessarily a restricted one, since he had no evidence, such as we must reckon with today, from subjects obtained outside North America and Europe. The chapters by Berry, Vernon and Klich in this volume would surely have interested him, as they provide data that challenge conventional approaches to measurement.

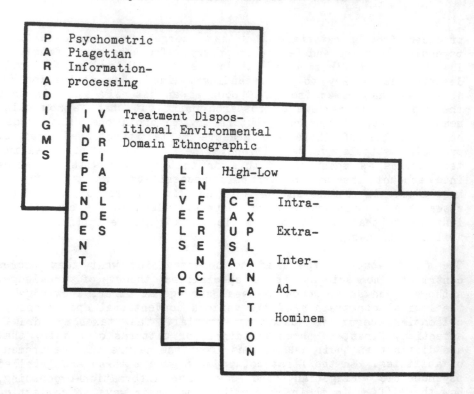

Figure 2   Taxonomy of Empirical Data Types

From the turn of the century Spearman derived a theory that depended upon a particular mathematical rule that could be observed in test correlations. All mental tests were thought to be in special relationships to each other. The essence of how test scores fitted Spearman's (1972) prescription is best described as the tendency for all tests of ability to be positively correlated. From the special patterns made by these test correlations, Spearman deduced that a pervasive and fundamental source of energy was at work in mental performance:

"....all the mental activity, just like the physical, consists in ever varying manifestations of one and the same thing, to which may be given the name of energy..." (p. 133).

This pervasive energy "factor" he called "g" because of its general nature. In essence, Spearman saw a relationship among test correlations that led him to assert that there was a single common factor among all mental tests that accounted for their

individual correlations with each other. But perhaps the best way
to understand what Spearman discovered is to begin with a set of
numbers that already illustrate this "one factor" relationship
among test correlations, and then to work backwards to the ideal
correlation matrix. No great mathematical skill is involved, just
a little patience while working through this example, based on a
set of six numbers.

.9   .8   .7   .6   .3   .1

Imagine these to be indices of the amount of general mental energy
used by a group of subjects to perform six different intellectual
tasks. We could use them, for example, as indicators of how much
a test score depended on this theoretical notion of mental energy,
.9 being the highest, and .1 the lowest. Another way of saying
this is to call this row of numbers "general factor loadings" or
"g" loadings. From this single row of six numbers one can make a
square matrix, very like a correlation matrix, by a method called
post-multiplication.

If we now multiply .9 by itself (.81) and then by every other
index ... (.9 x .8 = .72); (.9 x .7 = .63) and so on down the
line, the row looks like this

(.81)   .72   .63   .54   .27   .09

Another row can be produced by multiplying .8 by all the others.

.72   (.64)   .56   .48   .24   .08

This procedure can be repeated for all the other numbers to
produce a square matrix (Matrix A) of rows and columns that looks
this this:

MATRIX A

(.81)	.72	.63	.54	.27	.09
.72	(.64)	.56	.48	.24	.08
.63	.56	(.49)	.42	.21	.07
.54	.48	.42	(.36)	.18	.06
.27	.24	.21	.18	(.09)	.03
.09	.08	.07	.06	.03	(.01)

Now the next part is the interesting one. Spearman produced many square matrices of test correlations, and he thought that he could reduce every matrix to <u>one</u> row of figures, which, when post-multiplied by itself, could reproduce the correlations almost perfectly. A real correlation matrix (MATRIX B) would look like this compared to its reconstruction.

MATRIX B

1.0	.72	.63	.54	.27	.09
.72	1.0	.56	.48	.24	.08
.63	.56	1.0	.42	.21	.07
.54	.48	.42	1.0	.18	.06
.27	.24	.21	.18	1.0	.03
.09	.08	.07	.06	.03	1.0

The second matrix is exactly like the first, except that the diagonal now contains 1.0, representing the actual correlation of each test with itself, not a derived, or manufactured value. Without knowing beforehand, as we did , the square of the "perfect" row of numbers in the diagonal of Matrix A, one would have to <u>guess</u> a value for each 1.0 in the pattern, so that when the square root of each guessed diagonal value were obtained, it could serve as an estimate of the "g" loading that would reproduce the matrix perfectly, or as near perfectly as possible. We already have that set of values, since we manufactured it for the diagonal of Matrix A. The perfect guessed estimates for a single factor would be;

.81   .64   .49   .36   .09   .01

The square root of each diagonal value brings us back to the first row of numbers.

.9   .8   .7   .6   .3   .1

Using these numbers, the intercorrelations of Matrix B could be reproduced perfectly from post-multiplication of a singe "general factor" with these values. Some tests would have very high loadings, others hardly any at all, but these values could be calculated exactly.

Two interesting points can be observed in Matrix A. First, the rows and columns are all perfectly correlated with each other. Second, any block of four correlations also has a peculiar arithmetical relationship. If two diagonal correlations in any block of four are multiplied, say the .03 and the .03 of the lower right corner, the product (.0009) is equal to the product of the other diagonal pair (.01 and .09). Every block of four correlations (or tetrad) in Matrix A behaves like this, as a little checking will show.

From this, Spearman was able to derive his theory of two factors. What was always extracted in this way from a set of correlations was a single set of numbers, one for each test, representing g; and what might be left after the correlation due to g was accounted for was specific to each test, and uncorrelated with anything else.

This example illustrates the basic idea of factor analysis, which is to reduce the matrix of correlations parsimoniously to rows of numbers that, when post-multiplied, will reproduce the original matrix with least error. These mathematical functions can then be used to create new measures of individual differences. For all its insularity, the theory has survived as one against which data from Euramerican or "exotic" cultures are compared. Theories of the abilities of mankind must test the limits of this trend to positive correlation, whatever the cultural heritage of the sample of subjects. This challenge is apparent in the response of those who questioned what that trend implied, notably Thurstone (1938), Thomson (1951), Guilford (1959, 1969), Cattell (1971), Carroll (1976, 1983) Eysenck (1982) and Sternberg (1985a). Theories of abilities, whatever their outward appearance, tend to be like onions. The removal of a surface layer reveals a smaller core.

So far, only the obvious aspect of Spearman's model has been uncovered. That outer skin covers a more fundamental notion still: an inner psychophysical model of man's abilities that is independent of data from other cultures. This controls the very nature of data collection from any culture, since Spearman's psychometric theory came from a more fundamental theory of knowledge formed over a thirty year period. In that time, physics was the science, and energy its epicentre. In producing a new way of reasoning about mental life, Spearman attempted to link mental events with the physical world. His analogy between physics and mental life depended on the prior existence and use of a mathematical technology that manifested the parallel. By the turn of the century, it was there in the shape of an index of agreement among measures applied to the same set of individuals. Karl Pearson, who developed the coefficient upon which Spearman's theory was founded, called his index of covariation between two measures the product-moment correlation.

Some benefit accrues from looking closely at the name given to it
by Pearson. It requires that the covariation of individual
differences be calculated as a product of moments around a point:
specifically, deviations from the mean, which is a fixed point, or
fulcrum of a distribution of scores. How does this relate to the
physics of the Victorian and Edwardian eras? Perhaps the most
famous school text book of physics to deal with measurement of
forces around a fixed point is Loney's (1890), on statics and
dynamics. By 1964 it had gone through five editions and thirty
three printings. Loney describes moments very exactly, and (p.
61) has a diagram showing that a system is in equilibrium around a
fixed point when the sum of the products of force times distance
from the fixed point is zero. That very diagram provides the
analogy between energy in physics and energy in the mind, as
Spearman saw it. It underpins the whole concept of the
correlational technology of tests and testing. The amount of
mental energy for an individual can be captured in terms of a test
score's relative distance from a group mean. An individual
difference score is a moment around a point, as in physics.

Secondly, the deviation score in standard form was the building
block of a quantum theory of human abilities, standing in relation
to mental energy as moments of forces around a point did to the
physical world of mass and inertia. Although the correlation
coefficient begins with deviations from an average score, it is
itself an average value, specifically of the amount of consistent
deviation from the means that the same set of persons show when
measured twice. It is difficult to understand Spearman's concept
of the abilities of man, and those variations introduced by his
rivals and successors, unless one grasps the power of this method
of measurement as a model for an exact science of the mind. At
the very start of his theory construction, (Spearman, 1904), he
stressed what his theory demanded, and what the Pearson
coefficient appeared to give it ..." the first fundamental
requisite of correlation, namely, a precise quantitative
expression."

To derive scores based on deviations from a mean is only one way
to quantify individual differences. Other paradigms use other
procedures, but to point out how universal is the practice in
spite of theoretical differences is perhaps too easy. Since
Spearman's famous book, one theory of abilities has been produced
based on the correlation coefficient every ten years (see Figure
1) (Irvine, 1983a). Some of the protagonists of these theories,
such as Vernon, Carroll, Eysenck and Sternberg are able to write
for themselves in this book. It is unlikely that each one of
these theories was closely conscious of its epistemology; but in

their reliance on the assumptions of the index of correlation, they are, as Sternberg argues for quite different reasons, very much alike. They have wrongly, I think, been called structuralist theories. They are undoubtedly, as Stephenson (1981) points out, quantum theories. They are above all, as the book by Loney reminds us, static, and not dynamic theories of cognition, since they derive from a theory of objects that are fixed, not objects in motion.

Piagetian Observations

By 1927, the publication date of Spearman's book, the names of Rutherford and the Cavendish laboratory in Cambridge had become permanently linked with the knowledge that the atom could be split. Physics was changing dramatically. The previous year saw the publication in English of Piaget's book on language and thought in the young child (Piaget, 1926). Piaget's radical approach to the science of mental measurement was, as he and his disciples have insisted, that of genetic epistemology. This grandiloquent but complex and somewhat daunting phrase has produced as many interpretations as there are commentators. The key perspective on human abilities is derived from the important aspects of Piagetian research that give it a separate status in the taxonomy. These are its origins, aims and methods. Observations are not extensions of physics but of biology; not energy but growth "...Every psychological explanation comes sooner or later to lean either on biology or logic..." (Piaget, 1950, p.1). The aim of experiments relying on cognitive tasks is to define universal progressions from infancy to old age in the use of thought for adaptation to the environment. To do this in a Piagetian mould, the scientist requires absolute scales of measurement against which individuals can first be measured and then, after clinical interview, understood. Thus Piaget offers a theory of knowledge (epistomology) arising not from physics, but (genetic) out of the species itself - out of man's biological nature. Embryology has as much to offer as a key to understanding Piagetian emphases as physics has to understanding Spearman's arguments. Each stage of mental life is irreversible. Just as the embryo cannot revert to one of its earlier forms, there is no going back, except in the imagination, to what it is like to think like a child. The scale of measurement must reflect that irreversible trend. It is an absolute, testifying to qualitative differences in thought that are associated with different life-span stages.

A steady body of research in Europe and America from 1950 onwards speaks to the pervasive influence of Piagetian, as distinct from psychometric methods. There are some quite obvious differences between psychometric approaches whose empiricism yields a correlation, and one whose end point is a clinical judgement based on a standard form of interviews with the subject. First, the result of the application of a small number of tasks to a single subject is designed to determine the processes of thought in the developing organism. Next, there is no mean score by which to fix a personal deviation, positive or negative. A scale of mental life, analogous to egg, tadpole and frog, assures all of adult thinking status if they survive environmental hazards and censors. In Piagetian theory, normality is progression, not an IQ of 100. We will all get there sooner or later.

One must be careful to link and distinguish the two most influential schools of mental measurement in one other way. Individuals are assessed by trained psychologists on a one to one basis except when group tests, which are self report questionnaires in highly mechanised form, are administered. Far many more people have undergone standardised group testing than have been subjects of Piagetian or laboratory experiments in cognition. On the other hand, all forms of individual assessments resemble group tests in their quest for standard procedures. Apart from differences of scale, there is one important logical constraint on empirical observations, the condition of stimulus identity.

The need to control as much as possible stems from the development of experimental psychology from the laboratories of the hard sciences. Replication without standardisation is impossible. Cronbach (1957) drew attention to a split in psychology between those who exercise as much control as possible over the dependent variable in the laboratory, and those who let the subject do what he may on a number of dependent variables that are then correlated. Yet both test and laboratory cultures in the discipline pursue stimulus identity as a logical starting point. Without identical stimuli for each group of subjects, observed differences are impossible to interpret. All seem agreed on that point.

Cognitive information processing

The road to Piagetianism and psychometrics may well have started in a third path to knowledge, that of cognitive information-processing. The work of Wundt, as Eysenck (Chapter 8, this volume) asserts, may have paved the way for a theory of cognition. Neither physics nor biology is its focus, but the definition of the concept of intelligence by adopting a logical categorisation of mental activity from a precise theory of the transmission of information. This particular biometric emphasis appears in Spearman's work, although it was not a central method of measurement. Theoretical and operational consensus seems to vanish in the literature as the use of tests increases to define a specialist branch of psychology.

The divisions that Cronbach observed and drew attention to, however, did not begin to narrow until a conscious effort was made once again to apply cognitive theory, that derived from laboratory environments, to the measurement of individual differences. Such an effort emerged once more in the seventies, and is catalogued in the texts by Resnick (1976), Friedman, Das and O'Connor (1981), Sternberg (1985a) and, cross-culturally, by Irvine and Berry (1983). Eysenck (1982) sees the divisions in the quest for a structure of intellect somewhat differently. He takes a fundamentalist position. For him, the Binet-Simon and Wechsler testing approach based on item-analysis has been somewhat isolated from the rigour of experimental research. He argues that the quest for intelligence as a scientific construct requires biochemical and neurological models for the definition of information transfer. His model for intelligence is unique in its emphasis not on the apparent complexity of thought, but on the ease with which some of these indices of complexity, such as IQ scores, can be defined by "simple" measures of the speed and regularity of transmission of information through the cortex. The chronometric approach currently demonstrated by other contributors such as Sternberg, Hunt, and Pellegrino, is perceived by Eysenck as contributing to a rethinking of the parameters by which the abilities of mankind shall, and as he would argue, must be measured if the science of individual differences is to remain credible.

Perhaps Eysenck goes only part of the way towards a complete paradigm shift. A theory that refuted the whole correlational approach might serve us if not better, then differently. In tho seventies Sternberg (1977) produced component-theory and criticised the whole factor-analytic approach because it had not the power, scientifically, to advance our knowledge of intellect. Sternberg's paradigm avoided psychometric factors of any kind, and instead concentrated on defining the information content of reasoning in terms of stages of processing. Latency was used as a measure of the process. Sternberg is still, in his triarchic theory summarised in Chapter 3, concerned with the nature of human intelligence. In contrast to Eysenck, he emphasises not neurology but the constants in information-processing tasks that transfer across items in tests. It would appear that dynamic images are the metaphors considered useful. Take the definition of a component by Sternberg and Gardner (1982) as an example... "The component may translate a sensory input into a conceptual representation, transform one conceptual representation into another, or translate a conceptual representation into a motor output." Translations and transformations are dynamic mental concepts. These are seldom seen in the factor-analytic literature apart from Guilford's (1959) elaborate metaphor for the structure of intellect. That metaphor had a vogue for a while, like other structures of intellect, but never really became scientifically viable.

How unique is Sternberg's approach, and what are its points of contact with rival formulations? Has it a life expectancy of more than ten years? Sternberg's components are latency based, and in that they share with Eysenck's, Hunt's and Pellegrino's research a common concern for speed. Sternberg himself defines <u>duration</u>, <u>difficulty</u> and <u>probability of execution</u> as the markers for components. This can be compared with the much earlier transatlantic excursion by Furneaux, Eysenck and White (White 1982) into <u>speed</u>, <u>accuracy</u>, and <u>persistence</u> in relation to problem parameters such as difficulty and discriminating power. There is precious little between them in the long run.

In the short run the information-processing approach to the abilities of mankind will dominate the next decade of research. Two recent textbooks (Sternberg, 1985b; Kail and Pellegrino, 1985) reveal its popularity. Moreover, the lower cost of microcomputers has brought large-scale research to bear on the problems of construct validation. Success in this applied area has already been demonstrated by Fairbank, Tirre and Anderson (in press). Although the technology for expansion exists in networks of microcomputers, Spearman would still not find the basic mathematical approach to individual difference measurement foreign to him. Sternberg, Eysenck, Hunt and Fairbank are still calculating the very correlations he borrowed from Pearson, even if these are based on mean values of latencies instead of mean number correct. The mathematical bounds of the coefficient have not been challenged by paradigm shift. The dependent variable is still a deviation score from an average.

These three paradigms, traditional testing, neopiagetian interviews and information processing in experimental settings, are the epistemological bases of enquiry into the abilities of mankind. Although they seem distinct in some ways, they share affinities of scientific emphasis. The foundations of our taxonomy allow a rough sort of the empirical data base for building purposes. The paradigms say different things about mental life; and the question of the value of any one of them is answered only when one knows the scientist's aim.

Independent Variables and Levels of Inference

Often the scientist's aim is to explain what makes performance on tests or tasks easy for some and difficult for others. There is a good example in the extensive literature on the performance of different cultural groups on tests and tasks. Much of the flavour of that debate is present in the contributions by Berry (Chapter 10), Klich (Chapter 7) and Vernon (Chapter 9) in this book. Critics of such comparative studies demand proof of the status of the test score in each group (Berry, 1972). The dependent variables must mean the same thing from one group to another. Unless there is a method of satisfying that blanket restriction, an unfalsifiable veto is placed on all test use in different cultures.

Irvine (1965, 1966, 1979) specified the sources of variance that accompanied test use across cultures and also proposed ways of regulating these. He has provided (Irvine, 1983a) a system for proving a test or test series by considering the claims made for the validity of a test score in a context of independent variable types. This quasi-causal dimension serves to classify the kinds of evidence most commonly used to construct ability theory. This specification is found in the second frame of Figure 2.

First, he assumes that test scores or latencies can be used as dependent variables in situations where the cause of enhanced or restricted performance can be inferred without doubt. These are most easily recognised as treatments, such as in practice or coaching experiments, and are critical when motivational effects are linked with different testing conditions. Variables assumed to affect test performance "directly" in quasi-experimental contexts are usually, but not always, low-inference. The third frame of Figure 2 introduces this important distinction. The evaluative label low inference is not confined to laboratory manipulations. Any pre-selection of a group by previous performance likely to be related to current performance is a low-inference situation. Good teaching environments also enhance performance, although to adduce these as direct causes of group differences is a much harder task, or a longer leap from the immediate data. Culture as a direct cause is, like ethnic grouping, one of the highest inferences of all, yet it is one that is constantly being brought into play as a mechanism in theory construction.

A very important point to remember in the scrutiny of inferences from data is the lack of repeated measurements in the assessment of individual differences. Most test scores are derived from one application of the test. This real-world situation tends to encourage the post-hoc examination of variables that are assumed to influence performance. These variables, because they are post-hoc and static, are very often high-inference variables. Typical data types that can be evaluated in this way are variables based on streaming in schools; schools themselves; urban or rural residence; number of years of schooling; parental occupation and educational levels; ecological demand characteristics.

These are all (Figure 2, frame 2) environmental variables that could be either low or high inference independent variables. These may be distinguished from other data types that are not environmental, but dispositional. These include gender; broad comparison groups where little genetic similarity is present; and groups where genetic identity or bias may be assumed, such as in samples of identical twins. Dispositional variables have also been constructed from differences in the age of onset of some predisposing physical characteristic such as gynaecomastia, menarche, and even myopia.

Other, usually high inference variables of an even more complex, interactive nature include ethnic identity, or tribal groupings, structural and language characteristics. These are ethnographic in nature, and they can extend to meta-analysis of results, using the ethnic identity of the researcher as litmus test for bias in method, analysis or interpretation of findings (Irvine, 1986).

The point of this scheme is its potential for systematic analysis of evidence about causal influences on task performance. Each class of variable contributes quite different kinds of information about test scores, and they are not equal in their potential for causal attribution. So far we have distinguished one evaluative dimension, high-low inference that has causal properties, and four data types: treatments, environmental, dispositional and ethnographic.

Finally, the last kind of information about tests (Figure 2, frame 2) comes from the correlations of tests or tasks amongst themselves, whether as predictive or descriptive variables. This is taken as the last data type. An illustration from testing will suffice, but any paradigm can produce a domain study. When tests or tasks are subjected to correlation among themselves and factor analysed, the factors may be used as a means of classifying tests into broad families. The consistent appearance of the same test factors within subjects over many different samples and occasions becomes evidence for the validity of the constructs used by theorists to explain performance. Carroll shows the value of domain variables in his categorisation of factors derived from many independent correlational analyses. Each kind of study, whether it is psychometric, neopiagetian or information-processing, can concern itself with treatments, domain, environmental, dispositional or ethnographic variables. These fifteen ideal types can and do inform theory construction in quite different ways. Moreover, each type is capable of yielding low or high inference results: but the conclusions that can be attached to each type of finding do not simply depend on this classification, as we now illustrate.

Causal explanations

The taxonomy requires one other dimension for evaluation of the evidence from test score use. The type of causal explanation given by the researcher for any apparent difference between groups was determined by Irvine (1979). He showed that four classes of explanation have been produced to account for observed differences in test performance, as illustrated in Figure 2, frame 4. The first is intra-hominem. This relates observed differences in cognitive performance, individual or group, with the structural properties of the brain, its biochemistry or neurology. This kind of explanation is typical of laboratory experiments of "basic processes". The next is extra-hominem, and attributes performance differences to ecological press and the demands of survival in a particular environment: for example Arctic nomadic lifestyles versus pastoral subtropical subsistence farming are held to be polar opposites in their influence on spatial abilities, according to Berry, in Chapter 10. A third is termed inter-hominem, being a class of explanation that explains performance differences in terms of what people teach each other: language skills, educational curricula, values and behavioural norms.

A fourth is an ad-hominem appeal to common sense, often associated with anthropological vetoes that point to the development in local contexts of skills that tests and tasks fail to measure in standard formats. Ad-hominem explanations of effects are seldom scientific, but they have the effect of making psychologists justify their methods.

The taxonomy for systematic analysis of studies about the abilities of mankind can now be seen to have four dimensions. One is epistemological, recognising that its three classes, psychometrics, neopiagetianism and information-processing, are different ways of discussing the universe of mental abilities. They are different universes of discourse. The second is inferential, in that it describes the type of variable used to infer propositions about abilities. The other two classifications are concerned with causal explanations of data types. Some studies require long inferences, and others permit direct or short inferences about what causes any alteration in the dependent measure. All inferences from data are part of a persistent form of explanation for cause, of which four types have been specified.

It is possible to generate 120 ideal types. In fact, far fewer types are used for research purposes. This is a consequence of the frequent covariation of variable types, empirical and inferential; and the choice of any one empirical type may lead the experimenter to one class of explanation, though it need not logically do so. Nevertheless, validation of any ability construct might yet require evidence from all three epistemologies and all types of independent variable, leading inexorably to one class of explanation.

FUNCTIONS AND CONSTANTS

From this taxonomic approach to the understanding of data produced to validate theories of intellect comes the realisation that all models of the nature of human abilities are functions of their origins. The generic problems of the discipline in the past have originated from a lack of a method of delimiting the contributions from a variety of approaches. As Sternberg suggests, a lot of the debate has taken place on grounds that were inappropriate. That may have been an unforeseen, but abiding consequence of inexact theory.

There have, then, been many constants in the quest for individual differences, and some of these were not necessarily helpful. Those that have proved most troublesome to the conclusion of research in individual differences have been the common faults of the research enterprise. Among them have been the failure to follow known guidelines for construct validity. Much lip-service is paid to the multi-method and multi-trait approach. This requires the empirical test of a theory when all possible confounding elements have been removed, including the paradigm of data collection itself. A corollary of paying scant attention to construct validity is the pursuit of new names for the same measurements, or the production of many different measures for the same phenomenon, without investigating the claims of the old measures. There are many tests of intelligence, as well as various labels for scores from any single test of intelligence. The apparatus score from the WISC, for example, has been called non-verbal intelligence, fluid intelligence, simultaneous processing, field-dependence-independence. This practice of calling a test score something other than the last theoretician usually leads to the gravest fault of all, stipulative definiton. One would have hoped that the new techniques of measurement would have been able to avoid this; but it has emerged from new approaches to measurement, as the next example reveals.

This legacy has in recent years been brought home to those who might be tempted to search for a standard way to administer some of the elementary cognitive tasks (ECTs) that have been the vehicle of individual differences research. No sooner does one discover one way of administering a task than one finds the very experimenters who introduced it have themselves altered the instructions to their subjects in their latest versions, while stipulating the measure to be the same as it was in the previous experiment. We refer particularly to recent work by Stankov on divided attention (Stankov and Horn, 1980, Stankov 1983). Close reading of the Stankov series shows not only that instructions to subjects are modified without predicting the outcome of such changes, but that the products are assumed to be identical from experiment to experiment. More to the point, the editors of the journals concerned apparently see nothing wrong with this. They might also have asked what rival theory of attention has been excluded from the experiments, had construct validation crossed their minds.

However, editors of journals in individual differences have nothing to fear from their so-called hard cognitive colleagues. A quick glance at Welford's (1980) comprehensive book on reaction times demonstrates that whole careers have been built in experimental psychology by changing the rules within subjects for what appears to be the simplest of all cognitive tasks and then arguing bitterly with colleagues about the outcomes as if the products (latencies) from the subjects were the result of identical sequences of operations within them.

Similarly, Jensen's recent foray into individual differences (Jensen, 1982) using reaction times has now taken on the mantle of divided attention with a set of tasks that bears no generic or theoretical similarity to those of Stankov (Vernon, 1983; Vernon and Jensen, 1985). Neither Stankov's nor Vernon and Jensen's tasks are in any way comparable with those preferred by Lansman, Poltrock and Hunt (1983) in their pursuit of ability to focus and divide attention. In the space of a publishing year we have witnessed more tests of attention than have probably been developed in the past hundred years. The canon of parsimony has vanished in a cloud of neophilia. Some sanity may be returning to the movement if the critical notice served on Jensen's reaction time series is taken as more than a straw in the wind. Irvine (1983b) in a review of work by Jensen in Eysenck's (1982) collection made the point that the literature on reaction-time tasks is too voluminous to ignore, and that these tasks are neither pure nor simple.

Current Functions

It might well be argued that an expose of our past and present faults of theory and its operation in tests and tasks is neither constructive nor well informed, because the battleground has been changed beyond recognition by recent paradigm shifts owing little to traditional psychometrics. This point of view might reasonably place particular emphasis on the work of Sternberg (1985a) and of Eysenck (1982) and his colleagues. Nevertheless, if anticipation of any cogent objection is a sign of intelligence, perhaps judgement can be withheld for a little while yet, especially if we acknowledge that the work of these scientists should not be viewed outside the scientific prescriptions first advocated by Carroll (1976, 1980, 1983).

Sternberg's current theory of intelligence has had detailed comment and criticism from peers. Among several critics are those who say he extends his definitions to such an extent that they are incapable of falsification. Such a charge places severe limitations on any theory. Irvine (1984) has considerable sympathy with that view, drawing attention to the great difficulty with Sternberg's notion of a contextual subtheory. Context, according to Sternberg, embraces everything from the printed page to cultural values. The important aspects of context, though, seem to lie in the representation of a stimulus in the context of the subject's working memory. Those of us who recall Ferguson's (1954, 1956) essays on transfer and intelligence think that this unexplored relationship is the best ostensive definition of the kind of sleeping partnership between long and short-term memory that the Atkinson-Schiffrin model of information processing tacitly assumes. In brief, concentration of effort in STM operations will have only a limited life span in the quest for a definition of intelligence. Sternberg's emphasis on context reminds us that the subject has always brought with him to the task more than we could measure.

For all that, Sternberg's major achievement is likely to be his modernisation of "Donders" thinking about mental life as constituting measurable stages or components. The timing of stages in the execution of problem-solving tasks allows predictions about the contribution of individual differences in these stages to success on the task as a whole. In pursuit of this work in the seventies, Sternberg avoided factor analysis and traditional psychometric tasks as if they were apples in Eden. Consumption meant explulsion from his frame of reference. Nevertheless, two points seem to have escaped general notice. First, Sternberg uses produce-moment correlations, the generic tool of all psychometricians, thereby aligning his work with the psycho-physics model of means as fulcrums around which individual differences may be observed as moments. Next, given that the total time to solve a problem is the sum of its constituent parts, the parts themselves are not necessarily independent of each other. In fact, the ipsative nature of the components is a problem that Sternberg acknowledges but is powerless to solve. Some concern at the high multiple R values of the fits for his models would be diminished given proof of experimental independence in his measures. Nevertheless, observers will be glad to credit Sternberg with a bold approach, even if they regret its temporary abandonment before its implications have been worked through.

A second line of research with its roots in the Galton tradition has been extensively reported by Eysenck (1982) and his colleagues A.E. Hendrickson (1982) and D.E. Hendrickson, (1982). This work has two quite distinct parts, empirical relationships among measures, and the theory that explains them. The empiricism is easy enough to demonstrate. First, averaged evoked potentials of auditory stimuli were clinically determined for each subject by the experimenter, and the lengths of the wave in the first 256 ms. and the first 512 ms. following the onset of the stimulus were determined by an averaging algorithm. In addition the variance of the waves over all trials was calculated for each subject. When the results of these measures were correlated with IQ total, the 256 ms. length measures and variance measures each correlated .7 with the IQ total, and combined in a post hoc composite yielded .82. On the other hand, the composite 512 ms. measures produced a correlation of .59 (n=78) whose confidence limits are .72 and .43.

This disparity might cause some concern for those who desire that a part of a wave should not predict more than all of it, but this is a minor point when the theory of the evoked potential is considered. Hendrickson presents the view that the biochemical nature of pulse transmission presupposes a basic regularity in the pulse to ensure the smooth passage of information from stimulus receptor to the cortex. The more regular the pulse, the faster and more accurate the information transmission. Irregular pulses destroy clear messages. The AEP is a window on to that clarity. Long strings and small variances are the hallmark of efficient and regular biochemical pulses, the basic stuff of intelligent thought and action. String length and variance are transformations of that biochemical efficiency. Some veteran AEP watchers will know that Irvine (1983b) holds that the two measures are experimentally related, just as reaction times and their variances are, and family size and position. However, that is an empirical question, even if it prevents the use of the two measures in covariance analysis, factor analysis and the like.

Hendrickson's theory is applied by Eysenck in argument for the biological basis of intelligence. Some regard Eysenck's position as too fundamentalist. Sternberg (1984) produces a cogent rebuttal of physiological determinism that will do for the moment, since that red herring need not detain us. What has hitherto been missing is the knowledge that the theory of the evoked potential is by no means captured by Hendrickson's explanation. In fact, his work seems to be consistent with only one of two rival theories. The debate is about two different viewpoints. Simply expressed, the evoked potential wave represents either a reformulation of the amount of energy present in the trace before the onset of the stimulus, or has additional energy present in it. While Hendrickson's theory of biochemical regularity fits very well with a constant energy system, it would not fare nearly so well with an additive energy explanation.

Recent work in Plymouth by the Electrical Engineering Department on the harmonics of the evoked potential offers strong evidence for an additive energy system (Jervis, Nichols, Johnson, Allen and Hudson, 1983). Indeed it is not the only evidence on offer (Jervis, Allen, Johnson, Nichols and Hudson, 1984). My point is not, of course, that this detracts from the empiricism demonstrated by Eysenck and his colleagues; simply that the one explanation for the relationship between IQ and evoked potential put forward by Eysenck so far, cannot be accepted as the only plausible alternative. No scientist can ignore plausible rival alternatives for long, without doing the discipline a disservice. Eysenck will doubtless reconsider his theoretical position because the evidence about the increased amount of energy in the wave invalidates the kind of physiological perspective he has preferred. The shape of the wave does not in fact depend solely on system constancy, but signals how the system accommodates and enables energy increase. Spearman, in fact, was not far wrong in proposing mental energy mobilisation as one important area for investigation, even if tests and factor analysis were only blunt instruments.

Tools of interrogation and integration

Hendrickson's work would still be portentous even if it proved to be incorrect. Its significance would have more to do with the method of testing his pulse-train theory than its present status. He simulated the effects of irregular pulse-trains on a computer, arriving at wave forms resembling those of short, rounded evoked potential measures. His precise theoretical formulation allowed the design and execution of the experiment. Similar rigour in the field of mental testing is apparent in the work of J.B. Carroll (1976, 1980, 1983). A short account of his earlier work might be salutory as well as instructive, since it stands in sharp contrast to any programme of work mentioned so far. Wherein lie the differences, and what has happened to his prescriptions?

Carroll's (1976) watershed essay on tests as cognitive tasks was available in report form in 1974 and had been in preparation for some time prior to that. It emerges as the very first use by a psychologist of a computer to aid in the classification of test

items by means of a theoretical system. Nowadays the system would
be classified as a hybrid between an expert system and an empty
decision machine. Input from the psychologist was forced on a
predetermined grid derived form a theory of distributive memory.
The result was, indeed, a new structure of intellect (Carroll's
own sub-title); but there was not a correlation to be seen, not a
principal component conjured, and not a single subject
interrogated, except Carroll himself. Some might have described
this oracular performance had he not done it again in 1980. In
this extensive monograph he provides, and demonstrates the force
of, an improved system for the analysis and construction of
paradigms and of the tasks that define them.

Throughout this paper I have been suggesting that the discipline
as a whole has suffered for lack of such a framework. Perhaps I
have been particularly severe on reaction-time proponents. That
is partly due to Carroll's (1980) examples of how reaction time
measures can be seen to differ significantly in their demands on
the subject by adopting a computer based system of interrogation
of the task. The object is to relate experimenter events to the
corresponding mental events of the subject. The result is a Dual
Time Representation chart. Reaction time tasks, by this scheme,
show infinite variety. Carroll's approach has been extended in
this volume in Chapter 5. He has gone on to demonstrate that a
standard method of analysing data, and of constructing models for
it, is preferable to widespread idiosyncrasy. His contribution to
item difficulty is the start of the next focus in individual
differences. That, surely, is the question of what makes items
difficult.

Without tools of interrogation of data, such as the taxonomy we
present here, without new methods to validate old constructs, and
the power of computers to help in decision functions, the science
of individual differences will not improve. I have asserted, if
not demonstrated why I believe that human ability measurement is
not yet wholly credible. Some hope that we can achieve scientific
certainty in measurement because the distinguished contributors to
this book have pointed not one, but several ways to remove
barriers to progress. These are non-observance of construct
validation frameworks and methods; instrument variations whose
consequences are unexplained; ignorance of methods of task
specification; and disagreement on the priorities for paradigm
refinement. These were, indeed, the problems that divided
Spearman, Thurstone, Guilford, Cattell and others in the heyday of
tests. They have not disappeared with odysseys in the wine-dark
sea of cognitive tasks.

REFERENCES

Berry, J.W. (1972). Radical cultural relativism and the concept of intelligence. In L.J. Cronbach & P.J.D. Drenth, (Eds.), Mental tests and cultural adaptation. The Hague: Mouton.

Carroll, J.B. (1976). Psychometric tests as cognitive tasks: a new "Structure of Intellect." In L.B. Resnick, (Ed.), The nature of intelligence. Hillsdale, NJ: Erlbaum.

Carroll, J.B. (1980). Individual difference relations in psychometric and experimental cognitive tasks. Report No. 163, Thurstone Psychometric Laboratory, University of North Carolina, Chapel Hill, N.C.

Carroll, J.B. (1983). Studying individual differences in cognitive abilities: implications for cross-cultural studies. In S.H. Irvine & J.W. Berry, (Eds.), Human Assessment and Cultural factors. New York: Plenum.

Cattell, R.B. (1971). Abilities: their structure, growth, and action. Boston: Houghton-Mifflin.

Cronbach, L.J. (1957). The two disciplines of scientific psychology. American Psychologist, 12, 671-684.

Eysenck, H.J. (Ed.) (1982). A model for intelligence. New York: Springer-Verlag.

Ferguson, G.A. (1954). On learning and the abilities of man. Canadian Journal of Psychology, 10: 121-131.

Friedman, M.P., Das, J.P., & O'Connor, N. (1981) Intelligence and Learning. New York: Plenum.

Guilford, J.P. (1959). Three faces of intellect. American Psychologist, 14, 469-479.

Guilford, J.P. (1967). The nature of human intellect. New York: McGraw-Hill.

Hendrickson, A.E. (1982). The biological basis of intelligence. Part 1: theory. In H.J. Eysenck (Ed.), A model for intelligence. New York: Springer-Verlag

Hendrickson, D.E. (1982). The biological basis of intelligence. Part 2: measurement. In H.J.Eysenck (Ed.), A model for intelligence. New York: Springer Verlag.

Irvine, S.H. (1965). Adapting tests to the cultural setting: a comment. Occupational Psychology, 39: 12-23.

Irvine, S.H. (1966). Towards a rationale for testing abilities and attainments in Africa. British Journal of Educational Psychology, 36: 24-32.

Irvine, S.H. (1979). The place of factor analysis in cross-cultural methodology and its contribution to cognitive theory. In L.H. Eckensberger, W.H. Lonner, & Y.H. Poortinga, (Eds.), Cross-cultural contributions to psychology. Lisse: Swets & Zeitlinger.

Irvine, S.H. (1983a). Testing in Africa and America: the search for routes. In S.H. Irvine & J.W. Berry, (Eds.), Human assessment and cultural factors. New York: Plenum.

Irvine, S.H. (1983b) Has Eysenck removed the bottleneck in IQ? Essay review of "A Model for Intelligence", edited by H.J. Eysenck. New York: Springer, 1982. In: New Scientist, 99: 121-122.

Irvine, S.H. (1984). The contexts of triarchic theory. The Behavioral and Brain Sciences, 7: 293-294.

Irvine, S.H. (1986). Cross-cultural assessment: from practice to theory. In W. Lonner & J.W. Berry, (Eds.), Methods in cross-cultural psychology. New York: Sage.

Irvine, S.H. & Berry, J.W. (Eds.) (1983). Human assessment and cultural factors. New York: Plenum.

Irvine, S.H. & Berry, J.W. (Eds.) (1986). Human abilities in cultural context. (In press).

Jensen, A.R. (1982). Reaction time and psychometric g. In H.J. Eysenck, (Ed.), A Model for Intelligence. Springer-Verlag: New York.

Jervis, B., Allen, E., Johnson, T., Nichols, M. & Hudson, N. (1984). The application of pattern recognition techniques to the contingent negative variation for the differentiation of subject categories. IEEE Transactions on Biomedical Engineering, BME-31: 342-349.

Jervis, B., Nichols, M., Johnson, T., Allen, E. & Hudson, N. (1983). A fundamental investigation of the composition of auditory evoked potentials. IEEE Transactions on Biomedical Engineering, BME-30: 43-50.

Kail, R. & Pellegrino, J.W. (1985). Human intelligence: perspectives and prospects. New York: Freeman.

Lansman, M., Poltrock, S.E. & Hunt, E. (1983). Individual differences in the ability to focus and divide attention. Intelligence , 7: 299-312.

Loney, S.L. (1890). The elements of statics and dynamics. London: Macmillan.

Miles, R.T. (1957). Contributions to intelligence testing and the theory of intelligence. 1. On defining intelligence. British Journal of Educational Psychology, 27: 153-165.

Piaget, J. (1926). The language and thought of the child (trans. Marjorie Worden). New York: Harcourt Brace.

Piaget, J. (1950). The Psychology of intelligence. (English edition). London: Routledge.

Resnick, L.B. (Ed.) (1976). The nature of intelligence. Hillsdale, NJ: Erlbaum.

Spearman, C. (1904). "General Intelligence," objectively determined and measured. American Journal of Psychology, 14: 201-293.

Spearman, C. (1927). The abilities of man. London: Macmillan.

Stankov, L. (1983). Attention and intelligence. Journal of Educational Psychology, 75, 471-490.

Stankov, L. & Horn, J.L. (1980). Human abilities revealed though auditory tests. Journal of Educational Psychology, 72, 19-42.

Stephenson, W. (1981). Sir Cyril Burt. Letter to Editor. In Bulletin of the British Psychology Society, 34: 284.

Sternberg, R.J. (1977). Intelligence, information processing, and analogical reasoning: the componential analysis of human abilites. Hillsdale, NJ: Erlbaum.

Sternberg, R.J. (1984). Toward a triarchic theory of intelligence. The Behavioral and Brain Sciences, 7: 269-287.

Sternberg, R.J. & Gardner, M.K. (1982). A componential interpretation of the general factor in human intelligence. In H.J. Eysenck, (Ed.), A model for intelligence. New York: Springer-Verlag.

Sternberg, R.J. (1985a). Beyond IQ: a triarchic theory of human intelligence. New York: Cambridge.

Sternberg, R.J. (Ed.) (1985b). Human abilities: an information-processing approach. New York: Freeman.

Thomson, G.H. (1951). The factorial analysis of human ability. London: University of London Press. (5th Ed.)

Thurstone, L.L. (1938). Primary mental abilities. Psychometric Monographs, 1.

Vernon, P.A. (1983). Speed of information processing and general intelligence. Intelligence, 7: 53-70.

Vernon, P.A. & Jensen, A.R. (1985). Individual and group differences in intelligence and speed of information processing. Personality and Individual differences, 5: 411-423.

Welford, A.T. (1980). Reaction times. New York: Academic.

CHAPTER 2

HUMAN COGNITION AND INTELLIGENCE
TOWARDS AN INTEGRATED THEORETICAL PERSPECTIVE

JOHN M. VERSTER

Human Development Division, N.I.P.R, South Africa

INTRODUCTION

This chapter presents a selective review of theoretical
developments and empirical research results bearing on the nature
of human cognition and intelligence. An attempt is made to show
how concepts of cognition and intelligence have, historically,
formed focusses in quite separate universes of discourse in
scientific psychology. Cognition became a focal point in
experimental psychology, aimed at identifying universal laws of
mental function. Intelligence became the central concept in the
study of individual differences in mental competence, their
causes, correlates, and consequences. Only during the latter half
of the last decade have psychologists begun to make a concerted
effort to integrate knowledge and theory from the two formerly
separate sub-disciplines. The purpose of this report is to
appraise the progress being made towards this end and to highlight
implications and opportunities for new research.

Greater emphasis is given, in this chapter, to the individual
differences tradition, since the theoretical perspectives and
measuring instruments it has spawned have seen far wider
application in the real world, influencing social policy as well
as educational and vocational practice in many countries. Yet it
has been only recently, due to the gradual rapprochement between
experimentally based cognitive psychology and measurement-
oriented intelligence research, that psychologists and the general
public have begun to question in earnest the adequacy of the
theoretical base for many so-called intelligence and ability tests
in popular use.

Early Conceptions of Intelligence

A central theoretical question in cognitive psychology for over a
century has concerned the nature of human intelligence, its
origin, developmental course, structure, and function. The
implicit motive behind the question is to derive a theory capable
of explaining adequately both the nomothethic laws governing
manifest individual and group differences in cognitive ability,
and the ideographic variations in cognitive function that testify
to the psychological uniqueness of each individual. This
question, albeit in modified form, remains one of the major issues
in scientific psychology and it is of central relevance to the
theme of this report.

To gain an appreciation of the developmental sequence and pace at
which systematic thought pertaining to this question has
progressed, it will be necessary and instructive to regress
briefly in time and to take up the narrative at its logical
beginning.

Perhaps the most meaningful starting point lies in the enormously
insightful, if complex and speculative writings of Herbert Spencer
(1855). Spencer was, in essence, a biologist, physiologist, and
philosopher whose psychological thinking grew out of the
pre-evolution doctrine of associationism. Yet Spencer was
profoundly interested in the emerging notion of evolutionism,
publishing on this theme in the early 1850s before the appearance
of Charles Darwin's celebrated treatise on 'The Origin of
Species'. Spencer's chief concern was to create a "synthetic
philosophy" in which all natural things could be related in terms
of a unified principle of development. Included in this framework
was his concept of the human mind. In contrast to the prevailing
view espoused by the associationist school, that the mind was
composed of innumerable separate faculties acquired
mechanistically as a consequence of associations among incoming
sensory impressions, Spencer conceived of the mind as an
integrated whole, expressive of a single adaptive capacity. He
was the first to use the term <u>intelligence</u>, derived from Cicero,
with reference to the adaptive function of nervous and mental
processes. He was also first to elaborate the view that all
development involves differentiation, followed by integration at
successively higher, more complex levels of organisation. He
expressly applied this notion to the human mind, suggesting that
the mind (intellect) is organised hierarchically, with
developmentally simpler processes (reflexes) at the lowest level
(subconscious), and progressively more complex processes
(sensation, perception, association, relation) defining
progressively higher (conscious) levels of organisation and
function.

It will be seen later that Spencer's speculative views are remarkably close to contemporary conceptions in cognitive psychology, after the intervention of more than a century of empirical research and theoretical development.

A less successful theme in Spencer's work is his attempt to resolve the mind-body problem, a crucial issue which cannot be omitted from any comprehensive theory of intelligence. He was unable to find a means of relating mental events to physical processes in the brain. Eventually he resorted to the view that they represent a series of parallel events, both of which stem from a deeper underlying reality. This reality he regarded as unknowable. Yet he believed that mental and physical events are closely associated and somehow must be linked organically. He consistently qualified this view by emphasising that neither one should be treated as a cause of the other. Rather, they should both be seen to arise from the same unfathomable source.

Perhaps the forerunner of a truly scientific approach to the study of human intelligence is the nineteenth century British scholar and evolutionist, Sir Francis Galton, a cousin of Darwin. In his first major contribution to psychology, Galton (1869) sought to demonstrate the hereditary basis of genius, a term he applied to those commonly considered to have attained outstanding eminence in their respective fields. His work bore a very strong influence from the new theory of evolution which Darwin (1859) had published only a decade earlier. Galton was the first to apply Darwin's principles of variation, selection, and adaptation directly to human populations. He espoused the view that races (sub-species) evolve in response to differential environmental pressures operating over time on different segments of a population (species). By extending this view, Galton became the first to really develop the concept of _individual differences_, a central tenet of modern differential psychology.

Galton's conception of the human mind was based on the widely held belief that all mental events have three aspects: cognitive, conative, and affective. On the basis of his biographical studies of men of eminence, he came to the conclusion that all three components are essential to outstanding achievement. His pedigree analyses convinced him that all three were subject to the laws of heredity. Yet, he argued, of the three cognitive capacity is by far the most important, since it alone sets an upper limit to what can be accomplished by an individual. Galton accordingly decided to devote most of his attention to a detailed analysis of the nature of human cognitive ability. Like Spencer, he rejected the elaborate classification of mental faculties of the associationist school. In its place, he devised a system of constructs that amounts to a three-way cross-classification, in terms of which inborn tendencies (innate) are contrasted with acquired tendencies; a super-faculty (general ability) is set in opposition to special aptitudes; and cognitive capacity is distinguished from motivational and emotional tendencies. Out of this system grew the first specific definition of intelligence, as innate, general cognitive ability. This definition was to exert a strong influence on later psychologists, most notably Burt (1909-1975) and defenders of the IQ movement.

The Invention of Mental Tests

In his later work Galton (1883) concentrated on the development and refinement of quantitative methods for use in the study of mental phenomena. It is ironical that in so doing he helped lay the foundations for both traditions underlying what Cronbach (1957) has called the two disciplines of scientific psychology, the experimental and the differential. Only in the last decade (e.g., Carroll, 1980a) have these two traditions begun to converge effectively into the modern synthesis of cognitive science.

During the period 1879-80 Galton developed the first empirical framework for studying the phenomena of associationism and applied his principles to the study of free association. His experimental procedure was quickly adopted by Wundt, who had just founded his laboratory in Leipzig. Wundt's descendants became the bearers of the experimental tradition in psychology, which focusses on the establishment of general laws governing cognitive processes, but pays no heed to individual variations in task performance.

Galton's subsequent work (1880-1883) on mental imagery, involving the first use of the questionnaire method in psychology, concentrated on the quantification of individual differences and represents the beginning of the differential, or psychometric tradition in scientific psychology. But it was his development of simple tests of sensory judgements and reaction times, that heralds the first true attempt to measure intelligence. Galton's (1869) view of intelligence as a unitary capacity acquired through inheritance encouraged his belief that it could be measured objectively by quantifying individual differences in the simplest sensory processes. For this reason his attention was diverted from an attempt to sample the higher cognitive processes that today are viewed as the central components of intelligence.

Yet the significance of Galton's contribution should not be overlooked. His firm belief in the biological determination of all mental qualities, although today relegated to a pole position in the spectrum of views on the nature/nurture issue, nonetheless led to the development of important statistical concepts which have had a profound influence on the subsequent development of psychometric methodology. In particular, his theory of "atomic" or "particulate" inheritance, which was a remarkable anticipation of Mendelian genetics, led to the prediction that mental phenomena would follow the same laws of inheritance as physical phenomena. Hence in the same way that physical attributes such as weight or height were known to be distributed in the general population according to a symmetric, bell-shaped curve, so, Galton believed (1883), intelligence should be distributed according to what today would be called a normal distribution. This innovative view gave rise to the first normative psychometric scales, in which individual differences in intelligence were described in terms of standard deviation units about a mean value representing the average level of intelligence in the population. Galton's belief that intelligence followed a uniform rate of growth as a function of age, suggested the utility of expressing a child's intelligence in terms of the ratio between the deviation of his performance from the norm for his age, and his chronological age. This notion was the forerunner of the subsequent mental level of Binet and Simon (1908) and of the concepts of mental age and intelligence quotient (IQ) proposed by Stern (1912) and used widely by later psychologists.

It is worth observing, in passing, that if Galton's (1883) theory concerning the mechanism responsible for individual differences in intelligence is wrong, then there may be no longer any compelling reason to adhere to the convention of standardizing intelligence tests to yield a normal distribution of scores in the general population. Indeed, this time-honoured practice may be responsible for the concealment or distortion of important information regarding the true distribution of cognitive ability (or abilities) which might hold the key to a better understanding of the mechanisms underlying its (their) determination. If, for the sake of argument, intelligence is acquired largely through the agencies of environmental opportunity, is it not conceivable that the distribution of intelligence may deviate significantly from normality in the same way that, say, income usually does, showing marked skewness and kurtosis? This is an issue which has only just begun to receive the attention, however obliquely, of modern test theorists (e.g., Lord, 1969) but which has not yet been faced squarely by most users of tests in psychological practice.

The objective measurement of human ability became a focal point in the development of psychology as a scientific discipline around the turn of the century. In America, James McKeen Cattell (1890) of Columbia University coined the term "mental testing" and with his associates (Cattell and Ferrand, 1896) developed the first largescale mental test battery, which was administered to university students. Their tests provided measures of a variety of cognitive processes, including free and controlled association, simple sensory judgements, simple perceptual processes, reaction times, and memory span. Like Galton, however, they failed to devise ways of measuring the higher cognitive processes which exemplify modern intelligence tests and which would have provided the correlations they sought in vain with criteria of academic achievement.

Significant advances in mental testing soon followed, most notably in the seminal work of The Frenchmen Alfred Binet and Th. Simon (1905) who invented the first tests of higher cognitive processes. A careful reading of the frequently misconstrued theoretical position taken by these authors (Binet and Simon, 1916) reveals that they conceived intelligence to be a global capacity of the mind, but that its nature was multi-facetted, including "nearly all the phenomena with which psychology concerns itself, sensation, perception...as much as reasoning" (p.42). This formulation differs substantially both from Galton's (1883) unitary general cognitive capacity and from the doctrine of independent faculties which, in different guises, dominated much of eighteenth and nineteenth century thinking. Instead of repeating the mistakes of earlier mental testers, Binet and Simon (1916) perceived that "...in intelligence there is a fundamental faculty....This faculty is judgement,...the faculty of adapting one's self to circumstances" (p.42). They channelled their efforts towards the measurement of this higher adaptive capacity based on judgement and reasoning.

Analysis of the writings, testing strategy, and materials used by Binet and Simon (1916) indicates clearly that they held the view that the mental processes underlying intelligence are hierarchically organized. Intellectual development during childhood was considered to involve progressive adaptation to environmental demands by mastering successively higher forms of cognitive function until, in adolescence, the highest levels of judgement are attained. Unlike Galton, they emphasized the importance of environmental opportunity and learning in the development of intelligence. Their views, for the most part, are remarkably close to Spencer (1855) and differ in most important aspects from Galton (1883). Thus, like Spencer, they associate intelligence with a global entity, mind, not just its cognitive aspect. It is viewed as the major adaptive mechanism of the organism, capable of benefitting from experience. It can be broken down structurally into successive hierarchical levels, which progress from the simple to the complex, corresponding to major epochs of development.

This view seems a remarkable anticipation of contemporary developmental theories of intelligence, as exemplified in the work of Piaget (1964), Bruner (1957), Horn (1978), and others. These theories all recognise qualitative discontinuities between stages of growth, which give rise to structural changes in intelligence over time. They also recognise the dual importance of innate and environmental factors in the development of intelligence. Yet for at least half a century, Galton's extreme hereditarian views held sway over the more subtle and complex perspectives of Alfred Binet, leading the ill-fated IQ movement, which grew out of the latter's tests, into eventual embroilment in fruitless social polemics and ultimately to public disrepute.

The First Factor Model of Intelligence

Most authors would agree that the next major advance in the development of cognitive psychology as a quantitative discipline came with Spearman's (1904; 1912; 1927) development of the statistical method of factor analysis and its application to the problem of defining the structure of human intelligence.

Spearman (1904) was impressed by the potential he saw in Pearson's (1902) product-moment correlation coefficient which was a refinement of the earlier method of correlation proposed by Galton (1883). He saw it as a means of identifying the "hidden underlying cause" of the variations between individuals in mental function (p.74). He recognised that the coefficient of correlation between a pair of variables offered no basis for inferring whether one variable was the cause or effect of the other, although either condition might conceivably obtain. He regarded it as more appropriate, however, following J. S. Mill's fifth canon of the method of concomitant variation, that in the case of psychological variables the correlation coefficient should be interpreted as representing some common fact of causation, or common factor. Spearman recognised that by extending the measure of correlation between a pair of variables to an estimate of the common variation among a number of variables, it should be possible to discover the major common factors of the mind.

This line of thought had been independently pursued in the USA by Cattell and his collaborators (Cattell, 1890; Wissler, 1901). They had analysed data from student samples tested on measures of simple sensory and psycho-physical processes. Their results led them to conclude that there was no evidence of a common factor underlying performance on the tests, or between test performance and academic achievement. Spearman (1904) criticised their work, chiefly on the grounds that their samples were too homogeneous to exhibit large variations in intelligence. He administered similar measures to more heterogeneous, although smaller samples of school children. His data were analysed with the aid of Yule's (1897) formula for partial correlation and a correction formula of his own for attenuation due to measurement error. The results

revealed correlations equal to unity, leading Spearman to conclude
that he had demonstrated evidence of a common element underlying
all the specific forms of intelligence assessed by the tests. He
interpreted the common factor initially as general sensory
discrimination. His conclusion was hotly contested by Thorndike
(1909) who used apparently similar methods but came up with
zero-order correlations, re-affirming his belief in the presence
of distinct and independent intelligences. Clearly both
investigators could not be right. Future research would reveal
that the extreme discrepancy of results lay both in the choice of
experimental design and in the use of statistical methods favoured
respectively by Spearman (1904) and Thorndike (1909). As it would
eventually transpire, neither contestant in the bitter debate was
right.

In the same year that the debate flared up, new results were
published (Burt, 1909) offering qualified support for Spearman's
position. Unlike Cattell, Spearman, Thorndike, and others who had
until then used chiefly measures of simple sensory processes, Burt
(1909) had taken account of Binet's (Binet and Simon, 1905) work
and included in his study a wider variety of tests with a greater
emphasis on the higher cognitive processes. He used modified
statistical procedures in the analysis of his data and produced
correlations of less than unity, but significantly greater than
zero. He concluded that the common variation in the test scores
represented not the simplest common property of sensory
discrimination, but the highest common factor, which was exhibited
most clearly in those measures calling for logical thought and
judgement. Spearman readily accepted this interpretation,
building upon it in his own research. He recognised that in
addition to a factor common to performance on all mental tests,
there may be factors specific to each particular test, thus
accounting for the correlations of less than unity. Three years
later he formally propounded the famous two-factor theory of
intelligence, crystallizing this view (Spearman and Hart, 1912;
Spearman, 1914). The general factor, designated simply g to avoid
unwarranted confusion with previous notions of intelligence, was
considered to enter into all mental performance, but was most
purely measured in tests demanding the higher cognitive functions
of logic, judgement, and reasoning. The other factor, denoted s,
did not enter into the correlations between pairs of tests, but
reflected the residual variance specific to performance on each
test. After fifteen years of development, refinement, and bitter
controversy, Spearman (1927) published his definitive statement on
the two-factor theory of intelligence in his classic book "The
Abilities of Man".

Although this work was enormously influential at the time, a
number of shortcomings in Spearman's (1927) formulation are

evident. For a start, his elegant statistical criterion for a two-factor solution, which stipulates that all the "tetrad differences" in the intercorrelation matrix must be equal to zero, was not always satisfied by the data (Burt, 1940). More important from the viewpoint of psychological theory, the data base on which the two-factor model was erected is far from adequate to support a comprehensive theory of intelligence. The tests on which most of his intercorrelation matrices are based represent a meagre sample of the potential universe of human cognitive processes. In fact, he relied mainly upon measures of scholastic achievement. A rather extreme interpretation of his general factor, g, is consequently that it represents no more than overall scholastic achievement in the British school system of the time. Certainly Spearman had little grounds for going beyond this interpretation. Indeed, it is to his credit that he acknowledged he had no adequate explanation for the identity of g, allowing that it might represent merely "...some mathematical function of a large number of elements distributed by 'chance'" (Spearman, 1927, p.414).

It might be observed, parenthetically, that this view is ominously similar to Galton's (1883) "atomic" theory of the mechanism by which his general cognitive capacity is inherited, and which gave rise to his belief that it must be normally distributed. It is perhaps small wonder that Spearman's statistical factor, g, and Galton's theoretical construct, innate general cognitive capacity, became confused in the minds of many uncritical applied psychologists. It requires only a small leap of imagination to fuse these two unrelated and equivocal formulations into the "scientific" justification often cited in support of popular IQ tests as measures of a unitary intellectual quantity, intelligence (e.g., Brody and Brody, 1976; Matarazzo, 1976).

Spearman's (1927) more venturesome hypothesis, that g represents some form of mental energy, bears no relation to the empirical procedures used to derive it. At best, it serves as a vain attempt to resolve the mind-brain problem and enjoys no serious scientific support. His equally speculative characterization of the essence of g in terms of his three neogenetic principles of cognition (Spearman, 1923) was received with greater enthusiasm but remains, nonetheless, unsubstantiated to the present day. Moreover, it fails to account for the origin, structure, function, or development of g and is therefore of limited explanatory value.

His treatment of the s factor, which implies that there are as many specific abilities as there are tasks to perform and that each is independent of the other, as well as of the general factor, is, to say the least, extremely unparsimonious. More recent evidence, based on better test batteries and improved statistical procedures, suggests that the variance attributed by Spearman to g and s can be better accounted for by other models.

A final criticism of the two-factor model as a comprehensive theory of intellectual structure arises from Spearman's (1927) own awkward recognition of the need to append a number of extra constructs, which could not be accommodated without disrupting the model's elegant simplicity. These are the lesser known cognitive factors Spearman also considered to be universal and to possess functional unity, notably general inertia (c) and general oscillation. A last factor, w, was also considered to enter into all cognitive performance and its estimation, but was not in itself supposed to be cognitive. It was interpreted tentatively as 'self-control' (p.413).

Hierarchical Structure of the Mind

One of the most industrious and prolific of Spearman's former students was Cyril Burt, whose prodigious outflow of publications spans over six decades. Some of Burt's writings, particularly those bearing on the nature/nurture issue, have recently become the subject of a major public scandal (e. g., Dorfman, 1978) and no longer merit serious scientific consideration. But much of his earlier work on factor analysis has been left untouched by this ignominious debacle and will be considered here. Even if his data cannot be trusted, his methodological and theoretical contributions have had a significant impact on the quantitative study of intellectual structure and are pertinent to the present theme of discussion.

Burt's (1949) model of the structure of the mind developed from an interesting amalgam of the views of the major theorists considered in the preceding sections. From Spencer (1855) he took his central notion of a hierarchically organised intellect in which mental processes are located on structurally distinct levels corresponding to reflexes, sensations, perceptions, associations, and relations. Like Galton (1869) he distinguished between cognitive, conative, and affective aspects of the mind. He also chose to define intelligence in Galton's narrow sense of innate general cognitive ability and he interpreted the theoretically normal distribution of intelligence as evidence for its hereditary determination. Following the work of Binet and Simon (1905) he became convinced of the practical utility and theoretical significance of sampling mainly the higher cognitive processes in tests of intelligence (Burt, 1914). From his chief mentor, Spearman, he acquired the conviction that the most fruitful means of studying the structure of the mind was by factor-analytic methods. He was not wholly convinced, however, that Spearman's (1927) two-factor model of g and s was the best means of accounting for the variance in tables of intercorrelations based upon mental test scores.

In the decade or so following Spearman's (1927) classic publication, major modifications and improvements had been made to his factor-analytic method, culminating in a series of important extensions to the basic mathematical model (Thurstone, 1935; Holzinger, 1937; Thomson, 1939; and Burt, 1940). Burt's (1940) approach to the problem of factor analysis, in particular, was inspired by the findings of Stephenson (1931) and El Koussi (1935) which pointed to the presence of major group factors of intelligence distinct from g and s. Their data supported Burt's (1919) earlier hypothesis, following Spencer (1855), that the mind would exhibit a hierarchical structure, with group factors located on successive levels of generality intermediate between g and s. This hypothesis was strongly augmented by the work of MacDougal (1932) whose thinking was based in physiology. He argued that, as the individual evolves, new sub-systems of abilities gradually form and become differentiated from the initial general structureless state. These acquire a certain functional autonomy, yet remain integral sub-systems of the brain's global capacity. The progressive differentiation of abilities follows the course of maturation of major physiological structures, or sub-systems in the brain. These support, respectively, reflex, sensori-motor, perceptual, associative, and relational processes or functions. MacDougal (1932) acknowledged the heavy dependence of his theory on the original formulation of hierarchical structure outlined by Spencer (1855).

Burt (1945) was later to give a clear exposition to the proposed mechanism by which the mind becomes hierarchically structured. His formulation has become known as the differentiation hypothesis of intellectual development. A considerable volume of support for this hypothesis, in its various forms (e.g., Garrett, 1946) has been garnered in independent studies over the past several decades. These have been comprehensively reviewed by Reinert (1970) who concludes that there is sufficient evidence to indicate the existence of age-related changes in the factorial structure of intelligence, but that the data do not yet permit a clear-cut description of the nature of the changes.

In 1949 Burt published his major theoretical statement on the hierarchical structure of the mind. It represents a formidable integration of theory, method, and empirical results based on factor-analytic studies. He recognised evidence for the presence of at least 18 group factors, which could be located on successive hierarchical levels beneath the general factor, g. This in turn he identified as innate, general cognitive ability, a sub-set of the larger totality, mind. On the simplest level were factors associated with <u>sensory</u> processes of sight, hearing, smell, touch, and kinesthesis. On the next level he located factors representing <u>perceptual</u> and complex perceptual-motor processes. Factors at the next level, termed intermediate, represent <u>associative</u> thinking processes classified according to either form (e.g., productive association) or context (e.g., verbal, arithmetic, practical/spatial/mechanical). On the highest level he located <u>relational</u> cognitive processes as involved, for example, in scientific or logical thinking on the one hand, and in artistic or aesthetic judgement and appreciation on the other.

Although Burt's (1949) work falls short of the rigorous standards of modern factor-analytic research on many counts, his general model has served as a rich source of hypotheses for subsequent empirical verification and refinement. The powerful influence of his hierarchical model is still felt, albeit in modified form, in most currently prominent theories of intellectual structure based upon factor analysis (e.g., Vernon, 1959, 1961; Cattell, 1971; Horn, 1978; Royce, 1977). Factor analysis of the intercorrelations among sub-tests of widely used IQ tests such as the Wechsler Adult Intelligence Scale (WAIS) has revealed not a unitary intellective factor, but an hierarchical arrangement of abilities (Wallbrown, Blaha and Wherry, 1974). Even the most outspoken and longstanding adversary of hierarchical theories of intellectual structure, J.P. Guilford (1967; 1971) has capitulated in his most recent public statement (Guilford, 1980) conceding that the weight of available evidence favours a hierarchical interpretation. The principles of hierarchical organisation have been retained in theories of mental abilities which transcend factor-analytic methods (e.g., Sternberg, 1979) and which strive to integrate research findings from many disparate disciplines (e.g., Koestler, 1979).

Much of Burt's work after publication of his benchmark paper of 1949 was devoted to adducing evidence for his belief in the hereditary determination of the general factor at the apex of the intellectual hierarchy. The recently published authoritative biography of Cyril Burt by Hearnshaw (1979), who had access to Burt's own diaries, confirms that Burt perpetrated systematic fraud from about 1950 onwards. Data from his twin studies, in particular, are worthless. Burt's (1949) hypothesis that the general factor in his data matrices represents innate cognitive ability remains unfounded and recourse must be had to other sources in search of a resolution to the nature/nurture issue in intelligence.

Primary Mental Abilities

While Burt's (1949) model was acclaimed by British psychologists as a promising rapprochement between Spearman's (1927) two-factor theory and the growing evidence of group factors independent of g but more general than the specifics, it failed to satisfy many of the criteria necessary for a convincing scientific theory of mental structure. Not least, the factor-analytic procedures favoured by Burt lacked the desired degree of objectivity. His method of factor extraction leads inevitably to a hierarchical interpretation of the data with a general factor accounting for the greatest proportion of the variance. Factors beneath the general factor necessarily have both positive and negative loadings, making interpretation very problematic. Furthermore, his method allows only for the extraction of orthogonal factors, imposing unwarranted constraints upon interpretation and foreclosing the possibility of studying relationships that might exist among intellectual dimensions.

These and other shortcomings had been foreseen early on by L.L. Thurstone (1931), working at the University of Chicago in America, where he developed the statistical method of <u>multiple factor analysis</u>. As is often the case with important scientific developments, there were several independent precursors to Thurstone's formulation. According to Burt the essential idea of multiple factor analysis was clearly set out by the British statistician Karl Pearson in the first decade of the century, but was never followed up. The same principles were independently discovered and further developed by Garnett (1919) in an article published in the proceedings of the Royal Society. At about the same time American mathematicians were developing the methodology for principal components analysis, which Truman Kelly (1923; 1928; 1935) extended into multiple components analysis and applied for the first time to mental test data.

Yet there is general consensus that it was Thurstone's (1931; 1933; 1935; 1947) clear exposition of multiple factor analysis and its largescale application to psychological test data (Thurstone, 1936; 1938; 1944) that heralded a major turning point in the history of differential psychology. Henceforth the centre of developments shifted from the prestigious London group to America where it has remained to the present.

Thurstone's (1924) early views on the nature of intelligence developed, in part, as a reaction against mechanistic S-R theory. He viewed all mental life as action in the process of being formulated. He saw the origins of cognitive behaviour within the individual rather than as a response to external stimuli. He argued that the behaviourists' sequence of stimulus-person-response should be reformulated to read person-stimulus-response. This last insight has only recently regained currency in cognitive psychology, where it has been independently rediscovered, for example, by Tyler (1978) as the basis of her theory of individuality and personal choice. It also occupies a central position in some, but not all modern theories of information processing. Thurstone's extensive experience at the Carnegie Institute of Technology, with problems in educational and vocational prediction, greatly influenced his impatience with a single overall index of general intelligence. According to his biographer (Wood, 1962) he considered such indices as the IQ to be a "hodge-podge of unknown abilities combined at unknown weights". He was similarly disenchanted with other central concepts in the popular view of intelligence at this time. He exposed serious flaws in the rationale of the mental age concept (Thurstone, 1926) and rejected the pseudo-axiomatic assumption of Gaussian distributions underlying mental traits (Thurstone, 1927).

Against this background of his developing views on intelligence, the impetus for his methodological innovations must be seen, at least in part, to have arisen as a reaction against the restrictive confines of Spearman's (1927) theory of g and s and the methodology that evolved around it. Central to Thurstone's whole approach was a spirit of rigorous empiricism, founded on the premise that data must be permitted to guide theory development, subject to the accepted scientific principles of parsimony and objectivity. Instead of addressing himself to the debate on whether a table of correlation co-efficients supported mainly a general factor, mainly group factors, or some compromise between the two, he reformulated the basic factor-analytic problem. The central question for Thurstone was to determine how many factors need be postulated to account for the observed correlations. It was left to his method to determine whether the resultant factors should be construed as common or group, broad or narrow. In the course of developing his technique he introduced several major extensions to the basic factor-analytic method, including the concept of communalities, the notion of rotating the reference frame, the departure from orthogonality to admit oblique references axes, the procedures for second-order factor analysis, the principle of factorial invariance and, above all, the crucial idea of simple structure (Thurstone, 1940; 1947).

Thurstone (1936; 1938) first applied his method of multiple factor analysis to a matrix of intercorrelations among 56 tests that had been administered to 240 students at the University of Chicago. Instead of one general factor, his method revealed nine separate factors, seven of which could be readily interpreted. He identified the factors as spatial ability (S), perceptual speed (P), number facility (N), verbal meaning (V), rote memory (M), word fluency (W), and inductive reasoning (I).

The remaining factors he identified tentatively as deductive reasoning (D) and a restriction factor (R). A subsequently applied oblique rotation of the reference frame, guided by the criterion of simple structure (Thurstone, 1940) revealed low positive correlations among all but the two verbal factors (V and W) which were more substantially correlated.

Thurstone (1938) labelled his factors the primary mental abilities (PMAs) arguing that his statistical procedures justified, for the first time, a scientific interpretation of factors as real functional and causal entities. He was nonetheless cautious not to intimate that his abilities were necessarily primary in any ultimate neurological sense, nor that they should be regarded as empirically irreducible. He fully acknowledged the effects that sampling variables, both in terms of subject selection and test selection, might exert on the final factor solution. For the same reason he never claimed his list of PMAs was exhaustive of the potential repertoire of human abilities.

At first it seemed that Thurstone's (1939) results constituted a mortal blow to the British theory of g. A possible reconciliation was soon perceived, however, by R.B. Cattell (1941) who suggested that g might be obtained as a second-order factor among Thurstone's primaries. Until then no suitable methodology had been developed for second-order factor analysis, largely because prior to Thurstone no one had seriously entertained the notion of correlating factors at the first order.

In a subsequent study (Thurstone and Thurstone, 1941) the notion of oblique factors was taken an important step forward. It was argued that the maintenance of orthogonality among factors amounted to the imposition of an unnecessary and arbitrary mathematical constraint. From a scientific point of view it seemed more reasonable to expect that abilities might be correlated with one another, especially in particular experimental samples, but potentially also in the general population, just as the distinct physical attributes of weight and height tend to be correlated. The Thurstones accordingly left it to the data to determine whether and to what extent their factors would be correlated. The final solution to the factor rotation problem was left to the criterion of simple structure, which ensured a mathematically unique and scientifically meaningful solution.

In this study (Thurstone and Thurstone, 1941) ten factors were extracted from the intercorrelations among 60 tests administered to 710 eighth-grade children. The factors were rotated to an oblique simple structure. Cosines of the angular separations among the reference axes indicated substantially higher correlations than those found among primaries in the adult sample. Nevertheless the initial PMAs of N, W, S, V, M, I, and P seemed to have been replicated in the sample of school children, with minor differences in the patterns for different age groups. A second-order analysis of the correlations among the six most stable primaries (N, W, S, V, M, I) suggested that a single factor was sufficient to account for the common variance. The verbal and inductive primaries had the highest loadings of the second-order factor, while rote memory had the lowest loading. The factor was interpreted tentatively as a second-order general factor, which only further research in different samples, using independent tests, could corroborate or refute as a universal intellective factor analogous to Spearman's g.

In principle, at least, there thus seemed grounds for a resolution to the seemingly disparate British and American results, with the important concept of hierarchical organisation offering the framework needed for a theoretical reconciliation. Henceforth emphasis shifted from direct attempts to clarify the nature of the hypothetical construct, g, to the seemingly more profitable enterprise of uncovering the full range of primary mental abilities. The question of second-order factors was relegated, for the time, to a position of lesser importance.

TAXONOMIC SYSTEMS OF COGNITIVE PERFORMANCE

The Search for a Taxonomic System

The success of Thurstone''s early PMA studies led to the mounting of a large-scale search in pursuit of further primary abilities. At first, particular domains of cognitive behaviour, such as memory, verbal, perceptual, or spatial were systematically explored and new abilities were uncovered (e. g., Thurstone, 1944; Thurstone, 1950; Adkins and Lyerly, 1952; Pemberton, 1952). But as Thurstone's general approach became more widely known and his techniques more readily available beyond his laboratory, the search became less co-ordinated and more frenzied. Many new factors were thrown up, often as trivial by-products of studies with somewhat different aims. Often factors failed to emerge in independent attempts at replication, remaining specific to the particular data matrices that produced them (French, 1951). The clear perspective Thurstone had brought to bear on the problem of defining the ability domain clouded with his passing in the mid nineteen fifties, becoming progressively more confused by the clumsy efforts of less competent researchers.

A notable exception to the vogue of haphazardly proliferating ability factors that swept through the nineteen fifties and early sixties is to be found in the ambitious but co-ordinated research programme of J.P. Guilford (1956; 1967) and his many collaborators at the University of Southern California. Guilford's well-known three-dimensional model of the structure-of-intellect (S-I) was put forward in an attempt to bring order to the disarray that was rapidly overtaking the field of abilities research. The model arose partly as a systematic summary of empirical results Guilford had amassed in the course of his work in the American Armed Forces during the Second World War. But it was influenced to a great extent also by his intuitive insights and personal philosophy regarding the nature of human intellect. It is due to this element of arbitrariness underlying his principles of classification, that the model has never enjoyed the degree of acceptance accorded earlier to Thurstone's primary mental abilities.

Guilford's (1956; 1967) basic model comprises a cube defined by three dimensions he terms operations, products, and contents. He identifies five operations, namely cognition, memory, divergent production, convergent production and evaluation; six products, namely units, classes, relations, systems, transformations, and implications; and four contents, called figural, symbolic, semantic, and behavioural. The result is a three-way matrix of 120 cells each determined by a unique combination of operations, products, and contents. Each cell is considered to represent a unique intellectual ability. In some cases more than one ability per cell has been found, particularly when more than one sense modality (e.g., visual or auditory) is involved.

An important and highly controversial feature of the model is that the cells are treated as strictly orthogonal. This carries the implication that the intellect is composed of well over a hundred mutually independent abilities. For many this notion stretches scientific credulity too far. Moreover, it is at variance with the enormous weight of research findings from beyond Guilford's laboratory which points, with remarkable consistency, to a picture of significantly fewer, positively correlated ability factors (e.g., French, Ekstrom, and Price, 1963; Horn, 1976; Kline, 1979). One constructive critic of the S-I model (Varela, 1969) has proposed the interesting idea of replacing Guilford's cube with a cylinder to represent the closer relationships among factors. In a very recent statement, Guilford (1980) has relented in his insistence on orthogonality, allowing that factors may be correlated, indeed, in the real world. He does not see this admission as a criticism of the S-I model, however, preferring to view his model as the best available framework for constructing a hierarchy of abilities.

But the fundamental criticism remains that the initial principles of classification are derived largely on a priori grounds and are arbitrary. Alternative taxonomic principles have been proposed by other writers, notably Eysenck (1953; 1967), Guttman (1954; 1964) and Humphreys (1961) which are no less valid but have been subjected to far less empirical verification and have not had anything like the same impact on research in related areas of psychology. Indeed, one of the greatest strengths of Guilford's S-I model is its richness as a source of ideas for stimulating new research. Hence, in recent years attention has been directed at exploring the relations between S-I concepts and information-processing theory (Guilford and Tenopyr, 1968; Guilford and Bradley, 1970), while Michael (1968), Dunham and Bunderson (1969), and others have examined relationships between S-I factors, learning, and instruction methods. Guilford (1979) has recently provided a useful summary of these applications of the S-I model to more general problems in cognitive psychology.

It can be expected that the S-I model will continue to exert an influence on research at the interface between human abilities and other domains because of its convenient, logical dimensions. But as the basis for a theory of human intellect it has been found sterile and wanting in empirical support. In a major summary of work on the S-I model, Guilford and Hoepfner (1971) claim to have found support for a large number of the factors expected to fill the 120 cells. Yet few critics have been willing to accept the S-I factors as referents for meaningful abilities (e. g., Vernon, 1964; 1969b). Humphreys (1962) deplores Guilford's claim to have produced more factors than Thurstone (1938) had tests, due to the widespread view that the latter had sampled the ability domain carefully. Humphreys accuses Guilford of blowing up trivial or specific variance into factors by artful inclusion of closely similar tests. The critical evaluations of Horn (1967; Horn and Knapp, 1973) have exposed fundamental shortcomings in the factor-analytic methodology favoured by Guilford and his colleagues in seeking to verify their factors. In particular, their Procrustean methods of target rotation have been shown to provide no better support for factors predicted on the basis of the S-I model than for predictions from random models (Horn and Knapp, 1973).

Alternative Systems of Classification

Summaries of factor studies in the abilities domain by reviewers outside of Guilford's laboratory recognise support for significantly fewer primary abilities (French, Ekstrom, and Price, 1963; Pawlik, 1966; Horn, 1976; Kline, 1979). These reviewers would probably concur in settling on no more than about 30 and perhaps fewer established primary factors. Not all of these would be regarded as useful or widely applicable in the real world (Vernon, 1979) but they are nonetheless important from a scientific viewpoint. Most reviewers are also agreed that one of the most consistent findings in the psychometric literature is the positive manifold, or oblique structure among ability factors, as predicted by Thurstone. This is in sharp contrast to the orthogonal structure artificially imposed by Guilford as a mathematical constraint on his data. The positive correlations among ability factors should not be overhastily interpreted, however, as conclusive evidence of the pervasive influence of a general factor (g) at the second-order level. This remains an open question for empirical investigation. It is equally well established that correlations of near zero between particular pairs of tests, or factors, are frequently found. Moreover, the pattern of correlations among ability tests is known to vary somewhat as a result of sampling differences and test selection, leaving the question of factorial invariance over populations an open one.

The above considerations should serve to emphasize that the search for a good taxonomic system in the realm of human abilities is no mean task.

Eysenck (1953; 1967) is one of the first to have attempted the construction of an alternative and more parsimonious system to replace the S-I model. Like Guilford, he distinguishes among three major principles of classification, but he does not divide his resulting cube into mutually exclusive cells, or compartments. On one axis he distinguishes among different types of mental processes, such as reasoning, memory, or perception, based largely on Thurstone's (1938) PMAs. Along the second axis he recognises a distinction among different types of test materials, or task materials such as verbal, numerical, or spatial, again being guided by Thurstone's results. His third dimension reflects differences in the quality of response demanded. The major distinction here is between speed and power, following the insightful but complex work of Furneaux (1960). Eysenck's model appears to hold considerable merit as a more dynamic representation of the way different components of a task influence cognitive performance. But it was designed mainly with a view to explaining the determinants of scores on omnibus intelligence tests and to serve as the basis for constructing more effective tests. Unfortunately it has not been followed up by systematic research and evaluation.

A different system for classifying cognitive performance has been proposed by Guttman (1954; 1964) within the framework of his facet theory of intelligence. Although his model does not derive directly from factor-analytic results, it has been strongly influenced by this tradition of research and warrants brief mention here. Guttman (1950) seems to be one of the few to have heeded Thurstone's (1947, p.xiii) recommendation that a non-metric form of analysis, yielding rank order data, might be ultimately more suited to the problem of studying the structure of interrelations among intelligence tests. Application of his non-metric smallest space analysis (SSA) (Guttman, 1968) to data taken from Thurstone and Thurstone (1941) and Thurstone (1938) suggested that the space defined by the interrelations among tests could be described with reference to a roughly conical structure called a circumplex. This space is stratified cross-sectionally into a series of roughly concentric circles. Successive strata represent qualitative differences in test demands along a continuum Guttman (1965) characterises as varying from analytic at the core, to achievement at the circumference. The distinction between analytic and achievement depends on the nature of the relations that must be cognised by the test subject in order to produce a correct answer. Analytic relations are rule inferring and closely parallel Spearman's (1923) eduction of relations, while achievement relations are rule applying and resemble Spearman's eduction of correlates. The circumplex is divided radially into segments corresponding roughly to what Guttman (1965) calls languages of communication. These are analogous to the distinction in Eysenck's (1953) model among types of materials, notably verbal, numerical, and spatial/pictorial.

Guttman (1967; Guttman and Schlesinger, 1966) acknowledges many of the limitations inherent in his model. Particularly, that facet analysis cannot be applied to all kinds of tests and that the logical distinction between analytic and achievement items may not always be paralleled by a psychological distinction at the process level.

A somewhat related model has been proposed independently by Humphreys (1962) who acknowledges the dependence of his thinking on the initial stimulation he received from Guttman's (1954) formulation of facet theory. Humphreys' facet model in some respects also resembles earlier work by Godfrey Thomson (1939) and E.L. Thorndike, to both of whom he gives credit. Like their conceptions of mental structure, however, it is of no more than heuristic interest. It amounts to an a priori set of logical principles (facets and elements) for classifying mental tests or for designing new ones. Little empirical work appears to have been stimulated by this model and it has not been systematically pursued by Humphreys. As in the case of the arbitrary classification schemes of Guilford and Guttman it is doubtful whether even extensive empirical research would establish Humphreys' (1962) taxonomic system as a useful scientific representation of the organisation of human abilities.

Higher-order Systems of Abilities

While Guilford and his many followers concentrated chiefly on the extension of Thurstone's list of primary abilities, R.B. Cattell and his adherents have done more than any other group in developing Thurstone's notion of second- or higher-order structure among abilities. From the published literature it is difficult to determine who deserves credit for first proposing the idea of second-order factor analysis. Cattell (1971) claims priority dates back to his paper delivered to the 1940 annual meeting of the American Psychological Association (Cattell, 1941) which paved the ground for a reconciliation between the seemingly antithetical perspectives of Spearman (1927) and Thurstone (1938). Be that as it may, the first published application of second-order analysis is by Thurstone and Thurstone (1941).

Although the Thurstones took out only one factor at the second-order, Cattell's (1941) hypothesis was that there should be two. This hypothesis was more fully developed in a subsequent paper (Cattell, 1943), and has since become known as the theory of fluid and crystallized intelligence.

Ironically, the introduction of this theory coincided with the presentation in 1941 by D.O. Hebb (Hebb, 1942) of an independently derived but very similar set of conclusions, pointing to the likelihood that two distinct concepts of intelligence should be recognised. Hebb's theory, based on evidence from clinical neurology, proposed that an innate genotypic potential, termed intelligence A, should be distinguished from the phenotypic expression of realized intellectual capacity, termed intelligence B. Cattell (1963; 1971) has summarized the major similarities and differences between his theory and that of Hebb. Perhaps the most important difference, from the viewpoint of theory testing, is that both of Cattell's constructs can be directly assessed, whereas neither of Hebb's constructs can be measured independently. For this reason Cattell's theory has attracted wider scientific interest than Hebb's and has stimulated a greater volume of research.

It seems strange at first sight, therefore, that the theory was left dormant for two decades following its announcement, before being actively pursued. The reason for this, as Cattell (1963) suggests, is that a critical experiment to test the theory had to await crucial methodological developments in factor analysis and psychometrics. A somewhat related reason is that the theory's major proponent became engrossed, during the intervening period, in pioneering explorations of personality structure.

In its original formulation the structural theory of fluid and crystallized intelligence states that in a comprehensive sampling of human abilities, the effects of two major cognitive dimensions can be discerned. One of these, fluid intelligence (Gf) is a close behavioural correlate of basic neural-physiological capacity, as laid down initially by heredity and intra-uterine influences. Gf is not a direct referent for innate potential in the sense of Hebb's (1941) intelligence A, but reflects rather a pattern of behaviour resulting from the interaction of this potential with environmental-developmental influences common to members of any society. Crystallized intelligence (Gc) on the other hand, represents the level of cognitive development attained through accumulation of knowledge, skills, and strategies in the course of acculturation. A primary agent in the development of Gc is therefore formal learning in the context of education, whereas Gf is to a greater extent dependent on the incidental learning opportunities available in virtually any human culture.

Cattell (1963) is at pains to point out that Gc is not the same as general scholastic achievement (V ed) nor should Gf be equated with the Burt-Vernon group factor, K, practical intelligence.

Underlying both Gf and Gc are what Spearman (1923) termed the eduction of relations and eduction of correlates. Cattell considers the basic processes involved to depend upon two general concepts, identified respectively as anlage functions, reflecting the perceptual limits of an individual and generalised solution instruments or aids. Examples of anlage functions would include Spearman's (1923) span of apprehension, Hearnshaw's (1964) temporal integration, or Guilford's (1967) adaptive flexibility. Aids are likened to Harlow's (1949) learning sets, Piaget's (1946) operations, and to Bruner's (Bruner, Goodnow, and Austin, 1956) strategies. Aids are considered to range along a continuum from those that are essentially personal, idiosyncratic cognitive techniques, to those which have become the common possession of members of a culture. Aids may also range from those which virtually everyone has an opportunity to acquire, to those accessible to relatively few individuals, who have gained exposure to highly selective, usually organized, learning situations such as courses in advanced mathematics or musicology.

The principal theoretical distinction between Gf and Gc has to do with their location in this latter continuum. Although both involve anlage functions and aids, Gf reflects relatively greater influence of anlage functions, coupled with aids of an idiosyncratic nature relevant to the immediate environmental situation. On the other hand Gc reflects relatively more use of previously acquired aids and concepts available in memory stores. Moreover, the aids involved in Gf derive from relatively universal human experiences, whereas those in Gc are more specifically tied to a particular culture or socialization programme.

In the early nineteen sixties Cattell (1963) undertook a study he believed to constitute a critical check on the fluid-crystallized theory. The design of the experiment called for second-order factorization of the first-order factors found among a battery of culture-fair and culturally-embedded ability tests, together with a disproportionate number of non-ability variables. The latter were intended as markers for well established personality factors with a known structure at the second-order level (Cattell and Beloff, 1959). They were not of direct theoretical interest but were included in the design of the study for methodological reasons associated with factor rotation. Culture-fair measures included four perceptual tests from Cattell's (1957) IPAT Culture-fair Intelligence Scale 2a. Thurstone's PMA battery was used for measures of five culturally-embedded primary abilities, notably V, N, I, S and W. The latter two were considered relatively less culturally saturated and consequently likely to involve significant amounts of both Gf and Gc. The sample consisted of 277 junior high school boys and girls from Illinois. Altogether 44 variables were intercorrelated. Twenty-two primary factors were extracted and rotated to oblique simple structure. Intercorrelations between the primaries were determined from a transformation matrix and submitted to factoring at the second-order level. Four personality and two ability factors were identified at this order. The ability factors corresponded to the expected nature of general fluid and general crystallized intelligence. The former was defined by the culture-fair subtests plus space while the latter involved the four remaining PMAs, notably V, N, W, and I.

A subsequent study by Horn and Cattell (1966) using an adult sample brought further refinement to the definition of Gf and Gc. New evidence was brought to bear on four further general factors at the second-order level. These were identified as general visualization, fluency of retrieval, speediness, and carefulness. Positive manifold for the intercorrelations among the six second-order ability factors was interpreted as indicating "a social fact of interdependence between intra-person and environmental influences determining behavioural attributes" (Horn and Cattell, 1966, p. 253).

The work of Horn (1966) and Horn and Bramble (1967) provides further support for the six broad cognitive dimensions at the second-order level. Furthermore, their study was designed to assess the short-term stability of the factors as a check on their trait status. Tests were administered to the same subjects on ten separate occasions over five days. Special analyses were used to distinguish trait from state variance. Other than general speediness, all expected factors appeared in the analyses and all manifested substantial trait variance. Tests for fluid intelligence showed relatively more day-to-day covariation than crystallized measures, however, revealing some of the properties associated with psychological states. The short-term fluctuations in fluid ability were interpreted as evidence for its closer dependence upon basic neurophysiological processes.

On testing the lower limits of applicability of his theory Cattell (1967) found fluid and crystallized dimensions operating as distinct abilities as early as five to six years of age. This study also revealed a dimension resembling general visualization. Independent researchers have since produced evidence that the theory holds up in different socio-economic classes (Schmidt and Crano, 1974) in other national groups at a variety of ages (Undheim, 1976; 1978) and in a broad cross-section of distinct cultural populations (Hakstian and Vandenberg, 1976).

The weight of evidence in support of Cattell's structural theory of higher order ability organisation is impressive. Yet it would be vastly premature to accept the theory as a valid representation of the structure of human abilities. At best it is aimed in the right direction, but it is still at a very early and tentative stage of development. In its most comprehensive elaboration to date Cattell (1971) introduces major revisions and extensions, adding many new insights, hypotheses and technical terms. The outcome, known as the triadic theory of intelligence, has now been part of the psychological literature for a decade, but much of it has yet to be subjected to empirical verification. Influential critics such as Vernon (1979) and Guilford (1980) view its basic tenets with scepticism and choose to dismiss a good deal of Cattell's theorising as fanciful. Others, most notably Horn (1978) accept it in better faith as the best available system for integrating present knowledge and guiding future research in the realm of human abilities.

STABILITY OF COGNITIVE STRUCTURE

Life-span Changes in Cognitive Structure

For any model of intellectual structure to have an impact on the psychology of cognition as a whole, provision should be made for relating structure to function and for encompassing both within a developmental framework. How do certain structural features evolve, what are the underlying mechanisms and processes and to what extent do they become modified over the life-span? these are questions to which only some of the structural models considered in the preceding chapters have been addressed. Burt (1949; 1954) for example, developed his hypothesis of intellectual differentiation to explain the increasing structural complexity that accompanies growth during the childhood years. Thurstone and Thurstone (1941) were less explicit about the mechanisms of differentiation, but were equally ready to acknowledge that structural changes take place during childhood development. Guilford's S-I model with its mutually exclusive factors explicitly ignores the question of structural development. Only Cattell's (1963) fluid-crystallized theory and its extension in the form of triadic theory (Cattell, 1971) directly accommodate the question of development over the entire life-span, from birth to death. Most prominent developmental theories of cognition, conversely, pay little or no attention to the adult years and take insufficient account of the problems of structure as understood and explicated in the literature of differential psychology (Reinert, 1970).

One of the most indefatigable and insightful reviewers of the literature on human abilities and their structural development over the life-span is Cattell's former student and collaborator, J.L. Horn (1968; 1970; 1976; 1978). In a major review of research on the life-span development of human abilities prior to 1970, Horn (1970) attempts to draw together the threads of evidence from over six hundred studies. He is forced to acknowledge that the data are replete with inconsistencies, paradoxes, and unresolved issues. Yet certain broad consistencies are apparent that transcend sampling, theoretical and methodological differences across studies.

Perhaps the most notable consistency bears on the finding of a process of structural change in the composition and expression of human intellect over the life-span. There is broad agreement across researchers that the infant years (approximately the first two years of life) are characterized chiefly by the development of sensorimotor alertness (Bayley, 1943; Piaget, 1936; 1946; Hunt 1961). Transfer learning (Ferguson, 1954; 1956) and even trial-and-error learning appear to be unimportant influences on development during this period. Classical conditioning and frequent repetition appear to be the principal factors producing growth and change. Ability measurements taken during this period show generally low correlations, sometimes even negative, with measures taken during later periods of life.

The next phase of development appears to centre around the formation and attainment of basic concepts, or what Cattell (1963) has described as the acquisition of generalised solution instruments or aids. This activity begins some time during the second year of life and continues essentially throughout the life-span. But is is most prominent and intensive in the age range from two to six years (Hofstaetter, 1954). This period corresponds roughly to the preconceptual phase of the second major stage in the Piagetian scheme. Use is made primarily of perceptual processes for exploring and knowing the world. At first objects are represented idiosyncratically in terms of what might be called symbols. Gradually these become integrated with one another as complex symbol systems are formed. This process is facilitated by the simultaneous and interdependent development of language. Transfer learning plays an important role in the growth and structural evolution of intelligence during this period. The greater portion of reliable variance in measured abilities at this stage comes from tests of the processes implied in the Cattell-Horn notion of fluid intelligence. Substantial positive correlations are found with measures taken later in life, although these become progressively weaker as age increases.

Cognitive development and accompanying changes in intellectual structure are marked during the childhood years. From about age nine to fifteen emphasis shifts from the acquisition of basic concepts and aids and the mastery of language to a phase of growth characterised more by the intensive internalization of culture and a corresponding differentiation of the intellect. In a Western context the primary agent of acculturation shifts from the home to the school and the specialised abilities that evolve are those emphasised in the curricula of formal education. Most notable among these are the primary mental abilities first identified by Thurstone and Thurstone (1941). Relative to earlier periods, this phase is characterised by major growth in the abilities underlying crystallized intelligence. Cultural differences in values and emphasis exert important influences on the emerging intellectual structure during this period. For example, Levinson (1961; 1963) found that in Jewish-American homes and communities development of the primary ability V (verbal comprehension) is emphasised relative to the development of other primaries such as I (inductive reasoning), N (number facility) or S (space). A reverse pattern was found to hold in the case of Chinese-Americans. Similar factors have been advanced to account for the emergence of sex differences in ability patterns during this stage (Hill, 1967; Werts, 1976). Studies by Jensen (1967), Cattell, Feingold, and Sarason (1941), and many others serve to caution that the expression of intelligence during this period, although significantly influenced by acculturation, is more than just the product of formal learning and transfer. To a significant extent it is also still an expression of important unlearned anlage functions and of incidental learning. In Cattell's terms, fluid and crystallized intelligence must be seen as highly co-operative during this period.

Considerably less is known about the development and changing structure of intelligence in the adult years than in the case of childhood and youth. Yet a substantial volume of research has been addressed to this question, as testified by Horn's (1970) review. Consideration of the evidence suggests that despite the amount of work done, there is still too little clarity to come to

any firm conclusions. Two of the most hotly debated issues
concern, firstly, whether the structure of intellect remains
stable during adulthood, whether the process of differentiation
that characterises the pre-puberty and adolescent years continues
into adulthood and on into old age, or whether a structural
de-differentiation or neo-integration occurs. This issue revolves
around the problem of structure. The second issue has to do with
the level of intelligence. Does it remain constant, does it
continue to increase, or does it reach an asymptote and thereafter
decline? Both issues are compounded by the prevalence of
differences among cultures and between the sexes. For purposes of
the present discussion, only the first issue, pertaining to
structure, is of direct concern. (The interested reader is
referred to papers by Horn and Donaldson (1976), and Baltes and
Schaie (1976) for good expositions of the major opposing views
concerning the question of intellectual growth, stability, or
decline in adulthood. More recent statements on the differing
arguments in the debate are to be found in Horn and McArdle
(1980), and Cunningham (1981)).

On the question of structural change in the adult years, Reinert's
(1970) very comprehensive review suggests that the evidence is
weighted in favour of a de-differentiation hypothesis.
Particularly in the mature years (from about age 35 onwards) the
intellectual structure is characterised by a very strong first
factor, with a concomitant decline in the importance of subsequent
factors. Balinsky (1941) has described this finding as indicating
a re-organisation of the intellect towards a flexible complexity.
Horn (Horn and Cattell, 1967; Horn and Donaldson, 1976) argues
that the results are consistent with the predictions of Gf-Gc
theory, notably that crystallized intelligence increases in
importance during adulthood relative to fluid intelligence and
other abilities. Only qualified support for this view is offered
by a recent test of the Gf-Gc theory in old age (Baltes,
Cornelius, Spiro, Nesselroade, and Willie, 1980). The results of
this study do, however, clearly support the more general
hypothesis that in the late adult years (age range 60-89) a
neo-integration, or de-differentiation of psychometric
intelligence occurs. Recent work by Cunningham (1980b; 1981;
Cunningham and Birren, 1980) offers further, qualified support for
the de-differentiation hypothesis in late adulthood. This work
suggests that although the number of intellectual factors may not
decrease with ageing, factor covariances tend to increase,
implying a greater interdependence among abilities in late
adulthood.

The general hypothesis that emerges from the literature is thus
that the intellectual structure undergoes continual, if subtle,
change over the course of the human life-span. In the earliest

years biogenic factors are more important than environmental ones, exercising an <u>integrative</u> influence on cognitive development. At some stage during childhood intensive acculturation assumes paramount importance, bringing about structural <u>differentiation</u> and the growth of specialised abilities. As the individual matures in adulthood, a re-organisation of the intellect occurs, with abilities becoming <u>loosely integrated</u> in a complex, flexible structure.

This biosocial hypothesis of intellectual development is consistent with the general scientific notion of development in all living organisms (Scarr-Salapatek, 1975). Development, in a biological sense, usually refers to change, over time, in terms of both structure and function, in the direction of greater differentiation and of ·increasingly higher levels of organisation. Notwithstanding, careful reviews such as Reinert (1970) and Schaie (1970) warn against premature acceptance of this hypothesis until further evidence is available. They even discourage uncritical acceptance of the more general hypothesis that intellectual development is accompanied by structural changes of any kind. Yet both authors agree that the hypotheses are plausible in the light of available evidence and warrant further research.

Influential theorists including Piaget (1936; 1946) and his followers (Elkind and Flavell, 1969), as well as certain factor analysts (Hofstaetter, 1954) have interpreted the changing pattern of intellectual structure in terms of <u>stages of development</u>. It is indeed convenient to organise and evaluate data on the life-span development of intelligence in terms of major life-stages, as in the preceding discussion. Yet the integration-differentiation-neointegration hypothesis of structural change is not to be confused with stage developmental theories. Cronbach (1967), Nesselroade (1970), Schaie (1970) and others have pointed out that stage theories have yet to be adequately tested from a methodological viewpoint and that the available data are equally consistent with theories proposing that changes come about through continuous, imperceptibly small transformations.

The best available model to account for the observed pattern of development would seem to be that originally proposed by Anderson (1939) and subsequently extended by Humphreys (1960) and Horn (1978). It has come to be known as the <u>quasi-simplex model</u> of intellectual development (Horn, 1978). It provides a good account of the common finding that test-retest correlations based on repeated measurement over the life-span conform roughly to a pattern described by Guttman (1954) in mathematical terms as a simplex. That is to say, correlations tend to be highest for measures taken in adjacent years, but become progressively weaker as the time interval between measurements is increased, although they remain positive. This model and the findings that support it bear testimony to the lucidity of the early insights of Spencer and Alfred Binet, while suggesting that Galton's original thesis, of a unitary cognitive capacity developing at a uniform rate over time, was wrong.

Cross-cultural Comparisons of Cognitive Structure

The study of intellectual structure is rendered problematic not only as a result of ontogenetic changes over the life span, but also due to the effects of individual and group differences in biogenic and ecological circumstances. Since both sources of influence have been shown to modify the evolving intellectual structure within a given population, it seems reasonable to expect that variations in biological and ecological factors across populations might give rise to differences in intellectual structure in different populations.

This is a question of fundamental importance for psychology as a whole, since it touches on the quest for universally valid constructs that would help seal the discipline's status as a science. The branch of psychology most closely pre-occupied with this question has come to be known as cross-cultural psychology. This is an unfortunate label, because it carries with it the false connotation that interest is limited to explaining variations in behaviour in terms of cultural variables. As several prominent advocates of cross-cultural psychology have recently proclaimed, its scope must be understood to include the full spectrum of ecological and biological variables, as well as cultural variables, in the comparative study of behavioural variation (Berry, 1966; 1969; 1976; Dawson, 1969; 1971; Jahoda, 1970). Indeed, as Lijphart (1971) has pointed out, its scope is not defined in terms of content as in the case of other branches of psychology, but rather by its method. For this reason Berry (1980) has argued that a more appropriate label for this sub-discipline would have been comparative psychology, since it relies on use of the comparative method, in common with many other sciences. Regrettably the latter label, through an accident of history, has come to be associated exclusively with phylogenetic comparisons in psychology. Variations in psychological function related to culture, sex, language, age, or other factors have been excluded from the domain of comparative psychology, as this label has come to be used. An implicit identity thus needs to be made between the term cross-cultural in psychology and the term comparative in other disciplines including sociology, anthropology, economics, and political studies (Berry, 1980).

In keeping with this view, the goals of cross-cultural psychology have been variously enunciated and progressively extended by Biesheuvel (1958), Poortinga (1971), Ekensberger (1972), Triandis, Malpass, and Davidson (1972), Brislin, Lonner, and Thorndike (1973), Berry (1980) and others. It is clear from these formulations that the discipline needs to be distinguished from the superficially related, diehard nature/nurture tradition in intelligence research (Jensen, 1977).

The latter enterprise is characterised for the most part by the use of sophisticated statistical artifice in the estimation of so-called heritability ratios for such a theoretical behaviour indices as the IQ, without showing due concern for the problems of construct validity, cross-cultural comparability or measurement equivalence. Legitimate scientific enquiry into the hereditary and environmental determinants of cognitive structure and function over the life-span will have to await the application of such promising theoretical developments as exemplified in the work of Royce (1977) and his colleagues. Royce's conceptual schema takes account of the most recent developments in cognitive psychology, incorporating inputs from both experimental and psychometric research. The central analytic tool is the factor model, which is used to define a multidimensional, hierarchically organised cognitive system. The cognitive system can be specified in terms of both structural variables and process variables. The complex multiplicity of both genetic and environmental influences is also recognised and their respective effects on cognitive variables are specified in terms of a factor-gene model and a factor learning model. The models permit analysis of interactions among genetic and learning variables over the full span of ontogenetic development. The empirical work of Vandenberg (1977) and Vandenberg and Kuse (1979) represents a useful contribution to research on the hereditary basis of different mental abilities.

In contrast to Royce's concern with the partitioning of variance in cognitive behaviour between hereditary and environmental factors, cross-cultural psychologists are involved in the search for psychological universals (Dasen, 1977; Lonner, 1980) and are pre-occupied with the methodology for establishing criteria which will enable valid comparisons of psychological functions to be made across populations. Central to this endeavour is the need to develop procedures for defining constructs and processes cross-culturally. Constructs such as intelligence are not assumed or accepted on a priori grounds unless demonstrated empirically to meet criteria of dimensional identity (Frijda and Jahoda, 1966) across populations. Dimensional identity can be established either by the adoption of accepted universals from other disciplines, such as biology or linguistics, or by the empirical demonstration of <u>equivalence</u> in the data collected in different cultural populations.

Lonner (1980) has shown that there are many established universals in other disciplines which may serve as dimensions along which individuals or groups can be compared in cross-cultural psychology. There is considerably less agreement with regard to the procedures for demonstrating measurement equivalence. Different classifications of criteria of equivalence have been proposed by Berry and Dasen (1974), Poortinga (1975a), Brislin (1976), Irvine and Carroll (1980), and others. The persistent lack of consensus among these authors renders many published findings on cross-cultural differences in mean level of performance on behavioural dimensions of doubtful worth (e.g., Jensen, 1973). It would seem advisable for the enterprise of comparing performance levels cross-culturally to await further methodological developments and refinement of measuring procedures, as foreshadowed in the promising lead given by Van de Vijver and Poortinga (1982).

A somewhat less problematic, if in a sense less ambitious objective in cross-cultural research is the comparison of structural relations among dependent variables. Equivalence of structures has been identified by various writers (Irvine, 1966; Poortinga, 1975a; Bass and Royce, 1975; Irvine and Carroll, 1980) as a prerequisite for comparability of levels. The essential requirement is that patterns of covariation among variables within groups should be similar before comparisons of scores can be made across groups. This requirement is variously known as <u>scalar</u> equivalence, which is established by comparing correlation matrices (Poortinga, 1975) or <u>metric</u> equivalence which is best studied by comparison of factor structures across cultural populations (Irvine, 1966; Bass and Royce, 1975). Structural comparisons need not be made only with a view to the ultimate comparison of levels of performance on psychological constructs. They may be seen as a worthwhile scientific objective in their own right, as a means of evaluating hypotheses about structural invariance or as a means of testing more general theories of structural development cross-culturally. The study of structural congruence across cultures differs from the comparative study of performance levels in that the focus of interest in the case of the former is on the establishment of <u>similarities</u>, whereas the latter is more concerned with <u>differences</u> in the psychological make-up of different populations.

Vandenberg and Hakstian (1978) provide a useful review of factor-analytic studies in which cognitive structures are compared cross-culturally. Despite pervasive differences among studies in terms of methodological approach standards, these authors conclude that there is evidence of considerable similarity in cognitive structures across widely divergent cultures. Their conclusion is support by a re-analysis of data from Vernon's (1969) studies, undertaken in four different cultures which were administered essentially the same set of tests. Samples included Scots from the Hebrides, Ugandans, Canadian Eskimos, and Canadian Indians. Using a variety of procedures Vandenberg and Hakstian (1978) obtained factor structures for each sample separately from the original intercorrelation matrices provided by Vernon. These were rotated towards a common target considered to be the average factor matrix for the sample combined. Coefficients of factor congruence were estimated for each of seven common factors across the four samples using a formula first proposed by Tucker (1951). Congruence coefficients ranged from .71 to .88 indicating a generally high degree of agreement in the definition of factors between sample pairs. Interestingly, the factors themselves and their underlying oblique simple structure can be reconciled more readily with Thurstone's (1938) PMA model than with Vernon's (1961) own model in which the major portion of variance is attributed to a general factor at the apex of a branched hierarchy.

In a subsequent study based on the same data, Hakstian and Vandenberg (1979) sought to test the generalizability of Cattell's (1971) higher-order model of cognitive structure. Good support was found for four of the six postulated capacities, namely fluid and crystallized intelligences, general memory and general retrieval. In addition a strong Piagetian conservation factor was identified. No evidence for Cattell's second-order general cognitive speed factor was expected, or found, since no marker variables for this factor had been included in the original data. Once again it is interesting to note that Vernon's (1969) predicted general factor, g, did not materialise even at the second-order, despite the fact that Vernon himself had selected the initial measurement variables. Similarly, at the third-order not one but two very general factors were found, common to the different cultures. These were interpreted tenatively as original fluid intelligence and acculturation influences. The major dimension of discrimination among the four samples was highly dependent upon acculturation. Samples were rank-ordered in terms of mean level of performance on this dimension precisely according to independent assessments of their acculturation opportunities and familiarity with the English language.

Irvine (1979) has compiled a comprehensive survey of ninety-one studies using factor analysis to examine intellectual structure across cultures. Despite the diversity of cultures sampled, the range of different tests used, and the variations in factor-analytic methodology, broad consistencies are clearly apparent in the pattern of results. Factors reported lend themselves to parsimonious classification in six compound groupings, labelled reasoning, verbal abilities and skills, spatial/perceptual processes, numerical operations, memory functions, and physical/temperamental quickness. These groupings are strongly reminiscent of Thurstone's (1938) original PMAs.

A noteworthy relation was found by Irvine to obtain between the level of education of samples and number of mathematically extracted factors, regardless of the original number of variables on which analyses are based. This general finding lends support to the plausibility of the hypothesis that education facilitates psychological differentiation.

The degree of consistency in the pattern of factors across cultures, Irvine (1979) argues, permits a class of explanation defined as intra-hominem (p. 10). This implies support for the hypothesis of universal processing parameters in human cognition. These appear to transcend behaviour variations due to extra-hominem sources , attributable to ecological press (Witkin and Berry, 1975), or inter-hominem sources, arising from combinations of linguistic, educational, or social variables that mediate man's ability to communicate with other men (Irvine, 1979, p. 304).

Irvine emphasises that his logically constructed factor groupings are in no way intended to represent a theory of cognitive organisation. He also cautions that the groupings are internally complex and are not to be assigned status as psychological constructs. Not even the underlying mathematical factors, on which the groupings are based, should be identified automatically with psychological functions. Factors are not, in themselves, explanatory constructs. At best they are pointers to underlying sources of explanation in terms of information-processing parameters. These in turn require classification with the aid of independent experimentation, guided by cognitive theory from beyond the domain of factor analysis.

Sex Differences in Cognitive Structure and Function

The overall stability of intellectual structure across cultures must be understood at a molar level of analysis only. At the more molecular level some differences in structure seem inevitable. Even between sub-groups of a single, culturally homogeneous population, minor differences in cognitive structure may be manifest. Such differences would be expected where sub-groups differ marginally in terms of influences associated with cognitive structure, such as maturation rate (genes, hormones, nutrition), socialization (family structure, child rearing, role modelling), or specific learning opportunities (education, environment). But as in the case of cross-cultural differences in cognition, population sub-group differences are likely to be far less pronounced with regard to cognitive structure than other characteristics such as level of performance and variability. These propositions have been examined chiefly in comparative studies of population sub-groups differentiated on the basis of sex.

Money and Ehrhardt (1972), Maccoby and Jacklin (1974), Wittig (1979), and many others have pointed out that the individual attribute, sex, is less easy to define scientifically than is commonly accepted in everyday terms. There are several biological criteria that generally differentiate males from females. The most obvious and easily assessed of these include sex chromosomes, sex hormones, and reproductive organs. Inconsistencies among these biolological criteria can and do occur within an individual, if infrequently, detracting from their reliability and raising serious methodological problems for comparative gender research. The label of male or female is generally assigned at birth on the basis of external genitalia alone. This sex of assignment is most frequently used in sex research in psychology, but at least in some cases, it may conceal the confounding of effects on the variable under investigation due to inconsistencies between, say, sex chromosomes and sex hormones (Money and Ehrhardt, 1972). Sex of assignment does not show a perfect correlation with the psychological traits of masculinity and femininity (Bem, 1974), so that the attribution of observed sex-related differences in cognitive function socialization factors requires careful treatment. These and other methodological issues are not always accorded the attention they deserve in the literature on sex-related differences in cognitive behaviour. Findings of sex-differences in cognitive structure or function accordingly need to be interpreted with extreme caution, if the greater enterprise of understanding the effects of different sources of influence on human cognition is to profit from this literature.

As Petersen and Wittig (1979) have argued, the label of male or female is a highly salient characteristic of an individual. One study (Grady, 1977) has shown that of all characteristics used to describe strangers, sex was always noted and usually was the first characteristic to be mentioned. It would seem, accordingly, of the greatest importance to understand the ways in which sex is associated with relevant psychological and behavioural attributes. More accurately, the need is to understand which of the factors differentiating males from females is implicated, and through which mechanisms such factors exert their influence.

Unfortunately, the salience of sex as an individual attribute in everyday life has emotional and polemical overtones which are not always excluded from scientific discourse and laboratory investigation. It is noteworthy that while most earlier writers on the subject of behavioural sex-differences have been males, following in the tradition of Havelock Ellis's (1894) classical study, most prominent contemporary writers to challenge earlier theories are females (Anastasi, 1958; 1972; Tyler, 1965; Bem, 1974; Maccoby and Jacklin, 1975; Sherman, 1978; Waber, 1977; Wittig and Petersen, 1979).

It is regrettable that scientific debates should polarize contestants on the basis of their sex. Lehrke (1978) for example, deplores the fact that the longstanding hypothesis of greater male variability (greater female stability) in biological and cognitive traits, which can be traced back to Ellis's work, should come under increasing attack from an almost exclusively female lobby. Since scientists of both sexes frequently have to resort to the same limited body of empirical data to support their arguments, it must be assumed that the data themselves do not provide a clear-cut basis for supporting or rejecting the hypothesis. This is so despite the sophistication and plausibility of the explanatory biological mechanism proposed to account for the hypothesis (Lehrke, 1974) and the lack of alternative mechanisms in arguments rejecting the hypothesis on purely empirical grounds (Lehrke, 1978). This problem is apparent in relation to many other controversial issues in the sex difference literature. It necessitates particular alertness to the possibility of sex-linked experimenter bias when reviewing results.

Although the central issue in this discussion has to do with the stability of cognitive structure in relation to population differences, age, culture, or sex, it appears that little research has been addressed directly to the question of sex differences in cognitive structure. Most of the sex differences literature deals with comparisons of mean levels of cognitive performance, while a considerable volume of literature is also addressed to the issue of variability of cognitive function as discussed briefly above.

On the question of structural comparison, Cattell (1971) contends that there is no evidence to suggest the presence of important structural differences in intellectual make-up between the sexes, particularly as regards higher-order ability structure. With regard to structure at the level of primary abilities, he appears to recognise evidence for at least minor structural differences between the sexes, within certain restricted ability domains. Werdelin's (1959) often cited study is referred to as an example of evidence for possible sex-related structural differences in the domain of visuo-spatial thinking. In a sample of Swedish male

- 61 -

high school pupils, Werdelin found two distinct primary space factors underlying performance on tasks of geometric ability and spatial thinking, while only one factor could be identified for girls. The apparently greater differentiation of spatial abilities in the case of boys might point the way to an explanation for their generally higher performance levels on the spatial tests. On the other hand, some common underlying merchanism could be responsible for the observed sex differences in both structure and level. Bryden (1979), for example, has reviewed evidence in support of hypotheses that such differences might relate to differences in the neural organisation of the brain, particularly with regard to cerebral hemisphere asymmetry. He is obliged to conclude, like other reviewers in this field (Harris, (1978) that the evidence pertaining to sex differences in neural organisation is inadequate to account for the observed sex differences in spatial abilities.

It is surprising that no systematic attempt has been made to replicate or refute Werdelin's findings of structural differences in spatial abilities between the sexes. Until further evidence becomes available, this isolated result must be regarded as highly tentative, possibly an artefact of sampling error or research methodology. No similar finding has been forthcoming with regard to sex differences in ability structure in other cognitive domains. Major reviews of the sex differences literature (Maccoby and Jacklin, 1975; Sherman, 1978; Wittig and Petersen, 1979) make no mention of findings pertaining to structural differences. It is not clear whether this should be interpeted to imply that no noteworthy differences have been found in research, or whether research has not yet been directed at this question. A painstaking search through the literature suggests that the latter is a valid reflection of the state of research. A likely explanation is that most psychologists interested in sex differences in cognitive function seek explanations in terms of developmental theories. They criticize factor-analytic designs for reflecting the underlying structure of behaviour as a set of traits, rather than a true structure in the sense of a system of interacting units of behavioural operations (Cohen and Wilkie, 1979). While this criticism is valid for much of psychometric research, it is not a necessary criticism of theories based upon factor analysis, as in the case of stratified system theories (Catttell, 1971; 1977) both of which include a temporal dimension as an essential feature. Notwithstanding, available knowledge about performance distributions for males and females on different tests or tasks provides no reason to expect sex differences in cognitive structure. This may be viewed, perhaps, as a strong null hypothesis which has yet to be adequately tested. For the present, the question remains open for further research.

With regard to sex differences in level of cognitive performance, the literature is replete with claims and counter claims for the superiority of one sex or the other on abilities defined with varying degrees of methodological precision (Maccoby and Jacklin, 1975). In a recent careful appraisal of research evidence Sherman (1978) concludes that the most striking features to emerge are the "trivial and fragile nature of sex-related differences in cognition and flimsy quality of the theories of biological influence" (p. 172). These views are echoed and amplified in the more assertive conclusions of Fairweather (1976) who argues flatly that there is as yet no convincing evidence for sex-related differences in cognition, or in underlying cerebral organization.

Nevertheless, Sherman (1978) proceeds to argue that if any biologically based sex difference in cognitive performance exists, the most plausible claim would seem to be for the frequently cited female precocity in verbal skills. The likely explanation she considers to be found in some aspects of the accelerated biological maturation of females. This claim is not endorsed by Maccoby and Jacklin (1975), who show that at best it is subject to severe qualifications.

Sherman's "bent twig hypothesis" to account for female verbal precocity, is that girls show an early preference for verbal, left hemisphere, approaches to problem solution, which establishes a primacy for verbal, as opposed to visuo-spatial thinking. This primacy, or bending of the twig in favour of verbal processing, is encouraged through socialization since verbal activities are supposed to be sex-typed female. Visuo-spatial skills, on the other hand, are considered sex-typed male. Females are considered to lose their advantage in verbal skills towards the onset of adolescence, when males catch up "as they mature and as they are exposed to heavy educational intervention in verbal training" (Sherman, 1978, p.172).

The primacy hypothesis has something of a hen-or-egg argument about it, since it is not clear which comes first, an advantage favouring verbal over spatial processing in girls due to the developmental course or neural organisation between the hemispheres, or a culturally induced female disposition to verbal cognitive activity, which interacts with neural development. Although Sherman (1978) musters a good deal of evidence in favour of her claim for early female precocity in verbal skills, the observed sex differences are neither large nor consistent. In their review, Maccoby and Jacklin (1975) find that earlier, but not more recent studies, point to a small female lead on specific aspects of language acquisition prior to actual speech, before the age of three. Between ages three and eleven no reliable sex differences in verbal skills are apparent. After puberty, a clear female lead seems to develop in certain kinds of verbal tests, but not in others. These findings do not support hypotheses of sex differences in the development of hemisphere lateralization. Rather, they are consistent with hypotheses emphasizing sex role differentiation in the course of socialization, chiefly during the adolescent period.

A good number of technically complex biological hypotheses have been advanced or contested in attempts to reconcile the disparate results of research in relation to verbal sex differences (e.g., Buffery and Gray, 1972; Bryden, 1979; Carter-Saltzman, 1979; Dan, 1979; Nash, 1979; Petersen, 1979; Waber, 1979). It seems premature to attempt an evaluation of the various arguments, however, since the fundamental question of whether the sexes differ reliably in verbal skills has not been answered satisfactorily yet. The magnitude and direction of differences vary across studies. Many studies have failed to establish a significant sex difference in verbal skills; Maccoby and Jacklin (1975) list over one hundred researches that failed to establish a significant sex difference in the verbal domain. More than a dozen studies are listed showing a significant difference in verbal performance favouring males. The magnitude and direction of the differences shows some dependence upon age, as well as socialization factors. In studies undertaken outside of the U.S.A., for example in W. Germany (Preston, 1962), Zimbabwe (Irvine, 1966), and Tanzania (Drenth, Van der Flier, and Omari, 1979) results most frequently favour males. Presumably this has to do with the higher ratio of male to female teachers in these countries compared to America. The argument in this case would be that activities such as reading, essay writing, and other verbal pursuits are less obviously sex-typed female than in the U.S.A., or that they are sex-typed male. The trend favouring the hypothesis of female verbal precocity in the largely American literature may be simply an indication of a national socialization bias, and biological explanations need not be implicated.

Before leaving this question it is also important to consider, in more precise terms, which verbal skills are purported to differentiate the sexes. Omnibus "verbal intelligence" tests or verbal aptitude tests, in vogue amongst educational psychologists in the U.S.A., are of no value in relation to this question. It is necessary to restrict the analysis to only those data based on reliable measures of established primary factors in the verbal domain. The best known of these are Thurstone's (1938) original factors for word fluency (W) and verbal meaning (V). The former has to do with the production of words under appropriate constraints, such as listing in a short span of time as many words as possible conforming to a given prefix or suffix. The latter factor involves comprehension of the meaning of words, as in a vocabulary test, or reasoning about the meaning in written material, as in a test of reading comprehension. When verbal skills are appraised separately in terms of these factors, the evidence suggests that the advantage of American females is restricted to factor W (Cattell, 1971; Maccoby and Jacklin, 1975; Wittig and Petersen, 1979). Males outperform females on tests of factor V about as often as not, resulting in no clear trend favouring either sex when it comes to verbal ability based on knowledge and understanding (vocabulary), or reasoning (reading comprehension). But even the female advantage on factor W is not unequivocal (Wittig and Petersen, 1979; Maccoby and Jacklin, 1975). Further verification within and across different language-cultural groups, at different age levels, is required before the finding can be considered sufficiently established to warrant an explanation at the biological level. Moreover, it would have to be adequately demonstrated that the tests used in this research are unbiased and constitute a fair basis for comparisons to be made between the sexes. This problem is analogous to the issue of demonstrating measurement equivalence in cross-cultural comparative research, as discussed in the foregoing section.

The same may be said with respect to sex comparisons on most other ability factors, where the evidence of reliable sex differences is even more tenuous. Females, for example, are often but not always claimed to lead on speed of performance on simple motor and perceptual tasks (Broverman, Klaiber, Kobayashi, and Vogel, 1968), rote memory (Hobson, 1947), and deductive aspects of reasoning. Males are most often claimed to load on spatial, mechanical, inductive, and mathematical abilities, as well as problem-solving which requires originality (Cattell, 1971; Harris, 1978). The sexes appear well matched on quantitative abilities, with females being supposed slightly superior on speed or simple numerical calculations, males on spatial or geometric aspects. Maccoby and Jacklin (1975) as well as other reviewers provide ample examples of results counter to these claims. The direction of the differences depends on age factors, cultural factors, and on the nature of the particular test used to assess the ability in question. For example, a "reasoning test" may favour either females, or males, depending upon whether the task content emphasises deductive, or inductive problem solving (Cattell, 1971).

Cattell (1971) has argued that if there is a biological basis to observed sex differences in cognitive performance, it is more likely to be indirect, via the effects of sex-linked genetic differences on temperament factors, which influence cognitive behaviour. For example, the frequent claim that females achieve better scores than males on simple tasks requiring speediness, as in certain tests for factors N or P, is most likely due to genetically determined sex differences in the temperament factor, Corteria (U.I.22). The higher performance of males on inductive problem solving, requiring originality, may be due to genetic differences favouring males in the underlying personality factor, Independence (U.I.19). Despite Cattell's interesting proposition, however, it must be accepted that on present evidence the genetic basis of observed sex differences in temperament factors is no more clearly established than in the case of cognitive factors.

Several authors have argued that the only sex differences in cognitive function that appear with reliable consistency, even across cultures and race groups, are in the area of visual spatial thinking. In an intensive investigation of sex differences in the specific field of spatial abilities, McGee (1979) brings powerful evidence to bear on the hypothesis of male superiority. He offers no further evidence on Werdelin's (1959) finding of a sex-related structural difference in spatial abilities, but concludes that male superiority in level of spatial performance is "one of the most persistent and best documented findings in the mental abilities literature, contrary to reports by Sherman (1978) and Fairweather (1976)". Furthermore, he interprets findings of sex differences favouring males in various broader aspects of perceptual-cognitive functioning, such as mathematics and field dependence, as a secondary consequence of differences with respect to spatial abilities.

McGee's (1979) evaluation of the factor-analytic literature on abilities leads him to conclude that there is consistent evidence for two distinct abilities in the spatial domain. The first, spatial visualization, has to do chiefly with the mental manipulation of pictorially presented stimuli. This factor involves, in particular, the ability to rotate, twist, or invert pictorial material mentally. The second factor, spatial orientation, involves "comprehension of the arrangement of elements within a visual pattern, the aptitude for remaining unconfused by the changing orientations in which a configuration may be presented, and the ability to determine spatial relations in which the body orientation of the observer is an essential part of the problem" (p.4). Significant sex differences favouring males are commonly reported for both factors. There is no evidence to suggest that sex differences are greater or more consistent in the case of either factor. Nor do there appear to be developmental differences in the age at which sex differences reliably appear. In the case of both factors, reliable sex differences do not appear until puberty, although, where differences do appear in younger samples, boys typically show superiority on both factors. These findings are in essential agreement with the views of other authorities (Maccoby and Jacklin, 1974; Harris, 1978; Vandenberg and Kuse, 1979).

McGee (1979) is forced to conclude, in company with most writers in the field, that evidence pertaining to the various hypotheses advanced to explain male superiority on spatial factors, is far from clear-cut. The longest standing hypothesis, that the differences are genetically determined, through the action of a sex-linked recessive gene on the X chromosomes of males (O'Connor, 1943) has not stood up well under the critical scrutiny of recent, more sophisticated research designs (Bock and Kolakowski, 1973; Vandenberg and Kuse, 1979). This is so despite the demonstration that spatial abilities in the population at large have a high hereditary determination (Vandenberg, 1971), perhaps slightly higher in the case of orientation than visualization (Yen, 1975), but in both cases at least as high as verbal abilities (Vandenberg, 1977).

The hormonal hypothesis of sex differences in spatial abilities (Stern, 1960) remains equally unsubstantiated (McGee, 1979). This hypothesis is predicated on the observation that spatial abilities do not differ reliably between the sexes until the onset of adolescence. The developmental timing of such differences suggests the possible influence of genetically controlled sex differences in the release and balance of sex hormones, such as androgens and estrogens, which in turn have been linked to performance on spatial tasks (Petersen, 1976). Indications are that high somatic androgenicity may be associated with lower spatial scores, both within sexes and between the sexes, thus accounting for the lower scores of females.

Recent work by Waber (1977; 1979) has cast a new perspective on this hypothesis. Her experimental results suggest that individual differences in the rate of physical maturation override sex effects in the determination of variance on spatial tests. Late maturers of both sexes tend to perform better on spatial tests than early maturers. The highest performers, however, are late maturing, poorly androgenised boys whereas the poorest performers are early maturing girls and boys with high somatic androgenicity. This finding is consistent with the work of Broverman, Klaiber, Kobayashi, and Vogel (1968). Waber (1979) has linked her concept of maturation rate to individual differences in hemisphere lateralization, where it also appears to moderate the effects of sex differences.

In the light of her results, Waber (1979) has argued that apparent differences between the sexes in cognitive function cannot be assumed to represent a sexual dichotomy in behaviour. She proposes that it might be more fruitful to conceptualize the sexes as differentially arrayed along continuous biological dimensions.

This perspective would be similarly appropriate when considering hypotheses emphasising the effects of <u>socialization</u> variables on individual and group differences in behaviour. It is cognate with the work of Bem (1974) and others, who recognise <u>continuous psychological dimensions</u>. This perspective would be similarly appropriate when considering hypotheses emphasising the effects of <u>socialization</u> variables on individual and group differences in behaviour. It is cognate with the work of Bem (1974) and others, who recognise <u>continuous psychological dimensions</u> of Femininity and Masculinity. These may be present to a significant extent in the same individual, in the form of Androgyny. Using this perspective Welsh and Baucom (1977) for example, found significant correlations between Masculinity and Feminity and scores on a reasoning test, yet males and females did not differ significantly on the test.

The issues raised in this section hopefully serve to illustrate something of the complexities involved in unravelling sources of influence on cognitive function. It seems that hypotheses advanced to explain cognitive sex differences at a biological level are premature, since the differences themselves are not yet sufficiently established. Even in studies where differences do appear, too little is known about the meaning, in psychological terms, of the cognitive processes underlying the performance distributions, so that it is never quite clear just what is differentiating the sexes. Of even greater immediate concern is the fact that in virtually all published studies to date, the methodological issue of establishing comparability of measures between the two sexes is wholly ignored. Until such time as sex-fair tests are produced, there is little point in devoting further attention to the literature on sex-related cognitive differences.

For the present, scientific neutrality suggests the need to extend the null hypothesis put forward earlier in this section, with regard to structural differences, to the effect that there is as yet no good reason to believe that the sexes differ fundamentally in terms of either cognitive structure, or level of performance. It may be instructive, however, to consider in greater depth the state of contemporary knowledge regarding the biological substrate of cognition in general, and the nature of human information processing, in terms of parameters other than global scores on psychometric tests. These issues are discussed in the following sections.

NEUROLOGICAL BASIS OF COGNITIVE FUNCTION

On the Relation between Mind and Brain

The problem of relating psychic processes to underlying physiological processes has long excited and frustrated the imaginations of scholars and scientists. The mind-body problem, or psychophysical problem, has been a central debating point in philosophy since the time of Homer. Because of its relevance to an understanding of man's place in nature, it has provoked frequent and bitter controversy, especially between free thinkers and dogmatists.

Amongst classical scholars there was even confusion as to which organs of the body might be associated with the functions of the mind. Aristotle, for example, despite his sophisticated formulation of the principles of deductive logic, believed the heart to be the seat of reason. He called it the common sense, which received sensory inputs via the veins and transmitted responses via the arteries. He relegated the brain to the role of an air-cooled radiator for regulating body temperatures. Plato and Hippocrates, on the other hand, were among the first to associate the brain with mental processes, including consciousness or self-awareness, purposiveness, and moral judgement. It is interesting that Plato's concept of mind, or soul, incorporated the principle of hierarchical structure. At the top of the psychic hierarchy he placed reason, purposiveness, and consciousness. Below these he located various affective and energic processes and below these, bodily appetites, or basic physiological needs. This conception may be the earliest prototype of modern models of hierarchical structure in psychology. It seems a close forerunner, in particular, of Freud's original theory of mental structure, with three major levels corresponding to the superego, ego, and id.

Plato's notion of the mind-body relationship represents the first clear statement of the doctrine of psychophysical dualism. The mind, or soul, was conceived as something non-physical, divine, and immortal. Yet it was capable of interaction with the physical body. This doctrine was adopted by the early Christian theologians, most notably St Augustine in the fourth century, and it has survived as a tenet of Christian thinking until the present. The seventeenth century French philosopher, Rene Descartes, developed and extended the doctrine of psychophysical dualism into an influential theory which even physiologists could treat seriously. He saw a two-way interaction between mind and body, believing the link to lie in the pineal gland, an undivided structure behind the third ventricle of the brain. Although the function of the pineal has not yet been established, the theory of psychophysical dualism has survived to the present day, its most influential advocates being, perhaps, Popper and Eccles (1977).

Many influential thinkers since Descartes, however, have rejected
the theory of dualism. Kant (1724-1804) argued that a mind,
existing only in time and not in space, could not influence a
physical brain extended in space as well as time. Today this
argument takes the form that Descartes' dualism contradicts the
law of conservation of energy. Leibnitz (1649-1716) had attempted
to surmount this difficulty in proposing a theory of
psychophysical parallelism. Subsequent influential physiologists,
including Herbert Spencer (1855) and Hughlings Jackson (1887)
embraced this theory but it no longer has a following in
neurophysiology since it provides no explanation for the
correlation between psychic and physical events. Spinoza
(1632-1677) first gave expression to what is today the identity
hypothesis in which brain activity and mental processes are viewed
as merely different perspectives on the same thing, or opposite
sides of the same coin. This is somewhat analogous to the
complementarity principle in nuclear physics, in terms of which
sub-atomic phenomena may be explained simultaneously either as
waves or particles. The major alternative to the theory of
psychophysical dualism, however, arises from the strict
materialism of Thomas Hobbs (1588-1679). In this view the brain is
the organ of the mind. It is considered to produce mind much as a
gland produces a particular secretion. The idea of an incorporeal
substance is thereby wholly obviated. Modern neuroscience, it
would appear, chiefly favours some product of the materialism and
identity theories, although there is as yet no unanimity regarding
the precise form of the modern stance on the mind-body problem
(Armstrong, 1976; Pucetti, 1977; Kornhuber, 1978; Leibovic, 1979;
Hill, 1981).

Studies seeking to associate cognitive processes with specific
anatomical structures in the brain are usually founded on some
derivative of the materialism-identity hypotheses. Evidence,
particularly from clinical neuropsychology, at least offers
compelling reassurance that the major organ in terms of which
explanations for cognitive behaviour must be sought, is the brain
(Dimond, 1980).

Certain cognitive functions have been identified unequivocally
with particular loci in the brain. Contrary to expectations
raised by early phrenologists, the most clearly localised
functions are the simplest cognitive processes, involving the five
senses and muscular movement. Following the pioneering work of
Penfield and Rasmussen (1950), neuropsychologists have been able
to construct a fairly detailed map of the brain loci of sensory
and motor functions, including areas for sensory associations and
images (Penfield and Perot, 1963). More complex functions tend to
lack a specific location in the brain. Higher cognitive
capacities may overlap several sensory and movement areas,

depending upon the extent to which these are involved (Cattell, 1971). Nonetheless, the extremist theory of equipotentiality and mass action of brain matter, first propounded by Karl Lashley (1950), is rejected by most modern neuropsychologists (e.g., Gazzaniga and Le Doux, 1978). It is generally accepted that even among the higher cognitive functions, certain brain structures or areas are more closely involved than others (Dimond, 1980).

Perhaps the earliest and most dramatic discovery of a specifically localised higher cognitive function is that of French anthropologist and neurosurgeon, Paul Broca (1865). He identified an important language control centre involved in the production of words and articulation of speech. Broca's area, as it is widely known, lies on the cortical convexity of the left temporal lobe, just anterior of the Sylvian fissure. A second language centre was discovered shortly afterwards by Wernicke (1897) in the posterior part of the superior temporal convolution. Wernicke's area, which occurs also only on the left side of the brain in normal right handers, is involved in the semantic integration and verbal comprehension aspects of language use. A vast tract of fibres, the fasciculus arcuatus, connects the two speech centres.

Interestingly, the clinically verified functions of Broca's area and Wernicke's area have a striking, if superficial resemblance to Thurstone's (1938) independently discovered psychometric factors, W (Word Fluency) and V (Verbal Meaning).

The two verbal factors, which are positively correlated, are among the best established ability dimensions in the psychometric literature. Yet the close correspondence between them and the well researched language control centres of clinical neuropsychology appears not to have been noted or to have received much attention. One reason may be the problem of communication between these two highly specialised sub-disciplines of psychology. Another reason may be that the discovery of language centres in the left hemisphere of the brain sparked off a major research impetus in neuropsychology which has overshadowed what might otherwise have become important research leads.

Broca's early discovery of a language centre in the left cerebral hemisphere helped establish two of the major foundations of the study of higher brain functions. The first is the principle of localization considered briefly above. The second is the question of dominance. A theory gradually evolved in the literature to the effect that the superior capacity of the left hemisphere for language processing, verbal thought, and articulate speech, might give it an advantage over the right hemisphere in the competition for central processing time, or attention and control of the motor system. In this sense there would be a relationship of cerebral dominance, or a bilateral asymmetry of functional organisation in the brain. This view, in different forms, has served as a basic concept in theories of neural organisation in the brain for over a century.

The cerebral dominance hypothesis received major new impetus and support from the benchmark empirical findings of Anderson (1951) who used psychometric procedures to study the effects of brain injuries sustained by veterans of the two World Wars. He classified patients in one of two groups, depending on whether injury had occurred in the left (dominant) or right (non-dominant) cerebral hemisphere. Using the Wechsler-Bellevue Intelligence Scale (Version 1) he was able to show that injuries to the left hemisphere were associated with significantly greater loss of verbal capacity than injuries to the right hemisphere. Conversely, patients with non-dominant hemisphere damage suffered significantly greater performance capacity deficits than the group with dominant hemisphere damage. Despite the powerful impact of these results, however, cautious authorities two decades ago (e.g., Mountcastle, 1961) still distrusted the evidence from clinical patient populations and continued to question the existence of true lateral differences in cerebral organisation. The view 'that the two hemispheres are equal in functional potential at birth remained widely accepted (Glees, 1967).

These conservative views were radically altered by the remarkable studies of R. W. Sperry and his colleagues, published in the late nineteen sixties and early seventies (Sperry, 1968a; 1968b; 1969; 1970; Sperry, Gazzaniga, and Bogen, 1969). Sperry was given an opportunity of studying the psychological consequences of a rarely used operation in which the two hemispheres of the brain are surgically disconnected. The operation, known as commissurotomy, involves a sectioning of midline commissural tissue in the corpus callosum, a massive tract of more than 200 million fibres connecting left and right hemispheres. The operation was performed by neurosurgeons (Bogen, Fisher, and Vogel, 1965) as a last resort treatment for intractible epileptic siezures. It is less radical than the earlier practice of hemispherectomy, in which an entire hemisphere is removed.

The results of Sperry's ingenious tests on commissurotomy patients, following a recovery period of about two years, provide dramatic and convincing support for earlier hypotheses of cerebral dominance and lateral specialization. The two hemispheres appear to each have their own mode of thinking and processing information. As expected on the basis of earlier research, Sperry found the left to be more proficient at verbal, sequential, analytic thinking, the right to be more adept at space perception, global synthesis, and imagery. The disconnected left hemisphere, which controls the right hand and right visual half field, was found capable of speech, writing, and mathematical calculation.

The disconnected right hemisphere, which controls the contralateral hand and visual half field, remains essentially mute, alexic, agraphic, and unable to do calculations beyond simple additions to sums under 20. Abstract reasoning and symbolic thinking in the disconnected left hemisphere appear virtually unimpaired, apart from some weakening in mnemonic functions. The left hemisphere, even after commissurotomy, remains dominant, controlling the motor system and governing general behaviour unless information processing demands are directed specifically at the right hemisphere.

Sperry's (1973) findings led him to conclude that cerebral dominance and hemispheric specialization may be inherent principles of neural organisation, which are innately determined. Perhaps one of the most startling findings to come from Sperry's experiments, however, is that the two hemispheres appear to have independent identities, each with its own unique senses, feelings, thoughts, and aspirations. After disconnection, each continues to function autonomously and apparently normally, as if unaware that another half brain, with is own conscious mind, occupies the same skull. This amazing finding, that consciousness can be divided surgically, revolutionized thinking with regard to the mind-body problem in psychophysics. It has necessitated a complete re-evaluation of the relation between mind and matter.

On the basis of his results, Sperry (1968a; 1968b) has proposed a new theory of this relation, described as _emergent interactionism_. The theory states that conscious awareness is a dynamic emergent property of cerebral excitation, yet it is something more than just the sum of neural, physical, and chemical events. Conscious phenomena are considered to interact causally with physical brain processes, giving direction to the flow and pattern of cerebral excitation to which, in turn, conscious experience owes its existence. In placing mind over matter in this way, yet regarding it as an emergent product of matter, Sperry's theory achieves an elegant compromise between the extremes of mentalism and materialism, which subsequent neuroscientists have found very appealling.

More recent research has supported and amplified the essential features of Sperry's results with split-brain patients (Zangwill, 1974; Gazzaniga and Le Doux, 1978). Functional asymmetries of the two hemispheres have been related to genetic (Levy, 1971) and hormonal factors (Petersen, 1979), particularly as associated with sex differences (Gale, Brown, Osborne, and Smallbone, 1978; Wittig, 1979; Vandenberg and Kuse, 1979), and individual differences in physical maturation (Waber, 1977). Levy's (1974; 1978) excellent summaries of the differential cognitive functions associated with left and right hemispheres, however, serve to caution against unwarranted oversimplications and generalizations of the kind proliferated in recent, semi-popular literature. Lateralization of function must be understood in relative rather than absolute terms, except in a few important cases where functions are completely lateralized. Moreover, allowance must be made for considerable individual variability in the cerebral organisation of the brain and its attendant mental processes. It should be remembered, too, that normal humans have intact callosal fibres and as Bogen (1970) has argued, the corpus callosum regulates a continual flow of cross-talk between the hemispheres, integrating mental life and conscious experience. Dimond (1980) stresses that in addition to the two-way information flow achieved via the corput callosum, and despite the different areas of specialization in the cortex, all higher cognitive processes ultimately devolve onto a single regulatory control centre. This is a structure in the phylogenetically more primitive mid-brain, called the thalamus. He sees the role of the thalamus not as master of the cortex, but as its servant, much as a government is servant to its people.

Electrophysiological Correlates of Cognitive Performance

Experimental clinical neuropsychology has done much to establish associations between specific brain structures and particular cognitive functions (Geschwind, Galaburda, and LeMay, 1979; Dimond, 1980) and has provided a theory of the relation between physical brain processes and noetic phenomena, including consciousness (Sperry, 1968; Pucetti, 1977). But the neuroanatomical relationships and the psychophysical theory are not sufficient to explain the individual differences in cognitive ability that underlie psychometric theories of intelligence. Nor do they explain the mechanisms underlying different information-processing parameters in the experimental paradigms of cognitive psychology.

The search for explanations at this level must turn to evidence from studies in which measures of brain processes are correlated directly with measures of cognitive performance.

The earliest brain measures to be correlated with cognitive function were gross estimates of brain size, or cerebral capacity. These were generally studied in relation to assessments of intellectual capacity. Results typically supported the popular view that a large head is evidence of a good brain, or high intelligence. This line of research inevitably came to be applied to the comparative study of different human races. Hence, for example, data from Samuel George Morton's (d.1851) enormous pre-Darwinian collection of skulls were widely quoted in support of prevailing Caucasian prejudices regarding the rank order of intelligence of the races. Gould (1978) has recently demonstrated how unconscious manipulation of the data became a scientific norm in this tradition of research. His own careful re-analysis fails to provide support for the hypothesis of racial differences in cranial capacity, but underlines the more generally substantiated finding of sex differences. The last extensive review on the subject of brain size and intelligence (Hamilton, 1936) bolstered the belief in a positive correlation, but served to caution that the magnitude of the true coefficient is low, probably between .05 and .1. Cobb (1965) has more recently questioned values even of this order, pointing out that brains of equal mass may differ considerably in other respects, particularly texture. Yet such influential contemporary authorities on intelligence as Cattell (1971) still endorse the view that gross brain mass and intelligence are significantly correlated.

Far more interest and attention has been directed at attempts to measure internal brain processes and to correlate these with cognitive performance. The expectation that the workings of the brain could be measured somehow in electrical terms goes back to the classic studies of Galvani on frogs' nerves. In 1875 the English physiologist, Caton, using animals, demonstrated electrical potential waves during brain action for the first time. In the nineteen twenties, a German psychiatrist named Berger developed the technique of recording electrical brain waves from the human skull. Electroencephalograms, or EEG records as they are known today, have since become widely used in clinical neuropsychology and in research on the neural functioning of the brain. To some, it is as if records of the brain's electrical activity provide a window through which to peep and observe the actual information processing machinery at work. Cautious authorities such as Jacobson (1973) insist that what is being seen is not the processing of information but the transmission of signals. He uses the analogy of a telegraph system, in which messages are transmitted by signal in Morse code. Their information content has to be decoded by a receiver if the message is to be understood. The implication is that brainwave recordings provide a basis from which inferences can be drawn about the nature and significance of underlying processes.

The electrical currents that can be recorded from the brain with aid of scalp electrodes vary considerably in amplitude (measured in microvolts, V), frequency (measured in cycles per second, Hz), and other characteristics. The problem is to find the best means of reducing the waves to quantitative indices so that they can be studied in relation to other measures and their message be decoded by inferential means. Three general classes of approach to the problem of analysing brain waves have been developed.

One is a type of Fourier analysis, in which the wave form of the EEG is broken down into components, such as alpha rhythm (8-13 Hz), beta rhythm (14-35 Hz), delta rhythm (<3Hz), and theta rhythm (4-7 Hz), (Brazier, 1962). This method is currently used more widely for clinical purposes than for research. The quantitative data it provides are less than optimally reliable. A second method involves applying many reptitions of an external stimulus, or other process, and averaging the brain potential changes that follow stimulation over a given time interval. By this means an average curve of optimum reliability, called an evoked potential (EP), is obtained (Desmet, 1979). This method has come to be used more frequently than the former in contemporary research, although mostly within the framework of experimental, rather than correlational studies. In the third method, the measurable characteristics of the brain's electrical activity are treated as variables. These are measured across many subjects and submitted to factor analysis. The variations in amplitude, frequency, and other measures can be reduced by this means to a limited number of underlying dimensions, thus facilitating the problem of inferential interpretation (Cattell, 1971). This method, perhaps, lends itself best of all to research within the correlational tradition, but as yet it has not been used extensively.

In an early review of research on electroencephalography, Lindsley (1944) concluded that it is doubtful whether there is any high relationship between EEG component measures and psychometric intelligence. Ostow (1950) was more decisive in his review, stating that there is no relationship between EEG and intelligence in normal adults. Ellingson (1956) similarly concluded that available evidence failed to support the hypothesis of a relation between alpha rhythm or other EEG components and intelligence. Vogel and Broverman (1964) conclude their critical review on a more qualified note. They contend that evidence for a relation is strongest in samples of children, institutionalised geriatric patients, mental deficients, and brain injured persons. EEG indices were found to be more strongly related to mental age than IQ. Studies on which these conclusions are based are subject to serious methodological and theoretical criticism, however. Ellingson (1965) has disputed the claims of Vogel and Broverman 1964). He argues that evidence for a relation between normal brain wave phenomena and IQ in children and the mentally retarded is contradictory and inconclusive. The weight of available evidence suggests that there is no relation in the case of normal adults. Furthermore, Ellingson stresses, EEG abnormality and decreased intellectual capacity are both effects of organic brain disorders, hence they tend to be related to one another.

Claims for the existence of a correlation between <u>evoked potential</u> <u>measures</u> and psychometric intelligence appear to have greater support, although results are by no means conclusive. Chalke and Ertl (1965) published data indicating that high psychometric intelligence may be associated with short latencies in the later components of the visual evoked potential (VEP). This finding was replicated in a subsequent study by Ertl and Schafer (1969). Significant negative correlations in the range -.32 to -.35 were found between different IQ measures and late component latencies in the VEPs of a sample of 573 primary school pupils. It was concluded that "evoked potentials, which reflect the time course of information processing by the brain, could be the key to understanding the biological substrate of individual differences in behavioural intelligence" (p.422). Using a different experimental approach, Ertl (1972) found that high and low IQ subjects differ significantly in the amount of energy content in the early part of the evoked potential, prior to 150ms following stimulation. This finding is generally construed as support for Ertl's (1968) original hypothesis that the VEP reflects differences in <u>neural efficiency</u> between individuals. Independent studies corroborating the correlations of Ertl and his co-workers have been reported by Plum (1968) and Weinberg (1969). Rhodes, Dustman, and Beck (1969) found a non-significant trend in their results in the direction of a relation between late VEP component latencies and intelligence. Shucard and Horn (1972) acknowledge the foregoing evidence, but point out that the relationships in these studies are not replicated over a broad range of population; that use is made of omnibus measures of intelligence rather than measures of different human abilities; and that the findings are not integrated in a coherent theory.

In an attempt to redress these shortcomings, they undertook a comprehensive investigation of the relation between VEP measures and operationally independent forms of intelligence, based on the theory of fluid and crystallized intelligence (Horn, 1970). They included a large battery of psychometric tests referencing eleven primary ability factors and four second-order factors, namely fluid intelligence, crystallized intelligence, general visualization, and general mental speed. EEG recordings were taken from a set of eight electrode pairs in different placements. VEPs were recorded between F_4-P_4 and F_3-P_3, the former being considered equivalent to placements used by Ertl (1968) and Ertl and Schafer (1969). Three stimulus conditions were used for eliciting evoked potentials. These are described as "high extrinsic activation" (HEA), "medium extrinsic activation" (MEA) and "intrinsic activation" (IA) respectively (p.61). In the latter condition the subject is required to lie quietly and attend through nearly closed eyes to a stimulus consisting of diffuse light flashes with a randomly varied inter-stimulus interval between 1 and 4ms. A heterogeneous sample of 108 adults in the age range 16-68 years served as subjects.

Results of this study support expectations raised by the work of Ertl and his colleagues. In general, long VEP latency was associated with low ability, short latency with high ability. Correlations ranged between .05 and -.32 the majority being around -.15. Shucard and Horn (1972) conclude that a relation exists between cortical evoked potentials and human abilities, but that "the linear correlation which represents this is not very large" (p.63). Interestingly, the IA stimulus condition produced considerably more significant correlations than the MEA or HEA conditions. Correlations are most robust between late component VEP latencies and broad ability measures such as g, Gf, and Gc. Correlations with narrower abilities fall below significance when age effects are partialled out. No noteworthy differences occur in the pattern of correlations for separate speed and level measures of ability.

A general conclusion drawn from this study is that "short evoked potential latencies represent, in part, intellectual alertness that can be either self-induced or induced by external conditions" (p.66). Brighter individuals appear to show greater plasticity, or flexibility with regard to alertness, being better able than their dull counterparts to adjust levels of intrinsic activation to suit circumstances. This inference recalls, once again, Ertl's (1968) notion of neural efficiency, giving it an added dimension of meaning.

Shucard and Horn (1972) acknowledge that the interpretation of their results falls short of a complete explanation of the correlation between VEP latencies and human abilities. Nonetheless, they surmise that what is common to VEP latency, to simple abilities and to complex abilities is some process that can be understood and made operational in terms of relatively simple tests. It would seem instructive to pursue this observation using Carroll's (1980) subsequently defined notion of elementary cognitive tasks (ECTs).

Calloway (1973) reviewed literature on averaged evoked potentials and test intelligence and found three classes of relation to obtain. The first is that already noted, between VEP latency and ability measures. Evidence bearing on the second suggests that under low activation conditions bright subjects show greater VEP asymmetry (between left and right hemispheres) than dull subjects. Finally, VEP variability appears to be related to better test performance, particularly on perceptual measures. Calloway cautions that all three classes of relation appear to be a function of the cognitive operations a subject is carrying out during evoked potential testing and hence should not be interpreted as reflecting any immutable biological substratum of intelligence. Like most behaviour, he argues, evoked potentials reflect genetic, biological, and social influences.

Despite the recognised complexity of evoked potential waveforms and the likelihood of determinants being multidimensional, multivariate procedures have seldom been used in the analysis of evoked potential variables and their relationships with cognitive measures. Donchin and his associates (Donchin, 1966; Donchin and Lindsley, 1969; Donchin, Calloway, and Jones, 1970) used various multivariate techniques in their research but concentrated on within subject data. Bennett, MacDonald, Brace, and Nenoyama (1971) used principal components to study the dimensionality of certain VEP measures across subjects, but their sample was fairly small and they included relatively few VEP variables. Crawford (1974) used a much larger sample in studying relationships between VEP variables and intelligence test data, but limited his analysis to canonical correlations.

One of the first comprehensive attempts to study the structure of interrelationships among VEP variables with the aid of factor analysis is by Street, Perry, and Cunningham (1976). They recorded and inter-correlated 19 different VEP variables, as well as age, for a sample of 98 kindergarten children of both sexes. A variety of objective procedures was used to estimate the best number of factors for extraction. A seven-factor pattern was selected and rotated to orthogonal simple structure. Some factors were interpreted as specific to particular areas of the cortex, whereas others seemed general across cortical areas. Similarly, some factors appeared to be specific to particular experimental procedures of recording, whereas others seemed general across different recording procedures. More specific factors represented different dimensions of latency and complexity. The most general factor across conditions represented variance due to amplitude. Another fairly general factor was interpreted as representing linearity. The authors regard their results as conclusive evidence of the multidimensionality of the VEP domain.

In a subsequent study using the same data, a team from the same laboratory at the University of Florida (Perry, McCoy, Cunningham, Falgout, and Street, 1976) studied the multivariate VEP correlates of intelligence, using a variety of different psychometric tests and ability measures. The seven VEP factors were used as predictor variables in a series of multiple regression analyses, with different ability composites serving as criterion variables. In general, it was found that different combinations of VEP factors were needed to predict differently composed ability composites. The best single VEP predictor of an overall

intelligence composite was found to be a latency factor specific
to a particular diffuse stimulus recoding procedure. When the
four best VEP predictors of overall intelligence were included, a
multiple r of .38 (p <.01) was obtained. When intelligence was
broken down into separate verbal and performance scale scores, it
was found that the seven VEP variables provided a better
prediction of the latter (R= .38; p <.05) than of the former (R =
.29; p <.05). When the five best VEP predictors of the performance
scale score were analysed in conjunction with the five most highly
predicted performance sub-tests, a canonical correlation of Rc =
.49 (p <.01) was obtained. The highest single weight on the VEP
side came from a specific complexity variable, whereas the highest
weight on the psychometric side came from the Geometric-Design and
Block-Design sub-tests of the Wechsler Preschool and Primary Scale
of Intelligence (WPPSI), (Wechsler, 1967). The authors concluded
their study with the observation that relations between cortical
functioning and behavioural abilities must be understood in
multivariate terms, even when dealing with young, preschool
children. This conclusion echoes the general findings of Shucard
and Horn (1972) in a heterogeneous population of adults.

Woodruff (1978) has traced the life-span developmental pattern of
brain electrical activity and related it to behavioural change.
She notes that there is a high correspondence, in particular,
between behavioural changes in cognition and brain electrical
changes during development. Hence, for example, there is a marked
stabilization of EEG activity between the first and second years
of life and this coincides with the progression from dealing with
the environment purely in sensory and motor responses to dealing
with perceptual representations of the environment. Another
marked period of stabilization occurs after the eleventh year,
coinciding with the onset of conceptual thinking, or abstract
logical capacity. Dealing with averaged evoked potentials,
Woodruff outlines a number of hypotheses which appear consistent
with research evidence. The first is that early components in the
VEP reflect processing activity in the primary sensory system,
where the physical parameters of the stimulus are encoded.
Another hypothesis is that later components are associated with
more diffusely projecting pathways, believed to be involved in
more complex information processing. A third hypothesis, enjoying
strong support from experimental studies, is that the late
positive component, or P (Price and Smith; 1974) is clearly
related to complex information processing and decision making.

A striking new and as yet incompletely researched theory of the
relation between electrophysiological processes in the brain and
cognitive performance has been proposed by Hendrickson and
Hendrickson (1981). The theory is intended to explain the
biological basis of individual differences in intelligence. It

deals with the way information is converted, or transduced from the impinging physical environment into some mental code and with the way it is filtered, stored, and finally represented in some physical form which permanently alters the internal state of the biological system.

Central to the theme is a "pulse train hypothesis" (p.5). It deals with the manner in which the majority of stimuli are encoded as pulse trains, as information is conveyed from peripheral to central processes. Higher levels of abstract thought are considered to be encoded and processed within the brain in pulse train packets. In general, they contend, different species are expected to have pulse train packets with a different constant number of pulses. Humans, they suggest, have a constant of 22 pulses. In contrast to this, rodents, for example, have only about 16 pulses. Individual differences in intelligence are not a function of the number of pulses in a pulse train or packet, since this is constant for the species. Rather, they are the result of different classes of errors which can arise during the transmission of neural impulses within the system.

A simulation study relating this theory to electrophysiological measurement is reported. Based on the results of the simulation, a new electrophysiological measure of intelligence is proposed. The utility of this measure, which is essentially an index of evoked potential complexity, is tested empirically in a novel re-analysis of data from Ertl's (Ertl and Schafer, 1969) study. It is shown that high IQ is associated with greater complexity of the VEP waveform. A correlation of .77 between the two measures is reported. In a subsequent, as yet unpublished report by D.E. Hendrickson (1981) empirical replication of this result is claimed. In a sample of 219 high school children, a correlation of .72 is reported between a VEP complexity measure and full WAIS IQ.

It is too early to assess the value of the Hendrickson's theory of information processing in the nervous system. The technical complexity of the formulation, and specialized knowledge required to follow the theoretical arguments, render their work difficult to evaluate. Nonetheless, the theory deserves the serious attention of experts and students in the field of cognitive science. It is one of the few attempts to deal comprehensively with the central problems of how the brain processes information and why individuals differ in cognitive efficiency. Eysenck (chapter 8), presents an integrated perspective on this material.

THE CONTRIBUTION OF INFORMATTON PROCESS PARADIGMS

The pluralistic development of scientific psychology has been noted already. Two streams of research were traced to a common origin in the pioneering work of Francis Galton (1869; 1883) in the nineteenth century. Earlier sections of this review have traced the development of one stream, which focuses on individual differences and relies largely upon psychometric measurement and multivariate correlational analysis. The second stream, by contrast, uses analysis of variance methods to explain variations in dependent variables in relation to carefully selected independent variables. Tight experimental controls are used to nullify effects due to all possible extraneous variables. Samples are selected with a view to minimising within-group variance due to individual differences, since interest is on the establishment of general laws of behaviour that transcend individual variations. No attempt is made here to trace the developmental history of the experimental tradition in cognitive psychology. Suffice it to say that it evolved via the work of the early German experimentalists at Wundt's (1862) laboratory into an extremely diversified field which is characterised, if anything, by a lack of underlying theoretical unity.

It is worth noting in the present context, that one of the major influences on the experimental tradition in psychology, notably behaviourism, expressly denies the reality of covert mental events, or cognitive processes, as mediators of overt action. For this reason behaviourism, following Watson (1913), has had a serious detrimental effect on the theoretical development of cognitive psychology, despite the valuable contributions it has made to the experimental method in psychology. A somewhat less dominant school employing experimental methods, Gestalt psychology (Wertheimer, 1925; Kohler, 1929; Koffka, 1935) perhaps will be judged eventually to have had a far more profound and lasting influence on the growth of psychological knowledge in general and on an understanding of human cognition in particular.

For the purpose of the present discussion, however, interest goes back no further than the past decade or so, which has seen the rise of modern, experimentally-based cognitive psychology. It should be stated at the outset, that the focus of interest here is not directly on the models of cognitive processing generated by this tradition. Rather, it is on the contribution that process models can make to an understanding of the individual differences in cognitive performance that are responsible for the structural models considered in preceding sections.

Considering its recency, it is hardly surprising that the modern school still lacks a unified theory of human cognition. A major obstacle frustrating attempts at creating a synthesis of empirical results is that much of the research takes place within distinct paradigms which do not permit easy cross-referencing of results. Nonetheless, the paradigms themselves are founded on a common assumption, namely that the human brain is the organ responsible for the internal processing of information and that, if the processes cannot be observed directly, at least they can be inferred under strict experimental conditions that permit replication and generalization.

One important paradigm in the broadly defined domain of cognitive science which is not founded on this assumption is artificial intelligence, or AI (Miller, 1978; Simon, 1979). AI research is justified on the premise that the processing of information by machines can be studied as a worthwhile scientific end in itself. Although models of machine processing are recognised as a potentially rich source of hypotheses about human processing, there is no necessary implication that machine tested models are a valid representation of human processing characteristics. Winograd (1980), for example, has developed an impressive model of language processing by computer without claiming it as a valid account of human language processing. Closely related to AI but nonetheless recognised as a distinct paradigm is <u>cognitive simulation</u> (e.g., Szymanski, 1980). In this tradition, which preceded AI, computer processing is not of interest in its own right. Machine processing is used purely for the purpose of testing the feasibility of hypotheses developed to account for aspects of human information processing.

In all other paradigms of modern cognitive psychology, the human processor, man, is studied directly. Carroll (1980) has attempted a classification of research in experimental cognitive psychology in terms of the following eight distinct information-processing paradigms:

perceptual apprehension (e.g., Richards and Platnick, 1974);

reaction time and movement time (e.g., Jensen, 1979);

evaluation and decision (e.g., Anderson and Reder, 1974);

stimulus matching/comparison (e.g., Clark and Chase, 1972);

naming/reading/assocation (e.g., Stroop, 1938);

episodic memory read-out (e.g., S. Sternberg, 1969);

analogical reasoning (e.g., R. J. Sternberg, 1977); and

algorithmic manipulation (e.g., Hunt, Lunneborg, and Lewis, 1975).

With the possible exception of the episodic memory read-out paradigm, which deals chiefly with error probabilities, the focus of interest in the various paradigms of cognitive psychology is on the _time_ taken by each process. Posner (1978) introduced the generic term _mental chronometry_ to refer to this field of study. The general assumption in mental chronometry is that information processing proceeds in a _series of stages_ and that the total time observed from the initiation of a cognitive task can be analysed in terms of the time taken by each of the stages. From this it follows that if one were to use mental chronometry paradigms for studying individual differences in cognition, which has not been the emphasis thus far, one would attempt to measure _reliable variations in processing time_ over individuals for each hypothetical stage. A possible source of difficulty here lies in the fact that stages might overlap or interact in such a way that it would be difficult or meaningless to time them separately.

Nevertheless, this is the gist of what Carroll (1980) proposes as a major objective for cognitive psychology during the eighties. In his monolithic synthesis of literature, he attempts to analyse the major dimensions of individual differences (IDs) produced by the psychometric tradition (cognitive factors) in terms of the processing parameters of the mental chronometry paradigms in experimental cognition. This ambitious enterprise was initiated in an earlier report (Carroll, 1974) which heralds a watershed in the history of psychometric studies of cognition. In this report, for the first time, psychometric tests are formally treated as cognitive tasks and their processing demands are systematically analysed in terms of an experimentally derived model of human cognition. The model used is Hunt's (1971; Hunt, Frost, and Lunneborg, 1973; Hunt, Lunneborg, and Lewis, 1975) _distributive memory model_, based on an earlier model of Atkinson and Shifrin (1968), and modified to incorporate Newell's (1973) concept of a _production system_. Two randomly selected tests from each of twenty four factors in the widely-known kit of reference tests for cognitive factors (French, Ekstrom, and Price, 1963) are included in the analysis. A specially developed computer program is used to facilitate the prodigious undertaking.

Carroll (1974) attempts to interpret the task demands of tests with reference to the principal _memory store_ addressed in the processing. Following the distributive memory model, a distinction is made between long-term memory (LTM), intermediate-term memory (ITM), and short-term memory (STM). The role of _sensory and iconic_ buffers is considered and the major _strategies_ required for effective task performance are postulated. Where possible, _limits_ on performance due to individual differences in <u>speed</u>, or <u>operating capacity</u> are identified. Finally, an attempt is made to show how the information flow is controlled by an <u>executive</u> or <u>iterative production system</u> which may be a set of innate or learned processes, not necessarily always conscious, nor in the immediate focus of attention.

To date, few attempts have been made to use Carroll's (1974) new structure-of-intellect in the interpretation of factor analysis results, perhaps because of the daunting complexity of the task. One exception is a large-scale study undertaken at the National Institute for Personnel Research (Crawford-Nutt, 1977) in which, at the writer's suggestion, Carroll's framework for process analysis was applied. Irvine (1979) sees in Carroll's approach a challenge to the factor analyst to relate the definition of factors to reasons for their existence as differentiated psychological functions. This must be done with reference to different underlying process parameters and to differential processing stages. He argues that factors should be construed as complex dependent variables, whose demands may have more precise definition in terms of processes, by parameter measures that are not themselves tests.

Alternative systems (for elaboration see Chapters 3 and 4) for studying individual differences in cognitive performance, in the light of cognitive process models, have been proposed by Robert Sternberg (1977; 1978) and Earl Hunt (1978; 1979). The fundamental unit of analysis in Sternberg's theory is the component, defined as an <u>elementary information process</u>. Mental activity in the course of thinking and problem solving is reduced to its constituent components by means of a rational procedure termed <u>componential analysis</u>. Executive functions that have generality across task domains are known as <u>metacomponents</u>. Sternberg's emerging <u>componential theory</u> of intelligence has attracted much attention in recent literature, drawing both criticism and acclaim (Sternberg, 1980). Carroll's (1978) careful review is perhaps representative, commending Sternberg's work as courageous and ambitious, yet finding it inadequate as a general theory of intelligence on many counts. Rather like Guilford's S-I theory, it seems isolated from the main body of empirical and theoretical developments, in part due to the use of idiosyncratic and highly specialised terminology and tools of analysis. Unlike the case with Guilford's theory, however, these unique features may yet prove to be the salvation, rather than the undoing, of componential theory. In time they may become the corner-stones on which new theories of intelligence are erected. It is still too early to form judgement on this issue.

Hunt's emerging synthesis, if less creative than Sternberg's, is more eclectic and may prove, ultimately, to be of greater value. Three sources of individual differences in information processing are proposed, namely structure, strategy, and general attentional resources. Structural factors, relating to the architecture of the cognitive system, set limits on the effectiveness of specific information-processing steps. Strategy of problem solving accounts for the major portion of variance in test performance, particularly within homogeneous groups of subjects. Differences related to structure, on the other hand, may be more important in accounting for between-group differences in performance. The common finding that virtually all measures of cognitive competence are positively correlated is attributed to the hypothesis that all mental processes compete for general attentional resources and that individuals may differ in the attentional resources they can bring to bear on any cognitive task (see Ch.4).

Neither Sternberg nor Hunt has managed to produce a system that equals, in sheer comprehensiveness of scope and painstaking attention to detail, the synthetic analysis of Carroll (1980). Carroll's most recent analysis is an extension of earlier work (Carroll, 1974; 1978; Carroll and Maxwell, 1979). In the most recent report psychometric factors of intelligence are considered in terms of all eight major paradigms in experimental cognitive psychology. An attempt is made to explain the basis for individual differences (IDs) in a unit of analysis called elementary cognitive tasks (ECTs).

An ECT is defined as:

"Any one of a possibly very large set of tasks in which a person undertakes, or is assigned, a performance for which there is a specifiable class of 'successful' or 'correct' outcomes or end states which are to be attained through a relatively small number of mental processes or operations, and whose successful outcomes can differ depending upon the instruction given to, or the sets or plans adopted by, the person." (Carroll, 1980, p.11.)

A set of the ten most commonly assumed cognitive processes, across the eight task paradigms of cognitive psychology, is identified for detailed analysis. Carroll's list of cognitive processes is reproduced here, with brief descriptions taken from a summary article (Carroll, 1981, p.16).

The Monitor (MONITR) process is a cognitive set or "determining tendency" that guides the operation of other processes during the course of a task. Generally, it is embodied in the instructions given to the subject at the outset of an experiment or during the course of its performance.

The Attention (ATSTIM) process has to do with the subject's expectations regarding the types and numbers of stimuli that are to be presented.

The Apprehension (APSTIM) process has to do with the registering of a stimulus in a sensory buffer.

The Perceptual Integration (CLOZR) process concerns the perception of a stimulus, or the attainment of perceptual closure of a stimulus, and its matching with any previously formed memory representation.

The Encoding (REPFRM) process is that of forming a mental representation of a stimulus and its interpretation in terms of its attributes, associations, or meaning, depending on the requirements of a particular task.

The Comparison (TSTIM) process is that of determining whether two stimuli are the same, or of the same class.

The Co-representation Formation (FOCORP) process is that of establishing a new representation in memory in association with one with a longer history, often in terms of some rule that gives the basis on which the co-representation is formed.

The Co-representation Retrieval (FICORP) process is that of finding, in memory, a particular representation in association with another representation on the basis of some rule or other basis for the association.

The Transformation (TRAREP) process is that of transforming or changing a mental representation on some specified basis, for example, "mental rotation" of a visual stimulus.

The Response-Execution (XECUTR) process is that of operating on some representation in such a way as to produce either an overt or a covert response: a movement that presses a button, an uttered word, or a covert "rehearsal".

Carroll's (1980) analysis of these cognitive processes is achieved by simulating ECTs in each of the eight paradigms with the aid of a computer program, SIMCOG, and then assessing simulations of the processes involved in each ECT in terms of measures of processing time and, in some instances, error rates. After this instructive analysis, IDs in ECTs are appraised, respectively, against the background of knowledge from factor analysis, and task analysis. An attempt is made, finally, to integrate the results of the exercise in a broader body of psychological theory.

To undertake anything approaching a just evaluation of Carroll's analysis, which runs to about three hundred pages in fine print, would be well beyond the limits of the present discussion. It is clear, however, that this work represents a major step towards the much needed integration of psychometric and experimental cognitive theory. No longer will factor analysts be able to account for factors merely with reference to introspectively derived descriptions of assumed sources of variance underlying tests. Interpretations will have to consider processes similar to the ten studied by Carroll, relating them to different <u>memory stores</u>. We can thus expect to see factors described in terms of different sensory <u>encoding</u> processes, different processes of perceptual <u>transformation</u> in STM, different <u>strategies</u> for directing the flow of information between memory stores and different forms of <u>response execution</u>, or motor output. Different sources of test variance due to processing <u>time</u> and <u>error</u> rates, in the different processing stages, will need to be specified. The challenge implied is a considerable one, but the outcome may bring psychologists closer to an eventual understanding of the complex relation between intellectual <u>structure</u> and cognitive <u>function</u>. Carroll's current thinking can be followed in chapter 5.

Advances in Cognitive Measurement

Despite the growing body of theory pertaining to the manner in which the human brain processes information, cognitive psychologists have not yet invented a means of directly observing the processing of information in the nervous system. To experimentalists and psychometricians alike, the functioning brain remains a mystery, sealed in a "black box". Only the outcomes of its activity can be observed. Cognitive psychology, for the present, consequently remains at the level of an inferential science.

Nonetheless, if the information subjected to processing is carefully controlled and relevant parameters are used for measuring behavioural outcomes, considerable faith can be vested in the inferences made about underlying processes. It is accordingly worth noting the various measurement procedures and parameters in use and examining their respective merits as aids to an understanding of cognitive behaviour.

As recorded in the previous section, psychometricians and experimentalists have established different traditions of preferences regarding parameters for measuring cognitive behaviour. The former school has concentrated more on right and wrong responses, whereas the latter has made greater use of reaction times or response latency measures. Hence psychometric theories of human ability structure are generally founded upon multivariate correlational analyses of accuracy scores, obtained from tests administered with lenient time constraints. Experimentally-based theories of human cognitive processes, on the other hand, are more frequently guided by variance analyses in which the dependent variables are reaction times, or their reciprocals, speed of response. In these studies tasks of modest or inconsequential difficulty are mostly used. The implicit assumption underlying the psychometric tradition is that accuracy of response is a more important indicator of individual differences in intellectual ability than speed. The assumption in the experimental tradition appears to be that speed of response provides a more sensitive measure of differences in underlying mental processes than accuracy.

Cronbach (1957), NcNemar (1964), and numerous others have recognised that the advancement of cognitive psychology depends upon the extent to which the respective merits of two formerly independent traditions can be integrated into a comprehensive new research paradigm. The ideal paradigm is expected to be one informed by dynamic models of cognition, taken from experimental research on information processing, married to knowledge abut performance dimensions, established through factor analysis of individual differences on reliable psychometric tests. The paradigm should make provision for descriptions of cognitive behaviour in terms of separate parameters for speed, accuracy, and other characteristics. Although no such paradigm has been forged successfully yet, several useful leads have been developed. One noteworthy example is the work of the British team led by Professor Hans J. Eysenck during the nineteen fifties and sixties (Eysenck, 1953; 1967; Furneaux, 1960; Brierly, 1961; White, 1973). In this work a distinction is made between different behaviour parameters in the test situation, notably speed, accuracy, and persistence. Speed is measured as response time per item, accuracy is a function of right and wrong responses over the test, and persistence is a measure of the subject's willingness to persevere with difficult problems. Another parameter, level, is sometimes used in the work of this group to refer to the order of complexity a subject can manage given unlimited time.

In the views of this group, the central cognitive component in intelligence test performance is speed. In omnibus IQ tests, speed is averaged over different mental processes and accounts for the major portion of variance in scores. When more specialized tests are used, the underlying common variance, or g factor variance, is considered to represent chiefly individual differences in mental speed (Eysenck, 1967). Eysenck and Furneaux argue that the fundamental nature of mental speed can be demonstrated by plotting an individual's item response latencies against the difficulty level of the items concerned. When this is done, typically a negatively accelerated curve is obtained; when the time units are transformed logarithmically the plots for all individuals become linear and parallel. This finding is interpreted as evidence that the only source of differences among individuals on the items is the intercept on the abscissa of the graph, where log. time represents speed of response. The increase in log. time with increase in item difficulty has the same slope for all individuals tested. The slope of the regression is accordingly a constant, which, Eysenck claims, is one of the few demonstrated in psychology.

Furneaux (1960) suggests that central to all cognitive information processing is some kind of scanning mechanism the speed of which determines the probability of the right solution being brought into focus more or less quickly. This notion is developed by Eysenck (1967) to provide an explanation for the failure of simple reaction time experiments to correlate with intelligence. In the example cited, it is argued that in a task in which a subject must press a button in response to a light flash, no information is conveyed, by definition, when there is only one light/button combination. As the number of combinations increases the amount of information increases logarithmically, so that with two combinations one bit of information is conveyed, with four combinations, two bits, and eight combinations, three bits. Evidence is cited from studies by Hick (1952), Hyman (1953), and Schmidtke (1961) that response time increases linearly with increasing number of bits of information. Hence each subject's performance can be described graphically in terms of two parameters, the intercept on the ordinate, representing raw reaction time, and the rate of increase in reaction time with increasing amount of information processed, represented by the slope of the regression line when amount of information in bits defines the abscissa. In such a graph, simple reaction time, involving 0 bits of information, would show no correlation with speed of information processing. By equating speed of information processing with "intelligence", the lack of correlation between simple reaction time and "intelligence" is explained. The slope of the regression line, however, showing increase of reaction time with amount of information processed, would be expected to show a negative correlation with "intellignece". This prediction suggests that intelligent subjects would show less increase in reaction time with increases in the number of light/button combinations than dull subjects. Experimental evidence produced by Roth (1964) is cited as confirmation of these predicitons. A more recent, independent attempt at confirmation of predictions from the Eysenck/Furneaux theory of mental speed fails to provide unequivocal support (Seymour and Moir, 1980). Nonetheless, researchers at Eysenck's laboratory continue to show interest in the theory as the basis for an understanding of intelligence. In

one recent variant, for example, Hendrickson and Hendrickson
(1980) refer to research on Inspection Time (IT) as a promising
source of explanations for individual differences in IQ. In
particular, they cite the findings of Nettelbeck and Lally (1976)
who report a Spearman rank correlation of .92 between WAIS
performance IQ and an IT measure.

Brand (1979) has provided a useful and up-to-date review of the IT
literature. IT measures are based on simple tasks in which some
stimulus, usually visual, is presented for a brief, predetemined
time period, following which subjects must make some judgement
about the stimulus. The presentation time is lowered on
successive trials until the subject no longer can make reliable
judgements. This minimum exposure time is called the subject's
IT. A general finding noted by Brand is that high IQ subjects are
able to make good discriminations at much lower presentation times
than low IQ subjects.

Hendrickson and Hendrickson (1980) offer an explanation for this
finding with reference to their pulse train hypothesis. Their
argument is supported by some intriguing equations, which merit
close attention but which cannot be summarized usefully without a
detailed account of their theory of neural transmission being
presented. The gist of the argument is that higher IQ subjects
have fewer pulse transmission errors. A pulse train triggered by
a visual stimulus impinging on the retina is therefore likely to
have a higher probability of conveying reliable information to the
central nervous system in the case of a high IQ subject than in
the case of a low IQ subject. In subjects of lower IQ pulse
trains are likely to lose information or to convey distorted
information due to higher probabilities of transmission errors
occurring in the intervals between pulses. Hence fewer pulse
trains are required to convey reliable information about the
stimulus in high IQ subjects, and a shorter stimulus exposure time
is accordingly needed to permit reliable judgements to be made
about properties of the stimulus.

While this argument may provide a partial explanation of the
observed correlation between IT and IQ, it seems to fall short of
an explanation of the basis of intelligence. It deals merely with
the transmission of information in the peripheral visual system
and fails to address the more important issue of the processing
that takes place once the information reaches the central nervous
system. The explanation is confined, in this sense, to the first
of Spearman's (1923) three noegenetic laws of cognition, pertaining
to the apprehension of experience. It does not deal with his two
higher laws, having to do with the eduction of relations and

eduction of correlates. The Hendricksons have not yet correlated ITs with their electrophysiological complexity measure, although a high relationship would be essential to the validity of their theory of intelligence. Nor has their hypothesis been tested yet that IT measures should correlate highly with measures of fluid intelligence but not so highly with measures of crystallized intelligence. Research along these lines is being planned, and the results should prove of great interest.

Unlike their British counterparts, differential psychologists in America have, until recently, shown little interest in studying speed of performance as a parameter distinct from accuracy. The reason for this is presumably to be found in the fact that Thurstone's (1938) demonstration of PMAs eclipsed interest in Thorndike's (1926) fundamental work on speed and power in mental tests. Although one of Thurstone's original factors, P, is identified as perceptual speed, tests referencing this factor are scored for accuracy rather than speed. The score assigned to a subject represents the total number of items answered correctly over the test. The rationale for interpreting P as a speed factor is that the tests are administered under strictly timed conditions. In effect subjects are required to work at optimum performance in terms of both speed and accuracy in order to achieve a high score. The variance in the total score is thus some unknown function of speed and accuracy. It is impossible to partition the variance in such a score into separate speed and accuracy components. Hence two subjects achieving the same score on one of Thurstone's perceptual speed tests may differ markedly in terms of their speed and accuracy characteristics. Indeed, individuals may differ in the speed-accuracy tradeoff they make on a particular test and the speed-accuracy tradeoff function for a particular individual may differ across tests, depending upon the processing demands of the task in terms of content and complexity (Wickelgren, 1977).

Prominent American psychometricians in the human abilities field subsequent to Thurstone have similarly failed to distinguish operationally between speed and accuracy performance parameters. Guilford (1967) for example makes no explicit provision for speed factors in his S-I model, nor does speed merit a listing in the subject index of his most recent text on cognitive psychology, which purports to go beyond factor theory (Guilford, 1979). In the Horn-Cattell system of higher-order abilities, a general speediness factor is recognised as a broad second-order construct (Horn, 1968; Cattell, 1971). Marker variables used for this factor, however, are chiefly Thurstonian perceptual speed tests or similar instruments scored for number of right responses within a restricted time. Variables based upon reaction times, item-response latencies, or other true speed parameters are seldom

used. In their various writings it is clear that neither Cattell
nor Horn has firm views on the theoretical status of speed in
cognitive performance. Horn (1968) has suggested that speediness
may be an indication of endocrine functions, whereas Cattell
(1971) prefers to view speed as a non-cognitive temperament
factor. Both writers acknowledge that the dimensionality of speed
variance in cognitive performance is pooorly established. In
concert with many other factor analysts they have repeatedly
called attention to the need for more research on individual
differences in cognitive speed and for a clarification of the
relation between speed and other cognitive factors.

Notwithstanding, in a thorough review of recent literature on
individual differences in cognitive abilities, Carroll and Maxwell
(1979) devote no more than half a page to a section on cognitive
speed, citing only four references. Their excuse for this meagre
coverage is that considerations of speed enter into virtually all
other ability domains covered in their review and speed is not
treated in the literature as a distinct phenomenon. But they
argue that perhaps it <u>should</u> be treated as distinct in the
future. They refer to the excellent work of Egan (1976) on
spatial abilities as an example of the advantages that can be
expected if speed and accuracy are accorded status as separate
performance parameters.

Egan's (1976; 1978; 1979) work departs from the standpoint that
classic psychometric tests of abilities have been developed and
used without a deep understanding of the mental processes required
to do them. The approach he advocates to rectify this unhealthy
state is to design measures based upon information-processing
analyses of the ability domains in question. In his own work he
focuses on the spatial ability domain because of its topical
interest to information-processing theorists (Shepard and Metzler,
1971) and its established practical relevance to applied problems
(Smith, 1964). He regards his studies of spatial tasks, however,
merely as examples of a new class of research aimed at
understanding processes measured by ability tests. His approach
begins with the construction of an information-processing model of
the task of interest. This is done by observing the effects of
stimulus manipulations on a measure of task performance, usually
response latency. The model is successively adapted until it can
be demonstrated that the performance of a majority of subjects is
consistent with the patterns predicted by the model. Only then
are measures based on the model constructed to assess individual
differences in performance. Measurement parameters in the new
ability tests are typically <u>times</u> taken to complete the
hypothetical mental operations correctly. Accuracy, or error
probability measures may be used as well. Instead of the single
opaque score obtained on a traditional ability test, scores

derived from information-processing models represent estimates of performance on different hypothetical operations. There may be several such scores for any particular task, each describing performance on a different operation, or set of operations, each of which in turn is theoretically based.

Egan (1979) lists several potential benefits he considers to derive from the new generation of ability measures. First, new interpretations for classical psychometric concepts are made possible. The new interpretations have the advantage of being conceptual and process oriented rather than purely actuarial and statistically oriented. Second, theory-based mental tests suggest new directions for research on individual differences. One practical advantage in this regard is the possiblility of re-examining criterion scores in the light of better understood predictors for use in personnel and educational selection. Thirdly, understanding tests in terms of mental processes may lead to improved methods of assessing abilities, particularly in cases where response speed is important or where it is desirable to distinguish between speed and accuracy performance components.

Examples of models constructed from information-processing theory are presented for different spatial tasks, suggested by different psychometric factors in the spatial abilities domain. Common to each model is the assumption that tasks involve a set of distinct operations, usually performed sequentially. Even relatively simple tasks based on narrowly defined "pure" psychometric factors are assumed to be complex, involving distinct cognitive operations. A simple processing model for spatial visualization tasks, for example, is reproduced below in Figure 1.

This simple model (see chapter 6 for a review of different models of spatial abilities) may apply, at least in a general way, to a wide range of spatial visualization tasks. Visualization tasks typically require the mental manipulation of visual representations of an object. In a typical visualization test item, a subject has to choose from among, say, five alternatives, a drawing that best represents a spatially transformed version of the original object. In information-processing experiments, a subject usually has to make a two-alternative choice. Either the second object is judged to be a simple transformation of the original, in which case the response is "Same", or the second object is not considered a simple transformation of the original, in which case the response is "Different". The different stages of task performance implied by the processing model for spatial visualization include some kind of visual <u>encoding</u> of stimulus information, termed SEARCH in Fig. 1, followed by a TRANSFORM operation in which the code, in this case is <u>rotated</u> mentally and then <u>compared</u> with another visual stimulus. In the final stage,

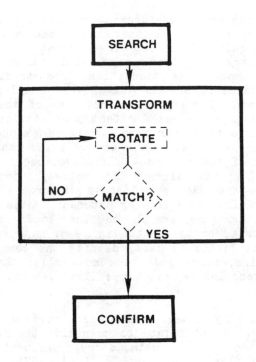

Figure 1   Processing model for spatial visualization tasks
(from Egan, 1979).

CONFIRM, an overt response is made, for example, by pressing a
button marked "Same".

Individuals may be assumed to differ in the speed and accuracy
with which each operation, or stage, is executed. Using tasks
based on a model of the above kind, Egan has produced results
suggesting that overall <u>accuracy</u> on spatial visualization tests is
influenced chiefly by variance in the <u>search</u> operation, whereas
overall <u>speed</u> is influenced mainly by variance in the
<u>transformation</u> stage. Generalization of this important finding
may account for the frequently observed lack of correlation
between global speed and accuracy measures on ability tests
(Carroll, 1981). These results provide compelling reasons why
cognitive tests should incorporate <u>separate</u> parameters for
measuring speed and accuracy on different component operations,
rather than traditional <u>global</u> measures such as overall proportion

correct or number of items attempted within a limited time.

Both cognitive theory and measurement methodology have advanced in the past decade to a level that makes the new generation of ability tests quite feasible. The advent of computer-based testing technology and the ready availability of inexpensive microprocessors makes the transition from traditional testing practically attainable and an unavoidable challenge to the new generation of cognitive psychologists. One of the most valuable advantages of using computers for test presentation, is that each subject's response times per item, or per task operation, can be recorded easily and reliably, as well as the accuracy or appropriateness of the response. The development of computerized testing technology is already an active, competitive field, particularly in the USA as evidenced in proceedings of recent conferences organized by a leading exponent (Weiss, 1977; 1980). A computerized literature search on the topic of computerized testing, instituted by the writer in 1976, has produced over one hundred relevant titles to date, despite the comparative recency of the enterprise, which goes back no earlier than the nineteen sixties (Greenwood and Taylor, 1965; Cleary, Linn, and Rock, 1968; Elwood, 1969).

The most noteworthy developments associated with computerized testing however, do not relate to cognitive theory but rather to measurement theory and methodology. Influential advances associated with flexi-level testing (Lord, 1971; 1977), adaptive testing (Weiss, 1973; 1974; Kingsbury and Weiss, 1980), and tailored testing (Samejima, 1977), provide outstanding examples. Despite the psychometric sophistication of this work, these authors display little interest in the recent advances associated with experimentally tested theories of cognitive processes. Their concerns centre around the statistical treatment of test scores representing the <u>products</u>, or outcomes of cognition. They do not address themselves to the substantive theoretical challenges related to the measurement and clarification of cognitive <u>processes</u>. A few noteworthy developments in this direction have begun to appear only very recently (Cory, Rimland, and Bryson, 1977; Dillon, 1981; Whitely and Schneider, 1981; Barratt, Alexander, Doverspike, Cellar, and Thomas, in press). The scope is still wide open for important advances to be made in the application of computerized testing technology and modern measurement methodology to the study of basic processes underlying human cognition.

Towards an Integrated theory of Human Cognition and Intelligence

Having duly appraised the findings of pertinent research in the foregoing sections, the question may be asked, what then is really known about human cognition and intelligence? The only fair answer, shared undoubtedly by most prominent researchers in the field, would seem to be that very little, indeed, is <u>known</u>.

It is known that the brain is the organ primarily responsible for the processing of information, but there is, as yet, no wide-spread agreement as to the mechanisms involved in information processing. Something is known about the operating characteristics of certain hypothetical processes, but there is still no well established set of cognitive processes in the literature. Several models have been proposed to describe information processing in the nervous system, but the true architecture of mental life is poorly understood. The presence of reliable individual differences underlying cognitive function is well established, but the causes of individual and group differences remain contentious debating points. The precise nature and meaning of the dimensions underlying human cognitive variations are not yet well established, hence it cannot be stated with certainty what the structure of their interrelations is, nor under which circumstances structural differences or structural changes can be expected. The effects of social, cultural, biological, and maturational influences on cognitive function are poorly understood. Even considerations of the most suitable procedures and parameters for measuring cognitive behaviour still appear open to subjective judgement, or taste.

One author, commenting recently on the state of knowledge in cognitive science, expressed his exasperation at the pace of progress, stating that he is "...struck by how little is known about so much of cognition" (Norman, 1979, p.10). Influential theorists looking in on progress from different vantage points have been forced to conclude similarly. At the start of his lengthy analysis of knowledge pertaining to human ability systems, Horn (1978), for example, laments that "compared with our knowledge what truthfully can be said about human abilities and their development is as a whisper in a gale" (p.212). On summing up his review of research on elementary cognitive tasks, Carroll (1981) likewise concludes that "...this kind of study is still in its infancy; at present, the few established findings, if any, constitute a puzzling mosaic that leaves a large residual of problems and gaps in knowledge" (p.21).

Yet there is optimism in many quarters that the pace of progress is accelerating (e.g., Glaser and Pellegrino, 1978). At least the issues, priorities, and prospects seem clearer now than when Cronbach (1957) first mooted a plea for the merger of multivariate differential and bivariate experimental psychology, or when McNemar (1964) re-emphasized the importance and urgency of the task.

Amongst major contributors to differential research there appears to be a general acceptance of the need to reinstate a theoretical basis for future psychometric work on abilities (Cattell, 1971; Eysenck, 1973; Horn, 1978; Guilford 1979; 1980; Royce, 1979; 1980; Carroll, 1980; 1981). There seems to be widespread agreement among these authors that classic psychometrics can contribute little to advance understanding beyond what is already known. For this reason, most of these writers have begun what might be referred to as putting psychology back in psychometrics. For the most part, this means infusing theoretical insights from the information-processing paradigms of cognitive psychology into new work on individual differences in abilities.

It is important to realise that this is a matter of re-introducing psychological theory as a foundation for psychometric research on individual differences. Cattell, (1971), Sternberg (1980), and others have made the point that the early pioneers of psychometric research on intelligence (Spearman, 1927; Thurstone, 1938) were in the first instance cognitive psychologists, interested in understanding human information processing (e.g., Spearman, 1923; Thurstone, 1924). They turned to psychometric methods as a means of clarifying and elaborating the structural aspects of intelligence. Unfortunately, neither lived long enough to complete the work he had begun, by integrating structural analyses of intelligence within the compass of a broader, process-oriented theory of human cognition. Their less visionary factor-analytic successors appear to have lost sight of the overall goals of the enterprise, resulting in the long period of stagnation characterising psychometric research on abilities, during the middle decades of this century. Only in the last decade have differential psychologists regained sight of the initial objective, and begun to re-examine factor models of intellectual structure from the broader theoretical perspective of a psychology of human cognition.

Experimental psychologists interested in cognition have not been as ready to re-appraise their traditional psychonomic methods and paradigms in the light of empirical findings on individual differences in intelligence. Yet a growing number of experimentalists, following the lead of Hunt, Frost, and Lunneborg (1973) are beginning to turn attention to the importance of accounting for individual differences on various measurement parameters of information processing. Leading contemporary theorists, such as Sternberg (1977; 1978; 1979; 1980) are seeking new methodologies for task analysis, which hopefully will permit not only a decomposition of cognitive tasks into theoretically meaningful subordinate components, but will enable, in addition, the measurement of individual differences in performance on processing components.

It seems thus that a start has been made towards the inevitable merger of psychometrics and psychonomic cognitive research, as a first step, indeed as a prerequisite, for the formation of an integrated theory of human cognition and intelligence. For the present, and the immediate future, it would seem necessary that researchers should retain full freedom in their approach to the common goal of creating a new theoretical synthesis. It is yet far too early to prescribe priorities for this ambitious programme, since it is by no means clear which of many avenues of approach will ultimately provide the greatest payoff.

Until the knowledge base for theoretical development has broadened, it would seem desirable that at least some research specialists within the separate sub-disciplines should continue with their respective programmes, without showing too much concern for the super-ordinate goal of integrative theory development. The imaginative psychometric work of Horn and his associates, for example, on factor-analytic explorations in the domains of auditory abilities (Stankov and Horn, 1980; Horn and Roy, 1980; Horn, Donaldson, and Engstrom, 1981), or structural modelling of aging effects on intellectual development (Horn and McArdle, 1980; McArdle and Horn, 1981), should continue unabated. Similarly, the creative research of experimental cognitive psychologists in the tradition of Shepard and his colleagues, on mental rotation and other perceptual transformations should continue to enjoy a high priority (Shepard and Metzler, 1971; Shepard and Feng, 1972; Cooper and Shepard, 1973; Metzler and Shepard, 1974; Cooper and Podgorny, 1976). The findings of this research are being used already by others in studies at the interface between experimental and psychometric research, as in the impressive work of Egan (1979), discussed in the preceding section. Until such time as the outline of a new theory for integrating knowledge about human cognition and intelligence becomes more clearly visible, reliance must be placed on some kind of wider conceptual framework for guiding research, and for organizing and integrating new data. Perhaps the most promising conceptual framework for this purpose is that being developed by Royce and his associates (Royce and Buss, 1976; Royce, 1979; Royce, 1980). This conceptual framework has the advantage of being accommodated within the overall context of general systems theory in science. The cognitive system is conceived to be organised on successive hierarchical levels, from molecular to molar. Structural features and process features of cognition are jointly accommodated and can be interrelated. A temporal dimension makes provision for the description and analysis of developmental change over the entire human lifespan, in response to both biological (genetic) and environmental (learning) causal influences.

The <u>cognitive system</u> is conceived as one of six interdependent systems making up the suprasystem of human personality, as a total psychological unit. The <u>affective system</u> (Royce and McDermott, 1977) is conceived as a processing unit similar to the cognitive system, both of which function as information transformers. The <u>style system</u> (Wardell and Royce, 1978) and <u>value system</u> (Schopflocher, Royce, and Meehan, in press) are also conceived as processing units, but their function has more to do with personality integration. The <u>sensory system</u> (Kearsley and Royce, 1977) and motor system (Powell, Katkzo, and Royce, 1978) are conceived as peripheral processing units that function as input/output transducers and encoders.

The six systems of personality are organised as a multilevel, hierarchical suprasystem in which there is a controlled-process stratum (sensory and motor), a learning-coping stratum (cognitive and affective), and an integrative stratum (style and value). Like the cognitive system, each of the remaining five systems is conceived as a multilevel, hierarchical system (Royce, 1979). Factor analysis is used as the major analytic technique for identifying the elements of the respective hierarchies. The elements (factors) in turn, may be used for further research either as independent, or as dependent variables, depending upon their treatment in the research design (Royce, 1980). Central to this conceptual framework, is the <u>information processing paradigm</u>, which Royce (1979) considers potentially best suited for generating a viable, dynamic theory of human variations in psychological function.

A recent empirical investigation by the writer (Verster, 1982a) may be seen as an attempt to build on the views and conclusions expressed above. The study is designed to evaluate a model of structural relations among major cognitive process variables. The model is informed by results from both the differential and experimental literatures considered in preceding sections. It is based, more specifically, on supplementary findings from pilot investigations (Verster and Steyn, 1973; Verster, 1975). In terms of the model, sequentially related information-processing stages are delineated and their expected locations indicated in a structured hierarchy of cognitive levels. Use is made in the study of a specially prepared battery of computerized cognitive process tests. The tests each give separate task performance measures for speed (item-response latencies) and accuracy (based on right and wrong responses). The computerized test battery is administered to three different, heterogeneous adult samples described as White Males (N=100), White Females (N=100), and Black Males (N=173). Speed and accuracy data are analysed separately, in the case of each sample, using modern structural equation modelling methods (Browne, 1981). The results provide statistically acceptable support for the validity and generality of the structural model of cognitive processes across cultural groups and between the sexes.

The lowest hierarchical levels in the model are defined by simple sensory and psychomotor processes. These are involved, respectively, in the <u>encoding</u> (input) and <u>response execution</u> (output) stages of information processing. Successively higher levels are defined, in turn, by more complex perceptual and conceptual processes. Perceptual processes (as, for example, in scanning, matching, rotation, closure) occur during the <u>transformation</u> stage of information processing. Conceptual (relational) processes (as, for example, in concept formation, analogical thinking, rule induction, logical inference) are involved in the <u>strategic</u> stage of information processing. The findings of this study are more fully discussed and evaluated elsewhere (Verster, 1982b; Verster, in preparation). In conjunction with other contemporary developments in the literature of cognitive psychology, they may be seen as a useful basis for further empirical work directed at the integration of knowledge about human cognition and intelligence.

ACKNOWLEDGEMENTS

This report was first prepared as part of project 4525.7, Cognitive Development, being undertaken in the human Development Division, NIPR. It is based on work included in a D Litt et Phil thesis accepted by the University of South Africa in 1982.

Thanks are due to Dr. G.K. Nelson, Director, NIPR, for permission to produce the report, and Mrs. P.G. Ferrey, Human Development Division, for typing the manuscript.

REFERENCES

Adkins, D.C., and Lyerly, S.B. (1952). <u>Factor analysis of reasoning tests</u>. Chapel Hill: University of North Carolina,

Anastasi, A. (1958). <u>Differential Psychology</u>. (3rd ed.) New York: MacMillan.

Anastasi, A. (1972). Four hypotheses with a dearth of data: Response to Lehrke's "A theory of X-linkage of major intellectual traits". <u>American Journal of Mental Deficiency</u>, <u>76</u>, 620-622.

Anderson, A.L. (1951). The effect of laterality localization on focal brain lesions on the Wechsler-Bellevue subtests. Journal of Clinical Psychology, 7, 149-153.

Anderson, J.E. (1939). The limitation of infant and preschool tests in the measurement of intelligence. Journal of Psychology, 8, 351-379.

Anderson, J.R., and Reder, L.M. (1974). Negative judgements in and about semantic memory. Journal of Verbal Learning and Verbal Behavior, 13, 664-681.

Armstrong, D.M. (1976). A materialist theory of the mind. London: Routledge and Kegan Paul.

Atkinson, R., and Shiffrin, R.M. (1968). Human memory: Proposed system and its control processes. In K.W. Spence and J.T. Spence (Eds.) The psychology of learning and motivation. Advances in research and theory, Vol. 2. New York: Academic.

Balinsky, B. (1974). An analysis of the mental factors of various age groups from nine to sixty. Genetic Psychology Monographs, 23, 191-234.

Baltes, P.B., Cornelius, S.W., Spiro, A., Nesselroade, J.R., and Willis, S.L. (1980). Integration versus differentiation of fluid/crystallized intelligence in old age. Developmental Psychology, 16, 625-635.

Baltes, P.B., and Nesselroade, J.R. (1973). The developmental analysis of individual differences on multiple measures. In J.R. Nesselroade and H.,W. Reese (Eds.) Life-span developmental psychology: Methodological issues. New York: Academic Press.

Baltes, P.B., and Schaie, K.W. (1976). On the plasticity of intelligence in adulthood and old age: Where Horn and Donaldson fail. American Psychologist, 31, 720-723.

Barratt, G.V., Alexander, R.A., Doverspike, D., Cellar, D., and Thomas, G.C. (1982). The development and application of a computerized information processing test battery. Applied Psychological Measurement.

Bayley, N. (1943). Mental growth during the first three years. In R.G. Barker, J.S. Kounin, and H.F. Wright (Eds.) Child Behaviour and Development, New York: McGraw-Hill.

Bem, S.L. (1974). The measurement of psychological androgyny. Journal of Consulting and Clinical Psychology, 42, 155-162.

Bennett, J.R., MacDonald, G.S., Brace, S.M., and Nenoyama, K. (1971). Some statistical properties of the visual evoked potential in man and their application as a criterion of normality. IEEE Transactions on Bio-medical Engineering, BME-18, 23-33.

Berry, J.W. (1966). Temne and Eskimo perceptual skills. International Journal of Psychology, 1, 207-229.

Berry, J.W. (1969). On cross-cultural comparability. International Journal of Psychology, 4, 199-128.

Berry, J.W. (1976). Human ecology and cognitive style: comparative studies in cultural and psychological adaptation. Beverly Hills: Sage/Halstead.

Berry, J.W. (1980). Introduction to methodology. In H.C. Triandis and J.W. Berry (Eds.) Handbook of Cross-cultural Psychology: Methodology (Volume 2). Boston: Allyn and Bacon.

Berry, J.W., and Dasen, P. (Eds.) (1974). Introduction to culture and cognition. London: Methuen.

Biesheuvel, S. (1958). Objectives and methods of African psychological research. Journal of Social Psychology, 47, 161-168.

Binet, A., and Simon, Th. (1916). The development of intelligence in children. Baltimore: Williams and Wilkens.

Binet, A., and Simon, Th. (1961). The development of intelligence in children. L'Annee Psychologique, 1905, pp. 163-191. Translated and reprinted in T. Shipley (Ed.) Classics in Psychology. New York: Philosophical Library, pp. 819-872.

Bock, R. D., and Kolakowski, D. (1973). Further evidence of sex-linked major gene influence on human spatial ability. American Journal of Human Genetics, 25, 1-14.

Bogen, J.E. (1970). Drugs and cerebral function. Springfield, Ill.: Thomas.

Bogen, J.E., Fisher, E.D., and Vogel, P.J. (1965). Cerebral commissurotomy: A second case report. Journal of the American Medical Assocation, 194, 1328-1329.

Brand, C. (1979). General intelligence and mental speed: their relationship and development. Paper read at NATO International Conference on Intelligence and Learning. York University, July.

Brazier, M.A. (1962). The analysis of brain waves. Scientific American, 206, 142-153.

Bierley, H. (1961). The speed and accuracy characteristics of neurotics. British Journal of Psychology, 52, 273-280.

Brimer, M.A. (1969). Sex differences in listening comprehension. Journal of Research and Development in Education, 3, 72-79.

Brislin, R. (1976). Comparative research methodology: cross-cultural studies. International Journal of Psychology, 11, 215-229.

Brislin, R. Lonner, W.J., and Thorndike, R. (1973). Cross-cultural research methods. New York: Wiley.

Broca, P. (1865). Du siege de la faculte de language articule. Bulletin de la Societe Anthropologie, 6, 377-393.

Brody, E.B., and Brody, N. (1976). Intelligence: Nature, determinants, and consequences. New York: Academic.

Broverman, D.M., Klaiber, E.L., Kobayashy, G., and Vogel, W. (1968). The role of activation and inhibition in sex differences in cognitive abilities. Psychological Review, 57, 23-50.

Browne, M.W.. (1981). Covariance structures. In D.M. Hawkins (Ed.) Topics in applied multivariate analysis, Vol.2. Technical Report TWISK 193, Pretoria: National Institute for Mathematical Sciences, January.

Bruner, J.S. (1957). Contemporary approaches to cognition. Cambridge, Massachusetts: Harvard University Press.

Bruner, J.S. (1964). The course of cognitive growth. American Psychologist, 19, 1-15.

Bruner, J.S., Goodnow, J.J., and Austin, G.A. (1956). A study of thinking. New York: Wiley.

Bryden, M.P. (1979). Evidence for sex-related differences in cerebral organization. In M.A. Wittig and A.C. Petersen (Eds.) Sex-related differences in cognitive functioning: Developmental issues. New York: Academic Press.

Buffery, A.W.H., and Gray, J.H. (1972). Sex differences in the development of spatial and linguistic skills. In C. Ounsted and D.C. Taylor (Eds.) Gender differences: theory, ontogeny and significance. Baltimore: Williams and Wilkens.

Burt, C. (1909). The experimental study of general intelligence. Child Study, 4, 78-100.

Burt, C. (1912). The inheritance of mental characters. Eugenics Review, 4, 1-33.

Burt, C. (1914). The measurement of intelligence by the Binet tests. Eugenics Review, 6, 36.

Burt, C. (1919). The development of reasoning in children. Journal of Experimental Prediatrics, 5, 68-77; 121-127.

Burt, C. (1938). The analysis of temperament. British Journal of Medical Psychology, 17, 158-188.

Burt, C. (1939). The factorial analysis of emotional traits. Character and Personality, 7, 238-254; 285-299.

Burt, C. (1940). The factors of the mind: An introduction to factor analysis in psychology. London: University of London Press.

Burt, C., (1945). The assessment of personality. British Journal of Educational Psychology, 15, 107-121.

Burt, C. (1949). The structure of the mind: a review of the results of factor analysis. British Journal of Educational Psychology, 19, 176-199.

Burt, C. (1954). The bearing of the factor theory on the orgnization of schools and classes. Unpublished Report to the London County Council, London, 1919. (Cited in Burt, C., The differentiation of intellectual ability. British Journal of Educational Psychology, 24, 76-90).

Burt, C. (1955). The evidence for the concept of intelligence. British Journal of Educational Psychology, 25, 158-177.

Burt, C. (1962). Mental and scholastic tests. (4th ed.)   London: Staples.

Burt, C. (1963). Is intelligence distributed normally?   British Journal of Statistical Psychology, 16, 175-190.

Burt, C. (1966). The genetic determination of differences in intelligence: a study of monozygotic twins reared together and apart. British Journal of Psychology, 57, 137-153.

Burt, C. (1975). The gifted child.   London: Hodder and Stoughton.

Buss, A., and Royce, J.R. (1975). Detecting cross-cultural commonalities and differences: intergroup factor analyses. Psychological Bulletin, 82, 128-136.

Butcher, G. (1969). Creativity in multivariate personality research. In R.M. Dreyer (Ed.) Contribution to the understanding of personality in honour of R.B. Cattell. Urbana: University of Illinois Press.

Calloway, E. (1973). Correlation between averaged evoked potentials and measures of intelligence. Archives of General Psychiatry, 29, 553-558.

Carroll, J.B. (1974). Psychometric tests as cognitive tasks: A new "structure-of-intellect". RB 74-16, Technical Report No. 4, Princeton: Educational Testing Service.

Carroll, J.B. (1978a). How shall we study individual differences in cognitive abilities?   Methodological and theoretical perspectives. Intelligence, 1, 2, 87-115.

Carroll, J.B. (1978b). Book review: "Intelligence, information processing and analogical reasoning: The componential analysis of human abilities" by Robert J. Sternberg. Hillsdale, N.J.: Eribaum. In Applied Psychological Measurement, 2 (4), 615-618.

Carroll, J.B. (1980). Individual difference relations in psychometric and experimental cognitive tasks. Report No. 163, AD A086057. Chapel Hill: University of North Carolina.

Carroll, J.B. (1981). Ability and task difficulty in cognitive psychology. Educational Researcher, 10, 11-21.

Carroll, J.B., and Maxwell, S.E. (1979). Individual differences in human cognitive abilities. Annual Review of Psychology, 30, 603-640.

Carter-Saltzman, L. (1979). Patterns of cognitive functioning in relation to handedness and sex-related differences. In M.A. Wittig and A.C. Petersen (Eds.) Sex-related differences in cognitive functioning: Developmental issues. New York: Academic Press.

Cattell, J.McK. (1890). Mental tests and measurements. Mind, 15, 373-381.

Cattell, JMcK. and Ferrand, L. (1896). Physical and mental measurements of the students of Columbia University. Psychological Review, 3, 618-648.

Cattell, R.B. (1941). Some theoretical issues in adult intelligence testing. Psychological Bulletin, 38, 592.

Cattell, R.B. (1943). The measurement of adult intelligence. Psychological Bulletin, 40, 153-193.

Cattell, R.B. (1957). The IPAR Culture Fair Intelligence Scales. Champaign, Ill.: Institute for Personality and Ability Testing.

Cattell, R.B. (1963). Theory of fluid and crystallized intelligence: A critical experiment. Journal of Educational Psychology, 54, 1-22.

Cattell, R.B. (1967). The theory of fluid and crysallized general intelligence checked at the 5-6 year-old level. British Journal of Educational Psychology, 37, 209-224.

Cattell, R.B. (1971). Abilities: their structure, growth, and action. Boston: Houghton Mifflin.

Cattell, R.B., and Beloff, H. (1959). The high school personality questionnaire. Champaign, Ill.: Institute for Personality and Ability Testing.

Cattell, R.B., Blewett, D.B., and Beloff, J.R. (1955). The inheritance of personality. A multiple variance analysis determination of approximate nature-nurture ratios for primary personality factors in Q-data. American Journal of Human Genetics, 7, 122-146.

Chalke, F.C.R., and Ertl, J.P. (1965). Evoked potentials and intelligence. Life Sciences, 4, 1319-1322.

Clark, H.H., and Chase, W.G. (1972). On the process of comparing sentences against pictures. Cognitive Psychology, 3, 472-517.

Cloary, T.A., Linn, R.L., and Rock, D.A. (1968). An exploratory study of programmed tests. Educational and Psychological Measurement, 28, 345-360.

Cobb, S. (1965). Brain size. Archives of Neurology, 1965, 12, 555-561.

Cohen, D., and Wilkie, F. (1979). Sex-related differences in cognitive functioning: Developmental issues. New York: Academic Press.

Cooper, L.A., and Podgorny, P. (1976). Mental transformations of visual comparison processes: Effects of complexity and similarity. Journal of Experimental Psychology: Human Perception and Performance, 2, 503-514.

Cooper, L.A., and Shepard, R.N. (1973). Chromometric studies of
    the rotation of mental images. In '.G. Chase (Ed.) Visual
    Information Processing. New York: Academic Press, 1973.

Cory, C.H., Rimland, B., and Bryson, R.A. (1977). Using
    computerized tests to measure new dimensions of abilities: An
    exploratory study. Applied Psychological Measurement, 1,
    101-110.

Crawford, C.B. A canonical correlation analysis of cortical evoked
    response and intelligence test data? Canadian Journal of
    Psychology, 28, 319-332.

Crawford-Nutt, D.H. (1977). The assessment of mental ability among
    Black teachers in Bophuthatswana. CSIR Confidential Contract
    Report C/PERS 257. Johannesburg: National Institute for
    Personnel Research.

Cronbach, L.J. (1957). The two disciplines of scientific
    psychology. American Psychologist, 12, 671-684.

Cronbach, L.J. (1967). Year-to-year correlations of mental tests:
    A review of the Hofstatter analysis. Child Development, 38,
    283-289.

Cunningham, W.R. (1980). Age comparative factor analysis of
    ability variables in adulthood and old age. Intelligence, 4,
    133-149.

Cunningham, W.R. (1981). Ability factor structure differences in
    adulthood and old age. Multivariate Behavioural Research,
    16, 3-22.

Cunningham, W.R., and Birren, G.E. (1980). Age changes in the
    factor structure of intellectual abilities in adulthood and
    old age. Educational and Psychological Measurement, 40,
    271-290.

Dan, A.G. (1979). The menstrual cycle and sex-related differences in cognitive variability. In M.A. Wittig and A.C. Petersen (Eds.) Sex-related differences in cognitive functioning: Developmental issues. New York: Academic Press.

Darwin, C. (1859). The origin of species. London: Murray.

Dasen, P.R. (1977). Are cognitive processes universal? A contribution to cross-cultural Piagetian psychology. In N. Warren (Ed.) Studies in cross-cultural psychology, Volume 1. London: Academic Press.

Dawson, J.L.M. (1969). Theoretical and research bases of bio-social psychology. University of Hong Kong Gazette, 16, 1-10.

Dawson, J.L.M. (1971). Theory and research in cross-cultural psychology. Bulletin of the British Psychological Society, 24, 291-306.

Desmedt, J.E. (Ed.) (1979). Cognitive components in cerebral event-related potentials and selective attention. Basel: Karger.

Dillon, R.F. (1981). Analogical reasoning under different methods of test administration. Applied Psychological Measurement, 5, 341-347.

Dimond, S.G. (1980). Neuropsychology: A text book of systems and psychological functions of the human brain. London: Butterworths.

Donchin, E. (1966). A multivariate approach to the analysis of average evoked potentials. IEEE Transactions on bio-medical engineering, BME-13, 131-139.

Donchin, E., Calloway, E., and Jones, R.T. (1970). Auditory evoked potential variables in schizophrenia, II. The application of discriminant analysis. Electroencephalography and Clinical Neurophysiology, 29, 429-440.

Donchin, E., and Lindsley, D.B. (Eds.) (1969). Average evoked potentials. Washington: NASA.

Dorfman, D.D. (1978). The Cyril Burt question: New findings. Science, 201, No. 4362, 117-1186.

Drenth, P.J.D., Van der Vlier, H., and Omari, I.M. (1979). The use of classroom tests, examinations and aptitude tests in a developing country. In L. Ekensberger, W. Lonner, and Y.H. Poortinga (Eds.) Cross-cultural contributions to Psychology. Lisse, Netherlands: Swets and Zeitlinger.

Dunham, G.L., and Bunderson, C.V. (1969). Effect of decision-rule instruction upon the relationship of cognitive abilities to performance in multiple-category concept problems. Journal of Educational Psychology, 60, 121-125.

Egan, D.E. (1976). Accuracy and latency scores as measures of spatial information processing. Research Report No. 1224. Pensacola, Florida: Naval Aerospace Medical Research Laboratory, February.

Egan, D.E. (1978). Characterizing spatial ability: Different mental processes reflected in accuracy and latency scores. Research Report No. 1250. Pensacola, Florida: Naval Aerospace Medical Research Laboratory.

El Koussi, A.A.H. (1935). The visual perception of space. British Journal of Psychology, Monograph Supplement, No. 20.

Ekensberger, L. (1972). The necessity of a theory for applied cross-cultural research. In L.J.C. Cronbach and P.J.D. Drenth (Eds.) Mental tests and cultural adaptation. The Hague: Mouton.

Elkind, D. and Flavell, J.H. (Eds.) (1969). Studies in cognitive development: Essays in honour of Jean Piaget. New York: Oxford University Press.

Ellingson, R.J. (1965). Relationship between EEG and test intelligence: A commentary. Psychological Bulletin, 65, 91-98.

Ellis, H. (1894). Man and Woman: A study of human secondary sexual characters. (4th ed.) London: Walter Scott.

Elwood, D.L. (1969). Automation of psychological testing. American Psychologist, 287-289.

Ertl, J.P. (1968). Evoked potentials, neural efficiency, and I.Q. Paper presented at the International Symposium for Biocybernetics, Washington, D.C.

Ertl, J.P. (1972) I.Q. evoked responses and Fourier analysis. Nature, 241, 209-210.

Ertl, J.P., and Schafer, E.W.P. (1969). Brain response correlates of psychometric intelligence. Nature, 223, 421-423.

Eysenck, H.J. (1953). Uses and abuses of psychology. London: Pelican.

Eysenck, H.J. (1967). Intelligence assessment: A theoretical and experimental approach. British Journal of Educational Psychology, 37, 81-98.

Fairweather, H. (1976). Sex differences in cognition. Cognition, 4, 231-280.

Ferguson, G.A. (1954). On learning and human ability. Canadian Journal of Psychology, 8, 95-112.

Ferguson, G.A. (1956). On transfer and the abilities of man. Canadian Journal of Psychology, 10, 121-131.

French, J.W. (1951). The description of aptitude and achievement tests in terms of rotated factors. Chicago: University of Chicago Press.

Frijda, N.H., and Jahoda, G. (1966). On the scope and methods of cross-cultural research. International Journal of Psychology, 1, 110-127.

Furneaux, W.D. (1960). Intellectual abilities and problem-solving behaviour. In H.J. Eysenck (Ed.) Handbook of Abnormal Psychology, Chapter 5. London: Pitman.

Gale, A., Brown, A., Osborne, K., and Smallbone, A. (1978). Further evidence of sex differences in brain organization. Biological Psychology, 203-208.

Galton, F. (1869). Hereditary genius. London: MacMillan.

Galton, F. (1883). Enquiries into human faculty and its development. London: MacMillan.

Garnett, J.C.M. (1919). On certain independent factors in mental measurement. Proceedings of the Royal Society, 26, 102-5.

Garrett, H.E. (1946). A developmental theory of intelligence. American Psychologist, 1, 372-378.

Gazzaniga, M.S., and Le Doux, J.E. (1978). The integrated mind. New York: Plenum.

Geschwind, N. Galaburda, A., and Le May, M. (1979). Morphological and physiological substrates of language and cognitive development. In R. Katzman (Ed.) Congenital and acquired cognitive disorders. New York: Raven.

Glaser, R., and Pellegrino, J.W. (1978). Uniting cognitive process theory and differential psychology: Back home from the wars. Intelligence, 2, 305-319.

Glees, P. (1967). Are both sides of our central nervous system of equal value? Triangle, The Sandoc Journal of Medical Science, 8, 101-108.

Gould, S.J. (1978). Morton's ranking of races by cranial capacity: unconscious manipulation of data may be a scientific norm. Science, 200, 503-509.

Grady, K.E. (1977). The belief in sex differences. Paper presented at Eastern Psychological Association Meeting, Boston.

Greenwood, D.I., and Taylor, C. (1965). Adaptive testing in an older population. Journal of Psychology, 60, 193-198.

Guilford, J.P. (1947). Printed classification tests. A.A.F. Aviation Psychology Report No. 5, Washington, D.C.: Government Printing Office.

Guilford, J.P. (1956). The structure of intellect. Psychological Bulletin, 53, 267-293.

Guilford, J.P. (1967). The nature of human intelligence. New York: McGraw-Hill.

Guildford, J.P. (1979). Cognitive Psychology with a frame of reference. San Diego: Edits.

Guilford, J.P. (1980). Fluid and crystallized intelligence: two fanciful concepts. Psychological Bulletin, 88, 406-412.

Guilford, J.P., and Hoepfner, R. (1971). The analysis of intelligence. New York: McGraw-Hill.

Guilford, J.P., and Tenopyr, M.L. (1968). Implications of the structure of intellect model for high school and college students. In W.M. Michael (Ed.) Teachings for creative endeavour. Bloomington: Indiana University Press.

Guttman,   L. (1950). Relation of scalogram analysis to other
           techniques. In S.A. Stoupfer et al., (Eds.) Measurement
           and prediction. New Jersey: Princeton University.

Guttman,   L. (1954). The radex: . A new apprach to factor
           analysis. In P. Lazarsfeld (Ed.) Mathematical thinking
           in the social sciences. New York: Columbia University
           Press.

Guttman,   L. (1955). A generalized simplex for factor analysis.
           Psychometrika, 20, 173-192.

Guttman,   L. (1965a). A faceted definition of intelligence. In R.
           Eiferman (Ed.) Scripta Hierosolymitana studies in
           pscyhology. Jerusalem: The Hebrew University, 14,
           166-181.

Guttman,   L. (1965b). The structure of interrrelations among
           intelligence tests. In Proceedings of the 1964
           Invitational Conference on Testing Problems. Princeton,
           New Jersey: Educational Testing Service.

Guttman,   L. (1967). The development of non-metric space analysis:
           A letter to Professor John Ross. Multivariate
           Behavioural Research, 2, 71-82.

Guttman,   L. (1968). A general non-metric technique for finding the
           smallest coordinate space for a configuration of
           points. Psychometrika, 33, 469-506.

Guttman,   L., and Schlesinger, I.M. (1966). Systematic construction
           of distractors for ability and achievement test items.
           Educational and Psychological Measurement.

Hakstian, A.R., and Vandenberg, S.G. (1979). The cross-cultural
           generalizability of a higher-order cognitive structure
           model. Intelligence, 3, 73-103.

Hamilton, J.A. (1936). Intelligence and the human brain. Psychological Review, 43, 308-321.

Harlow, H.F. (1949). The formation of learning sets. Psychological Review, 56, 51-65.

Harris, L.J. (1978). Sex differences in spatial ability: possible environmental, genetic, and neurological factors. In M. Kinsbourne (Ed.) Asymmetrical function of the brain. New York: Cambridge University Press.

Hearnshaw, L.S. (1979). Cyril Burt: Psychologist. London: Hodder and Stoughton.

Hearnshaw, L.S. (1964). A short history of British psychology. London: Methuen.

Hebb, D.O. (1942). The effects of early and late brain injury upon test scores and the nature of normal adult intelligence. Proceedings of the American Philosophical Society, 89, 275-292.

Hendrickson, A.E. (1982) The biological basis of intelligence. Part I: Theory. London: Department of Psychology, Institute of Psychiatry.

Hendrickson, D.E. (1981). The biological basis of intelligence. Part II: Measurement. London: Department of Psychology, Institute of Psychiatry.

Hendrickson, D.E., and Hendrickson, A.E. (1980). The biological basis of individual differences in intelligence. Personality and Individual Differences, 1, 3-33.

Hick, W. (1952). On the rates of gain of information. Quarterly Journal of Experimental Psychology, 4, 11-26.

Hill, D. (1981). Mechanisms of the mind: a psychiatric perspective. British Journal of Medical Psychology, 54, 1-13.

Hill, J.P. (1967). Similarity and accordance between parents and sons in attitudes towards mathematics. Child Development, 38, 777-791.

Hobson, J. R. (1947). Sex differences in primary mental abilities. Journal of Educational Research, 41, 126-132.

Hoepfner, R., Guilford, J.P., and Bradley, P.A. (1970). Information-transformation abilities. Educational and Psychological Measurement, 30, 785-802.

Hofstatter, P.R. (1954). The changing composition of intelligence. A study in T-technique. Journal of Genetic Psychology, 85, 159-164.

Holzinger, K.J. (1937). Student manual of factor analysis. Chicago: Department of Education.

Horn, J.L. (1967). On subjectivity in factor analysis. Educational and Psychological Measurement, 27, 811-20.

Horn, J.L. (1968). Organization of abilities and the development of intelligence. Psychological Review, 75, 242-259.

Horn, J.L. (1970). Organization of data on life-span development of human abilities. In L.R. Goulet and B.P. Baltes (Eds.) Life-span Development Psychology. New York: Academic Press.

Horn, J.L. (1971). Integration of concepts of reliability and standard error of measurement. Educational and Psychological Measurement, 31, 57-74.

Horn, J.L. (1976a). Human abilities: A review of research and theory in the early 1970's. Annual Review of Psychology, 27, 437-485.

Horn, J.L. (1976b). Progress report on a study of speed, power, carefulness, and short-term learning components of intelligence and changes in these components in adulthood. Army Research Institue, Grant No. DAHC 19/74-5-0012. Denver: University of Denver.

Horn, J.L. (1978). Human ability systems. Life-span Development and Behaviour, 1, 211-256.

Horn, J.L., and Bramble, W.G. (1967). Second-order ability structure revealed in rights and wrongs scores. Journal of Educational Psychology, 58, 115-122.

Horn, J.L., and Cattell, R.B. (1966). Refinement and test of the theory of fluid and crystallised general intelligence. Journal of Educational Psychology, 57, 253-270.

Horn, J.L., and Donaldson, G. (1976). On the myth of intellectual decline in adulthood. American Psychologist, 31, 701-709.

Horn, J.L., Donaldson, G., and Engstrom, R. (1981). Apprehension, memory, and fluid intelligence decline in adulthood. Research on Aging, 3, 33-84.

Horn, J.L., and Knapp, J.R. (1973). On the subjective character of the empirical base of Guilford's structure-of-intellect model. Psychological Bulletin, 80, 33-43.

Horn, J.L., and McArdle, J.J. (1980). Perspectives on mathematical/statistical model building (MASMOD) in research on aging. In L.W. Poon (Ed.) Aging in the 80's: Psychological issues. Washington, D.C.: American Psychological Association.

Horn, J.L., and Stankov, L. (1981). Auditory and visual factors of intelligence. Unpublished Research Report, University of Denver, Denver, Colorado.

Humphreys,   L.G. (1960). Investigations   of   the   simplex.
    Psychometrika, 25, 213-323.

Humphreys, L.G.(1961). The   organization   of   human   abilities.
    Presidential Address, Division 5 of American Psychological
    Association. New York: American Psychological Association.

Humphreys, L.G. (1962). The organization of human abilities.
    American Psychologist, 17, 475-483.

Hunt,   E. (1971). What kind of computer is man? Cognitive
    Psychology, 2, 52-98.

Hunt, E. (1978). Qualitative sources of individual differences in
    complex problem-solving. In J.M. Scandura and C.J. Brainerd
    (Eds.) Structural/process models of complex human behaviour.
    The Netherlands: Sitjhoff and Noordhoff.

Hunt, E. (1979). Intelligence as an information processing
    concept. Research Report 04206. Department of Psychology,
    University of Washington: Seattle, Washington.

Hunt, E. Forst, N., and Lunneborg, C. (1973). Individual
    differences in cognition: A new approach to intelligence. In
    G. Bower (Ed.) The psychology of learning and motivation,
    (Vol.7). New York: Academic Press.

Hunt, E., Lunneborg, C.E., and Lewis, G. (1975). What does it mean
    to be high verbal? Cognitive Psychology, 7, 194-227.

Hunt, J. McV. (1961). Intelligence and Experience. New York:
    Ronald.

Hyman, R. (1953). Stimulus information as a determinant of
    reaction time. Journal of Experimental Psychology, 45,
    188-190.

Irvine, S.H. (1966). Towards a rationale for testing attainments
    and abilities in Africans. British Journal of Educational
    Psychology, 36, 24-32.

Irvine, S.H. The place of factor analysis in cross-cultural methodology and its contribution to cognitive theory. In L. Eckensberger, Y. Poortinga and W. Lonner (Eds.), Cross-cultural Contributions to Psychology. Lisse: Swets and Zeitlinger.

Irvine, S.H., and Carroll, W.K. (1980). Testing and assessment across cultures: Issues in methodology and theory. In H.C. Triandis and J.W. Berry (Eds.) Handbook of Cross-cultural Psychology. Volume 2: Methodology. Boston, Massachusetts: Allyn and Bacon.

Jackson, G.H. (1887). Remarks on evolution and dissolution of the nervous system. Journal of Medical Science.

Jacobson, E. (1973). Electrophysiology of mental activities and introduction to the psychological process of thinking. In F.G. McGuigan and R.A. Schoonover (Eds.) The psychophysiology of thinking: Studies of correct procedures. New York: Academic Press.

Jahoda, G.A. (1970). A cross-cultural perspective in psychology. The Advancement of Science, 27, 1-14.

Jensen, A.R. (1967). Estimation of the limits of heritability of traits by comparison of monozygotic and dizygotic twins. Proceedings of the National Academy of Science, 149-157.

Jensen, A.R. (1973). Level I and Level II abilities in three ethnic groups. American Educational Journal, 4, 263-276.

Jensen, A.R. (1977). The problem of genotype-environment correlation and the estimation of heritability from monozygotic and dizygotic twins. Acta Geneticae, Medicae and Gemellologiae.

Jensen, A.R. (1979). g - Outmoded theory or unconquered frontier? Creative Science and Technology, 2, 16-29.

Kearsley, G. and Royce, J.R. (1977). A multi-factor theory of sensation: individuality in sensory structure and sensory processing. Perceptual and Motor Skill, 44, 1299-1316.

Kelly, T.L. (1923). Statistical Method. New York: MacMillan.

Kelly, T.L. (1928). Cross roads in the mind of man. Stanford: Stanford University Press.

Kelly, T.L. (1935). Essential traits of mental life. Harvard: University Press.

Kingsbury, G., and Weiss, D.J. (1980). A comparison of adaptive, sequential, and conventional testing strategies for mastery decisions. Research Report 80-4, AD A094478, Minneapolis: University of Minnesota.

Kline, P. (1979). Psychometrics and Psychology. London: Academic Press.

Koestler, A. (1979). Janus: A summing up. London: Pan Books.

Koffka, K. (1935). Principles of gestalt psychology. London: Routledge and Kegan Paul.

Kohler, W. (1929). Gestalt psychology: An introduction to new concepts in modern psychology. New York: Liveright, 1947.

Kornhuber, H.H. (1978). A reconsideration of the mind-brain problem. In P.A. Buser and A. Rougeuel-Buser (Eds.) Cerebral correlates of conscious experience. Inserm. Symposium No.6. Amsterdam: North Holland Biomedical Press.

Lashley, K. (1950). In search of the engram. . Symposium of the Society of Experimental Biology, 4, 454-482.

Lehrke, R.G. (1974). X-linked mental retardation and verbal disability. In The National Foundation - March of Dimes, Birth Defects Original Article Series, 10.

Lehrke, R.G. (1978). Sex linkage: A biological basis for greater male variability in intelligence. In R.T. Osborne, C.E. Noble, and N. Weyl (Eds.) Human variation: the biopsychology of age, race, and sex. New York: Academic Press.

Levinson, B.M. (1961). Sub-cultural values and I.Q. stability. Journal of Genetic Psychology, 98, 69-82.

Levinson, B.M. (1963). The W.A.I.S. quotient of sub-cultural deviation. Journal of Genetic Psychology, 100, 103-131.

Levy, J. (1971). Lateral specialization of the human brain: Behavioural manifestation and possible evolutionary basis. 32nd Annual Biology Colloquium on the biology of behaviour. Corrali, Oregon: Oregon State University.

Levy, J. (1974). Psychobiological implications of bilateral asymmetry. In S.J. Dimond and J.G. Beaumont (Eds.) Hemisphere function in the human brain. London: Elek. Science.

Levy, J. (1978). Lateral differences in the human brain in cognition and behavioural control. In P.A. Buser and A. Rougeuel-Buser (Eds.) Cerebral correlates of conscious experience. Inserm. Symposium No. 6. Amsterdam: North Holland.

        Lijphart, A. (1971). Comparative politics and comparative method. American Political Science Review, 65, 682-693.]

Lindsley, D.B. (1944). Electroencephalography. In J. McV. Hunt (Ed.) Personality and the behaviour disorders, Vol.2. New York: Ronald Press.

Lonner, W.J. (1980). Introduction to basic processes. In H.C. Triandis and W.J. Lonner (Eds.) Handbook of Cross-cultural psychology: Basic processes (Volume 3). Boston: Allyn and Bacon.

Lord, F.M. (1969). Estimating true score distributons in psychological testing. Psychometrika, 34, 259-299.

Lord, F.M. (1971). The self-scoring flexilevel test. Journal of Educational Measurement, 8, 147-151.

Lord, F.M. (1977). A broad-range tailored test of verbal ability. Applied Psychological Measurement, 1, 95-100.

Maccoby, E.E., and Jacklin, C.N. (1974). The psychology of sex differences. Stanford, California: Stanford University Press.

Maccoby, E.E., and Jacklin, C.N. (1975). The psychology of sex differences. Stanford, California: Stanford University Press.

Matarazzo, J.D. (1976). Wechsler's measurement and appraisal of adult intelligence (5th ed.). Baltimore: Williams and Wilkens.

McArdle, J.J., and Orn, J.L. (1981). Structural equation models of Gf-Gc Intelligence theory. Paper presented at American Psychological Association Annual Meeting. Los Angeles.

McDougal, W. (1932). Energies of men. London: Methuen.

McGee, M.G. (1979). Human spatial abilities: sources of sex differences. New York: Praeger.

McNemar, Q. (1964). Lost: our intelligence. Why? American Psychologist, 19, 871-882.

Metzler, J., and Shepard, R.N. (1974). Transformational studies of the internal representation of three dimensional objects. In R.L. Solso (Ed.) Theories in cognitive psychology: the Loyola symposium. New York: Wiley.

Michael, W.B. (Ed.) (1968). Teaching for creative endeavour. Bloomington: Indiana Univesity Press.

Miller, L. (1978). Has artificial intelligence contributed to an understanding of the human mind? A critique of arguments for and against. Cognitive Science, 2, 111-127.

Money, J., and Ehrhardt, A. (1972). Man and woman, boy and girl. Baltimore: John Hopkins University Press.

Mountcastle, V.B. (1961). Outer hemispheric relations and cerebral dominance. Baltimore, Maryland: Johns Hopkins Press.

Nash, S.C. (1979). Sex role as a mediator of intellectual functioning. In M.A. Wittig and A.C. Peterson (Eds.) Sex-related differences in cognitive functioning: Developmental issues. New York: Academic Press.

Nesselroade, J.R. (1970). Application of multivariate strategies to problems of structuring long-term change. In L.R. Goulet and P.B. Baltes (Eds.) Life-span developmental psychology: Research and theory. New York: Academic Press.

Nettelbeck, T. and Lally, M. (1976). Inspection time and measured intelligence. British Journal of Psychology, 67, 17-22.

Newell, A. (1973). Production systems and control processes. In W.G. Chase (Ed.) Visual information processing. New York: Academic Press.

Norman, D.A. (1979). Twelve issues for cognitive science. Technical Report AD 80992. Centre for Human Information Processing, University of California: San Diego, La Jolla.

O'Connor, J. (1943). Structural vizualization. Boston: Human Engineering Laboratory.

Ostow, M. (1950). Psychic function and the electroencephalogram. Archives of Neurological Psychiatry, 64, 385-400.

Pawlik, K. (1966). Concepts in human cognition and aptitudes. In R.B. Cattell (Ed.) Handbook of multivariate experimental psychology. Chicago: Rand McNally.

Pearson, K. (1902). On the influence of natural selection on the variability and correlation of organs. Phil. Trans. Roy. Soc., 200, 1-66.

Pemberton, C. (1952). The closure factors related to other cognitive processes. Psychometrika, 17, 267-288.

Penfield, W.,M and Perot, P. (1963). The brain's record of auditory and visual experience. Brain, 86, 595-695.

Penfield, W., and Rasmussen, T. (1950). The cerebral cortex of man: A clinical study of the localization of functions. New York: MacMillan.

Perry, N.W., McCoy, J.G., Cunningham, W.R., Falgout, J.C., and Street, W.J. (1976). Multivariate visual evoked response correlates of intelligence. Psychophysiology, 13, 323-329.

Petersen, A.C. (1976). A physical androgyny of cognitive functioning in adolescence. Developmental Psychology, 12, 524-533.

Petersen, A.C. (1979). Hormones and cognitive functioning in normal development. In M.A. Wittig and A.C. Petersen (Eds.) Sex-related differences in cognitive functioning: Developmental issues. New York: Academic Press.

Petersen, A.C., and Wittig, M.A. (1979). Sex-related differences in cognitive functioning: an overview. In M.A. Wittig and A.C. Petersen (Eds.) Sex-related issues in cognitive functioning: Developmental issues. New York: Academic Press.

Piaget, J. (1936). The origin of intelligence in children. New
    York: International Universities Press.

Piaget, J. (1946). The psychology of intelligence. London:
    Routledge and Kegan.

Piaget, J. (1964). The early growth of logic in the child.
    Translated by E.A. Lunzer and D. Papert. London: Routledge
    and Kegan Paul.

Plum, A. (1968). Visual evoked responses: their relationship to
    intelligence. Unpublished doctoral dissertation. University
    of Florida.

Poortinga, Y. (1971). Cross-cultural comparison of maximum
    performance tests: Some methodological aspects and some
    experiments with simple auditory and visual stimuli.
    Psychologia Africana Monograph Supplement, 6, 1-100.

Poortinga, Y. (1975a). Some implications of three different
    approaches to intercultural comparison. In J.W. Berry and
    W.J. Lonner (Eds.) Applied cross-cultural psychology.
    Amsterdam: Swetz and Zeitlinger.

Poortinga, Y. (1975b). Limitations on international comparison of
    psychological data. Netherlandse Tijdschrift voor de
    Psychologie, 30, 23-39.

Popper, K.R., and Eccles, J.C. (1977). The self and its brain.
    New York: Springer International.

Posner, M.I. (1978). Chronometric explorations of mind.
    Hillsdale, New Jersey: Erlbaum.

Powell, A., Katzko, M., and Royce, J.R. (1978). A
    multi-factor-system theory of the structure and dynamics of
    motor function. Journal of Motor Behaviour, 10, 191-220.

Preston, R.C. (1962).Reading achievement of German and American children. School and Society, 90, 350-354.

Price, R.L., and Smith, D.B.D. (1974). The P300 wave of the averaged evoked potential. A bibliography. Physiological Psychology, 2, 381-391.

Pucetti, R. (1977). Bilateral organization of consciousness. In S.J. Dimond and D.A. Blizard (Eds.) Evolution and lateralization of the brain. Annals of the New York Academy of Sciences, 229, 448-458.

Reinert, G. (1970). Comparative factor analytic studies of intelligence throughout the human life-span. In L.R. Goulet and P.B. Baltes (Eds.) Life-span developmental psychology: Research and theory. New York: Academic Press.

Rhodes, L.E., Dustman, R.E., and Beck, E.C. (1969). The visual evoked response: A comparison of bright and dull children. EEG Clinical Neuropsychology, 27, 364-372.

Richards, L.G., and Platnick, D.M. (1974). Word-recognition thresholds as a function of word length. American Journal of Psychology, 87, 65-70.

Roth, E. (1964). Die Geschwindigkeit der Verarbeitung vond Information und ihr Zusammenhang met Intelligenz. Zeitschrift fur Experimentelle und Angewandte Psychologie, 11, 616-622.

Royce, J.R. (1980). Factor analysis is alive and well. American Psychologist, 35, 390-393.

Royce, J. R. (1977). Genetics, environment and intelligence: A theoretical synthesis. In A. Oliverio (Ed.) Genetics, environment and intelligence. Elsevier: North Holland Biomedical Press.

Royce, J.R., and Buss, A.R. (1977). The role of general systems and information theory in multi-factor individuality theory. Canadian Psychological Review, 17, 1-21.

Royce, J.R. (1979). Toward a viable theory of individual
    differences. Journal of Personality and Social Psychology,
    37, 1927-1931.

Royce, J.R., and McDermott, J. (1977). A multi-dimensional system
    dynamics model of affect. Motivation and Emotion, 1,
    193-224.

Samejima, F. (1977). A use of the information function in tailored
    testing. Applied Psychological Measurement, 1, 223-248.

Scarr-Salapatek, S. (1975). Genetics and the development of
    intelligence. In F.D. Horowitz (Ed.) Review of Child
    Development Research, Vol.4. Chicago: University of Chicago
    Press.

Schaie, K.W. (1970). A re-interpretation of age-related changes in
    cognitive structure and functioning. In L.R. Goulet and P.B.
    Baltes (Eds.) Life-span developmental psychology: Research
    and theory. New York: Academic Press.

Schlopflocher, D.A., Royce, J.R., and Meehan, K. (1979). A
    multi-factor theory of values (Center Paper). Unpublished
    manuscript, University of Atlanta: Edmonton, Canada.

Schmidt, F.L., and Crano, W.D. (1974). A test of the theory of
    fluid and crystallized intelligence in middle- and
    low-socio-economic-status children: A cross-lagged panel
    analysis. Journal of Educational Psychology, 66, 255-261.

Schmidtke, H. (1961). Zur Frage der informations theoretischen
    Analyse von Wahreaktionsexperimenten. Psychologische
    Forschung, 26, 157-178.

Seymour, F.H.K., and Moir, W.L.M. (1980). Intelligence and
    semantic judgement time. British Journal of Psychology, 71,
    1, 53-61.

Shepard, R.N., and Feng, C.A. (1972). A chronometric study of mental paper folding. Cognitive Psychology, 3, 228-243.

Shepard, R.N., and Metzler, J. (1971). Mental rotation of three-dimensional objects. Science, 171, 701-703.

Sherman, J.A. (1978). Sex-related cognitive differences: An essay on theory and evidence. Springfield, Illinois: Thomas.

Shucard, C.W., and Horn, J.L. (1972). Evoked cortical potentials and measurement of human abilities. Journal of Comparative and Physiological Psychology, 78, 59-68.

Simon, H.A. (1979). Information processing models of cognition. Annual Review of Psychology, 30, 363-396.

Smith, I.M. (1964). Spatial ability. San Diego: Robert P. Knapp.

Spearman, C. (1904). "General Intelligence", objectively determined and measured. American Journal of Psychology, 15, 201-293.

Spearman, C. (1914). The theory of two factors. Psychological Review, 21, 101-115.

Spearman, C. (1923). The nature of "intelligence" and the principles of cognition. London: MacMillan.

Spearman, C. (1927). The abilities of Man: Their nature and measurement. London: MacMillan.

Spearman, C., and Hart, B. (1912). General ability: Its existence and nature. British Journal of Psychology, 5, 51-84.

Spencer, H., (1855). The principles of psychology. London: Williams and Norgate.

Sperry,   R.W. (1968a). Mental   unity   following   surgical
disconnection of the cerebral hemispheres. The Harvey Lectures,
Series 62. New York: Academic Press.

Sperry, R.W (1968). Hemisphere deconnection and unity in conscious
awareness. American Psychologist, (b), 23, 723-733.

Sperry,   R.W. (1969). A   modified   concept   of   consciousness.
Psychological Review, 76, 532-636.

Sperry, R.W. (1970). Cerebral dominance in perception. In F.A.
Young and D.B. Lindsey (Eds.) Early experience in visual
information processing in perceptual and reading disorder.
Washington, D.C.: National Academy of Science.

Sperry, R.W. (1973). Lateral specialization of cerebral function
in the surgically separated hemispheres. In F.J. McGuigan and
R.A. Schoonover (Eds.) The psychophysiology of thinking. New
York: Academic Press.

Sperry,   R.W.,   Gazzaniga,   M.S.,   and   Bogen,   J.E. (1969).
Interhemispheric relationships: The neocortical commissures:
syndromes of hemisphere disconnection. In P.J. Vinken and G.W.
Bruyn (Eds.) Handbook of clinical neurology, Vol. 4. Amsterdam:
North Holland, 273-290.

Stankov,   L.,   and Horn,   J.L. (1980). Human abilities revealed
through auditory tests. Journal of Educational Psychology, 72,
(1).

Stankov, L., Horn, J.L., and Roy, T. (1980). On the relationship
between Gf/Gc theory and Jensen's Level I/Level II theory.
Journal of Educational Psychology, 72, 796-809.

Stephenson,   W. (1931). Tetrad   differences   for   non-verbal
subtests. Tetrad differences for verbal subtests relative to
non-verbal subtests. Journal of Educational Psychology, 22,
167-185; 225-267; 334-350.

Stern, C. (1960). Human Genetics. San Francisco: Freeman.

Stern, W. (1914; 1912). The psychological method of testing intelligence. Translated by G.M. Whipple. Baltimore: Warwick and York (1912).

Sternberg, R.J. (1977). Intelligence, information processing, and analogical reasoning: The componential analysis of human abilities. Hillsdale, New Jersey: Erlbaum.

Sternberg, R.J. (1978). Intelligence research at the interface between differential and cognitive psychology. Intelligence, 2, 195-222.

Sternberg, R.J. (1979). The nature of mental abilities. American Psychologist, 34, 214-230.

Sternberg, R.J. (1980). Claims, counterclaims, and components: A counter critique of componential analysis. Technical Report No. 25 AD 8086797. New Haven: Department of Psychology, Yale University.

Sternberg, S. (1969). Memory scanning: Mental processes revealed by reaction-time experiments. American Scientist, 57, 421-457.

Street, W.J., Perry, N.W., and Cunningham, W.R. (1976). A factor analysis of visual evoked responses. Psychophysiology, 13, 352-356.

Stroop, J.R. (1938). Factors affecting speed in serial verbal reactions. Psychological Monographs, 50, (5), 38-48.

Szymanski, A. (1980). Computer simulation of human thought - its perspectives and constraints. Kybernetics, 9, 9-13.

Thomson, G.H. (1939). The factorial analysis of human ability. London: University of London Press.

Thorndike, E.L. (1909). The relation of accuracy in sensory discrimination to general intelligence. <u>American Journal of Psychology</u>, <u>20</u>, 364-369.

Thorndike, E.L. (1926). <u>The measurement of intelligence</u>. New York: Teachers' College, Columbia University.

Thurstone, L.L. (1924). <u>The nature of intelligence</u>. London: Routledge and Kegan Paul.

Thurstone, L.L. (1926). The mental age concept. <u>Psychological Review</u>, <u>33</u>, 268-278.

Thurstone, L.L. (1927). A unit of mental meausrement. <u>Psychological Review</u>, <u>34</u>, 415-423.

Thurstone, L.L. (1931). Multiple factor analysis. <u>Psychological Review</u>, <u>38</u>, 406-427.

Thurstone, L.L. (1933). <u>The theory of multiple factors</u>. Chicago: Author.

Thurstone, L.L. (1935). <u>The vectors of the mind</u>. Chicago: Univeroity of Chicago.

Thurstone, L.L. (1936). The factorial isolation of primary abilities. <u>Psychometrika</u>, <u>1</u>, 175-182.

Thurstone, L.L. (1938). Primary mental abilities. <u>Psychometric Monographs, No. 1</u>. Chicago: University of Chicago.

Thurstone, L.L. (1940). Experimental study of simple structure. <u>Psychometrika</u>, <u>5</u>, 153-168.

Thurstone, L.L. (1944). A factorial study of perception. <u>Psychometric Monographs</u>, <u>4</u>, vi-148.

Thurstone, L.L. (1947). Multiple factor analysis: A development and expansion of "Vectors of the Mind". Chicago: University of Chicago.

Thurstone, L.L. (1950). Some primary abilities in visual thinking. Proceedings of the Americal Philosophical Society, 94, 517-521.

Thurstone, L.L., and Thurstone, T.G. (1941). Factorial studies of intelligence. Psychometric Monographs No.2. Chicago: University of Chicago.

Triandis, H.C., Malpass, R.S., and Davison, A. (1972). Cross-cultural psychology. Biennial Review of Anthropology.

Tucker, L.R. (1951). A method for synthesis of factor-analytic studies. PRS Report No. 984, Department of the Army, Adjutant General's Office, Personnel Research Section: Washington, D.C.

Tyler, L.E. (1965). The psychology of human differences (3rd ed.). New York: Appleton.

Tyler, L.E. (1978). Individuality, human possibilities and personal choice in the psychological development of men and women. San Francisco: Jossey-Bass.

Undheim, J.O. (1976). Ability structure in 10-11 year-old Children and the theory of fluid and crystallized intelligence. Journal of Educational Psychology, 68, 411-423.

Undheim, J.O. (1978). Broad ability factors in 12 to 13 year-old children and the theory of fluid and crystallized intelligence and the differentiation hypothesis. Journal of Educational Psychology, 70, 433-443.

Vandenberg, S.G. (1977). Hereditary abilities in man. In A. Oliverio (Ed.) Genetics, environment, and intelligence. Elsevier: North Holland Biomedical.

Vandenberg, S.G., and Hakstian, A.R. (1978). Cultural influences on cognition: A reanalysis of Vernon's data. International Journal of Psychology, 13, 251-279.

Vandenberg, S.G., and Kuse, A.R. (1979). Spatial ability: A critical review of the sex-linked major gene hypothesis. In M.A. Wittig and A.C. Petersen (Eds.) Sex-related differences in cognitive functioning: Developmental issues. New York: Academic Press.

Van de Vijver, F.J.R., and Poortinga, Y.H. (1982). Cross-cultural generalization and universality. Journal of Cross-cultural Psychology, 13, 387-408.

Varela, J.A. (1969). Elaboration of Guilford's S-I model. Psychological Review, 76, 332-336.

Vernon, P.E. (1950). The structure of human abilities. New York: Wiley.

Vernon, P.E. (1961). The structure of human abilities (2nd ed.). London: Methuen.

Vernon, P.E. (1964). The psychology of intelligence and g. In J. Cohen (Ed.) Readings in psychology. London: Allen and Uwin.

Vernon, P.E. (1969a). Intelligence and cultural environment. London: Methuen.

Vernon, P.E. (1969b). Cross-cultural applications of factor analysis. Proceedings of the 26th International Congress of Applied Psychology. Amsterdam: Swets and Zeitlinger.

Vernon, P.E. (1979). Intelligence: Heredity and Environment. San Francisco: Freeman.

Verster, J.M. (1975). A dimension of conceptual speed. Psychologia Africana, 16, 45-58.

Verster, J.M. (1982a). The structure, organization, and correlates of cognitive speed and accuracy: a cross-cultural study using computerized tests. In S.H. Irvine and J.W. Berry (Eds.) Human assessment and cultural factors. New York: Plenum.

Verster, J.M. (1982b). A cross-cultural study of cognitive processes using computerized tests. Unpublished D. Litt. et Phil. thesis, Pretoria: University of South Africa.

Verster, J.M. Evaluation of a structural model of cognitive processes: an empirical investigation in different populations using computerized tests. Johannesburg: National Institute for Personnel Research, in preparation.

Verster, J.M., and Steyn, D.W. (1973). The development of a high level symbol Groups Test of determinative induction. Part Two: Psychometric Properties and interim standarization of test. CSIR Special Report PERS 196. Johannesburg: National Institute for Personnel Research.

Vogel, W., and Broverman, D.M. (1964). Relationship between EEG and test intelligence: A critical review. Psychological Bulletin, 63, 132-164.

Waber, D.P. (1977). Sex differences in mental abilities, hemispheric lateralization, and rate of physical growth at adolescence. Developmental Psychology, 13, 29-38.

Waber, D.P. (1979). Cognitive abilities and sex-related variations in the maturation of cerebral cortical functions. In M.A. Wittig and A.C. Petersen (Eds.) Sex-related differences in cognitive functioning: Developmental issues. New York: Academic Press.

Wallbrown, F.H., Blaha, J., and Wherry, R.J. (1974). The hierarchical factor structure of the Wechsler Adult Intelligence Scale. British Journal of Educational Psychology, 44, 47-56.

Wandel, D., and Royce, J.R. (1978). Toward a multi-factor theory of styles and their relationships to cognition and affect. Journal of Personality, 46, 474-505.

Watson, J.B. (1913). Psychology as the behaviourist views it. Psychological review, 20, 158-177.

Wechsler, D. (1967). Wechsler preschool and primary scale of intelligence. New York: Psychological Corporation.

Weinberg, H. (1969). Correlation of frequency spectra of averaged visual evoked potentials and verbal intelligence. Nature, 224, 813-815.

Weiss, D.J. (1973). The stratified adaptive computerized ability test. AD 768376/OGA. Minneapolis: University of Minnesota.

Weiss, D.J. (1974). Strategies of adaptive ability measurement. Research Report 74-5. Minneapolis: University of Minnesota. NTIS No AD A004270.

Weiss, D.J. (1978). Proceedings of the 1977 Computerized Adaptive Testing Conference. Minneapolis: University of Minnesota.

Weiss, D.J. (1979). Proceedings of the Computerized Adaptive Testing Conference (1979) held at Wayzata, Minnesota. Minneapolis: University of Minnesota.

Welsh, G.S., and Baucom, D.H. (1977). Sex, masculinity-femininity, and intelligence. Intelligence, 1, 218-233.

Werdelin, I. (1959). Geometrical ability and the space factors. Lund, Sweden: University of Lund.

Wernicke, C. (1874). Der aphasisiche Symptomenkomplex. Breslau: Cohn and Weigert.

Werts, C.E. (1967). Paternal influence on career choice. National Merit Scholarship Corporation Research Reports, 3, 19.

White, P.O. (1973) Individual differences in speed, accuracy, and persistence: A mathematical model for problem solving. In H.J. Eysenck (Ed.) The measurement of intelligence. London: Tinling.

Whiteley, S., and Schneider, L.M. (1981). Information structure for geometric analogies: A test theory approach. Applied Psychological Measurement, 5, 383-397.

Wickelgren, W.A. (1977). Speed-accuracy trade-off and information processing dynamics. Acta Psychologia, 41, 67-85.

Winograd, T. (1980). What does it mean to understand language? Cognitive Science, 4, 209-241.

Wissler, C. (1901). The correlation of mental and physical tests. Psychological Review Monograph Supplement, 3, (6).

Witkin, H.A., and Berry, J.W. (1975). Psychological differentiation in cross-cultural perspective. Journal of Cross-cultural Psychology, 6, 4-87.

Wittig, M.A. (1979). Genetic influences on sex-related differences in intellectual performance: Theoretical and methodological issues. In M.A. Wittig and A.C. Petersen (Eds.) Sex-related differences in cognitive functioning: Developmental issues. New York: Academic Press.

Wittig, M.A., and Petersen, A.C. (1979). (Eds.) Sex-related differences in cognitive functioning: Developmental issues. New York: Academic Press.

Wood, D.A. (1962). Louis Leon Thurstone: Creative thinker, dedicated teacher, eminent psychologist. Princeton: New Jersey.

Woodruff, D.S. (1978). Brain electrical activity and behaviour relationships over the life-span. In P.B. Baltes (Eds.) Life-span Development and Behaviour, Vol. 1. New York: Academic Press.

Wundt, W. (1862). On the methods of psychology. Translated from Beitrage zur Theorie der Sinneswahrnegnung. Leipzig: C.F. Winton.

Yen, W.M. (1975). Sex-linked major gene influences on selected types of spatial performance. Behaviour Genetics, 5, 281-298.

Yule, G.U. (1897). On the significance of Bravais Formulae for regression, etc., in skew correlation. Proceedings of the Royal Society, 60, 477-489.

Zangwill, O.L. (1974). Consciousness and the cerebral hemispheres. In S.L. Dimond and J.G. Beaumont (Eds.) Hemisphere function in the human brain. London: Elek. Science.

CHAPTER 3

SYNOPSIS OF A TRIARCHIC THEORY OF HUMAN INTELLIGENCE

ROBERT J STERNBERG

Yale University

INTRODUCTION

Theories of intelligence are not all theories of the same thing. Rather, they tend to be theories of different aspects of intelligence. To make matters worse, the theorists who propose these theories almost never make it clear just what aspects of intelligence their theories embrace. Consequently, it is difficult to know in what respects the claims of the various theories are complementary, and in what respects these claims are antagonistic. The end result is a continual state of "theory warfare" in which different kinds of theories are pitted against each other, whether or not they are truly competitive.

This chapter seeks to contribute toward the resolution of this state of "theory warfare" by proposing a unified framework in which to view theories of intelligence, and by proposing a unified theory that utilizes this framework, and in so doing, highlights what are argued to be remarkable convergences among theories. In proposing yet another theory, therefore, I seek not to add yet another warring party to the existing conflict, but to contribute toward the resolution of that conflict and the rechanneling of energies into more productive directions.

The chapter is divided into four major parts. First, I discuss some of the history of theories of intelligence, noting convergences as well as conflicts in the literature. These theories are placed into a metatheoretical framework that provides a useful means for seeing in what respects the theories diverge, on the one hand, and converge, on the other. Second, I present the proposed triarchic theory, which is an attempt to integrate and expand upon past theorizing. This theory is shown to draw upon all aspects of the proposed metatheoretical framework. Third, I discuss the relations between past theories and the triarchic theory, arguing that in many instances these past theories are in some sense special cases of this new theory. Finally, I summarize the main points of the chapter, and draw some conclusions.

THEORIES OF INTELLIGENCE: A CAPSULE HISTORY

The basic thesis of this section of the chapter is straightforward: Because theorists of intelligence have dealt with different aspects of the phenomenon of intelligence without acknowledging that they are dealing only with aspects of the whole phenomenon, and because they have failed to separate differences in methods from differences in substance, artificial competitions have been set up among theories that are not truly competitive at all. This unfortunate turn of events dates back to the beginnings of modern theorizing with Galton and Binet.

In his seminal work on intelligence, Galton (1883) proposed to view intelligence in terms of basic psychophysical abilities, such as various kinds of sensory acuities and discriminations. Many of his measures, such as strength of grip, probably had nothing to do with intelligence, but others, such as various measures of reaction time, probably did relate to intelligence in some way. More important than the particular measures Galton chose to use was his conception of intelligence in terms of very basic, "bottom-up" kinds of psychophysical, and especially mental, skills. Because Galton's measures were inadequate, initial tests of his theory yielded disappointing results (e.g., Wissler, 1901). But there may well have been more in his basic theoretical view than in his measures, because Galton's ideas about intelligence have been revived and rejuvenated in recent times (e.g., Carroll, 1976; Hunt, Frost, & Lunneborg, 1973; Jensen, 1982). For example, most contemporary theorists of intelligence are in consonance that mental speed has something to do with intelligence, although there is considerable disagreement as to just what this something is, and as to how it relates to measurements of mental speed.

Competing with the ideas of Galton were those of Binet and Simon (1916), which represented a more "top-down", judgment-based view of intelligence. According to Binet and Simon, intelligence is best understood in terms of one's ability to comprehend, evaluate, and act upon the world in which we live. Binet and Simon's tests of reasoning, problem solving, and judgment proved to be more highly correlated with a variety of external criteria, such as school performance and career attainments, than did Galton's.

The respective approaches to intelligence of Galton and Binet were never incompatible. Galton's measures were almost certainly inferior to Binet's, and the importance of his kinds of measures for predicting everyday competencies would almost certainly have been lower than that of Binet's kinds of measures, even if Galton had used more refined tests. But intelligence almost certainly involves both bottom-up, basic processes, and top-down, high-level processes in interaction. For example, reading comprehension depends upon and interacts with perception of the written word. Listening comprehension depends upon the rate at which one can take in information. If one is too slow in comprehending, the words will pass one by before one is able fully to encode them, and one may lose the stream of thought the speaker is attempting to convey. Reasoning under any kind of time pressure at all - whether internally or externally imposed - requires speed as well as high levels of judgment. The point to be made is that intelligence cannot possibly be understood fully except at <u>multiple levels of the processing of information</u>.

Any approach to understanding intelligence that is based solely upon individual differences in test performance may miss this important fact. Certain kinds of tests may swamp others in terms of accounting for observed variation among individuals in test scores. But a process analysis of test performance should reveal the importance of multiple levels of processing. In fact, not all process analyses will reveal all levels of processing, because task analyses are typically constructed to decompose stimulus variance only at a single level of processing. For example, typical decompositions of analogy test performance (such as that of Sternberg, 1977) deal with processes more at the level studied by Binet than at the level studied by Galton. The processes not isolated by a given task analysis are lumped into an undifferentiated "regression constant". Perhaps because so much of the richness of information processing is typically lumped into the constant, such residual components have often shown high correlations with external measures of intellectual abilities (see, e.g., Mulholland, Pellegrino, & Glaser, 1980; Sternberg, 1977).

It is important to note also that the contributions of various levels of processing - both in their effects upon person variance and in their effects upon stimulus variance - may differ over the life span. For adults who have largely automatized bottom-up information processing, top-down processes may contribute most of the variance both to person and to task differences. For children who have not fully automatized the basic processes, such processes may appear statistically to be more important. Thus the effects of age can lead to confusion in understanding of mental phenomena. For example, reading disabilities, which are almost inevitably multi-faceted in any case, have appeared to be more bottom-up in origin in some studies, and more top-down in origin in others. A review of the literature suggests, however, that the bottom-up processes contribute more at earlier ages, and the top-down processes contribute more at later ages (Spear & Sternberg, in press). Hence, limitations in ranges of ages studied can lead to systematic misinterpretations of the loci of reading difficulties.

The conflict between Galton and Binet was followed by conflicts among factor theorists of intelligence. In an attempt to place the study of intelligence on a more solid and scientific footing, theorists used factor analysis to help them identify what they believed would be fundamental latent sources of individual differences in intelligence. These "factors of the mind" were essentially structural in nature, although what the structures were remained something of a mystery. Spearman (1927) proposed a so-called "two-factor" theory, according to which the intellect comprises a general factor common to all intelligent performances and a set of specific factors, each of which is limited to influencing performance on a single test. Thurstone (1938) proposed a theory of primary mental abilities, according to which abilities such as verbal comprehension, verbal fluency, number, spatial visualization, and inductive reasoning are viewed as central to the intellect. Guilford (1967) proposed an elaborated version of Thurstone's theory, according to which the mind comprises 120 factors that differ in the processes, products, and contents involved.

Although the debates among factor theorists were always lively and at times acrimonious, these debates, too, were probably not well-founded.

Differences in obtained factor structures depended largely upon rotations of axes in the factor space obtained for a given set of tests. There is no evidence that the factor spaces differed much: Rather, what differed among theorists was the way in which each chose to assign reference axes for interpreting the factors. But these various rotations of the given space are all mathematically comparable with respect to the fit of the factor model to the data. Although some theorists even to this day argue that certain rotations of axes are psychologically superior to others (e.g., Carroll, 1980), I think it is becoming increasingly evident that assignment of axes is a matter of convenience, depending upon the use to which the factor-analytic data will be put. If one wishes a global, parsimonious assessment of intellectual performance on a group of tests, the general factor obtained from an unrotated factorial solution is particularly useful. If one wishes a more differentiated, but less parsimonious view of abilities, the simple structure of Thurstone may well be more useful. If one wishes to view abilities hierarchically, successively higher orders of factors may be extracted in order to highlight the interrelations among factors at successive levels of generality (as in the hierarchical theories of Vernon, 1971, or Cattell, 1971).

In brief, the debates among factor theorists were probably not well founded. These theorists were debating over different and ultimately isomorphic interpretations of the same basic data. The question was not who was right, but rather who was right for what purpose. As theories of intelligence, most of the factor theories, with the possible exception of Guilford's, are structually isomorphic. Again, we see in the history of theorizing about intelligence the emergence of ill-motivated conflicts.

The conflicts that have emerged in theorizing about intelligence are not limited to the psychometric approach. Information-processing psychologists have renewed the conflict between Galton and Binet in a modern-day guise. For example, in the 1970s, an obvious competition arose among advocates of the so-called cognitive-correlates approach, on the one hand, and of the so-called cognitive-components approach, on the other (Pellegrino & Glaser, 1979). Advocates of the former approach, such as Hunt (1978) and Jensen (1979), believed that intelligence should be studied in terms of basic, low-level processes of cognition, such as speed of lexical access or choice-reaction speed. Advocates of the latter approach, such as Sternberg (1977), Pellegrino and Glaser (1980), and Snow (1980), believed that intelligence should be studied in terms of higher processes, such as those contributing to performance on psychometric tests of intelligence. Examples of such processes would be inferring relations and applying relations. As time went on, it became progressively clear that these two approaches were no more in conflict than were the approaches of Galton and Binet (Caruso & Sternberg, 1984). Rather they dealt with different levels of processing in the same cognitive system, where all of the different levels are consequential for intelligent performance.

The disputes among theorists of intelligence have occurred not only within paradigms, but between paradigms as well. In the 1970s, attempts to integrate psychometric and information-processing theorizing tended to be at the expense of psychometric theorizing. Sternberg (1977), for example, expressed considerable scepticism regarding the role of factor analysis in theory and research on intelligence. It later became clear, however, that the two approaches are complementary: Factors and components of information processing are two different ways of parsing essentially the same mental phenomena. Both are useful for different purposes, depending upon whether one wishes to concentrate upon structure or upon process (Sternberg, 1980).

Yet another conflict was that between Piaget (e.g., Piaget, 1972), on the one hand, and psychometrics, on the other. Piaget developed his theory partly in response to his dissatisfaction with the procedures of Binet. He saw Binet as interested primarily in why children answer problems correctly, whereas he was interested as well in why children answer problems incorrectly. Piaget developed a theory that focused upon the roles of maturation and experience in intelligence. In particular, he discussed stages of development and mechanisms by which this development might take place. This kind of theorizing is actually complementary to psychometric as well as information-processing theorizing, in that either kind of theory needs to consider development as well as end states.

Perhaps the most significant conflict has been that between cognitivists, broadly defined, and contextualists. Cognitivists, who would include all of the theorists so far mentioned, have stressed the importance of understanding intelligence in terms of the mental mechanisms of mind. Contextualists, such as Berry (1972) and the members of the Laboratory of Comparative Human Cognition (1982) have emphasized the importance of contextual factors in understanding intelligence. Berry suggested a radical contextualist view according to which intelligence may well, and probably does, mean a somewhat different thing in each culture. Cole and his colleagues in the Laboratory of Comparative Human Cognition have suggested that there may be no fundamental universals in intelligence, although they have not taken a position as radical as Berry's. In some respects, the conflict between cognitivists and contextualists has not been as apparent as that between, say, various psychometricians or between these psychometricians as a group, on the one hand, and information-processing psychologists on the other. The reason for this is that the two camps have more or less ignored each other. The cognitivists, especially, have often seemed unaware of cross-cultural work being done, or what its implications are for their own theory and research. But again, this conflict is a misguided one. Irvine (1969, 1979) was among the first to note that a rapprochement between the two views is not only possible, but desirable. He has combined psychometric, factor-analytic methodology with sensitivity to cultural differences in cognitive task performance, with the result that it has been possible to go beyond merely saying that intelligence is all relative or that it is all universal. One of his main goals has been to specify just what is relative and what is universal. More recently, Goodnow (1976) and Sternberg (1984) have followed up on this approach by also attempting to specify what aspects of intelligence might be universal, and what aspects might not be. So that once again, an integrative rather than segregative view of perceiving the differences between positions has been the more useful one. To conclude, then, these debates, which are representative but not exhaustive of those that have occurred among theorists of intelligence, illustrate the importance of considering complementarity as well as conflict among theories and approaches. The appearance of difference has stemmed largely from two confusions.

The first confusion is over domain of discourse. Some theories, such as the psychometric and information-processing ones, have emphasized the role of internal mental mechanisms in intelligence. Other theories, such as the contextualist ones, have emphasized the role of external context. Still other theories, such as that of Piaget (1972), have emphasized the role of experience. The theories have differed primarily in terms of universe of discourse, rather than in terms of empirical or theoretical claims within any one domain. The theorists have been talking not against each other, but past each other. A full theory of intelligence would interrelate and integrate the role of intelligence as it occurs in each of these three domains.

A second source of conflict has been with respect of methodology, or the kind of information used to draw theoretical inferences. Some theorists, especially the psychometric ones, have emphasized "between subjects", or individual-difference variation. Other theorists, especially the information-processing ones, have emphasized "main effect", or stimulus variance. The two sources of variance are not in conflict: They are independent. A full theory of intelligence, again, would have to take into account the role of both sources of variance in intelligence, and interactions among "main effects". The triarchic theory presented below attempts to provide these various kinds of integration.

THE TRIARCHIC THEORY OF HUMAN INTELLIGENCE

The triarchic theory of human intelligence seeks to explain in an integrative way the relationships between (a) intelligence and the internal world of the individual, or the mental mechanisms that underlie intelligent behavior; (b) intelligence and the external world of the individual, or the use of these mental mechanisms in everyday life in order to attain an intelligent fit to the environment; and (c) intelligence and experience, or the mediating role of one's passage through life between the internal and external worlds of the individual. Consider some of the basic tenets of the theory.

Intelligence and the Internal World of the Individual

Psychometricians, Piagetians, and information-processing psychologists have all recognized the importance of understanding what mental states or processes underlie intelligent thought. In the triarchic theory, this understanding is sought through the identification and understanding of three basic kinds of information-processing components, which are referred to as metacomponents, performance components, and knowledge-acquisition components.

Metacomponents. Metacomponents are _higher order_, executive processes used to plan what one is going to do, to monitor it while one is doing it, and to evaluate it after it is done. These metacomponents include (a) deciding upon the nature of the problem confronting one, (b) selecting a set of lower order processes to solve the problem, (c) selecting a strategy into which to combine these components, (d) selecting a mental representation upon which the components and strategy can act, (e) allocating one's mental resources, and (f) monitoring one's problem solving. Consider some examples of each of these higher order processes.

Deciding upon the nature of a problem plays a prominent role in intelligence. For example, with young children as well as older adults, their difficulty in problem solving often lies not in actually solving a given problem, but in figuring out just what the problem is that needs to be solved (see, for example, Flavell, 1977; Sternberg & Rifkin, 1979). A major feature distinguishing retarded persons from normal ones is the retardates' need to be instructed explicitly and completely as to the nature of the particular task they are solving and how it should be performed (Butterfield, Wambold, & Belmont, 1973; Campione & Brown, 1979). The importance of figuring out the nature of the problem is not limited to children, older adults, and retarded persons. Resnick and Glaser (1976) have argued that intelligence is the ability to learn from incomplete instruction.

Selection of a strategy for combining lower order components is also a critical aspect of intelligence. In early information-processing research on intelligence, including my own (e.g., Sternberg, 1977), the primary emphasis was simply on figuring out what subjects do when confronted with a problem. What components do subjects use, and into what strategies do they combine these components? Soon, however, information-processing researchers began to ask the question of why subjects use the strategies they choose. For example, Cooper (1982) has reported that in solving spatial problems, and especially mental-rotation problems, some subjects seem to use a holistic strategy of comparison whereas others use an analytic strategy. She has sought to figure out what leads subjects to the choice of one strategy or another. Siegler (in press) has actually proposed a model of strategy selection in arithmetic computation problems that links strategy choice to both the rules and mental associations one has stored in long-term memory. MacLeod, Hunt, and Mathews (1978) found that high-spatial subjects tend to use a spatial strategy in solving sentence-picture comparison problems, whereas high-verbal subjects are more likely to use a linguistic strategy. In my own work, I have found that subjects tend to prefer certain strategies for analogical reasoning over others because they place fewer demands upon working memory (Sternberg & Ketron, 1982). Similarly, subjects choose different strategies in linear-syllogistic reasoning (spatial, linguistic, mixed spatial-linguistic), but in this task, they do not always capitalize upon their ability patterns so as to choose the strategy most suitable to their respective levels of spatial and verbal abilities (Sternberg & Weil, 1980). In sum, the selection of a strategy seems to be at least as important for understanding intelligent task performance as is the efficacy with which the chosen strategy is implemented.

Intimately tied up with the selection of a strategy is the selection of a mental representation for information. In the early literature on mental representations, the emphasis seemed to be upon understanding how information is represented. For example, can individuals use imagery as a form of mental representation (Kosslyn, 1980)? In more recent research, investigators have realized that people are quite flexible in their representations of information. The most appropriate question to ask seems to be not how is information represented, but which representations are used what circumstances? For example, Sternberg (1977) found that analogy problems using animal names can draw upon either spatial or clustering representations of the animal names. In the studies of strategy choice mentioned above, it was found that subjects can use either linguistic or spatial representations in solving sentence-picture comparisons (MacLeod et al., 1978) or linear syllogisms (Sternberg & Weil, 1980). Sternberg and Rifkin (1979) found that the mental representation of certain kinds of analogies can be either more or less holistic, depending upon the age of the subjects. In short, flexibility in the use of mental representations seems to be a hallmark of intelligence. People have available a variety of representation: The more intelligent ones know when to use which representations.

As important as any other metacomponent is one's ability to allocate one's mental resources. Different investigators have studied resource allocation in different ways. Hunt and Lansman (1982), for example, have concentrated upon the use of secondary tasks in assessing information processing, and have proposed a model of attention allocation in the solution of problems that involves both a primary and a secondary task. In my work, I have found that better problem solvers tend to spend relatively more time in global strategy planning (Sternberg, 1981). Similarly, in solving analogies, better analogical reasoners seem to spend relatively more time encoding the terms of the problem than do poorer reasoners, but to spend relatively less time in operating upon these encodings (Sternberg, 1977; Sternberg & Rifkin, 1979). In reading as well, the better readers are better able than the poorer readers to allocate their time across reading passages as a function of the difficulty of the passages to be read, and of the purpose for which the passages are being read (Wagner & Sternberg, 1983).

Finally, monitoring one's solution processes is a key aspect of intelligence 9see also Brown, 1978). Consider, for example, the Missionaries and Cannibals problem, in which the subjects must "transport" a set of missionaries and cannibals across a river in a small boat without allowing the cannibals an opportunity to eat the missionaries, an event that can transpire only if the cannibals are allowed to outnumber the missionaries on either side of the river bank. The main kinds of errors that can be made are either to return to an earlier state in the problem space for solution, or to make an impermissible move (Simon & Reed, 1976; see also Sternberg, 1982b). Neither of these errors would result if a given subject closely monitored his or her solution processes. For young children learning to count, a major source or errors in counting objects is to count a given object twice, an error that, again, can result from a failure in solution monitoring (Gelman & Gallistel, 1978). The effects of solution monitoring are not limited, or course, to any one kind of problem. One's ability to use the strategy of means-ends analysis (Newell & Simon, 1972) - that is, reduction of differences between where one is in solving a problem and where one wishes to get in solving that problem - depends upon one's ability to monitor just where one is in problem solution.

Performance components. Performance components are lower order processes that execute the instructions of the metacomponents. These lower order components solve the problems according to the plans laid out by the metacomponents. Whereas the number of metacomponents used in the performance of various tasks is relatively limited, the number of performance components is probably quite large. Fortunately, many of these performance components are relatively specific to narrow ranges of tasks, and hence not particularly interesting psychologically (Sternberg, 1979, 1985). The performance components of greatest interest are those that are general across a variety of cognitive tasks. When one limits oneself to the study of these performance components, the number of such components is quite manageable, because the same components appear again and again (Sternberg, 1983).

One of the most interesting classes of performance components is that found in inductive reasoning of the kind measured by tests such as matrices, analogies, series completions, and classifications. These components are important because of the importance of the tasks into which they enter: Induction problems of these kinds show the highest loadings on the so-called g, or general intelligence factor (Jensen, 1980; Snow & Lohman, 1984; Sternberg & Gardner, 1982). Thus, identifying these performance components can give us some insight into the nature of the general factor. In saying this, I am not arguing for any one factorial model of intelligence (i.e., one with a general factor) over others: To the contrary, I believe that most factor models are mutually compatible, differing only in the form of rotation that has been applied to a given factor space (Sternberg, 1977). The rotation one uses is a matter of theoretical or practical convenience, not of truth or falsity.

The performance components of inductive reasoning can be illustrated with reference to an analogy problem, such as LAWYER : CLIENT :: DOCTOR : (A) PATIENT, (B) MEDICINE. In encoding, the subject retrieves from semantic memory semantic attributes that are potentially relevant for analogy solution. In inference, the subject discovers the relation between the first two terms of the analogy, here, LAWYER and CLIENT. In mapping, the subject discovers the higher order relation that links the first half of the analogy, headed by LAWYER, to the second half of the analogy, headed by DOCTOR. In application, the subject carries over the relation inferred in the first half of the analogy to the second half of the analogy, generating a possible completion for the analogy. In comparison, the subject compares each of the answer options to the mentally generated completion, deciding which, if any, is correct. In justification, used optionally if none of the answer options matches the mentally-generated solution, the subject decides which, if any, of the options is close enough to constitute an acceptable solution to the examiner, whether by means of pressing a button, making a mark on a piece of paper, or whatever.

Two fundamental issues have arisen regarding the nature of performance components as a fundamental construct in human intelligence. The first, mentioned briefly above, is whether their number simply keeps expanding indefinitely. Neisser (1983), for example, has suggested that it does. As a result, he views the construct as of little use. But this expansion results only if one considers seriously those components that are specific to small classses of problems or to single problems. If one limits one's attention to the more important, general components of performance, the problem simply does not arise, as shown, for example, in Sternberg and Gardner's (1983) analysis of inductive reasoning, or Pellegrino and Kail's (1982) analysis of spatial ability. The second issue is one of the level at which performance components should be studied. In so-called "cognitive-correlates" research (Pellegrino & Glaser, 1979), theorists emphasize components at relatively low levels of information processing (Hunt, 1978, 1980; Jensen, 1982). In so-called "cognitive components" research (Pellegrino & Glaser, 1979), theorists emphasize components at relatively high levels of information processing (e.g., Mulholland, Pellegrino, & Glaser, 1980; Snow, 1980; Sternberg, 1977). Because of the interactive nature of human information processing, it would appear that there is no right or wrong level of analysis. Rather, all levels of information processing contribute to both task and subject variance in intelligent performance. The most expeditious level of analysis depends upon the task and subject population: Lower level performance components might be more important, for example, in studying more basic information-processing tasks, such as choice reaction time, or in studying higher level tasks, but in children who have not yet automatized the lower level processes that contribute to performance on these tasks.

Knowledge-acquisition   components. Knowledge-acquisition components are used to learn how to do what the metacomponents and performance components eventually do. Three knowledge-acquisition components appear to be central in intellectual functioning: (a) selective encoding, (b) selective combination, and (c) selective comparison.

Selective encoding involves sifting out relevant from irrelevant information. When new information is presented in natural contexts, relevant information for one's given purposes is embedded in the midst of large amounts of purpose-irrelevant information. A critical task for the learner is that of sifting the "wheat from the chaff": recognizing just what information among all the pieces of information is relevant for one's purposes (see Schank, 1980).

Selective combination involves combining selectively encoded information in such a way as to form an integrated, plausible whole. Simply sifting out relevant from irrelevant information is not enough to generate a new knowledge structure. One must know how to combine the pieces of information into an internally connected whole (see Mayer & Greeno, 1972).

My emphasis upon components of knowledge acquisition differs somewhat from the focus of some contemporary theorists in cognitive psychology, who emphasise what is already known, and the structure of this knowledge (e.g., Chase & Simon, 1973; Chi, 1978; Keil, 1984). I should point out, again, therefore, that these various emphases are complementary. If one is interested in understanding, for example, differences in performance between experts and novices, clearly one would wish to look at the amount and structure of their respective knowledge bases. But if one wishes to understand how these differences came to be, merely looking at developed knowledge would not be enough. Rather, one would have to look as well at differences in the ways in which the knowledge bases were acquired. It is here that understanding of knowledge-acquisition components will prove to be most relevant.

We have studied knowledge-acquisition components in the domain of vocabulary acquisition (e.g., Sternberg, in press; Sternberg & Powell, 1983). Difficulty in learning new words can be traced, at least in part, to the application of components of knowledge acquisition to context cues stored in long-term memory. Individuals with higher vocabularies tend to be those who are better able to apply the knowledge-acquisition components to vocabulary-learning situations. Given the importance of vocabulary for overall intelligence, almost without respect to the theory or test one uses, utilization of knowledge-acquisition components in vocabulary-learning situations would appear to be critically important for the development of intelligence. Effective use of knowledge-acquisition components is trainable. I have found, for example, that just 45 minutes of training in the use of these components in vocabulary learning can significantly and fairly substantially improve the ability of adults to learn vocabulary from natural-language contexts (Sternberg, in press).

To summarize, then, the components of intelligence are an important part of the intelligence of the individual. The various kinds of components work together. Metacomponents activate performance and knowledge-acquisition components. These latter kinds of components in turn provide feedback to the metacomponents. Although one can isolate various kinds of information-processing components from task performance using experimental means, in practice, the components function together in a highly interactive, and not easily isolable, way. Thus, diagnoses as well as instructional interventions need to consider all three types of components in interaction, rather than any one kind of component in isolation. But understanding the nature of the components of intelligence is not, in itself, sufficient to understand the nature of intelligence, because there is more to intelligence than a set of information-processing components. One could scarcely understand all of what it is that makes one person more intelligent than another by understanding the components of processing on, say, an intelligence test. The other aspects of the triarchic theory address some of the other aspects of intelligence that contribute to individual differences in observed performance, outside of testing situations as well as within them.

The Experiential Subtheory

Components of information processing are always applied to tasks with which one has some level of prior experience (including the null level) and in situations with which one has some level of prior experience (including the null level). Hence, these internal mechanisms are closely tied to one's experience. According to the experiential subtheory, the components are not equally good measures of intelligence at all levels of experience. Assessing intelligence requires one to consider not only components, but the level of experience at which they are applied.

During recent years, there has been a tendency in cognitive science to study script-based behavior (e.g., Schank & Abelson, 1977), whether under the name of "script" or under some other name, such as "schema" or "frame". There is no longer any question that much of our behavior is scripted, in some sense. However, from the standpoint of the present subtheory, such behavior is nonoptimal for understanding intelligence. Typically, one's actions when one goes to a restaurant or a doctor's office or a movie theatre do not provide good measures of intelligence, even though they do provide good measures of scripted behavior. What, then, is the relation between intelligence and experience?

According to the experiential subtheory, intelligence is best measured at those regions of the experiential continuum that involve tasks or situations that are either relatively novel, on the one hand, or in the process of becoming automatized, on the other. As Raaheim (1974) pointed out, totally novel tasks and situations provide poor measures of intelligence: One would not want to administer, say, trigonometry problems to a first-grader of roughly six years of age. But one might wish to administer problems that are just at the limits of the child's understanding, in order to test how far this understanding extends. In order to measure automatization skill, one might wish to present a series of problems - mathematical or otherwise - and to see how long it takes for solution of them to become automatic, and to see how automatized performance becomes. Thus, both slope and asymptote (if any) of automatization are of interest.

Ability to deal with novelty. Several sources of evidence converge upon the notion that the ability to deal with relative novelty is a good way of measuring intelligence. Consider three such sources of evidence. First, we have conducted several studies on the nature of insight, both in children and in adults (Davidson & Sternberg, 1984; Sternberg & Davidson, 1982). In the

studies with children (Davidson & Sternberg, 1984), we separated
three kinds of insights: insights of selective encoding, insights
of selective combination, and insights of selective comparison.
Use of these knowledge-acquisition components is referred to as
insightful when they are applied in the absence of existing
scripts, plans, frames, or whatever. In other words, one must
decide what information is relevant, decide how to put the
information together, or decide how new information relates to old
in the absence of any obvious cues on the basis of which to make
these judgements. A problem is insightfully solved at the
individual level when a given individual lacks such cues. A
problem is insightfully solved at the societal level when no one
else has these cues either. In these studies, our hypothesis was
that children who are intellectually gifted are gifted in part by
virtue of their insight abilities, which represent an important
part of the ability to deal with novelty.

Children were administered quantitative insight problems, of the
kinds found in puzzle books, that measured primarily either
selective encoding skill, selective combination skill, or
selective comparison skill. We manipulated the need for such
insights experimentally. Problems were either administered uncued
(standard format) or precued. The form of precueing depended upon
the kind of insight being assessed. For selective encoding, we
precued what information was relevant for solving a given problem
by highlighting all information that was relevant for solving each
problem. Thus, we eliminated the need for selective encoding by
pointing out to the children just what information was relevant
for each given problem. In the selective-combination condition,
precueing consisted of information telling the children how to
combine the given information selectively. For example, a table
might be drawn showing how the various terms of the problem
interrelated. In the selective-comparison condition, the need for
selective comparison was manipulated by varying the examples in
the introduction to the problems. Precued conditions ranged from
one in which examples were given but their relevance to the later
problems not pointed out, to examples that were explicitly stated
to be relevant for solution of the later problems, to examples
that were indicated as relevant to designated problems in the set
of problems that needed to be solved. The basic design,
therefore, was to test children either identified as gifted or not
so identified, and to administer problems that either required
insights of one of the three kinds or that did not require such
insights because the insights were provided to the children. The
critical finding was that providing insights to the children
significantly benefited the nongifted, but not the gifted
children. (None of the children performed anywhere near ceiling,
so that the interaction was not due to ceiling effects.) In other
words, the gifted children spontaneously had the insights and

hence did not benefit from being given these insights. The nongifted children did not have the insights spontaneously, and hence did benefit. Thus, the gifted children were better able spontaneously to deal with novelty.

In a very different paradigm, adult subjects were given what I call conceptual projection problems (Sternberg, 1982a). In these problems, one has to make predictions about future states of objects based upon incomplete and sometimes partially faulty information about the current states of the objects. These problems generally employed a science-fiction type of scenario. For example, one might be introduced to four kinds of people on the planet, Kyron: One kind of person is <u>born young and dies young</u>, a second kind of person is <u>born young and dies old</u>, a third kind is <u>born old and dies old</u>, and fourth kind is <u>born old and dies young</u>. Given incomplete information about the person in the present, one has to figure out what kind of person the individual is (names such as "kwef", "pros", "balt", and "plin" were used) and determine what his or her appearance would be twenty years later. Performance on the conceptual-projection task was experimentally decomposed, and the mathematical model of task performance accounted for most of the stimulus variance (generally 90+%) in task performance. Each of the these component scores was then correlated with performance on a variety of psychometric tests, including tests of inductive reasoning ability, which are primary measures of general intelligence. The critical finding was that the correlation of overall response time (generally at the level of about -.6, negative because response times were correlated with numbers correct) with psychometric test scores was due to correlations stemming from those performance components tapping the ability to deal with novelty, for example, changing conceptual systems from a familiar one (born young and dies old) to an unfamiliar one (e.g., born old and dies young). These correlations held up without regard to the particular surface structure of the problem, of which the scenario about birth and death states was only one of four. Thus, it was the ability to deal with novelty, rather than other abilities involved in solving the problems, that proved to be critical to general intelligence.

A third source of evidence for the proposed hypothesis derives from the large literature on fluid intelligence, which is in part a kind of intelligence that involves dealing with novelty (see Cattell, 1971). Snow and Lohman (1984; see also Snow, Kyllonen, & Marshalek, 1984) have multidimensionally scaled a variety of such tests and found the dimensional loadings to follow a radex structure. In particular, tests with higher loadings on g, or general intelligence, fall closer to the centre of the spatial diagram. The critical thing to note is that those tests that best measure the ability to deal with novelty fall closer to the

centre, and tests tend to be greater removed from the centre as
their assessment of the ability to deal with novelty becomes more
remote.   In sum, evidence from the laboratories of others as well
as myself supports the idea with the various components of
intelligence that are involved in dealing with novelty, as
measured in particular tasks and situations, provide particularly
apt measures of intellectual ability.

Ability to automatize information processing Although we are only
now testing the second aspect of the experiential subtheory, that
of the ability to automatize information processing, there are
several converging lines of evidence in the literature to support
the claim that this ability is a key aspect of intelligence.   For
example, Sternberg (1977) found that the correlation between
People-Piece (schematic-picture) analogy performance and measures
of general intelligence increased with practice, as performance on
these items became increasingly automatized.   Skilled reading is
heavily dependent upon automatization of bottom-up functions, and
the ability to read well is an essential part of crystallized
ability, whether as viewed from the standpoint of theories such as
Cattell's (1971) or Vernon's (1971), or from the standpoint of
tests of crystallized ability, such as the verbal portion of the
Scholastic Aptitude Test. Poor comprehenders can be those who have
not automatized the elementary, bottom-up processes of reading,
and hence who do not have sufficient attentional resources to
allocate to top-down comprehension processes.   Theorists such as
Jensen (1982) and Hunt (1978) have attributed the correlation
between tasks such as choice reaction time and letter matching to
the relation between speed of information processing and
intelligence.   Indeed, there is almost certainly some relation,
although I believe it is much more complex than these theorists
seem to allow for.   But a plausible alternative hypothesis is that
at least some of that correlation is due to the effects of
automatization of processing: Because of the simplicity of these
tasks, they probably become at least partially automatized fairly
rapidly, and hence can measure both rate and asymptote of
automatization of performance. In sum, then, although the
evidence is far from complete, there is at least some support for
the notion that rate and level of automatization are related to
intellectual skill.

The ability to deal with novelty and the ability to automatize
information processing are interrelated, as shown in the example
of reading above.   If one is well able to automatize, one has more
resources left over for dealing with novelty.   Similarly, if one
is well able to deal with novelty, one has more resources left
over for automatization.   Thus, performance at the various levels
of the experiential continuum are related to one another.

These abilities should not be viewed in a vacuum with respect to the componential subtheory. The components of intelligence are applied to tasks and situations at various levels of experience: The ability to deal with novelty can be understood in part in terms of the metacomponents, performance components, and knowledge-acquisition components involved in it. Automatization, when it occurs, is of these components. Hence, the two subtheories considered so far are closely intertwined. We need now to consider the application of these subtheories to everyday tasks, in addition to laboratory ones.

The Contextual Subtheory

According to the contextual subtheory, intelligent thought is directed toward one or more of three behavioral goals: adaptation to an environment, shaping of an environment, or selection of an environment. These three goals may be viewed as the functions toward which intelligence is directed: Intelligence is not aimless or random mental activity that happens to involve certain components of information processing at certain levels of experience. Rather, it is purposefully directed toward the pursuit of these three global goals, all of which have more specific and concrete instantiations in people's lives.

Adaptation. Most intelligent thought is directed toward the attempt to adapt to one's environment. The requirements for adaptation can differ radically from one environment to another - whether environments are defined in terms of families, jobs, subcultures, cultures, or whatever. Hence, although the components of intelligence required in these various contexts may be the same or quite similar, and although all of them may involve, at one time or another, dealing with novelty and automatization of information processing, the concrete instantiations that these processes and levels of experience take may differ substantially across contexts. This fact has an important implication for our understanding of the nature of intelligence. According to the triarchic theory, in general, and the contextual subtheory, in particular, the processes and experiential facets and functions of intelligence remain essentially the same across contexts; but the particular instantiations of these processes, facets, and functions can differ, and differ radically. Thus, the content of intelligent thought and its manifestations in behavior will bear no necessary resemblance across contexts. As a result, although the mental elements that an intelligence test should measure do not differ across contexts, the vehicle for measurement may have to differ. A test that measures a set of processes, experiential facets, or intelligent functions in one context may not provide equally adequate measurement in another context. To the contrary, what is intelligent in one culture may be viewed as unintelligent in another.

A nice example of this fact can be found in the work of Cole, Gay, Glick, and Sharp (1971). These investigators asked adult Kpelle tribesmen to sort twenty familiar objects into groups of things that belong together. Their subjects separated the objects into functional groupings (e.g., a knife with an orange), as children in Western societies would do. This pattern of sorting surprised the investigators, who had expected to see taxonomic groupings (e.g., tools sorted together and foods sorted together) of the kind that would be found in the sortings of Western adults. Had the investigators used the sorting task as a measure of intelligence in the traditional way, they might well have labeled the Kpelle tribesmen as intellectually inferior to Western adults. However, through persistent exploration of why the Kpelle were sorting in this way, they found that the Kpelle considered functional sorting to be the intelligent form of sorting. When the tribesmen were asked to sort the way a stupid person would so so, they had no trouble sorting taxonomically. In short, they differed on this task not in their intellectual competence vis a vis Western adults, but in their conception of what was functionally adaptive. Indeed, it takes little thought to see the practicality of sorting functionally: People do, after all, use utensils in conjunction with foods of a given category (e.g., fruits) on a frequent basis.

In the case of the Kpelle tribesmen, different contextual milieux resulted in a different conception of what constitutes intelligence: The particular difference illustrated above is in what is considered to be adaptive, rather than in the ability to act adaptively. But different contextual milieux may result in the development of different mental abilities. For example, Puluwat navigators must develop their large-scale spatial abilities for dealing with cognitive maps to a degree that far exceeds the adaptive requirements of contemporary Western societies (Gladwin, 1970). Similarly, Kearins (1981)' found that Aboriginal children probably develop their visuo-spatial memories to a greater degree than do Anglo-Australian children, who are more likely to apply verbal strategies to spatial memory tasks than are the Aborigines, who employ spatial strategies. In contrast, participants in Western societies probably develop their abilities for thinking abstractly to a greater degree than do societies in which concepts are rarely dealt with outside their concrete manifestations in the objects of the everyday environment.

One of the most interesting differences among cultures and subcultures in the development of patterns of adaptation is in the matter of time allocation, a metacomponential function. In Western cultures, in general, budgeting of time and careful allocation of one's time to various activities is a prized commodity. Our lives are largely governed by careful scheduling at home, in school, at work, and so on. There are fixed hours for certain activities, and fixed lengths of time within which these activities are expected to be completed. Indeed, the intelligence tests we use show our prizing of time allocation to the fullest. Almost all of them are timed in such a way as to make completion of the tests a nontrivial challenge. A slow or very cautious worker is at a distinct disadvantage.

Not all cultures and subcultures view time in the same way that we do. For example, among the Kipsigi, schedules are much more flexible, and hence these individuals have difficulty understanding and dealing with Western notions of the time pressure under which people are expected to live (Super & Harkness, 1980). In Hispanic cultures, such as Venezuela, my own personal experience indicates that the press of time is taken with much less seriousness than it is in typical North American cultural settings. Even within the continental United States, though, there can be major differences in the importance of time allocation. Heath (1983) describes young children brought up in the rural community of "Trackton", in which there is very little time pressure and in which things essentially get done when they get done. These children can have great difficulty adjusting to the demands of the school, in which severe time pressures may be placed upon the children for the first time in their lives.

The point of these examples has been to illustrate how differences in environmental press and people's conceptions of what constitutes an intelligent response to it can influence just what counts as adaptive behavior. To understand intelligence, one must understand it not only in relation to its internal manifestations in terms of mental processes, and its experiential manifestations in terms of facets of the experiential continuum, but also in terms of how thought is intelligently translated into action in a variety of different contextual settings. The differences in what is considered adaptive and intelligent can extend even to different occupations within a given culture milieu. For example, Sternberg (1984a) has found that individuals in different fields of endeavor (art, business, philosophy, physics) view intelligence in slightly different ways that reflect the demands of their respective fields.

Shaping. Shaping of the environment is often used when adaptation fails, as a backup strategy. If one is unable to change oneself so as to fit the environment, one may attempt to change the environment so as to fit oneself. For example, repeated attempts to adjust to the demands of one's romantic partner may eventually lead to attempts to get the partner to adjust to oneself. But shaping is not always used in lieu of adaptation. In some cases, shaping may be used before adaptation is ever tried, as in the case of the individual who attempts to shape a romantic partner with little or no effort to shape him or herself so as better to suit the partner's wants or needs.

In the laboratory, examples of shaping behavior can be seen in strategy selection situations where one essentially molds the task to fit one's preferred style of dealing with tasks. For example, in comparing sentence statements to pictures that either do or do not accurately represent these statements, individuals may select either a verbal or a spatial strategy, depending upon their pattern of verbal and spatial abilities (MacLeod, Hunt, & Mathews, 1978). The task is "made over" in conformity to what one does best. Similarly, I find that in multivariate statistics, my graduate students tend to view problems either algebraically or geometrically, depending upon their pattern of abilities and preferences. My own presentation of the subject is, again, "made over" to conform to their needs and desires.

Because people operate in groups as well as in isolation, attempts by group members to shape in different ways can result in products that either profit or lose from the group effort. I have recently attended a rather unstructured meeting in which a group of individuals attempted to accomplish a variety of agendas. But because of limited resources, not all of the agendas could be realized. The result was that practically none of them were, because of attempts by individuals to realize their own agendas at the expense of other people's. A more salutary result has eventuated from my collaborations with one of my graduate students. In research, I tend to be a "selective comparer", constantly seeking to relate new theories and facts to old ones. I am probably less careful, however, about selective combination, that is, about fitting together the various facts at my disposal. As a result, I may neglect to deal with those facts that do not quite fit into the framework I establish for them. My graduate student tends to be more a selective combiner than comparer. She is less concerned with relating new facts to old facts or theories, but more concerned with making sure that the various new facts can be fitted together into a coherent account that deals with them all. In our collaborations in research, we each attempt to shape the outcomes of the research in accordance with our preferred style of working. In this case, the two styles complement each other, as one individual makes sure that the research is not conducted in isolation from past research or ideas, whereas the other individual makes sure that inconvenient experimental results are not shunted to the side. Indeed, it is such results that may result in the true breakthroughs in research. Thus, in this case, the attempts to shape the environment in two different ways result in a healthy tension that improves rather than harms the final outcome.

In some respects, shaping may be seen as the quintessence of intelligent thought and behavior. One essentially makes over the environment rather than allowing the environment to make over oneself. Perhaps it is this skill that has enabled humankind to reach its current level of scientific, technological, and cultural advancement (for better or for worse). In science, the greatest scientists are those who set the paradigms (shaping), rather than those who merely follow them (adaptation). Similarly, in art and in literature, the individuals who achieve greatest distinction are often those who create new modes and styles of expression, rather than merely following existing ones. It is not their use of shaping alone that distinguishes them intellectually, but rather a combination of their willingness to do it with their skill in doing it.

Selection. Selection involves renunciation of one environment in favour of another. In terms of the rough hierarchy established so far, selection is sometimes used when both adaptation and shaping fail. After attempting both to adapt to and to shape a marriage, one may decide to deal with one's failure in these activities by "deselecting" the marriage, and choosing the environment of the newly single. Failure to adjust to the demands of a work environment, or to change the demands placed upon one so as to make them a reasonable fit to one's interests, values, expectations, or abilities, may result in the decision to seek another job altogether. But selection is not always used as a last resort. Sometimes one attempts to shape an environment only after attempts to leave it have failed. Other times, one may decide almost instantly that an environment is simply wrong for oneself, and feel that one need not or should not even try to fit into it or to change it. For example, we get, every now and then, a new graduate student who realizes almost immediately that he or she came to graduate school for the wrong reason, or who finds that graduate school is nothing at all like the continuation of undergraduate school he or she expected. In such cases, the intelligent thing to do may be to leave the environment as soon as possible, in order to pursue activities more in line with one's goals in life.

Environmental selection is not usually directly studied in the laboratory, although it may have relevance for certain experimental settings. Perhaps no research example of its relevance has been more salient than the experimental paradigm created by Milgram (1975), who, in a long series of studies, asked subjects to "shock" other subjects (who were actually confederates and who were not shocked). The finding of critical interest was how few subjects either shaped the environment by refusing to shock their victims, or employed the device of selection by simply refusing to continue with the experiment and walking out of it. Milgram has drawn an analogy to the situation in Nazi Germany, where obedience to authority created an environment whose horrors continue to amaze us to this day, and always will. This example is a good one in showing how close matters of intelligence can come to matters of personality. In fact, many Jews refused to leave Nazi-occupied territories for fear of losing their property, their peers, and so on. Their refusal may have been due to personality factors, but for many of them, their decision to stay was in some respects the supreme act of unintelligence, as it resulted in their death, not through choice, but later through having no choice at all in the matter.

To conclude, adaptation, shaping, and selection are functions of intelligent thought as it operates in context. They may, although they need not, be employed hierarchically, with one path followed when another one fails. It is through adaptation, shaping, and selection that the components of intelligence, as employed at various levels of experience, become actualized in the real world. In this section, it has become clear that the modes of actualization can differ widely across individuals and groups, so that intelligence cannot be understood independently of the ways in which it is manifested.

RELATION OF TRIARCHIC THEORY TO OTHER THEORIES

The goal of the triarchic theory is not to replace previous theories of intelligence, but rather, to incorporate them, and particularly, their best aspects. I argued in the first major section of this chapter that most theories of intelligence are inter-compatible, and this argument applies to the triarchic theory as well, vis a vis other theories of intelligence. Consider why.

Psychometric Theories.

The earliest psychometric theory was Galton's. Galton placed heavy stress upon psychophysical measures, and many of these, such as strength of grip, are given no credence today, except perhaps in Gardner's (1983) description of multiple intelligences, according to which strength might be part of kinesthetic intelligence. However, Galton's mental measures of attributes such as reaction time were a step in the right direction. These measures probably assessed, in some degree, speed of performance-componential functioning as well as speed of performance component execution, and both of these attributes are of some importance to intelligence. If Galton's and, later, Cattell's measures were not highly correlated with anything else, one would expect such low correlations due to the very narrow aspect of intelligence that these measures assessed.

The triarchic theory is more in line with the theory of Binet and Simon (1973), with its emphasis upon judgment. Binet emphasized higher order thinking in his theory, and his tests involve substantial investment of both metacomponents and performance components. Some of these tests, moreover, apply these components in novel situations. A few even apply them in contextually relevant ones. Hence, Binet's theory was more in the spirit of later theories of intelligence, including the triarchic one.

The first major factor theory of intelligence was that of Spearman (1923, 1927). Spearman's theory had two parts, the purely psychometric part, according to which intelligence is understood primarily in terms of a general factor, and an information-processing part, which specified three of the mental processes Spearman believed to be central in general intelligence. These three processes - apprehension of experience, eduction of relations, and eduction of correlates - are essentially identical to the performance components of encoding, inference, and application, respectively, that appear in the componential theory of induction. We, too, have found these components to be of central importance in the understanding of general intelligence (Sternberg & Gardner, 1982). We believe, with Spearman, that there is more to general intelligence than these three processes, however. This something more would include metacomponential functioning as well as the execution of general components of information processing (including components from all three categories) that are common across almost all information-processing tasks.

Thurstone's (1983) theory of primary mental abilities was originally seen by many as conflicting with Spearman's theory. It has become clear in recent hierarchical theories, and especially Gustafsson's (1984), that Spearman's and Thurstone's theories may be viewed as compatible, simply because they deal with factors at different levels of a hierarchy of decreasing generality. I view Thurstone's theory as tapping primarily the class components that apply to certain classes or groups of tasks (e.g., spatial tasks, verbal comprehension tasks, memory tasks) but not others (Sternberg, 1980). The performance component involved in mental rotation of objects is limited to spatial tasks and reasoning tasks that involve mentally rotating figures. Thus, this theory, too, is in some sense a subset of the triarchic one.

Probably the most well-known hierarchical theories are those of Cattell (1971) and of Vernon (1971). The theories are rather similar revealing Burt's influence, and I shall not try to deal with all aspects of either theory. In Cattell's theory, the most well-known part of it deals with two subfactors of general intelligence, _fluid ability_ and _crystallized ability_. Fluid ability is best measured by tasks requiring abstract reasoning, whereas crystallized ability is best measured by tasks requiring demonstration of accumulated knowledge, such as vocabulary. From the standpoint of the triarchic theory, fluid ability tests measure primarily metacomponential functioning, performance-componential functioning (and particularly, the performance components of induction), and the application of these various components to relatively novel situations. The tasks may or may not be novel to particular individuals, depending upon their past history and experience with such tasks. Crystallized ability tests measure primarily the products, rather than the processes of knowledge acquisition. They are thus indirect measures of componential functioning. I believe it is because these tests emphasize the measurement of products rather than processes that they are relatively more immune to age-related decline than are fluid ability tests (Horn, 1968).

Guilford's (1967) theory of intelligence has always been something of an anomaly. The factor-analytic evidence that has been offered in favour of it is of questionable validity (Horn & Knapp, 1973), and hence it is easy to dismiss the theory. But Guilford's theory makes certain important contributions that are unusual in factor-analytic theories. First, it explicitly builds the notion of process into the factors of intelligence, something no previous theory had done. Although the various postulated processes may not all be independent psychometric factors, they are at least recognized as distinctly contributing to the factor model. In the triarchic theory, of course, processes are also accorded a major role in understanding the nature of intelligence. Second, Guilford was among the earliest theorists to recognize the importance of everyday behavioral competence in intelligence. His theory was not limited in its scope merely to the academic side of intelligence. This emphasis appears in the contextual subtheory of the triarchic theory. Finally, the theory explicitly includes within the structure-of-intellect cube abilities having to do with dealing with novelty, in particular, the divergent thinking abilities. Although I question the validity of some of the tests Guilford has used to measure this construct, I applaud his recognition of the importance of dealing with novelty to intelligence. There are other positive features of Guilford's theory that could be mentioned, but I would hope the point is clear: Whether or not the theory is correct in its details (which I doubt), it is one of the most progressive psychometric theories of intelligence to have been proposed.

Information-Processing Theories.

Information-processing theories of intelligence differ primarily
in the level of information processing that they emphasize. As
noted earlier, theories such as Jensen's (1982) emphasize lower
levels of processing, whereas theories such as Sternberg's (1980)
or Snow's (1979) emphasize higher levels of processing. In the
triarchic theory, intelligence is understood in terms of the
interaction of all of these levels. Hence, a complete theory of
intelligence would have to account for individual differences in
choice reaction time as well as individual differences in complex
problem solving, as in complex analogies. This is not to say that
all levels of processing contribute equally to individual
differences in all societies, at all ages, or in all possible
groups. I doubt this to be the case. But the question here is of
degree of componential contribution rather than of kind of
componential contribution, and also of the degree to which the
execution of the various component processes is automatized. The
various information-processing theories serve a useful function in
highlighting the various levels of analysis that are possible in
understanding intelligent processing of information

Piagetian Theory

Piaget's theory of intelligence (e.g., Piaget, 1972) has so many
aspects that it would not be possible to deal with all of them
here. The richness of this theory is probably unmatched in any
other theory of intelligence. I will dwell here on only two
aspects of the theory, the mechanisms of equilibration and the
stages of development.

In Piaget's theory, adaptation to the environment occurs through
two mental mechanisms: assimilation and accommodation. In
assimilation, one fits a new stimulus into one's existing mental
structures. In accommodation, one alters one's mental structures
in order to understand the new stimulus. The mechanism of
equilibration (i.e., the balance between assimilation and
accommodation) thus highlights the role of dealing with novelty in
ecologically valid situations. The triarchic theory does not have
two processes that directly correspond to assimilation and
accommodation. Rather, it has three components of knowledge
acquisition - selective encoding, selective combination, and
selective comparison - that can be applied to tasks and situations
at differing levels of novelty and cognitive preparedness.
Whether or not a given process results in a new cognitive
structure is viewed as a representational issue rather than one of
process: In the triarchic theory, application of a process of

knowledge acquisition may or may not change one's mental representations or structures without changing the process involved. But this theory, like Piaget's, deals with the aspect of intelligence involving learning new information in tasks and situations that are relatively novel, and that are ecologically valid.

The triarchic theory does not postulate stages of intellectual development, although it does postulate a series of mechanisms by which cognitive development takes place (see Sternberg, 1985). I doubt that anything like discrete stages exist in cognitive development, and the bulk of recent evidence seems consistent with this doubt (see, e.g., Gelman & Baillargeon, 1983). In the triarchic theory, it is possible for sets of components to become available or increasingly accessible at about the same time, and such increases in availability and accessibility might render an appearance, at least in a rough sense, of a stagelike progression of cognitive development.

Contextual Theories

Some theorists of intelligence have emphasized the role of environmental context both in determining what intelligence is and in shaping one's level and kinds of intelligence (e.g., Berry, 1972; Laboratory of Comparative Human Cognition, 1982). These theories are partially consistent with the contextual subtheory of the triarchic theory, which also emphasizes how context shapes intelligence and intelligence shapes context. If there is a difference, it is in the triarchic position, shared by Irvine (1979), that there are constancies in intelligence across cultures that can help protect us from a position of total relativism.

CONCLUSIONS AND IMPLICATIONS

The triarchic theory consists of three interrelated subtheories that attempt to account for the bases and manifestations of intelligent thought. The componential subtheory relates intelligence to the internal world of the individual. The experiential subtheory relates intelligence to the experience of the individual with tasks and situations. The contextual subtheory relates intelligence to the external world of the individual.

The elements of the three subtheories are interrelated: The components of intelligence are manifested at different levels of experience with tasks and in situations of varying degrees of contextual relevance to a person's life. The components of intelligence are posited to be universal to intelligence: Thus, the components that contribute to intelligent performance in one culture do so in all other cultures as well. Moreover, the importance of dealing with novelty and automatization of information processing to intelligence are posited to be universal. But the manifestations of these components in experience are posited to be relative to cultural contexts. What constitutes adaptive thought or behavior in one culture is not necessarily adaptive in another culture. Moreover, thoughts and actions that would shape behavior in appropriate ways in one context might not shape them in appropriate ways in another context. Finally, the environment one selects will depend largely upon the environments available to one, and the fit of one's cognitive abilities, motivations, values, and affects to the available alternatives.

The triarchic theory has certain implications both for the assessment and the training of abilities. With regard to assessment, a full assessment battery would necessarily tap all of the abilities specified by the triarchic theory, something no existing test even comes close to. Although I am pursuing the development of a triarchic test of intelligence, even a test explicitly designed to measure intelligence according to the triarchic theory will be only an approximation to an ideal test, if only because the relativity of the contextual subtheory renders any one test adequate only for a limited population. Similarly, I have developed a training program for understanding and improving intellectual skills based on the theory (Sternberg, in press). But the training program could not possibly develop all of the skills posited by the theory, especially because contextual skills can be so variable across environments.

In conclusion, the triarchic theory offers a relatively complete account of intelligent thought that draws upon and partially subsumes many existing theories. This new theory, like all other theories, is only an approximation, one that will serve a constructive purpose if it, too, is eventually subsumed by a more complete and accurate theory of human intelligence.

REFERENCES

Berry, J.W. (1972). Radical cultural relativism and the concept of intelligence. In L.J. Cronbach & P. Drenth (Eds.), _Mental tests and cultural adaptation_. The Hague: mouton.

Binet, A. & Simon, T. (1916). _The development of intelligence in children_. Baltimore: Williams & Wilkins.

Binet, A. & Simon, T. (1973). Classics in psychology: The development of intelligence in children. New York: Arno Press.

Brown, A.L. (1978). Knowing when, where and how to remember: A problem of metacognition. In R. Glaser (Ed.), Advances in instructional psychology (Vol 1). Hillsdale, N.J.:Erlbaum.

Butterfield, E.C., Wambold, C. & Belmont, J.M. (1973). on the theory and practice of improving short-term memory. American Journal of Mental Deficiency, 77, 654-69.

Campione, J.C., & Brown, A.L. (1979). Toward a theory of intelligence: Contributions from research with retarded children. In R.J. Sternberg & D.K. Detterman (Eds.), Human intelligence: Perspectives on its theory and measurement. Norwood, N.J.:Ablex.

Carroll, J.B. (1976). Psychometric tests as cognitive tasks: A new "structure of intellect." In L.B. Resnick (Ed.), The nature of intelligence. Hillsdale, N.J.: Erlbaum.

Carroll, J.B. (1980). Individual difference relations in psychometric and experimental cognitive tasks. (NR 150-406 ONR Final Report). Chapel Hill, NC: L.L. Thurstone Psychometric Laboratory, University of North Carolina.

Caruso, D., & Sternberg, R.J. (1983). An information-processing model of individual differences in intelligence. Manuscript submitted for publication.

Cattell, R.B. (1971). Abilities: Their structure, growth and action. Boston: Houghton Mifllin.

Chase, W.G. & Simon, H.A. (1973). The mind's eye in chess. In W.G. Chase (Ed.), Visual information processing. New York: Academic Press.

Chi, M.T.H. (1978). Knowledge structures and memory development. In R.S. Siegler (Ed.), Children's thinking: What develops? Hillsdale, N.J.: Erlbaum.

Cole, M., Gay, J., Glick, J., & Sharp, D.W. (1971). The cultural context of learning and thinking. New York: Basic Books.

Cooper, L.A. (1982). Strategies for visual comparison and representation: Individual differences. In R.J. Sternberg (Ed.), Advances in the psychology of human intelligence. (Vol. 1). Hillsdale, N.J.:Erlbaum.

Davidson, J.E., & Sternberg, R.J. (1984). The role of insight in intellectual giftedness. Gifted Child Quarterly, 28, 58-64.

Flavell, J.H. (1977). Cognitive development. Englewood Cliffs, N.J.: Prentice-hall.

Galton, F. (1883). Inquiry into human faculty and its development. London: Macmillan

Gardner, H. (1983) Frames of mind: The theory of multiple intelligences). New York: Basic Books.

Gelman, R., & Baillargeon, R. (1983). A review of some Piagetian concepts. In P. Mussen (Series Ed.) & J. Flavell & E. Markman (Vol. Eds.), Handbook of child psychology. New York: Wiley.

Gelman, R., & Gallistel, C.R. (1978). The child's understanding of number. Cambridge MA: Harvard University Press.

Gladwin, T. (1970). East is a big bird. Cambridge, MA: Harvard University Press.

Goodnow, J.J. (1976). The nature of intelligent behavior: Questions raised by cross-cultural studies. In L.B. Resnick (Ed.), The nature of intelligence. Hillsdale, N.J.: Erlbaum.

Guilford, J.P. (1967). The nature of human intelligence. New York: McGraw Hill.

Gustafsson, J.E. (1984). A unifying model for the structure of intellectual abilities. Intelligence, 8, 279-203.

Heath, S.B. (1983). Ways with words. New York: Cambridge University Press.

Horn, J.L. (1968). Organization of abilities and the development of intelligence. Psychological Review, 75, 242-259.

Horn, J.L., & Knapp, J.R. (1973). On the subjective character of the empirical base of Guilford's structure-of-intellect model. Psychological Bulletin, 80, 33-43.

Hunt, E.B. (1978). Mechanics of verbal ability. Psychological Review, 85, 109-130.

Hunt, E.B. (1980). Intelligence as a information-processing concept. British Journal of Psychology, 71, 449-474.

Hunt, E.B., Frost, N., & Lunneborg, C. (1973). Individual differences in cognition: A new approach to intelligence. In G. Bower (Ed.), The psychology of learning and motivation (Vol. 7). New York: Academic Press.

Hunt, E., & Lansman, M. (1982). Individual differences in attention. In R.J. Sternberg (Ed.), Advances in the psychology of human intelligence (Vol. 1). Hillsdale, N.J.: Erlbaum.

Irvine, S.H. (1969). Factor analysis of African abilities and attainments: Constructs across cultures. Psychological Bulletin, 7 , 20-32.

Irvine, S.H. (1979). The place of factor analysis in cross-cultural methodology and its contribution to cognitive theory. In L. Eckensberger & Y. Poortinga (Eds.), Cross-cultural contributions to psychology. Lisse, Netherlands: Swets & Zeitlinger.

Jensen, A.R. (1979). g: Outmoded theory or unconquered frontier? Creative Science and Technology, 2, 16-29.

Jensen, A.R. (1980). Bias in mental testing. New York: Free Press.

Jensen, A.R. (1982). Reaction time and psychometric g. In H.J. Eysenck (Ed.), A model for intelligence. Berlin: Springer-Verlag.

Kearins, J.M. (1981). Visual spatial memory in Australian aboriginal children of desert regions. Cognitive Psychology, 3, 434-460.

Keil, F.C. (1984). Mechanisms of cognitive development and the structure of knowledge. in R.J. Sternberg (Ed.), Mechanisms of cognitive development. San Francisco, Freeman.

Kosslyn, S.M. (1980). Image and mind. Cambridge, MA: Harvard University Press.

Laboratory of Comparative Human Cognition. (1982). Culture and intelligence. In R.J. Sternberg (Ed.), Handbook of human intelligence. New York: Cambridge University Press.

MacLeod, C.M., Hunt, E.B., & Matthews, N.N. (1978). Individual differences in the verification of sentence-picture relationships. Journal of Verbal Learning and Verbal Behavior, 17, 493-507.

Mayer, R., & Greeno, J.G. (1972). Structural differences between learning outcomes produced by different instructional methods. Journal of Educational Psychology, 63, 165-173.

Milgram, S. (1975). Obedience to authority. New York: Harper & Row.

Mulholland, T.M., Pellegrino, J.W., Glaser, R. (1980). Components of geometric analogy solution. Cognitive Psychology, 12, 252-284.

Neisser, U. (1983). Components of intelligence or steps in routine procedures? Cognition. 15, 189-197.

Newell, A., & Simon, H. (1972). Human problem solving. Englewood Cliffs, N.J.: Prentice-hall.

Pellegrino, J.W., & Glaser, R. (1979). Cognitive correlates and components in the analysis of individual differences. In R.J. Sternberg & D.K. Detterman (Eds.), Human intelligence: Perspectives on its theory and measurement. Norwood, N.J.:Ablex.

Pellegrino, J.W., & Glaser, R. (1980). Components of inductive reasoning. In R. Snow, P. A. Federico, & W. Montague (Eds.). Aptitude, learning and instruction: Cognitive process analyses of aptitude (Vol. 1). Hillsdale, N.J.: Erlbaum.

Pellegrino, J.W., & Kail, R., jr. (1982). Process analyses of spatial aptitude. in R.J. Sternberg (Ed.), Advances in the psychology of human intelligence.

Piaget, J. (1972). The psychology of intelligence. Totowa, N.J.: Littlefield Adams.

Raaheim, K. (1974). Problem solving and intelligence. Oslo: Universitetsforlaget.

Resnick, L.B., & Glaser, R. (1976). Problem solving and intelligence. In L.B. Resnick (Ed.), The nature of intelligence. Hillsdale, N.J.: Erlbaum.

Schank, R. (1980). How much intelligence is there in artifical intelligence? Intelligence, 4, 1-14.

Schank, R.C., & Abelson, R.P. (1977). Scripts, plans, goals, and understanding. Hillsdale, N.J.: Erlbaum.

Siegler, R.S. (in press). Unitites of thinking across domains. In M. Perlmutter (Ed.), The development of intelligence: 1984 Minnesota symposium on child psychology. Hillsdale, N.J.: Erlbaum.

Simon, H., & Reed, S. (1976). Modeling strategy shifts in a problem-solving task. Cognitive Psychology, 8, 86-97.

Snow, R.E. (1979). Theory and method for research on aptitude process. In R.J. Sternberg & D.K. Detterman (Ed.), Human intelligence: Perspectives on its theory and measurement. Norwood, N.J.: Ablex.

Snow, R.E. (1980). Aptitude processes. In R.E. Snow, P.A. Federico, & W.E. montague (Eds.), Aptitude, learning and instruction: Cognitive process analyses of aptitude (Vol. 1). Hillsdale, N.J.: Erlbaum.

Snow, R.E., Kyllonen, P.C., & Marshalek, B. (1984). The topography of ability and learning correlations. In R.J. Sternberg (Ed.), Advances in the psychology of human intelligence (Vol. 2). Hillsdale, N.J.:Erlbaum.

Snow, R.E., & Lohman, D.F. (1984). Toward a theory of cognitive aptitude for learning from instruction. Journal of Educational Psychology, 76, 347-376.

Spear, L.C., & Sternberg, R.J. (in press). An information-processing framework for understanding reading disabilities. In S. Ceci (Ed.), Handbook for cognitive, social, and neuropsychological aspects of learning disabilities (Vol. 2). Hillsdale, N.J.: Erlbaum.

Spearman, C. (1923). The nature of 'intelligence' and the principles of cognition. London: macmillan.

Spearman, C. (1927). The abilities of man. New York: Macmillan.

Sternberg, R.J. (1977). Intelligence, information processing, and analogical reasoning: The componential analysis of human abilities. Hillsdale, N.J.: Erlbaum.

Sternberg, R. J. (1979). The nature of mental abilities. American Psychologist, 34, 214-230.

Sternberg, R.J. (1980). Sketch of a componential subtheory of human intelligence. Behavioral and Brain Sciences, 3, 573-584.

Sternberg, R.J. (1981). Intelligence and nonentrenchment. Journal of Educational Psychology, 73, 1-16.

Sternberg, R.J. (1982a). Natural, unnatural, and supernatural concepts. Cognitive Psychology, 14, 451-488.

Sternberg, R.J. (1982b). Reasoning, problem solving, and intelligence. In R.J. Sternberg (Ed.), Handbook of human intelligence. New York: Cambridge University Press.

Sternberg, R.J., & Davidson, J.E. (1982). The mind of the puzzler. Psychology Today, 16, June, 37-44.

Sternberg, R.J., & Gardner, M.K. (1982). A componential interpretation of the general factor in human intelligence In H.J. Eysenck (Ed.), A model for intelligence. Berlin: Springer-Verlag.

Sternberg, R.J. (1983). Components of human intelligence. Cognition, 15, 1-48.

Sternberg, R.J. (1984a). Implicit theories of intelligence, creativity, and wisdom. Manuscript submitted for publication.

Sternberg, R.J. (1984b). Toward a triarchic theory of human intelligence. Behavioral and Brain Sciences, 7, 269-287.

Sternberg, R.J. (1985). Beyond IQ: A triarchic theory of human intelligence. New York: Cambridge University Press.

Sternberg, R.J. (in press-a). The psychology of verbal comprehension. in R. Glaser (Ed.), Advances in instructional psychology (Vol. 3). Hillsdale, N.J.: Erlbaum.

Sternberg, R.J. (in press-b). Understanding and increasing your intelligence. San Diego: Harcourt, Brace, Jovanovich.

Sternberg, R.J., & Gardner, M.K. (1983). Unities in inductive reasoning. Journal of Experimental Psychology: General, 112, 80-116.

Sternberg, R.J., Guyote, M.J., & Turner, M.E. (1980). Deductive reasoning. In R. E. Snow, P.A. Federico, & W. Montague (Eds.), Aptitude, learning, and instruction: Cognitive process analyses of aptitude (Vol. 1). Hillsdale, N.J.: Erlbaum.

Sternberg, R.J., & Ketron, J.L. (1982). Selection and implementation of strategies in reasoning by analogy. Journal of Educational Psychology, 74, 399-413.

Sternberg, R.J., & Powell, J.S. (1983). Comprehending verbal comprehension. American Psychologist, 38, 878-893.

Sternberg, R.J., & Rifkin, B. (1979). The development of analogical reasoning processes. Journal of Experimental Child Psychology, 27, 195-232.

Sternberg, R.J., & Weil, E.M. (1980). An aptitude-strategy interaction in linear syllogisitic reasoning. <u>Journal of Education Psychology</u>, <u>72</u>, 226-234.

Super, C., & Harkness, S. (1980). The infant's niche in rural Kenya and metropolitan America. In L.L. Adler (Ed.), <u>Issues in cross-cultural research</u>. New York: Academic Press.

Thurstone, L.L. (1938). <u>Primary mental abilities</u>. Chicago: University of Chicago.

Vernon, P.E. (1971). <u>The structure of human abilities</u>. London: Methuen.

Wagner, R., & Sternberg, R.J. (1983). Executive control of reading. Manuscript submitted for publication.

Wissler, C. (1901). The correlation of mental and physical tests. <u>Psychological Review, Monograph Supplement</u>, <u>3</u>, No. 6.

Author Note

Preparation of this chapter was supported by Contract N000148K0013 from the Office of Naval Research and Army Research Institute.

A COGNITIVE MODEL OF INDIVIDUAL DIFFERENCES, WITH AN APPLICATION TO ATTENTION

Earl Hunt

The University of Washington

INTRODUCTION

There is virtually universal agreement that people differ in their mental competencies. Such variations are captured under the rubric "intelligence". But what does this mean? Natural philosophers have speculated about the nature and cause of intelligence for more than two thousand years. (There are explicit references to the concept in the Iliad.) No agreement has been reached. Similarly, over one hundred years of scientific study have failed to provide a generally accepted theory of either the nature or causes of individual difference in mental competence. Why?

The problem may be that we are casting our net too widely. The subject matter of "intelligent behavior" has been based largely on an informal folk psychology of the sort of phenomena that count as cognitive behavior. The influence of popular notions upon measurement procedures was explicit in Binet's development of the original intelligence test (Binet and Simon, 1905; for a review see Carroll, 1982), and is reflected in the tests derived from it, such as the Wechsler Adult Intelligence Scale (Matarazzo, 1972). The items on Binet's tests were originally drawn from knowledgable observers' ideas about what the "average" (or dull, or smart) person could do. Not surprisingly, the criterion for a good test has become the test's utility as a predictor of some social index of mental success, usually school grades. Such indices are global amalgamations over very many cognitive behaviors, and are caused by cognitive, non-cognitive, and even non-individual variables. Given the nature of the index, it is not surprising to find that the best predictors are non-specific global assessments of cognitive abilites. Wechsler (1975), the developer of what is probably the most successful of these tests, has been quite frank in saying that the Wechsler Adult Intelligence Scale (WAIS) is a standardized interview that samples representative cognitive

- 177 -

behaviors. And "representative", here, means representative in terms of social utility rather than representative in terms of what a person's mind can do.

Psychometric theories of intelligence are based on a more formal theory. Thurstone (1938) asserted that there exists a set of primary mental abilities, and then developed tests that were supposed to measure them. Cattell (1971) and Guilford (1967) made different assertions, but followed the same procedure. The psychometricians have also developed powerful inductive methods, such as factor analysis, to check on their intuitions about tests and their distributions. For the present purposes, though, this is something of a technical aside. While Thurstone and his followers did move away from a strict folk psychology, they did not take another step that I believe is essential. The psychometricians viewed patterns of correlations between test scores as sufficient evidence for their theories of the structure of intellect, but did not evaluate their intuitions about the processes that produced those scores. Put more directly, to a psychometrician a good test is one that provides the proper entries in a correlation table. By extension, a good theory of intelligence is one that succinctly summarizes the information in tables of correlations between tasks. But, as McNemar (1964) pointed out some years ago, providing a psychological interpretation for the mathematically defined factors is more than science.

The psychometric approach also has the characteristic of being fragmented. Individual tasks are justified as being tests of rather loosely-defined abilities, without providing any model of how the mind unites different abilities to perform a task. This point can be illustrated by considering a psychometric model for reading; imagine what might be constructed from the Cattell and Horn framework of "fluid" and "crystallized" intelligence (Cattell, 1972; Horn and Donaldson, 1979). This theory postulates, among other things, that there are abilities for "crystallized intelligence": the ability to use previously acquired knowledge, short term retention, and rapid perceptual detection of overlearned patterns. Now suppose that people are asked to take tests of these three factors, and are also to take a test of their comprehension of newspaper articles. It is conceivable to me that one could find that virtually all of the variance on the reading test was predicted by the tests of crystallized intelligence, short term memory, and perceptual identification. Quibbling a bit over words, however, none of the variance in reading would have been accounted for by the predictor tests, because no model of the process of reading had been offered. The point can be driven home by an athletic analogy. It may be possible to predict the variance in points scored by professional basketball players by

regressing their scoring on height, speed, and age. Accounting
for the variance is going to require some process model of outside
shots, foul shooting, and slam-dunks.

Here I shall argue for a process oriented approach. My thesis is
that one should begin with a theory of the process of cognition,
and use that theory to determine how cognition should be
measured. In an ideal world the general theory would lead to the
development of models of specialized tasks designed to provide
crucial tests of the theory itself. The models of the specialized
tasks would define estimates of the parameters characterizing an
individual's mental capacities. ('Parameter' is to be understood
to refer to a characteristic of the individual. It need not be a
number.) The pattern of correlations between parameter estimates
would become a thing to discover, but not a source of evidence for
validating a measure. Arguing by analogy again, blood pressure is
a measurement that is justified by our understanding of the
cardiovascular system, not by its correlation with weight or
longevity. Indeed, one might discover that a theoretically
understandable measure showed virtually no between subjects
variability, or that it was uncorrelated with measurements derived
from the folk psychology (e.g. school grades). In the
psychometric tradition such a finding is grounds for drumming the
measurement out of the regiment of tests. In a theory oriented
tradition the measurement remains as long as the theory does, and
the presence or absence of a correlation becomes a fact to be
explained.

An emphasis upon a process theory should not be construed as an
argument against either folk psychology or psychometric models.
The folk psychology models were developed for a practical purpose,
tho prediction of success in various social institutions. This is
a legitimate goal, and we need such tests. The psychometric
approach stands somewhere in-between. It provides a framework
that is extremely useful for sharpening both the folk psychology
tests and their use in describing practical changes in mental
competence. Because this point is important I offer two examples
of the compromise that psychometric theories present.

Horn's (1982) argument that crystallized intelligence increases
and fluid intelligence decreases with advancing age is a better
description of changes in adult intelligence than the generalized
observation that there are declines on the WAIS or similar tests.
The accuracy of this description has implications both for social
policy and for the study of geriatric cognition. But it is not a
statement about the changes in the process of cognition between
seventeen and seventy.

Moving to a more pragmatic example, flying a modern high-performance jet aircraft takes a good deal of "intelligence". However the type of mental skills required are not well evaluated by giving aviation cadets standard omnibus intelligence tests. The standardized tests rate verbal reasoning factors too heavily. Specialized tests that place more emphasis on spatial reasoning do a better job of prediction. So the specialized tests are useful. But they do not provide process models of how a pilot reasons, nor do they relate parameters of a person's cognition to their performance as an aviator.

These examples illustrate both the strength and the weakness of the psychometric approach. Obviously the remarks here will tend to stress its weaknesses. The strengths should not be gainsaid. Psychometric theories can be used to develop excellent, pragmatically useful systems of personnel classification. Furthermore, I do not really expect the development of process oriented theories to improve upon the prediction of performance in any spectacular way. Why, then, should a process model be explored?

Plato is said to have described science as the business of carving up Nature at her natural joints. In less colourful language, Pylyshyn (1983) has argued that scientific explanations first identify systems of variables that interact in a regular fashion, and then provide compact descriptions of these systems. The identification stage is central. Ashby (1960) defines a closed system as a set of variables whose values are determined by their mutual interaction, independent of the values of any variables outside the system. Therefore the first step in a scientific analysis is to establish a conceptual scheme that identifies a putatively closed system. The second, empirical step is to show that the system does indeed behave as it is expected to. What is being advocated is a deductive approach to the study of intelligence. First a process model of thought is postulated. Once this model has been defined, measurement procedures that are justified with respect to the model become the operational measure of "intelligence". More properly, they become the operational definition of identifiable processes within the model itself. This is the major point at which the deductive and inductive (psychometric) approach part company. The deductive approach may define measures that are important within the particular theoretical framework, but do not fit the folk definition of intelligence. It is equally possible that measures that are considered to be central to intelligence, within the folk tradition, are simply not well defined within the theory.

Let us return to the analogy of athletic performance. There is a folk definition of an "athletic ability". It stresses the ability to play certain games well. As anyone who watches televised sports knows, there are more than ample statistics on how well specific individuals play specific games. There are also theories of anatomy and physiology, that generate a variety of anthropometric measures of people, both as mechanical and biochemical systems. These measures are quite different from the measures recited by sports anouncers. While there is some correlation between sports performance and anthropometric measures, no one claims that athletic performance is determined solely by physical capacity, i.e. the sports and physiological measures do not jointly define a closed system. However the physiological anthropometric measurement system is closed within itself, and thus is a legitimate object for scientific study.

The analogy between athletic ability and anthropometric measurement carries over almost exactly to the relation between folk definitions of intelligence and scientific analyses of cognition. The folk definition of intelligence strongly stresses the perception of a person as having suceeded in certain "white collar" occupations, including but not limited to academic performance. Personal cognitive abilities are only one of several factors that establish such success. Since the variables that establish the folk definition of intelligence almost certainly do not form a closed system, their scientific analysis is virtually impossible. What can be done is to establish a scientific theory of individual differences in mental competence, using measures that may or may not correlate with the measures of folk psychology.

The following section of this essay presents a deductive approach to intelligence. First a theory of cognitive processing will be developed. The theory will then be applied to the study of individual differences in a partiuclar branch of cognition, the control of attention. (For a similar application to verbal comprehension, see Hunt (1987)). The essay closes with an evaluation of the model.

A MODEL OF COGNITION

The theoretical model to be described might be called the "modal" theory of Cognitive Science. It is based upon the concept of thought as rule governed behavior, in which rule execution is driven by pattern recognition. Early discussions of the concepts are found in Newell and Simon (1972), in which the notation system was introduced to psychologists, and in Newell (1973). Various specifications of the standard theory exist (Anderson, 1983; Hunt, 1981; Hunt and Lansman, in press; Thibadeau, Just, and Carpenter, 1982) that differ in terminology and the detailed assumptions that are made. For the present purposes the distinction between the different varieties of the modal theory do not matter. In the rest of the discussion the terminology of the Hunt and Lansman paper will be used. The theory itself will be referred to as the Standard Theory of Cognitive Science.

The standard theory is based on the idea that cognition can be modeled by computation (Pylyshyn, 1983). Computational models are divided into three logically distinct parts; algorithms that state the rules that the model "follows" in solving problems, a virtual machine that executes the algorithms, and a physical machine that provides the physical realization of the virtual machines. In this case the physical machine is said to emulate the virtual machine.

The distinction between the virtual machine and the algorithms is roughly analogous to the distinction between a programming language and a set of programs written in the language. The language provides primitive operations which the programs organize into problem solving sequences. The virtual machine - physical machine distinction is like the mind - body distinction. The physical machine provides devices that execute the logical functions of the virtual machine.

To apply this reasoning to individual differences, let us imagine a set of robots who were to be programmed to do some task. The robots are all assumed to utilize the same programming language. However, they may have been constructed by different manufacturers, using different quality material, and they may have been programmed by different programmers. This means that individual differences between robots can arise from two sources; the efficiency of the elementary processes provided by the language and the efficiency of the programs that the robots contain. The robot's overall efficiency as a problem solver will depend upon three different sources of "individual differences". These are the extent to which its programs represent an efficient method of analyzing the task at hand, the extent to which the programs are written to make the most efficient use of the robot's machinery, and the power of that machinery itself.

The cognitive science approach is made more specific by describing a particular virtual machine, and then exploring the problem solving algorithms provided for it. The machine that will be considered here is depicted, in outline, in Figure 1. This figure is the schematic for an abstract device that can communicate with its environment and manipulate internal representations of it.

Communication with the environment is accomplished by a set of channels, each of which can contain some object of the device's apperception. More formally, the information in the model's

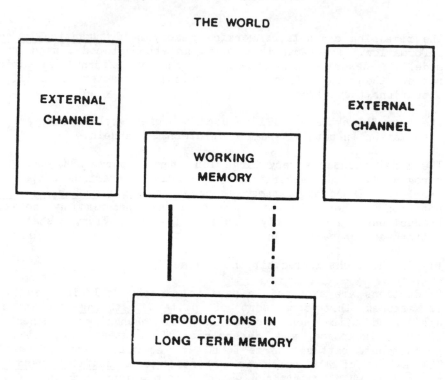

THE WORLD

Figure 1   A schematic for a robot mind

<u>external</u> channels is determined by the environment. By analogy to a human system, I shall speak of the auditory and visual sensory-perceptual systems as being represented by external channels. Note that this implies that information on channels will be coded in some form appropriate to that channel; e.g. visual and auditory codes.

The model contains an additional set of channels that will be referred to, collectively, as <u>working memory</u>. The working memory consists of one visual and one auditory channel, and an unspecified number of "semantic" channels. There are two distinctions between the working memory and the external channels. The first is that the contents of the working memory channels are always determined by actions of the model itself, rather than by the external environment. The second distinction deals with the codes used by the working memory channels. The auditory and visual channels contain objects in auditory and visual codes. These channels play a role roughly analogous to the echoic and iconic buffers in Baddeley's (1976) model of memory.

The remaining channels of working memory hold <u>semantically coded</u> information. The semantic code is an abstract code, used by the model to describe its interpretations of external situations, rather than to reflect the physical characteristics of the situations themselves.

The term "blackboard" will be used to refer, collectively, to the information in both external and internal channels.

The model assumes a very large long term memory (LTM) that holds "programs", i.e. algorithms for solving various types of problems. These algorithms are organized in a <u>production system</u> notation rather than in conventional programming notation. Productions are simply rules for behavior, stated as pattern-action pairs. An example is the simple rule for driving:

(1) If the light is red hit the brakes.

Productions are executed in parallel in the following sense. It is assumed that some sort of <u>pattern matching</u> mechanism is associated with each production. The mechanism examines the entire blackboard and determines the extent to which the production's pattern can be found in the blackboard information. The extent of the match is reported to a <u>conflict resolution</u> <u>mechanism</u>, which determines which, and how many, productions will be selected for execution. "Executing a production" means taking the actions specified in the action part of the production. In the example given, if rule (1) were made active a person (robot) would brake his/her/its car. Actions can be of two types. One, exemplified by (1), is the taking of some external action. The other action is to set some set of symbols into the channels of working memory. This is illustrated by the following rules:

(2) If a police vehicle is in sight place the goal "obey traffic laws" in semantic working memory.

(3) If a semantic channel contains the goal "obey traffic laws" and a pedestrian puts one foot in a crosswalk bring the car to a stop.

Examples (2) and (3) illustrate two points in addition to showing how actions place information in working memory. Goal states may be represented in symbolic form, and the goal states themselves can be used to guide actions.

The basic assumption of the standard theory is that thinking can be modeled by creating an appropriate system of productions. The sufficiency of the production notation as a model of thinking is not in question, for an unrestricted production system is equivalent to the Turing Machine. This is something of a problem, since a system with such computational power is an unrealistic system for human thought. The problem is usually handled by placing some restriction on the production executing mechanism, for instance by restricting the size of working memory.

The production system models proposed by Anderson and by Hunt and Lansman modify the "pure" production execution mechanism just described. In the pure model, as represented by Newell and Simon (1972) and Thibadeau et al. (1982), productions are always selected by the explicit recognition of patterns in the information on the blackboard. Thus passing of information from one production to another always involves working memory, and is influenced by a limit on the size of channels or of working memory itself. Following Schneider and Shiffrin's (1977) terminology, this will be referred to as <u>controlled</u> information processing.

The models of Anderson and Hunt and Lansman include a second form of information processing, based loosely on the idea of semantic activation (Collins and Quillian, 1969, Collins and Loftus, 1975). In the amplified model each production can be thought of as being embedded in a "semantic network" of productions. That is, the nodes of the network represent productions and the links in the network represent connections between related productions. When one production becomes aroused (typically by matching some information contained in the blackboard) activation is spread to other, related productions automatically, i.e. without regard to any match between the receiving production's pattern and the information on the blackboard. To take a much used example, suppose LTM contained a production of the form:

(4) If the visual symbol DOCTOR is observed place the semantic term for "doctor" in working memory

and

(5) If the visual symbol NURSE is observed place the semantic term for "nurse" in working memory.

Activation of the pattern for (4) would cause a spread of activation to the pattern for (5), making it more easily matched to subsequent information in working memory. Because the activation mechanism influences production activation without requiring explicit matching to information on the blackboard, it is usually considered a model for what Schneider and Shiffrin (1977) refer to as <u>automatic</u> information processing.

The standard model is a gross description of an information processing machine capable of supporting what Pylyshyn refers to as psychologically realistic computer programs. To move beyond gross description one has to state what those algorithms are, and show that the model is capable of supporting these algorithms. Indeed, it has been claimed that until one does so the model is capable of supporting these algorithms. Indeed, it has been claimed that until one does so the model is no more than a computationally stated fiction (Kolers and Smythe, 1984). Various forms of the model have been programmed both by Anderson (1983) and by Hunt and Lansman (in press). Presenting their studies, however, would be somewhat apart from the point of the current paper. The purpose here is to use this model as a way of organizing our knowledge about the sorts of individual differences that do and do not appear in studies of various mental phenomena.

If the standard production system model is accurate three processes should be basic to virtually all thought. The first is pattern recognition, i.e. the ability to recognize that an example of a production's pattern part is present in the information on the blackboard. The second key process is the ability to maintain information in working memory itself. What are the limits on storing and accessing information in the blackboard? How well does a person manage to focus attention on the information appropriate for solving the problem at hand? The third process of interest is the spread of activation in the automatic processing system. How rapidly does information spread from one memorial pattern to another? And how are the automatic and controlled processes co-ordinated in actual problem solving? Measures of these three processes, if they could be obtained, would play a role in the study of intelligence that is analogous to measures of heart rate and systolic and diastolic blood pressure cardiology.

If the analogy between psychology and cardiology were exact there would be behavioral paradigms that produced pure measures of the various information processing systems. Such paradigms would be analogous to pulse measurements and blood pressure cuffs. Unfortunately the world is not that simple. One of the problems is introduced by the concept of codes. Recall that codes refer to the fact that information may be stored using "visual", "auditory", or "abstract semantic" codes. It appears to be necessary to have at least this many codes to account for many of the observations about human thought (Anderson, 1983; Kosslyn, 1980, but for a contrary opinion see Pylyshyn, 1983, chapter 7). Now let us suppose, for the moment, that the model is an exactly correct description of human thought, and that the brain is a physical instantiation of the appropriate virtual machine. It does not necessarily follow that the same physical mechanisms would operate on information in each of the different codes. Indeed, there is a substantial amount of neuropsychological evidence to indicate that different processes operate upon auditory and visual codes. Thus a paradigm for assessing, say, acoustic short term memory, may not be appropriate for assessing visual short term memory. This point will be discussed at some length below, in dealing with measures of auditory and visual attention.

The use of an information processing model to assess individual differences is made still more difficult, both conceptually and practically, by the fact that individual differences in performance can arise either from individual differences in the parameters describing the "underlying virtual machine" or from individual differences in the efficiency of the algorithms being used to solve a problem. It has already been pointed out that it would be difficult to infer facts about the individual differences in the parameters of robot brains from robot performance, because performance is based upon the interaction between the properties of an algorithm and the properties of virtual machines, and not on either sort of property alone. The same principle applies to the analysis of human performance. Chase and Ericsson's work with skilled mnemonists provides an excellent example. Chase and Ericsson (1978) studied a person who could display an apparent digit span of in excess of eighty digits. If the ability to recite arbitrary lists of digits is taken as an infallible, direct measure of working memory size, this would be truly superhuman performance. In fact, though, Chase and Ericsson's participant relied entirely on a specialized algorithm that was useful solely for memorizing digits. If his memory span was tested by other devices, such as asking him to recite lists of letters or words, the results were well within the normal range.

There is no easy answer to the question of how to obtain "basic" measurements of cognition. Since perfect paradigms are unlikely to be developed we shall no doubt have to rely on converging measurements in many situations. This does not present an insurmountable measurement problem. Indeed, this is a situation in which psychometric techniques for theory verification can well be combined with cognitive process models (Gieselman, Wounwarn, and Beatty, 1982; Palmer, MacLeod, Hunt, and Davidson, 1985). Furthermore, the situation here is no different from the situation in many other areas of science. Even in so vast a topic as cosmology it may be necessary to take alternative measurements of the same theoretical construct (Hodge, 1984).

Three points have been made. First, the "folk" and "psychometric" approaches to the study of intelligence were commented upon. Then an argument was made for a different approach, based upon a theory of the process of cognition. Such an argument is vacuous in the absence of a specific process model, so one has been offered. It must be admitted that this model contains a great many "degrees of freedom", using that term rather more generally than in the technical, statistical sense. This poses something of a paradox. Kolers and Smythe (1984) have claimed, probably correctly, that computational models typically contain so many opportunities for adjustment that the models can never be defeated by the data from any conceivable experiment. I must agree; computational models cannot be defeated outright by experimental observations. However, I am less bothered by this than Kolers and Smythe are. The mind probably is very flexible, and any model of its action will have to capture that flexibility. How, then, are we ever to evaluate a computational model? The evaluation has to be based upon the model's utility as a device for organizing observations, rather than its role as a theory that dictates them.

In the next section an attempt will be made to use the standard model to organize some facts about individual differences in the control of attention.

ATTENTION

What is Attention? The folk definition of attention is that it is a commodity to be paid, and that when it is paid, one thinks better. Furthermore, some people seem better able to control this commodity than are others. We often say that certain people are better at paying attention than are others. The popular press has not hesitated to comment about the allegedly short attention span of some of our candidates for very high office. There are stereotypes of successful executives, who direct the activities of all those about them, and unsuccessful executives, who are defeated by the complexities of walking and talking.

The good and bad executives may be apocryphal. There is another real life example that many of us can observe. Commerical airline pilots sometimes allow passengers to listen in on air-ground communications during takeoff. Those readers who are not aviators may find it instructive to do so the next time they have the chance. The communications are cryptic and fairly complex. Different aircraft, identified by remarkably similar call signs, are given instructions that could easily be confused. The pilot must decode these instructions while performing a rather complex psycho-motor task: operating the controls that get the aircraft off of the ground. Commerical aviators vitually always get all the instructions right. How do they manage to do so? Is it due to training, or do pilots have to have some of "the right stuff" before they begin their careers?

The remainder of this section is devoted to an exploration of attention, within the framework of the modified cognitive science theory introduced in the first section. The presentation will be in three parts. First certain concepts that have evolved from the experimental analysis of attention will be placed within the framework of the cognitive science theory. Stress will be laid upon the progressive elaboration of the concept by different theoreticians. The resulting analysis will then be applied to observations about individual differences in performance on attention demanding tasks. The relevant literature is not large, but enough findings have emerged to make one think about the appropriate theory. It will be shown that there is a parallel between different conceptualizations of attention and the sorts of questions that have been asked about individual differences. Unfortunately, though, some of the empirical studies that purport to present findings on individual differences could have benefitted from a deeper conceptual analysis of what was being sought. For that reason, some space will be devoted to comments on the appropriate design of individual differences research in this field.

Conceptual Approaches to Attention

The scientific study of attention is based on three well documented findings. The first of these is the deleterious effect of information overload. Since this is a particularly important idea, it will be illustrated in some detail, using visual scanning as an example.

In a visual scanning experiment an observer is shown a stimulus panel that may or may not contain a target object. The observer's task is to indicate whether or not the target was present. The main dependent variable is the time that the observer needs to inspect the stimulus panel in order to detect targets reliably. Figure 2 depicts one widely used procedure. Before the beginning of a trial, the observer was told what target is to be detected. For instance, imagine that the observer was told to detect the figure "2", which actually does appear in the display. After the observer understands what the target is the trial beings. First the observer is shown a fixation panel, the first set of asterisks in the figure. Then the observer is shown the stimulus panel which is displayed very briefly. A typical display interval might be from 100 to 500 milliseconds. Under some conditions even briefer display intervals are used. The stimulus panel is then replaced by a masking panel (the right hand set of asterisks in the figure), and the observer indicates whether or not the target was present. The experimenter manipulates the display interval to locate the briefest interval at which the observer can maintain some preset level of accuracy.

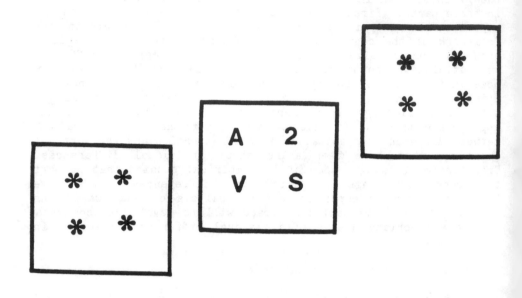

Figure 2   A Visual scanning paradigm

There are two independent variables in a visual scanning experiment; the number of items in a display panel (four in Figure 2) and the number of targets being scanned. For instance, in the hypothetical experiment described above the observer might be asked to detect the presence of a "2" or a "7". Providing that different targets are presented on each trial (the so-called "variable mapping" paradigm), the display interval required to detect targets rises linearly with the number of items on the display panel and the number of targets being searched for (Schneider and Shiffrin, 1977). This observation is best accounted for by assuming that targets are located by a limited capacity scanning device that operates in series on both the set of targets and the set of figures on the display panel. One can think of this situation as measuring the speed with which visual attention can be brought to bear on the comparison process. In spite of the "non-intellectual" nature of this task (it certainly is not as complex as a typical intelligence test) correlational studies have shown that the time required to locate targets in a visual scanning study is correlated with the general (g) factor extracted from conventional tests. At least among college student populations, high g scores are associated with rapid visual scanning (Ackerman and Schneider, 1985).

Dual task experiments provide a second source of evidence for some sort of attentional commodity. In these experiments the participant is asked to do two or more subtasks at once. For example, a person might be asked to monitor a light to see if it flickered, and at the same time to listen for a quiver in a tone. In many (but not all) such cases performance on the component tasks will deteriorate below that expected when either task is done alone. An idealized case is shown in Figure 3, which plots performance on one task as a function of performance on another. Norman and Bobrow (1975) referred to such plots as Performance Operating Characteristics (POCs), by analogy to the receiver operating characteristic of signal detection theory. They pointed out that a performance operator characteristic would trace out the form shown in Figure 3 if the participant could (a) improve his/her performance on each task, alone, by "directing attention" to it, and (b) if the participant was able to shift attention from one task to another on demand.

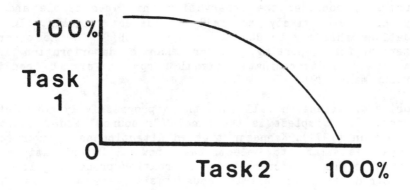

Figure 3   Idealized Performance Operating
Characteristic Curve

The third class of arguments in favour of a concept of attention is based on a more general observation. At the phenomenological level, people exhibit lapses of attention in a variety of situations. Fatigue, time of day, illness, or drug states can all induce alterations in the ability to detect and/or respond quickly to stimuli (Davies and Parasuraman, 1982.) The colloquial expression that we cannot pay attention when tired, or drunk, or ill, or elderly expresses the notion of a sensitive limited capacity mechanism for information processing.

Unfortunately, closer examination of virtually all of these phenomena leads to problems with the simple notion of attention as a resource to be shifted from one task to another. The deterioration in target detection may often simply be a reflection of the fact that the probability of error is increased when several less-than-perfect mechanisms are activated in parallel, even though the effectiveness of the individual mechanisms is independent of the number of other active devices (Duncan, 1980). Practice may sometimes greatly alter the attentional demands in a scanning task, or may exert almost no influence, depending upon precisely what is practised (Schneider and Shiffrin, 1977). Whether or not performance operating characteristics such as those shown in Figure 3 are obtained will depend upon what the tasks are, and how the observer has learned to control them. Finally, the phenomenological observations concerning attention wandering are often quite difficult to confirm in a controlled manner. To illustrate, consider the observation that when people are tired they are more likely to fail to detect signals. In many situations this may be due to an upward shift in the observer's criterion for reporting, rather than a deterioration in the capacity to discriminate signal from no-signal conditions (Parasuraman 1979).

Theories of attention fall into three progressively more detailed classes. The simplest is the single "resource" model introduced by Kahneman (1971). Kahneman treated attention as a power source, somewhat similar to electrical power. Deteriorations in performance due to increases in information processing load or to the introduction of simultaneous tasks were seen as due to exhausting the supply of power, as if the mental batteries had been overloaded. This view of attention has an interesting analogy to the concept of general intelligence. Are we to have "a" as well as "g"? Probably not, for further consideration has forced amplications of the concept of generalized attention that, in some respects, parallel the applications that have been required in the concept of general intelligence.

The biggest challenge to a generalized attention theory is that two tasks that fit the criteria for "demanding attention", singly

(Norman and Bobrow, 1975), may not exhibit mutual interference. Kerr, London and MacDonald (1983) offer a particularly good example. Balancing on one leg interferes with a spatial memory task but not a verbal memory task. In order to handle such observations, resource theory has been modified to include multiple pools of resources (Navon and Gopher, 1979). In the modified theory resources become more akin to economic commodity bundles than to an all purpose power source. The general concept of inter-task interference still holds, but the extent of the interference between any two tasks will be determined by their demand for common resources.

The problem with a multiple resource theory is that it is too rich. It is hard to imagine any observation that could not fit into a multiple resource model, if the theoretician was free to postulate as many resource pools as needed. To address this problem Wickens (1979, 1984) took the necessary step of defining the pools. He identified three general classes of resource. The first, encoding processes, deals generally with the structures and processes required to recognize objects in the environment. The second, central processes, deals loosely with the ability to construct mental representations. Any process that utilizes working memory appears to be a heavy user of this resource, so measurements of the extent to which a task interferes with the retention of information in working memory (or vice versa) provides a way of measuring the task's central process demands. Wickens' third class of resources are those involved in response selection and production. Although response production is often ignored in theories that concentrate on "perception" and "cognition" (and theories of intelligence are certainly among these), the attentional demands of response selection can be considerable.

Wickens' discussion of different sorts of resource structure clearly envisages a particular type of information processing machine. This welcome level of specificity is carried somewhat further in the structural interference approach to attention. Conceptually, structural interference theories see inter- and intra-task interference as arising not from a drain on attention as a power source, but rather as arising from competition for time on a specific information processing machine. Thus the analogy is more to a repair work job-shop, or perhaps a tool rental agency, than to a power system. Wickens himself argues that his notion of multiple resources is a structural one. Posner's (1978) approach exemplifies a generalized structural interference theory. Posner assumes that there exists a "central processing unit" that is required to do conscious tasks, but that a considerable amount of parallel processing can be done by perceptual units outside of the central processor, and hence on a non-interfering basis. At this level of generality the theory can be criticized as being vacuous. An unspecified "central processor" is no more scientific than an unspecified resource. The theory becomes less vacuous by developing a series of experimental studies that trace out the power of the various peripheral processes. For instance, Posner and his colleagues (Posner, Nissen, and Klein, 1976) present a case for assuming that there is a substantial amount of peripheral processing in audition, while cognitive analyses of visual stimuli are more tightly controlled by the central processing mechanism.

The cognitive science approach to attention is clearly based upon a notion of structural interference. There is nothing in the models of Anderson (1983), Hunt and Lansman (1983), or Thibadeau et al. (1982) that corresponds to a power source, but all these models do permit some form of competition for specific information processing mechanisms. Indeed, the idea of competition is implicit in any computational model based on production execution, because such models contain the implicit assumption that a particular stimulus situation can be "recognized" by at most only one production at any one time   (McDermott and Forgy, 1979).

The Hunt and Lansman (in press) modification of production system theories is the only model that deals with interference mechanisms other than generalized production competition. Hunt and Lansman explicitly introduce the idea of "channels" for the passage of information into the system from the external world. The channels are further grouped into sets of channels that use the same code. Production competition is restricted to productions within a code type. Thus at any one time there is intra-code competition between the auditory, visual, and semantic productions, but no competition for resources across code types. This could be looked upon as a modification of structural theory that instantiates Wickens' notion of multiple resource pools associated with peripheral input and central processes. However, Hunt and Lansman do not carry their ideas to the point of discussing response competition.

For the sake of completion, one more class of attention models should be mentioned. These will be called "confusion" models. Confusion models arise from the fact that, with sufficient practice, people can learn to perform very complex dual tasks. It can be shown that part of what is learned is how to execute the two tasks together, not just how to do them well on an individual basis (Damos and Wickens, 1980). Hirst, Spelke and Neisser's (1980) report is an extreme example. Some people can learn to take dictation while reading an unrelated text. Allport (1980) and Hirst et al. (1980) argue from these observations that people have a virtually unlimited capacity for processing concurrent information about different tasks, providing that they can recognize what information is relevant to which task, and providing that the actions required do not compete for use of a specific information processing mechanism. This is an important observation, for two reasons. First, it undoubtedly does capture one possible source of interference. Second, the explanation, and the observations on which it is based, highlight the important interactions between learning and attentional demands. A task that may be extremely attention demanding in an unlearned state may have trivial attentional demands after expertise has been achieved. To return to an example given earlier, when I (a non-aviator) listen in on air traffic control transmissions, I have trouble sorting out the messages to various aircraft. Fortunately commercial pilots are more experienced than I. Does this mean that the pilots have more attentional resources than I do, in general, or is it more correct to say that they have become very proficient in processing the messages in a specialized linguistic environment?

Studies of Individual Differences

Studies of individual differences in attention have generally paralleled the theoretical developments just outlined. That is, most studies can be classified as studies that examine individual variation in the total amount of attentional resources available, studies that examine people's ability to allocate their attention in dual task situations, and studies that examine individual variations in specific processes involved in attention allocation. What are the facts about individual differences in attention, and how do these facts amplify the cognitive science view of intelligence?

One of the defining characteristics of an attention demanding task is that performance on the task deteriorates in the face of increasing information load. A series of studies by Jensen and his collaborators (Jensen, 1981, 1982; Vernon, 1983) are relevant to this definition. What Jensen and his collaborators have done is to look at the time required to execute simple choice tasks. The paradigm most used is a task in which a person observes a display of matched lights and buttons, and presses a button when the corresponding light is illuminated. Although this task is not what one intuitively thinks of as an intellectual one, speed of choice has consistently been found to have a moderate, positive relation (r about .3) with much more intellectual behavior, such as performance on academic aptitude tests. Jensen has interpreted his findings as indicating that there is a generalized ability to classify internal representations rapidly. Since pattern recognition is a basic step in production execution, any individual differences in the pattern recognition process would be expected to have widespread, though not necessarily large, effects

on virtually all mental processes. Jensen has argued that this is
the case.

While this argument does establish a connection between concepts
of attention and intelligence, the argument is incomplete in two
ways. From the viewpoint of intelligence theory, it is not
correct to equate rapidity of decision making with good decision
making. There is ample evidence that in at least some situations
the intelligent go slowly (Sternberg, 1982). This is probably
related to the concept of an intra-individual speed-accuracy trade
off (Pachella, 1974). People maximize their mental competence by
monitoring their own performance as they exchange speed and
accuracy. From the viewpoint of attentional theory, looking only
at speed of decision making fails to address questions about a
person's ability to make a sensible allocation of attention to
different tasks.

The deployment of attentional resources is studied in various
forms of the Dual Task paradigm, in which people are given two
separate tasks to perform. The tasks are chosen so that there is
no obvious interference due to competition for physical
structures. Obviously finding that it is difficult to type while
playing the piano would be of little psychological interest. In
the secondary task version of a dual task paradigm one of the
tasks is identified as being of primary importance, while the
other task is to be done with one's "spare capacity". For brevity
these will be referred to as tasks A and B, respectively.
According to the resource view of attention, a participant will
first allocate sufficient attention to task A to ensure that it is
done at an optimal level, and then perform task B with whatever
resources are left over. Thus task B performance can be regarded
as a measure of the spare capacity left after Task A has been
performed.

This idea may be used to indicate that 'non-intellectual' and
intellectual tasks do draw on the same source of attentional
resources. In a study in our own laboratory (Hunt, 1980) students
solved problems from the Raven Matrices test of non-verbal
reasoning (Raven, 1941). The problems were presented in ascending
order of difficulty. While the people worked on the problem they
also attempted to hold a small lever between two posts. (The
lever position was indicated auditorily, to avoid visual
structural interference.) As the problems became harder hand
tremor increased. In fact, the degree of hand tremor could be
used as a sign that a person was about to make an error on the
mental problem.

A subsequent study used a somewhat more sophisticated variant of
the dual task design. Task A was a verbal memory task, and task B

was a button pressing response to a visual probe. The verbal memory task could be either an easy or a hard one. Performance on the _hard_ version of the verbal memory task was predicted by combining performance on the easy verbal memory task, done alone, and performance on the response task when done in conjunction with the easy verbal memory task. The rationale was that a measure of the spare capacity available during the easy version of the primary task should predict how much more attentional power could be brought to bear if the primary task became harder. In general the predictions were borne out. Easy memorization task performance and the reaction time to the probe provided independent contributions to the prediction of performance on the hard version of the memory task, done alone. This was interpreted as evidence that the hard version of the task taxed participants in two ways; by drawing on their task specific memorization skills and by drawing on their general attentional resources (Lansman and Hunt, 1982).

Studies such as this are fine when they work. Indeed, it is possible to consider using the secondary task paradigm to measure spare capacity in situations in which a person could not be tested directly by increasing the processing load in the primary task. On the other hand, there are a number of methodological problems associated with the interpretation of results when the "easy to hard" paradigm does not produce positive results. For instance, in our own work the "easy to hard" prediction was not confirmed when a visual memory task was substituted for the verbal memory task (Lansman and Hunt, 1982). The failure to find results in specific versions of the "easy to hard" paradigm is probably due to the simplistic, single resource view of attention on which the paradigm is based. The logic of a secondary task study required that each task draw upon the same, generalized attentional resources. This is the reason that very simple tasks, such as probe reaction tests are used as secondary tasks. The experimenter wants to minimize individual differences in the skills required to execute the secondary task, so that it becomes a pure measure of generalized attention. Unfortunately, even an apparently innocuous change in a task can alter its resource demands drastically. For instance, suppose that the primary task is a stimulus matching task similar to those illustrated in Figure 2, and the secondary task is either auditory or manual identification of probe. The reaction times of manual responses will be increased if the probe is presented during the stimulus comparison stage, but auditory response times are not influenced (McLeod, 1978). Such results cannot be reconciled with the view that attention is a unitary resource. But if one wants to argue for a multiple resource theory some rules must be given for specifying what the various resource pools are, and what sorts of tasks draw upon each pool. Another problem with the direct measurement of attentional capacity in the dual task paradigm is that the instructions themselves provide participants with a logical paradox. The participant is told to give first priority to ensuring performance on the primary task, and to do the secondary task with whatever resources are left over. From a strictly logical viewpoint, why should the secondary task be done at all? Kerr (1973) pointed out that the only way the experimenter can be sure that the participant is literally following instructions is to show that performance on the primary task, in the presence of the secondary task, is equivalent to performance on the primary task alone. In fact, some deterioration in primary task performance is almost always observed. This means either that the participant is not following instructions or that the participant does not have complete control over the allocation of attention to the two tasks. Of course, individual differences in the ability to control attention represent an interesting source of variation in themselves, as discussed below. However individual variations in the control of attention are not logically identical to individual differences in attentional capacity.

In spite of the appeal of the concept of attention as mental power, it appears that behavioral measures of attentional capacity do not greatly illuminate our understanding of individual differences in attention. The problem seems to be that the link between performance and attention allocation is so mediated by strategies, experience, and individual differences in the priority given to a task that performance itself is an inadequate measure of the attention committed to a task. It is possible that a physiological measure of attention, such as the pupillary response (Ahern and Beatty, 1981) could serve as a measure of an individual's commitment of attention to a task. Before such measures could be terribly useful in research that is based on an anlysis of individual differences, however, it will be necessary to develop a fairly complete measurement model relating the physiological observations to one's concept of attention.

Time Sharing

An alternative to equating attention with power is to study the ability to control attention when people are asked to do multiple tasks more or less simultaneously. The presumed trait of managing multiple tasks will be referred to as "time sharing ability", by analogy to the management of multiple users in a time-shared computing system. But does the putative ability exist? One can imagine a straightforward way to answer this question. Consider two tasks, A and B, that can be performed either alone or simultaneously. Let r(alone) be the correlation between the two tasks, measured alone, and r(together) be the correlation between the two tasks when done simultaneously. The first correlation should depend only upon the correlation between abilities required to do each task, while the second correlation should depend upon this correlation and the subject's ability to "time share" concurrent activities. Hence if the latter ability exists the r(together) correlation should be greater than the r(alone) correlation.

To be concrete, let us consider a study by Stankov (1983 a,b) of time sharing of auditory memory tasks. In his chord memory task people heard two chords, and were to indicate whether there had been a pitch change. The tonal memory required memory for the order of a series of tones. In the dual task conditions the stimuli for both tasks were given. Following stimulus presentation the subjects were cued to respond to one or the other task. Stankov found that between task correlations in the dual condition did, indeed, increase beyond those found in the single task condition. This finding was replicated, (with some reservations) in a subsequent study that used more tasks, and that paired memory for letter and tone series, (Fogarty and Stankov, 1982). Stankov has argued that such findings indicate that the dual task must depend more on a general factor than do the single tasks. In fact, he has suggested that this is evidence that competing tasks draw on a general intelligence factor (Stankov, 1983b, p. 480).

Unfortunately, it is not at all clear that Stankov's results are consistent with a 'power' concept of either intelligence or attention. Stankov (1983 a,b) has argued that when faced with a dual task people adopt consistent (over trials) strategies for attacking them. Suppose that this is true, and that both tasks draw on the same attentional resources. Since the two components of a dual task compete for attention there would be a built-in within-subjects negative correlation between performance on each component, across trials. The more attention is focused on one task, the worse performance on the other task should be. The within subjects negative correlation would generalize across subjects if different people consistently adopted different priorities for each task. This is not what was observed; component correlations increased or stayed the same in the dual task condition.

There is an alternative model that can explain Stankov's results by assuming only specific task abilities and an ability to control attention allocation. Consider again two individuals working on a letter and a tonal memory task. This time, though, suppose that the two people differ in their ability to do the tonal memory task, but are identical in their ability to perform the letter memory task, and in their attentional resources. Since there would be no variance in the letter memory task, done alone, its correlation with tonal memory would be zero. However, in the dual task condition the person with superior tonal memory might be able to attain a given level of performance on that task with a low expenditure of attentional resources, thus leaving more resources available for the letter memory task. Depending upon the priorities that each individual assigned to the two tasks, and the particular form of the relationship between component task performance and attentional resources assigned to that component, correlations between any pair of dual task components might increase, decrease, or stay the same. Note that this is true in a situation in which it has been assumed that there is no specific time sharing ability and in which subjects are assumed to be equal in general attentional resources.

Stankov's work is only one example of a number of studies that have attempted to define a time sharing ability by examination of changes in pairwise correlations between tasks done alone and as components of a dual task. In addition to a simple examination of changes in correlations, various methods have been proposed to extract "pure" measures of time sharing ability by computing some joint function of scores on two tasks done together and alone.

Ackerman, Schneider, and Wickens (1984) presented a critique of much of this work, and developed a good case for regarding all of the measures as deficient. They concluded that the case for the existence of a time sharing ability was neither made nor disproven by the study of alterations in correlations between pairs of tasks.

Ackerman et al. went on to point out that if a time sharing ability exists it should appear in a variety of different combinations of tasks. Consider, for example, a study with four tasks, A, B, C, and D. The tasks can be combined in six different ways, producing twelve additional scores, A(B) for the score on task A when done in combination with task B, A(C) for the same tasks done in combination with task C, and so forth. If a general time sharing factor exists it should contribute to the variance in performance of all tasks done in the presence of other tasks, and might or might not be correlated with performance on the various tasks done alone. Figure 4 illustrates this reasoning graphically.

Ackerman et al. used the Procrustean method of factor analysis to see if a time sharing factor defined in this way could be in data that had previously been reported as failures to obtain evidence for time sharing from the pattern of pairwise correlations. A factor structure similar to that shown in Figure 4 was found, although the contribution of the time sharing factor to

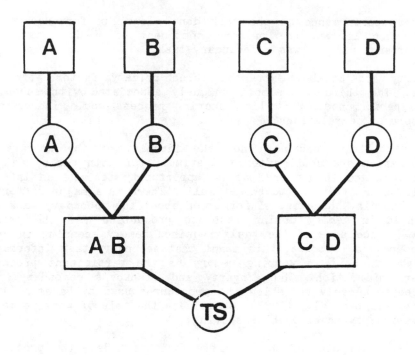

Figure 4   Timesharing across tasks

performance on the various tests was small.

Stankov (whose work was not reviewed by Ackerman et al.) made a similar use of factor analysis to define a time sharing factor in his studies. The results reported in his first study (Stankov, 1983a) are rather ambiguous. Some of the results of the second study (Fogarty and Stankov, 1982) lead to an interesting conjecture about the process of time sharing. To explain the problem, the procedure of the Fogarty and Stankov study must be considered in some detail.

In the dual task conditions of the Fogarty and Stankov study participants were first presented with the stimuli from both components of the dual task; e.g. both a sequence of tones and a sequence of letters. They were then given a cue indicating which task was to be given priority. The participant then gave the responses appropriate for that task. After the response for the priority tasks had been made the participant gave the responses required for the secondary task. Thus each task produces three scores; performance on the task done alone, performance on the task when it was the primary component of a dual task, and performance when it was a secondary task.

Fogarty and Stankov extracted three primary factors from the data. The third was almost uniquely associated with secondary task performance. What time sharing process would induce this pattern of correlations?

The participant did not know the identity of the primary and secondary tasks until after the stimuli for both tasks had been received, and thus there was no opportunity to make an informed decision in attending to the stimuli. There is a major difference in responding, however. Information about the secondary task must be held in memory during response production for the primary task. Since some of the tasks required memory scanning in order to compose a response, this meant that secondary task information had to be held in working memory as the participant processed other information. Thus Fogarty and Stankov's secondary task procedure closely resembles the procedures used by Daneman (1984) and by Klapp et al. (1983) to evaluate the role of working memory in various types of problem solving.

From the viewpoint of the cognitive science model, the procedures used by Fogarty and Stankov, Daneman, and Klapp et al. tap an information processing feature that must be vital in any time sharing activity. Return again to the example of an aviator flying in heavy traffic. The aviator must be able to hold messages from air traffic control in working memory while operating the aircraft. On demand information from one source must be used to construct a response to a query from another source. All this must be done without confusing identities of various packets of information in working memory. As was pointed out earlier, there is something to the confusion theory of dual task performance.

In discussing the role of working memory in dual task execution we have moved away from trying to determine the existence of a time sharing ability to considering the information handling processes that make up the ability. The next subsection considers some relevant studies.

The Processes of Attention

In terms of the cognitive science model, "paying attention" to a task means that pattern recognition, production execution, and action are controlled by task relevant information. But this is an outcome. What are the processes that support it? The studies reported by Daneman, Fogarty and Stankov, and Klapp et al.

provide evidence that the ability to retain information in memory in the face of competing activities is one of the key aspects of attention. Are there other processes?

Gopher and his colleagues (Gopher and Kahneman, 1971; Gopher, 1982; Kahneman, Ben-Ashai, and Lotan, 1973) have argued that a major aspect of the control of attention, and by extension time-sharing ability, is the ability to shift attention from one component task to another. In terms of the cognitive science model, this means doing whatever is necessary to change the "program" (i.e. production system) that is controlling behavior from one task to another, when an appropriate signal is detected in the external environment. One need only consider the importance of an automobile driver's being able to shift attention from the radio to the road to appreciate how important attention shifting can be.

Gopher's case for the primacy of attention shifting rests almost exclusively on a series of studies using the dichotic listening paradigm. Gopher and Kahneman (1971) considered a two-part dichotic listening task. In the first part the participant memorised the numbers presented to one ear, ignoring letters or numbers presented to the other ear. Suppose that the right ear is to be monitored, and the stimulus sequence is

RIGHT EAR A,8,B,4,C,T

LEFT EAR T,B,5,A,6,R

At this point the listener should have responded with the sequence (8,4). After the sequence has been presented, but without warning, the listener receives a signal that either indicates that monitoring should continue in the right ear or that the listener should switch to the left ear. Suppose that the left ear is indicated. Digits are then presented in either ear, as in the example

RIGHT EAR 5,9,2

LEFT EAR 7,3,1.

At this point the listener should respond with the sequence (7,3,1). Since the successive numbers are presented rapidly (at about a one second interval between numbers) the listener must reorient him/herself to the appropriate input channel following receipt of the signal indicating the start of the second part of the experiment. Thus the number of errors made on the second part of the task is taken as an indication of the efficiency with which this orientation takes place.

The early papers on using this task reported some interesting between-groups differences that seemed to validate the task as a measure of attention. Pilots who flew high performance military aircraft were found to perform better on the task than did transport pilots, even though pilots as a group did quite well (Gopher and Kahneman, 1971). Correlations were also found between test performance and the accident records of professional drivers (Kahneman et al., 1973). Based on these studies the test has been studied as a potential device for selecting aviation candidates. The correlations between test performance and completion of military flight school are reliable but moderate (r = .3, Gopher, 1982).

Our interests here are in the theoretical interpretation of the dichotic listening task, rather than in its use as a personnel selection device. Gopher (1982) regards the task as a measure of the ability to direct attention in general, rather than as a measure of ability to attend to auditory signals. Put another way, Gopher has treated individual differences in dichotic listening as being due to the execution of an abstract information handling process, and not as being due to facility in handling a particular type of sensory signal.

Findings by Lansman, Poltrock, and Hunt (1983) indirectly question this view. Lansman and her colleagues observed that attention demanding tasks could be broken down into three general classes. In **monitoring** tasks one simply listens or watches for a target stimulus. In **focussed attention** tasks the observer monitors the occurence of targets on a particular channel, ignoring information on the other channel. Finally, in **divided attention** tasks the observer monitors two or more channels at once, and must report targets wherever they may appear. Obviously, though, this classification of tasks in terms of process is orthogonal to a classification of tasks in terms of stimulus modality. One can think of monitoring, divided, and focussed attention tasks in either the visual or auditory modality.

In Lansman et al.'s study observers performed six different tasks: monitoring, focussed and divided attention tasks involving either visual or auditory stimuli. Several factor structures were explored as summaries of the between task correlations. Figure 5 shows the factor structure that was by far the best fit to the data. This structure contains correlated factors for visual and auditory attention, but it does not contain factors for the separate processes. Most importantly, the two factors for "auditory" and "visual" attention, although correlated, are clearly distinct. Lansman and her colleagues found that a single factor model could not fit their data.

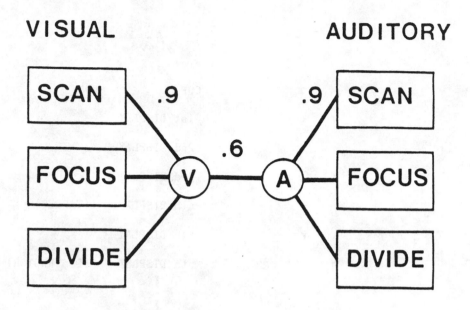

VISUAL

AUDITORY

Figure 5 Lansman et. al's factor
structure

Lansman et al.'s conclusions are contrary to Gopher's contention that there is a cross-modality "attention shifting" trait that, in effect, is the essence of attention. Lansman et al. did not use the precise one developed by Gopher, and for what reason their findings are not directly inconsistent with his. Hunt and Farr (1984) addressed the issue somewhat more directly.

Hunt and Farr combined Gopher's exact task with a visual analog of it. The procedure for the visual analog is shown in Figure 6. Each trial consisted of the presentation of two arrows, one pointing up and one pointing down, followed by either two letters or a letter and a number. Prior to the trial, the observer was told to report any numbers that appeared immediately following an upward (or downward) pointing arrow. Thus "direction of preceeding arrow" plays the role of "ear" in the Gopher paradigm. In part II of the trial the observer was either signalled to continue monitoring numbers that followed the same arrow, or the observer was switched from the "up" to the "down" arrow or vice versa.

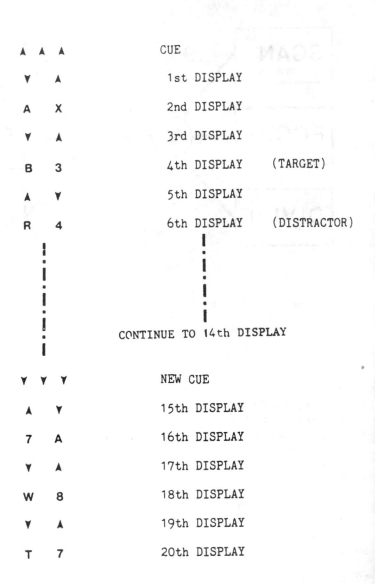

Figure 6 Hunt & Farr procedure

There was a correlation of .48 between performance on the auditory and visual attention switching tasks. While this correlation is substantial, it is less than would be expected if the tasks measured exactly the same trait. (In this case the between task correlation should approximate the product of the reliabilities of the two tasks, i.e. a correlation of about .7 should be observed.)

Hunt and Farr then constructed what amounted to a semantic attention switching task. Observers were asked to verify the truth of arithmetic statements. To illustrate, a sequence might be

$$8 + 1 = 9$$
$$3 + 5 = 7$$
$$4 + 2 = 6$$
$$2 \times 4 = 6.$$

Obviously the answers to the verification questions are True, False, True, and False. But consider the last item. The answer to this item would be "True" if the operation were addition instead of muliplication. Hunt and Farr's sequence of presentation first established a "set" for one type of arithmetic operation, and then switched to another. Because the subject had to override the established set, Hunt and Farr referred to such items as "Stroop" problems. There was a correlation of .45 between the time required to solve "Stroop" problems and the number of errors committed in Part II of the Gopher auditory attention switching procedure.

In summary, the ability to control attention seems to be partly a modality specific effect, and partly a general ability. To the extent that the general ability is involved, the key processes seem to be the management of information in working memory and the ability to switch rapidly from attending to one type of stimulus to attending to another. But is this all that there is to attention? The cognitive science model at least suggests that the experimental studies may have ignored an important variable. Describing what it might be provides a way to reprise much of the argument for a cognitive science view of intelligence.

Strategies and attention. Some speculative remarks

A computational approach to cognition stresses two things about any task; the effectiveness of the functional machinery that the person applies to the task, and the appropriateness of the cognitive program that controls the machinery. Studies of complex problem solving, where individual differences are very large, have shown that variation in both a person's functional machinery and controlling programs exert influences on gross performance. In some cases efficiency in one area can be traded for inefficiency in another.

Studies of attention have focussed almost exclusively on individual differences at the functional machinery level. This may be because studies of attention have developed from an experimental psychology/human engineering tradition rather than an academic selection tradition. In experimental psychology experiments are typically set up so that the way in which the subject has to do the task is under the control of the experimenter. Our interest is in how well a person performs some information processing act, conditional upon our having specified what that action is. In time sharing studies, for instance, great effort is made to ensure that the subject knows what the intra-task priorities are, and how well he or she is maintaining these priorities. Damos, Smist, and Bittner (1983) commented that the resulting experiments have yielded no evidence whatsoever for a "control of attention" trait. Given the results we have cited, several of which were published after Damos et al.'s statement, this position is a bit extreme. It is true that the generally small effect of time sharing and/or generalized attentional traits confounds our intuitions about individual differences in attention.

The experimental psychologists' efforts to control the situation may have thrown at least part of the baby out with the bath. To the extent that individual differences in the strategic way that people deal with time sharing situations control behavior, the sorts of tasks that have been studied are simply the wrong tasks. Damos and her collaborators (Damos and Wickens, 1980; Damos et al., 1983) have illustrated this by examining the effect of response strategies on a dual task. The task itself involved simultaneous presentation of a visual classification problem on one side of a computer screen, and a digit memory task on the other side. Participants could either respond more or less simultaneously to the stimuli in each task, or could mass a number of responses to one task, followed by a burst or responses to the other. Subjects adopted one or the other strategy. Performance on the simultaneous strategy was much more effective in the dual task mode (Damos and Wickens, 1980). Furthermore, people who spontaneously adopted the massed strategy had difficulty shifting to the alternating strategy. Since there were no differences between subjects in performance on either task, done singly, the observed difference was clearly in the qualitative way in which the participants reacted to the combined task, rather than in their ability to do the individual tasks.

The classification and memory task that Damos used is well within the experimental psychology tradition of rapid stimulus presentation and highly speeded responding. If subject strategies are a major factor in dual task performance in this sort of situation, they are probably much more important in extra-laboratory dual task performance. Think again of the often-used example of driving a car while talking or listening to the radio. Part of the trick in safe driving is to know when to stop talking and/or to turn off the radio. Even in aviation there are relatively few situations in which responses to two separate tasks must be made within fractions of a second. Both pilots and busy executives have some freedom to schedule their activities. The study of how they use this freedom is in its infancy.

CONCLUDING REMARKS

Although the idea that there are important individual differences in attention is an old one, the formal study of these differences is a relatively recent development. The early studies were attempts to show that a presumed trait existed, and to find good measures of it. Subsequently research has been directed at cataloging the microscopic information handling processes that underlie the trait, and finding which of them are responsible for individual differences at a more global level. Reviews of studies of other fields of cognition, such as verbal comprehension, spatial reasoning, induction, or deductive reasoning, would show the same sequence of events.

As the sequence unfolds what happens to the concept of attention? Or of verbal comprehension? Or of intelligence itself? The idea of a trait gives way to a very complex picture of somewhat correlated component skills that have to be assembled to do any one task. This sequence of events has been questioned by Jensen (1984), who has argued that the existence of a substantial positive manifold in measures of intellectual performance, plus the observed correlation between a general intelligence test factor and fairly simple tests of choice reaction time, can be taken as evidence that nature is fairly simple and that it is possible to speak of a generalized intellectual capacity.

The contrast between Jensen's position and the cognitive science position is not based on a (major) disagreement over facts. The general factor in intelligence tests clearly exists, and this statistical fact may be useful in personnel classification. The cognitive science approach is to try to understand why it exists. According to the standard theory espoused here, cognitive performance is produced by a program of the mind, using the mind's functional machinery. The brain's actual machinery determines how they will be used. Since the program is dependent on learning, human cognition is not pre-ordained by the physical state of the brain. Nor is cognition independent of that state. Some learned programs can greatly alter the effectiveness of a fixed machine, but in the end, the characteristics of the machine will determine what programs are possible.

The cognitive science approach will be of great help in tracing out these complex interactions. It will not help in providing a simple, easily understood measure of intelligence. The search for such a measure may well be misguided.

Acknowledgement Note

Preparation of this paper was supported by The Office of Naval Research, Contact Number N00014-84-K-0003 to the University of Washington. The opinions expressed are solely those of the Author.

REFERENCES

Ackerman, P.L. & Schneider, W. (1985). Individual Differences in Automatic and Controlled Processing. In R.F. Dillon (Ed.). Individual Differences in Cognition. New York: Academic Press

Ackerman, P.L., Schneider, W. & Wickens, C.D. (1984). Deciding the existence of time-sharing ability: A combined methodological and theoretical appraoch. Human Factors, 26, (1) 71-82.

Ahern, S. & Beatty, J. (1981). Physiological Evidence that demand for processing capacity varies with intelligence. In M.P. Friedman, J.P. Das, and N. O'Connor (Eds.) Intelligence and Learning. London: Plenum.

Allport, D.A. (1980). Attention and Performance. In Claxton, G. (Ed.) Cognitive Psychology: new Directions. London: Routledge and Kegan Paul.

Anderson, J.R., (1983). The Architecture of Cognition. Cambridge, MA: Harvard University Press.

Ashby, W.R. (1960). Design for a brain. (2nd Ed.). New York: Wiley.

Baddeley, A.D. (1976). The Psychology of Memory. New York: Basic Books.

Binet, A., and Simon, T. (1905). The Development of Intelligence
    in Children. L'Annee Psychologie, 163-244.

Carroll, J.B. (1982). The Measurement of Intelligence. In R.J.
    Sternberg (Ed.) Handbook of Human Intelligence. Cambridge,
    England: Cambridge University Press.

Cattell, R.B. (1971). Abilities: Their Structure, Growth, and
    Action. Boston: Houghton-Mifflin.

Chase, W.G. & Ericsson, A. (1978). Acquisition of mnemonic system
    for digit span. Paper presented at the meeting of the
    Psychonomic Society, San Antonio, Texas.

Collins, A. & Loftus, E.F. (1975). A spreading-activation theory
    of semantic processing. Psychological Review, 82, 407-428.

Collins, A. and Quillian, M.R. (1969). Retrieval time from
    semantic memory. Journal of Verbal Learning and Verbal
    Behavior, 8, 240-247.

Damos, D.L., Smist, T.E., and Bittner, A.C. (1983). Individual
    differences in multiple task performance as a function of
    response strategy. Human Factors, 25, (2), 215-226.

Damos, D.L. and Wickens, C.D. (1980). The identification and
    transfer of timesharing skills. Acta Psychologica, 46,
    15-39.

Daneman, M. (1984). Why some people are better readers than
    others: A process and storage account. In R.J. Sternberg
    (Ed.) Advances in the Psychology of Human Intelligence. (Vol.
    2). Hillsdale, N.J: L. Erlbaum Associates.

Davies, D.R. & Parasuraman, R. (1982). The Psychology of
    Vigilance. London: Academic Press.

Duncan, J. (1980). The locus of interference in the perception of
    simultaneous stimuli. Psychological Review, 87, 272-300.

Fogarty, G. & Stankov, L., (1982). Competing tasks as an index of
    intelligence. Personality and individual differences, 3,
    407-422.

Gieselman, R.E., Woodward, J.A. and Beatty, J. (1982). Individual
    differences in memory performance: A test of alternative
    information processing models. Journal of Experimental
    Psychology: General, 111, 109-134.

Gopher, D. (1982). A selective attention test as a predictor of success in flight training. Human Factors, 24, (2) 173-183.

Gopher, D. and Kahneman, D. (1971). Individual differences in attention and the prediction of flight criteria. Perceptual and Motor Skills, 33, 1335-1342.

Guilford, J.P. (1967). The nature of human intelligence. New York: McGraw-Hill.

Hirst, W., Spelke, E.S., Reaves, G.C., Caharack, G., & Neisser, U. (1980). Dividing attention without alternation or automaticity. Journal of Experimental Psychology: General, 109, 98-117.

Hodge, P.W. (1984). The Universe of the Galaxies. San Francisco: Freeman Press.

Horn, J.L. (1982). The theory of fluid and crystalized intelligence in relation to concepts of cognitive psychology and aging in adulthood. In Aging and Cognitive Processes. F.I.M. Craik & S. Trehumb (Eds.) Plenum Publishing Corporation.

Horn, J.L. & Donaldson, G. (1979). Cognitive development II: Adulthood development of human abilities. In O.B. Brim, Jr. and J. Kagan (Eds.) Constancy and change in human development. New York: Academic Press.

Hunt, E., (1980). Intelligence as an information processing concept. British Journal of Psychology, 71, 449-474.

Hunt, E., (1981). The design of a robot mind: A theoretical approach to issues in intelligence. In M. Friedman, J.P. Das, & M. O'Connor (Eds.), Intelligence and Learning. New York: Plenum.

Hunt, E. and Farr, S. (1984). Individual Differences in Attention Proceedings of the Psychonomoic Society Annual Meeting (abstract).

Hunt, E. (1987). The next word on Verbal Ability. In P.E. Vernon (Ed.) Speed of Information Processing and Intelligence. New Jersey: Ablex.

Hunt, E. & Lansman, M. (1982). Individual differences in attention. In R.J. Sternberg (Ed.) Psychology of Human Intelligence. Hillsdale, NJ: Erlbaum Associates.

Hunt, E. & Lansman, M., (1985). A unified model of attention and problem solving   Psychological Review (in press).

Jensen, A.R. (1984). Test Validity: g versus the specificity doctrine. Journal of Social and Biological Structure, 7, 93-118.

Jensen, A.R., (1982). The Chronometry of intelligence. In R.J. Sternberg (Ed.) Recent Advances in Research on Intelligence, Vol. I. Hillsdale, NJ: Erlbaum Associates.

Jensen, A.R. (1981). Reaction time and intelligence. In M. Friedman, J.P. Das & N. O'Connor (Eds.) Intelligence and Learning. New York: Plenum.

Kahneman, D. (1973). Attention and effort.   Englewood Cliffs, N.J: Prentice-Hall.

Kahneman, D., Ben-Ishai, R. and Lotan, M. (1973). Relation of a test of attention to road accidents. Journal of Applied Psychology, 58, 113-115.

Kerr, B. (1973). Processing demands during mental operations. Memory and Cognition, 1, 901-912.

Kerr, B., Condon, S. & McDonald, L.A., (1985). Cognitive spatial processing and the regulation of posture. Journal of Experimental Psychology: Human Percpetion and Performance, 11, (5) 617-622.

Klapp, S.T., Marshburn, L.E.A., & Lester, P.J., (1983), Short term memory does not involve the 'working memory' of information processing: The decline of a common assumption, Journal of Experimental Psychology: General, 112, 240-264.

Kolers, P.A. & Smythe, W.E. (1984). Symbol manipulation: Alternative to the computational view of mind. Journal of Verbal Learning and Verbal Behavior, 23, 289-314.

Kosslyn, S.L. (1980). Image and Mind. Cambridge, MA: Harvard University Press.

Lansman, M. & Hunt, E. (1982). Individual differences in secondary task performance. Memory & Cognition, 10, 10-24.

Lansman, M. Pultruck, S.E. & Hunt, E.B. (1983). Individual differences in the ability to focus and divide attention. Intelligence, 7, 299-312.

McLeod, P.D. (1978). Does probe RT measure central processing demands? Quarterly Journal of Experimental Psychology, 30, 83-89.

McDermott, J. & Forgy, C. (1978). Production system conflict resolution strategies. In D.A. Waterman & F. Hayes-Roth (Eds.) Pattern directed inference systems.. New York: Academic Press.

McNemar, Q. (1964) Lost: Our Intelligence? Why? American Psychologist, 19, 871-882.

Matarazzo, J.D. (1972). Wechsler's measurement and appraisal of adult intelligence. (5th Ed.) Baltimore: Williams and Wilkins.

Navon, D. & Gopher, D. (1979). On the economy of the human processing system. Psychological Review, 86, 214-255.

Neisser, U. (1976). Cognition and reality. San Francisco: Freeman Press.

Newell, A. (1973). Production Systems: Models of control structures. In W.G. Chase (Ed.) Visual Information Processing. New York: Academic Press.

Newell, A. & Simon, H. (1972). Human Problem Solving, Englewood Cliffs, NJ: Prentice-Hall, Inc.

Norman, D.A. & Bobrow, D.B., (1975). On data limited and resource limited processes. Cognitive Psychology, 7, 44-64.

Pachella, R.G., (1974). The interpretation of reaction time in information processing research. In B.H. Kantowitz (Ed.) Human Information Processing: Tutorials in Performance and Cognition. Hillsdale, NJ: Erlbaum Associates.

Palmer, J.C., MacLeod, C.M., Hunt, E. & Davidson, J. (1985). Information processing correlates of reading. Journal of Verbal Learning and Verbal Behavior.

Parasuraman, R. (1979). Memory load and event rate control sensitivity decrements in sustained attention. Science, 31, 924-927.

Pylyshyn, Z.W. (1983). Computation and Cognition. Cambridge, Mass: Bransford Press.

Posner, M.I., (1978), Chronometric explorations of mind. Hillsdale, NJ: Erlbaum Associates.

Raven, J.C. (1941). Standardization of progressive matrices 1938. British Journal of Medical Psychology, 19, 137-150.

Schneider, W. & Shiffrin, R.M. (1977). Controlled and automatic human information processing: I. Detection, search and attention. Psychological Review, 84, 1-66.

Spearman, C. (1927). The abilities of man. New York: MacMillan.

Stankov, L., (1983)(a). The rule of competition in human abilities revealed through auditory tests. Multivariate Behavioral Research Monogrpahs, 83-1.

Stokov, L. (1983)(b) Attention and Intelligence J. Educational Psychology, 75 (4) 471-490.

Sternberg, R.J. (1982). Reasoning, problem solving and intelligence. In R.J. Sternberg (Ed.) Handbook of Human Intelligence. Cambridge: Cambridge University Press.

Sternberg, R.J. Conway, B.E., Ketron, J. L. and Bernstein, M. (1981). People's conceptions of intelligence. Journal of Personality and Social Psychology, 91, (1) 37-55.

Thibadeau, R., Just, M.A., & Carpenter, P.A. (1982). A mind of the time course and content of reading, Cognitive Science, 6, 157-203.

Thurstone, L.L., (1938). Primary mental abilities. Psychometric Monographs, No. 1. Chicago: University of Chicago Press.

Vernon, P.E. (1983). Speed of information processing and general intelligence. Intelligence, 7, 53-70.

Wechsler, D. (1975). Intelligence defined and redefined: A relativistic appraisal. American Psychologist, 30, 135-139.

Wickens, C.D. (1979). The structure of attentional resources. In R.S. Nickerson (Ed.) Attention and Performance VIII. Hillsdale, N.J: L. Erlbaum Assoc.

Wickens, C.D. (1984). Engineering Psychology and Human Performance, Columbus, Ohio: Merrill.

CHAPTER 5

PSYCHOMETRIC APPROACHES TO COGNITIVE ABILITIES AND PROCESSES

JOHN B. CARROLL

The L.L. Thurstone Psychometric Laboratory

University Of North Carolina, U.S.A.

INTRODUCTION

In formulating an approach to the study of intelligence and cognitive abilities that will be in harmony with present theoretical and empirical trends, I believe it is essential to build upon what has been said and done on this topic in the past. In the 80 years since Spearman's (1904) introduction of a truly psychometric approach to intelligence, there has been much activity - an almost overwhelming outpouring of empirical findings, theory, and speculation. It would be foolhardy and indeed tragic to regard all this as being for naught; surely there is much that can be depended on, much to savour and reconsider, much to guide our current efforts. But there is also the need to re-evaluate the work of the past, to consider it in the light of methodologies that have become refined and much advanced over those utilized in former days. I begin with a reassessment of past work, based largely on a series of reanalyses of previously reported studies. That is followed by an exposition of a test analysis procedure that I believe has promise for bridging the gap that has often been recognized between purely psychometric approaches and approaches from experimental cognitive psychology. Finally, I attempt to outline the possible directions that future work might take in attempting better to understand the nature of cognition and cognitive ability.

My somewhat limited goal is, in fact, merely to arrive at a perspective on the nature of cognition, on the fact of individual differences in cognitive abilities and in individual's rates of development in these abilities, and on ways of assessing and measuring these things. Whether all this can lead to what can be called a theory of intelligence, I am not sure. I intend at least to outline my personal approach to the development of such a theory; the reader may judge the extent to which my approach has promise, in the light of other presentations and discussions in this volume.

FACTOR ANALYTIC INVESTIGATIONS OF COGNITIVE ABILITIES

Much of what we know, or think we know, about intelligence and
cognitive abilities derives from factor-analytic investigations
using psychological tests, and occasionally, other kinds of
observational data. Such investigations have been conducted in
several waves. We are all aware of the work of various British
statistical psychologists, principally Spearman (1927), in
indentifying a "general" factor of intelligence along with several
so-called group factors. Some of this work was echoed in the
United States with investigations by Kelley (1928) and by
Holzinger (1936). A second wave began with the classic work of
Thurstone (1931, 1938, 1947) culminating, one may say, in a series
of "kits" of factor-analytic marker tests of cognitive abilities
identified by Thurstonian methods and published by Educational
Testing Service (French, Ekstrom, & Price, 1963; Ekstrom, French,
& Harman, 1976). A third wave, overlapping with the second, and
indeed inspired by it, was initiated chiefly by J.P. Guilford,
first with his factor-analytic studies of aircrew classification
tests in World War II (Guilford & Lacey, 1947) and then with a
twenty-year study of "higher-level aptitudes" summarized in two
major publications (Guilford, 1967; Guilford & Hoepfner, 1971). A
fourth wave, perhaps not as vigorous as Guilford's but of serious
interest and promise, came with the work of Cattell and Horn on
cognitive abilities, summarized by Horn (1976, 1978) but
continuing with several major studies of recent vintage (Hakstian
& Cattell, 1974, 1978). It is perhaps unjust to speak of these
developments as "waves", for they are interrelated in complex
ways. Also, we must recognize that these waves, if such they
were, had parallels in factor-analytic work by investigators other
than those mentioned, in various countries - not only the United
States and Great Britain, but also including Australia, Canada,
France, Germany, Spain, Sweden, Yugoslavia, and even the Soviet
Union. I have attempted to compile a bibliography of
factor-analytic studies that have been done throughout the world;
I estimate that there are some 2000 studies relevant to cognitive
abilities, and even a greater number of datasets that have been
factor-analyzed and that might be candidates for further study and
analysis.

The basic scientific motives underlying these studies, it appears,
have been two: (a) the attempt to identify the "basic dimensions"
of cognitive abilities, and (b) the search for a meaningful and
interpretable "structure" of these abilities that would lead to a
theory of intelligence and cognition.

In the attempt to answer the first question - what are the basic
cognitive abilities? - the responses have ranged all the way from
Spearman's <u>initial</u> proposal that there is only one basic cognitive

ability, g, to Guilford's claim that there may be as many as 120
or more such abilities. To the outsider to the field, the
multiplicity of answers seems overwhelming, puzzling and even
suspect. Obviously, there is a need for clarity and resolution
here.

On the second question also - as to the "structure of abilities",
many proposals have been offered. The answer provided by Spearman
and his immediate followers - that there is a general factor, a
small number of group factors, and many specific factors - is
still recognized by some as the basis for an acceptable theory,
and certainly there is still much interest today in the nature and
importance of the general factor of intelligence (e.g., Detterman,
1982; Eysenck, 1982; Humphreys, 1979; Jensen, 1984). Thurstone did
not live to see the ways in which his theory of the structure of
intelligence developed into a kind of hierarchical theory, with
different levels of strata; the Cattell-Horn-Hakstian theory
concerning six or seven broad group factors, possibly but not
certainly dominated by a general factor, is only one
exemplification of this, represented at one stage in Cattell's
(1971) "triadic" theory of mental abilities. Vernon's (1961)
hierarchical theory is another exemplification of the same general
idea, although its methodological origins were different. The
answer took a markedly different form in Guilford's "Structure-of
Intellect" model, which he still defends staunchly (Guilford,
1979) even though he has recently admitted the existence of
"higher-order abilities" (Guilford, 1981). Obviously the question
of the "structure of intellect" needs further investigation and
resolution.

It can be debated, I suppose, whether these questions can ever be
answered in a satisfactory way, or even whether the questions
themselves are meaningful. If one reads some critics of factor
analysis (e.g. Sternberg, 1977, Chap. 2), one might conclude that
limitations of factor-analytic method preclude arriving at
satisfactory answers to either of the two questions I have
mentioned. I grant that there are certain limitations in factor
analytic method - partly connected with its technical
difficulties, and partly arising out of the fact that at least in
the usual R-technique it must necessarily deal with data from
groups of subjects. I do not feel, however, that these
limitations are so serious as to suggest dismissing
factor-analytic results altogether; quite the contrary. With
proper use, factor analysis can yield replicable and verifiable
findings that command respect. I also believe that
factor-analytic methodology has advanced and matured sufficiently
to permit deriving, through examination of past studies, at least
some reasonably secure answers to both the questions I have
mentioned above - answers that will contain clear and important

information for furthering the study of cognitive abilities. It will of course be necessary to supplement this information from other sources, some of which I will mention, but the factor-analytic information cannot be dismissed as irrelevant or meaningless.

Acting on these beliefs, I have undertaken to examine, and in many cases to reanalyze, data from a substantial proportion of the major factor-analytic investigations extant in the literature, going back even to studies completed in the early days of this type of inquiry. For this purpose I have selected approximately 300 datasets to look at, a "dataset" consisting of a correlation matrix for a specified number of variables as applied to a specified sample of individuals. At this time I can make only a preliminary, somewhat impressionistic report of my findings, partly because my project is still in progress, and partly because the sheer volume of results attained thus far is already far greater than I could include here.

Methodology

Some remarks are in order concerning the methodology I have been employing. In the main, I have used techniques of <u>exploratory</u> rather than <u>confirmatory</u> factor analysis, not only because these techniques are more traditional and well-advanced, but also because they are easier and less expensive of time, money and effort to apply (Carroll, 1985). Also, I believe that ready use of confirmatory techniques requires preliminary analyses by exploratory techniques, and that the pattern of results attained by exploratory techniques can approximate those verified by confirmatory techniques. I have adopted certain standard exploratory procedures, which include the following principal steps, from which I must omit many details:

1. Principal factoring (rather than principal component analysis) of the original correlation matrix with iteration for communalities until no difference between successive communalities exceeds .0005 in absolute value.

2. Choice of the number of factors, in the principal factoring procedure, according to several guidelines, including Cattell's (1966, 1978) screen test and Montanelli and Humphreys' (1976) parallel analysis criterion. Generally, several values of the number of factors are tried, and the final solution is based upon the largest number of factors that produces acceptable convergence of communalities (without a Heywood case) and also at least two loadings, for each factor, that are absolutely highest for a variable, and thus "salient". This guideline tends to restrict analysis to the larger, more important factors and to eliminate

many specific and presumably unimportant factors.

3. Rotation to oblique simple structure, where this seems to be called for, by an objective, replicable procedure that seems most generally to lead to the most acceptable second- and higher-order structures. For this purpose I have used a procedure recently developed by Tucker and Finkbeiner (1981), called "direct artificial personal probability function rotation" (DAPPFR). As the result of experimentation with this method on a variety of datasets I have, however, chosen parameters for it different from those initially recommended by these authors.

4. Where appropriate, hierarchical analysis of second- and higher-order structures with orthogonalization of rotated factor matrices by the method of Schmid and Leiman (1957).

It may be of interest to mention that my factor-analytic procedures have been programmed for a microcomputer (Apple II+), and except for the initial factoring of large matrices (generally, those with more than 30 variables), my computations have been performed by microcomputer - thus, incidentally, saving considerable computer expense despite the somewhat increased time required.

Findings

My account of findings must be prefaced with some remarks on the various difficulties I have encountered in attempting to examine, re-analyze, and synthesize the studies extant in the literature. First of all, I may mention that many studies are not sufficiently well reported, in an accessible form, to make me feel that I know exactly what was done in these studies. Even when the reports appear to be very full and extensive, there are usually details missing, largely because space limitations in journal articles, monographs, and project reports appear to have precluded giving those details. For example, tests are often mentioned only by name; one must search other literature for adequate descriptions. Even when a test is described in more detail, with illustrative items, one cannot really be confident in inferring what the test as a whole was like, or what it measured. Interpretation of factorial findings is therefore fraught with the danger of making misinterpretations solely due to lack of complete information.

Secondly, it is difficult to make generalizations across studies because the studies are often inherently noncomparable. For a particular study, batteries of tests and other variables have been assembled with a particular design in the investigator's mind - a design that may have been reasonable for the investigator's purpose, but that does not lead well to comparisons with designs and results of other studies. A factor that appears in one study may or may not be truly the same as one that appears in another study, even though there may have been some overlapping in the selections of test variables.

Comparison of studies becomes particularly difficult in assessing higher-order structures. Higher-order factors can be well defined only when there is a good selection of lower-order factors, i.e., in the usual case, "primary" or first-order factors. This is possible only with studies involving a large number of variables selected to define both first- and higher-order factors. As yet we have only a very few such studies, for obvious logistic reasons. Even Guilford's large correlation matrices are generally defective in this respect because most of them are focused on a limited domain of abilities, such as domains of reasoning, fluency, creativity, or memory, and contain insufficient markers of factors in other domains. Here I must rely considerably on hunches and speculative interpretation of available findings. There is clearly a need for further empirical work to specify more precisely how abilities are structured at the higher-order levels.

I could mention many other sorts of difficulties - for example, errors in published correlation matrices and test descriptions, insufficient specifications of samples tested, and factor-analytic procedures that I consider unwise or inappropriate. Of course, whenever in my opinion the factor analysis has been incomplete, or has been mishandled, I proceed to reanalyze the correlation matrix, sometimes dropping variables where I cannot correct errors. But in the frequent absence of information on the distribution characteristics of the variables and the linearity of regressions, I can only assume that matters have been properly taken care of in these respects.

In short, I have reluctantly come to the conclusion that despite its enormous volume, the factor-analytic literature is not truly adequate as a basis for reaching firm conclusions about the dimensionality and structuring of cognitive abilities. My findings and interpretations will necessarily be tentative and provisional at many points. It is not that I am faulting those who have poured their efforts into such investigations in the past; many of the gaps I now perceive have come to light only through my attempts to compare, reanalyze, and synthesize the available findings.

The dimensionality of cognitive abilities

Somewhat contrary to the presuppositions I had at the outset of my project, I am now inclined to conclude that the dimensionality of cognitive abilities is relatively limited. Certainly I find that there exists nothing like the large number of abilities postulated and claimed by Guilford (1967; Guilford & Hoepfner, 1971). When my criteria for number of factors are applied to the correlation matrices reported in Guilford's project, I find many fewer factors than he and his collaborators did. For example, in reanalyzing six of their datasets in the general domain of verbal ability and fluency, whereas the number of factors found by them ranged from 12 to 18, I found from 6 to 10. Even some of the factors I identified by my number-of-factors criteria turn out to be "specific" doublet factors associated with pairs of highly similar tests, such as alternate forms of the same test. I conclude that a large number of the factors claimed by Guilford and his associates are artifacts of their methods, or spurious resultants of inappropriate selections of variables to analyze. Although I have not yet taken the opportunity to apply statistical tests through LISREL-type confirmatory factoring, I believe that such an approach would support my supposition that many of the factors claimed by Guilford could not be upheld. At the same time, many of the factors that I <u>can</u> confirm from the Guilford studies are comparable to factors that I can confirm from studies of other investigators. Since I do not confirm Guilford's "structure-of-intellect", I see no need to use his tripartite system of designating those factors. (For example, his factor CMU - "cognition of semantic units"-is much more readily interpreted as identical or related to the Verbal or Verbal Comprehension factor found by many investigators.)

I am hesitant to list or describe the small number of factors that I believe can be confirmed from the available factor-analytic literature, because as previously stated, my project is not complete. Nevertheless, I present a highly provisional and deliberately incomplete list in Table 1, mainly in order to set the stage for later discussion. It will be seen that this list contains most (but not all) of the factors listed, for example, by Ekstrom (1979) in her review of the literature. The list is not unlike that presented more than thirty years ago by French (1951).

It appears that since the publication of French's review, few "new" factors have been disclosed, and factor interpretations have not been much refined. In some ways, this is discouraging; in other ways it is encouraging. It is discouraging because one would have thought that scientific efforts over more than thirty years would have been able to advance our knowledge to a greater extent than appears to have been the case. Does this mean that scientific efforts have been too limited, misguided, or otherwise deficient, or does it mean that the dimensionality of abilities is

Table 1

Tentative List of Factors, at Different Orders, Confirmed
by Re-analyses of Extant Factor-Analytic Literature
(First-order factors arranged under second-order factors)

"g" (3rd-order) General intelligence

Gf (2nd-order, possibly identical to g) Fluid intelligence
    I Induction
   RG General reasoning (mainly deductive)
   RL Logical reasoning
  IPA Information-processing accuracy
 IPSA Accuracy of semantic information processing

Gc (2nd-order) Crystallized intelligence
    V Verbal comprehension
   LX Lexical knowledge
   WS Word Sense (knowledge of properties of words)
   PC Phonetic coding
   GS Grammatical Sensitivity

Gv (2nd-order) General visual perception
   SR Spatial relations
   VZ Visualization
   CF Flexibility of closure
   CS Speed of closure

Ga (2nd-order) General auditory perception
   TT Temporal tracking
  DSP Discrimination among Sound Patterns (Pitch sense)
  SPD Speech Preception under Distraction
  MJR Maintaining and Judging Rhythm

Gs (2nd-order) General speed
    P Perceptual speed
   NA Naming speed
   RT Reaction time

Gi (2nd-order) General idea production (fluency)
   FA Associative fluency
   FE Fluency of expression
   FF Figural fluency
   FI Ideational fluency
   FS Speech fluency
   FW Word fluency
   FP Practical ideational fluency (sensitivity to problems,
                                        conceptual foresight)
    O Originality

Gm (2nd-order) General memory capacity
   MA Associative memory
   ME Episodic memory
   MS Memory span
   MV Visual memory

inherently so limited that even the best and most exhaustive scientific efforts would be unable to extend it? I am not yet sure of the answer to this question. In some areas or domains of ability, I believe the answer is that no effort could substantially modify the listings of factors available in the 1950s. In other domains - particularly those pertaining to temporal, speed, and auditory phenomena, for example, I believe that our efforts have been inadequate, and that there is much to be learned through careful empirical investigation.

The avowedly tentative conclusion that the dimensionality of cognitive ability is small and limited is encouraging, however, in the sense that it implies that we have less to deal with than we might have thought, in further studies of abilities - studies of their origins, their development, their modifiability, their uses and implications, and their theoretical interpretation. If there are no more than something like two or three dozen basic cognitive abilities, one can be more comfortable in contemplating such further studies than if, say, Guilford's claim of more than a hundred abilities were to turn out to be correct.

The structure of cognitive abilities

By the term "structure", I have reference to the factor-analytic model whereby abilities may be classified at different orders or "strata" such that some are more general than others, in short, the hierarchical model espoused by various writers like Vernon (1961) and Cattell (1971). A model of this general character is implied by the Schmid and Leiman (1957) method of hierarchical analysis that my research team has utilized whenever our rotational procedures yield factors that are substantially correlated. Let us recognize first of all that there is nothing sacred or fixed about the order at which a factor appears in the analysis of a particular dataset. A factor can appear at a primary or first order in one study, but at a second or higher order in another study, depending on what kinds of variables have been involved in the study. But further, I believe one should not assume that hierarchical structure implies what might be called a "strict" hierarchy whereby a factor at a higher order inherently subsumes factors at a lower order. Rather, I believe, hierarchy merely implies that some factors are more general than others, in the sense that they have loadings on a wider variety of variables (tests, or whatever). From the standpoint of factorial interpretation, this implies that some abilities enter into a wider variety of tasks than others. If there is a "general" factor of ability, as I believe is the case, it is the ability - whatever it is - that enters into the widest variety of cognitive tasks. But it is not the case that such a factor necessarily enters into all tasks, nor is it necessarily the case that a general factor subsumes all other cognitive factors. It is only a convenience to depict abilities through a "tree structure", as is often done, where each node dominates only a specific set of lower order abilities. The structure needs to be depicted more complexly, with crossovers between groups of factors shown as subsumed by different higher-order factors.

As I have already intimated, it has been very difficult to synthesize findings from the available literature to develop the true structure of factors of cognitive ability. Using evidence from different studies is a little like fitting together the pieces of a jigsaw puzzle, but actually much worse than that, because the pieces are at once incomplete, overlapping, and seemingly inconsistent. The difficulties stem not only from the incompleteness of the evidence but also from certain technical difficulties in applying hierarchical analysis. Nevertheless, certain findings begin to become clear.

It will probably be no surprise to report that there clearly exists a general factor of intelligence, that is, a source of variance that enters into a very wide variety of cognitive tasks, and into a very wide variety of factors at lower levels in the hierarchical structure. I am not in a position yet to say whether it enters into all cognitive tasks or factors; that would in any event be a matter of degree. That is, one should look at the proportion of variance in a particular variable that is accounted for by a general factor, if that general factor can be clearly identified in a particular dataset. Quite often, for example, one can identify only two uncorrelated 2nd-order factors in a study - looking like, say, the fluid and crystallized intelligences postulated by Cattell (1971); these factors can appear uncorrelated because of selectivity in the sample, or for other reasons. However, if these 2nd-order factors appear correlated, their covariance can be distributed into a 3rd-order factor, and depending on the interpretation of the 2nd-order factors, the 3rd-order factor can be regarded as a general factor. But the precise nature of the general factors found in different studies will depend upon the selection of variables in the study. Caution must be exercised in making too hasty cross-identifications of such factors.

Despite these difficulties and reservations, I will reiterate that the evidence appears to support the existence of a source of variance that is very general across cognitive tasks, whether they be of a "power" or "speed" variety. The proportions of variance accounted for in variables do vary widely, however, partly due to varying reliabilities of variables and partly due to inherent task characteristics.

At this point I wish to interject a comment on the widespread practice of reporting "proportions of total variance" accounted for by different factors in factorial studies. For example, it is frequently noted or reported that a general factor accounts for a very large proportion of total variance - e.g., 80%, while primary or group factors account for very little - e.g., 4 or 5 per cent apiece. Such a report leads many psychologists to believe that lower-order factors, especially first-order factors, are of little importance. Such a conclusion, I claim, is fallacious. The large proportion of total variance is replicated over many more variables, while the low proportions associated with primary or group factors is replicated over only a few variables. A more meaningful assessment of the relative importance of factors at different levels in the hierarchy can be made by considering the average proportions of variance contributed by factors at different levels. Examining a large number of datasets, I find that higher-level factors account on the average for only about half the common factor variance of the variables. In other words, higher- and first-order variables contribute about equal amounts of variance, and first-order or "group" factors deserve attention at least equal to that accorded to general factors.

While in a sermonizing mode, let me also state that I regard the frequent arguments over methods of factor analysis - e.g. the contrast between the methods of Burt and of Thurstone - as pointless. Using the hierarchical analysis method of Schmid and Leiman (1957), as I have been doing, one can convert a Thurstonian analysis almost precisely into one that would be achieved by Burt's methods. All my final interpretations are based on "orthogonalized" factor matrices with separate columns containing weights for factors at different levels in the hierarchy. Such matrices, when multiplied by their transposes, reproduce the corresponding correlation matrices precisely in the same way as do the corresponding unrotated principal factor matrices of equivalent rank. The number of columns in the orthogonalized matrices is, of course, greater than their rank. The advantage of these orthogonalized matrices is that the squares of the factor weights for a given variable immediately yield proportions of variance accounted for. These facts appear to have been overlooked in much factor-analytic literature, giving rise to unnecessary methodological controversy.

I am at this time really not in a position to specify the higher-order structure of cognitive abilities, that is, to list or recount the major sources of higher-order variance that I hope to identify in the factorial literature. My impression is, however, that besides a very general "g" factor the several "second-stratum" abilities identified by Hakstian and Cattell (1978) will be confirmed, perhaps not in the precise forms suggested by these authors, but at any rate in their general characteristics. "Fluid intelligence" frequently dominates primary factors of reasoning, induction, spatial relations, visualization, and perceptual speed - that is, any factor involving tasks demanding noticing and dealing with relationships. There will be a problem in deciding whether "fluid intelligence" (Gf) is really the same as Spearman's "g", as appears to be the case in a recent study reported by Gustafsson (1984). Gustafsson also confirmed the "crystallized intelligence" (Gc) and "visualisation capacity" (Gv) factors reported by Hakstian and Cattell. Crystallized intelligence tends to appear in tasks involving things learned from culture, such as vocabulary, general factors about mathematical and geometric relationships, and general information about the world. The visualization capacity factor tends to dominate tasks (and primary factors) involving visual perception.

Other second-order factors reported by Hakstian and Cattell include "general perceptual speed" (Gps), "general memory capacity" (Gm), and "general retrieval capacity" (Gr). My analyses suggest that factors similar to these can be confirmed in a wide variety of studies. For example, I can confirm a general memory capacity factor in reanalyses of studies by Kelley (1954) and by Underwood, Boruch, and Malmi (1978). Hakstian and Cattell's (1978) Gps factor seems to appear more generally as a "general speed factor" - with no necessary association with visual perceptual processes, however. Hakstian and Cattell's "general retrieval" (Gr) factor shows up in reanalyses of a number of Guilford and Hoepfner's (1971) studies, except that I prefer to call it something like "facility in production of ideas" or possibly, using Guilford's term, "divergent thinking". Undoubtedly still other important second-order factor sources of variances will appear in my reanalyses; I regret to say that I cannot yet suggest what these will be.

I do not find many surprises in my reanalyses; the picture of the structure of intelligence that emerges is very similar to those suggested by Cattell (1971; Horn, 1978) and by Vernon (1961). I would assume that my reanalyses might enable one to decide between these two models, or to achieve a higher-order synthesis (in the Hegelian sense - no pun intended).

DEFINING ABILITIES THROUGH THE PERSON CHARACTERISTIC FUNCTION

Factor analysis aids in identifying the dimensions of ability, and in understanding something about how general or specific these

abilities are with respect to the domain of possible cognitive
tasks. The mathematical parts of factor analysis do not, however,
indicate what these abilities are, or anything about their
nature. Traditionally, information of this character has been
developed by largely subjective interpretations of test content.
The procedure has been to examine the tests or variables having
high loadings or weights on a particular factor, contrasting these
tests with those having low or vanishing loadings on that factor.
One then attempts to infer what common elements are involved in
the high-loading tests and not in the low-loading tests or
variables. The elements (I use the term loosely and very
generally) might be areas of knowledge, strategies of test
performance, sensitivities to particular kinds of stimulus
characteristics, common aspects of motor response, and so on,
almost indefinitely. For example, it may appear that a group of
variables all put demands on knowledge of the subjects' native
language, especially its vocabulary and grammatic structure; the
inference is made, therefore, that these tests measure a factor of
"verbal ability". Another group of variables may appear to
require subjects to recall, from long term memory, and to write
down within a specified time-limit, as many instances as possible
of some category. The inference is therefore made, for example,
that these tests measure an "ideational fluency" factor.

This loose inferential process is involved also in the
construction of batteries for factor analysis studies. One
attempts to select or devise groups of variables that will
correlate highly among themselves, and thus define a factor,
because they all put similar demands on a particular hypothesized
ability, the ability being conceptualized in terms of some
particular common process, area of knowledge, or what not. Many
factor analysts have presumed that it is possible to test
hypotheses about the nature of abilities by devising tests that
contrast in particular ways, hoping to verify the hypothesized
contrasts through finding different factors associated with the
contrasting groups of variables. One can find in the factorial
literature at least some instances where this procedure seems to
have been successful. I do not believe, however, that it has been
carried through sufficiently. That is, there has been a failure
to conduct systematic and successsive factor-analytic
investigations to the point of arriving at definitive confirmation
or disconfirmation of alternative hypotheses. For example, with
regard to the above-mentioned verbal and ideational fluency
factors, there are still unresolved questions concerning the
extent and nature of these abilities, and of the best means of
measuring them. With regard to verbal ability, we do not know
with sufficient precision the role of basic linguistic competence

- perhaps in Chomsky's sense - as possibly opposed to sheer general vocabulary knowledge, listening ability, reading ability, inferential ability, and many other aspects of performance on tests in the verbal domain. Factor analysts have tended to persist in using the same traditional tests of verbal ability, such as written vocabulary and reading comprehension, without attempting to pull apart the separate aspects of verbal ability that I have suggested. Similarly, with regard to ideational fluency, we do not yet have good information about the generality of the ability over different areas of content, the role of different strategies of recall, or the role of writing speed in the tests commonly employed for this factor.

In short, from my survey of factor-analytic literature, I conclude that the promises of factor analysis are far from being completely fulfilled because there has not been enough work with the technique, with careful and insightful construction of tests and cognitive tasks and with suitable procedures of testing hypotheses. I make this observation with full realization that there are large logistic difficulties in conducting factor-analytic investigations and in finding funds to support them. Nevertheless, I believe differential psychologists need to be made aware of the many possibilities that still exist in pursuing factor-analytic investigations that have promise of making contributions to our knowledge of cognitive abilities, and that they need to be stimulated and encouraged to probe more deeply into the nature of cognitive abilities than they have in the past.

My concern at the moment is to draw attention to certain procedures of investigation and .interpretation that have little to do with factor analysis as such, except to the extent that they may be guided by factor-analytic findings and at the same time provide stimulus to further factor-analytic investigations.

The methodology of what has come to be known as mental test theory has many unrealized possibilities in the study of intellectual abilities. To be sure, various procedures arising in mental test theory have been routinely applied to all manner of ability tests. Tests are "item analyzed" and constructed with an eye to appropriate distributions of item difficulty and item discrimination indices. The reliabilities and validities of tests are determined, and much effort is put into establishing score scales, test norms, and other things recommended in standard manuals for constructing tests. But something is missing.

What is missing is the realization that data on test items should be capable of telling us something about the nature of the abilities that are being tested. Put in another way, these data should tell us something about whether an ability actually exists, and about how an ability functions. Current debates about the nature of human abilities are marred by confusion and lack of clarity because their participants lose sight of what kinds of data are needed to establish the existence of an ability. The kinds of data needed arise in the item analysis of tests, but these data need to be treated and interpreted in a special way that I will describe momentarily.

This idea is probably not really new. Early developers of intelligence tests, like Binet and Terman, were at least dimly aware that data collected on how well children of different ages could perform test items or intellectual tasks could be used to investigate the nature of the abilities tested. Also, I have found that E.L. Thorndike and his colleagues, in their 1927 book entitled The Measurement of Intelligence, were strikingly perceptive in their analysis of how variations in the difficulty of intellectual tasks were related to task characteristics. But for the most part, their work has been ignored. It is only in very recent years that some workers have again started to examine what makes for variations in intellectual task difficulty, and to try to infer from such data something about the nature of the abilities tested.

To make my presentation clear and concrete, I shall consider some data that I collected some years ago, and that I have recently analyzed more thoroughly, on an ability that is probably largely independent of "intelligence", namely musical pitch discrimination. The advantage in considering this ability is that is presents a "clear case" that can become a model for studying other kinds of abilities, including the abilities generally thought of as comprising "intelligence".

Pitch discrimination ability can be tested by one of the subtests, called "Sense of Pitch", of the Seashore Tests of Musical Talents. The data that I shall describe come from an administration of the 1919 edition of this subtest to some 1100 college undergraduates. Let me remind you of the nature of this test. It consists of ten sets of items, each at a different level of pitch difference. In each set, there are ten items, each consisting of two tones presented one after the other. The subject is to indicate whether the second tone of the pair is higher or lower than the first. The easiest set has tones that differ by 30 Hz, which is about a semitone at the pitch of the standard tone used. The other sets of items range down to a pitch difference of .5 Hz, which is so difficult for most people to detect that the distribution of scores on that item set is essentially a chance distribution. Obviously, there is a chance guessing factor of 50%; that is, chance guessing of responses may be expected to result in scores of 50%.

On a priori grounds, it can be assumed that the 100 items of this test measure the same ability, that is, ability to detect pitch differences. J.P. Guilford (1941) published an article claiming to show that this test measured three different abilities, but it can be shown that such a conclusion is due purely to an artifact in analyzing the data (Carroll, 1983). High scorers can detect much smaller pitch differences than low scorers can, and scores can be directly related to the threshold of pitch difference that the examinee can detect. This can be most easily seen in Figure 1.

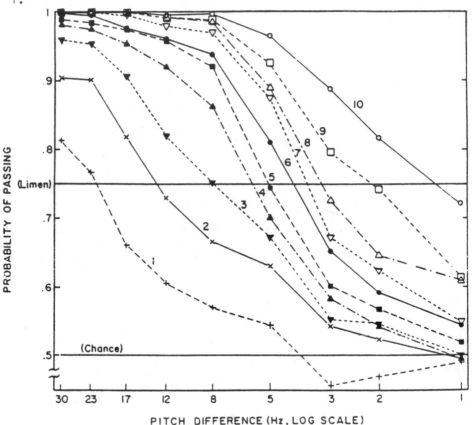

PITCH DIFFERENCE (Hz, LOG SCALE)

Figure 1   Person characteristic functions for the Seashore Sense of Pitch test, averaged for deciles of the total score distribution. (Data collected by Carroll; N = 1082)

What I have done is to divide the total score distribution into deciles, and then to plot, for each decile, the probability of passing items in each subset. For example, at the upper right, for the curve labelled "10" we have the probability of passing items with different pitch differences for the top tenth of the total score distribution. (Data for the most difficult subset of items, for a pitch difference of .5 Hz, were omitted from the analysis because the scores were essentially chance.) For the easiest subtests, the top scorers made essentially perfect scores; their curve drops down to probabilities of less than unity only for the more difficult subsets; the curve crosses the limen or threshold of 75% correct somewhere around a pitch difference of about 1.25 Hz. The limen is set at 75% because it is halfway between chance and perfect performance. In contrast, persons in the bottom tenth of the score distribution have a threshold of pitch discrimination at about 20 Hz, a little less than a semitone. Persons at near the median test score (represented by the line labelled "5") have a limen of about 5 Hz or about 1/6th of a semitone. The baseline is laid off in logarithmic units of pitch difference, and the curves shown all approximate normal ogives, a finding which is to be expected from psychophysical theory.

I cannot claim that plotting this kind of curve is original with me, although I arrived independently at this mode of plotting some years ago. From a recent review by Trabin and Weiss (1983) it appears that similar functions have been studied by Mosier (1941), Weiss (1973), and Lumsden (1977), although for somewhat different purposes. Weiss has used the term person response curve, but I prefer to call them person characteristic functions (PCFs). They show the relation between task difficulty (in this case, identified with pitch difference) and probability of correctly performing the task for a particular person. It can be assumed that each person taking this test has his or her own person characteristic function; the person characteristic functions of a population of individuals differ mainly in the position at which they cross the limen or threshold. They do not differ in the slopes of these functions; it appears that the slopes are essentially the same. Although I will not go into the mathematical details, I may say that it is possible to find a parameter that describes the steepness of the slope, and that this parameter can be estimated independently of the reliability of the test.

To me, this suggests an important hypothesis, namely that the slope of the person characteristic function is associated with the particular ability being measured. The value of the slope parameter characteristic of the ability can be regarded as an important scientific measurement, analogous, say, to the atomic weight of a chemical element.

In effect, the concept of the person characteristic function offers a model that is different in important respects from item response theory, which (as developed for example by Lord, 1980) is the major model investigated in current versions of mental test theory. In item response theory, the concern is with the probabilities of passing single items as a function of ability. In Figure 2, I show typical item response functions.

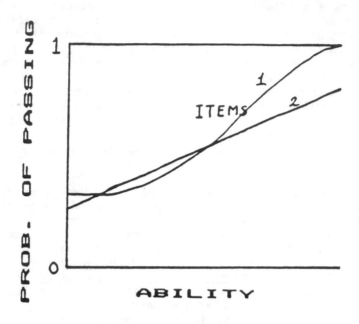

Figure 2   Item response curves for two items

It is seen that as ability increases, the probability of successful performance increases. The slope is steeper for item 1 than for item 2; one would conclude that item 1 is a better measure of whatever ability (or complex of abilities) is being measured. Also, note that item 1 has a "floor" greater than zero, presumably because persons with little ability can still pass the item guessing.

Person characteristic function theory, in contrast, concerns the probability of passing items or tasks as a function of the characteristics of those tasks. Typical person characteristic functions are shown in Figure 3; the curves shown are for two individuals.

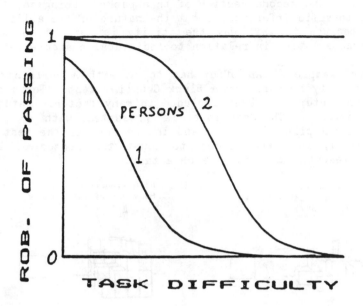

Figure 3   Person characteristic functions for 2 persons

Because the position of the curve for individual 2 is to the right of that for person 1, it is evident that person 2 has higher ability. Person characteristic theory is dependent on the assumption, or empirical evidence, that all tasks on the task difficulty continuum measure the same ability (or complex of abilities). It is evident that our example from the pitch discrimination test is in accord with this assumption. But person characteristic function theory enables and indeed encourages the investigator to examine the task characteristics that make for ease or difficulty. In the case of pitch discrimination data, the relevant variable is very clearly the difference in pitch of tones. Pitch discrimination ability can thus be <u>defined</u> in terms of individual differences in the magnitude of pitch difference at which the individual has 50% probability of detecting the difference (after correction for any chance guessing effect).

My principal suggestion here is that this model can be applied to any kind of ability, and to data from any kind of cognitive ability test, including tests of the various factors of ability discussed in the second section of this paper. Doing so, I claim, can lead to valid inferences about the nature of the ability being tested, because in this way the ability is defined in terms of task characteristics in relation to individual characteristics.

One other example I can offer has to do with a certain type of spatial ability measured by a Block Counting test. Tests of this general character have been included in many factorial studies of spatial ability. The examinee is presented with a picture representing a pile of blocks, and in the form of the test that I have studied, is asked simply to count the number of blocks. Figure 4 presents examples of such a task.

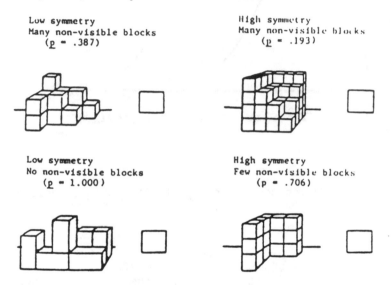

Low symmetry
Many non-visible blocks
(p = .387)

High symmetry
Many non-visible blocks
(p = .193)

Low symmetry
No non-visible blocks
(p = 1.000)

High symmetry
Few non-visible blocks
(p = .706)

Figure 4   Sample Block Counting test items, arranged to suggest the effect of symmetry and of the number of nonvisible blocks on item difficulty (p = proportion of 10th grade students giving correct answer). Ss are instructed to give the number of blocks in each pile, and are told that all blocks in a given picture are of the same shape.

The examinee is told that all the blocks are assumed to be of the same size and shape. There is virtually no guessing element in this tasks, since the examinee is asked to give a free response, that is, the number of blocks in the pile. Items can vary widely in difficulty. In Figure 5, I show person characteristic functions derived from Block Counting test data for 119 school children in the 10th grade.

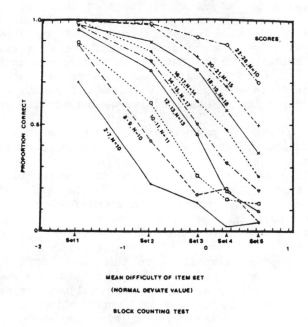

Figure 5   Person characteristic curves for Block
Counting test data, averaged over noniles
of the total score distribution (N = 119
children in the 10th grade).

The test used had 32 items, but 6 items were dropped from
consideration because they had low discrimination indices against
total score. The remaining 26 items were grouped into 5 sets
varying in difficulty, as indicated along the baseline, set 1
being the easiest and set 5 being the hardest. The total score
distribution on these 26 items was then divided into 9 groups of
approximately equal size. As may be seen, high scorers had almost
perfect probabilities of answering the easier items correctly, and
as the item became harder these probabilities were somewhat
reduced. Low scorers had considerable difficulty even with easy
items, and were generally unable to give correct answers for the
harder items. The person characteristic functions were generally
of similar shape. Now, the important thing about these data has
to do with what makes for task difficulty, since whatever makes
for task difficulty is the variable that gives rise to differences
in ability, and thus leads to a definition of that ability.

Examination of the items discloses that they vary mainly on two characteristics: (1) the proportion of blocks that are not visible, and (2) the apparent "symmetry" of the piles. The first of these variables has the greatest influence on item difficulty, but it interacts with the second, which also has an influence. In Figure 4 I have arranged 4 sample items in such a way as to suggest how these variables affect item difficulty as indicated by "p", the proportion of examinees answering an item correctly.

We are now ready for psychological interpretation, which I would offer as follows. First, when some of the blocks are not directly visible, the examinee is required to visualize where these blocks are and to note what other blocks they support. Second, when there is a good deal of "symmetry" in the pile of blocks, the subject can often determine the number of blocks in the pile by simple arithmetical processes such as multiplication and subtraction, and when this is possible it can be that visualization of blocks is of less importance. Indeed, it seems that the "symmetry dimension" in this task tends to distort the assessment of the subject's ability to visualize missing blocks, making the task partly one of arithmetical processing. Possible a better test could be devised by constructing all items with a minimal amount of symmetry, and also deliberately making the nonvisible blocks in some items easy to visualize and hard to visualize in others.

Despite its title, this test does not measure the ability to count blocks, as such. Rather, it measures the ability to visualize where the hidden, nonvisible blocks are in the total configuration of a pictured pile of blocks. This conclusion arises from a psychological analysis of what makes for task difficulty.

Suggested by these findings, further questions could arise and be answered by appropriate investigations. Is the ability to visualize hidden blocks in a drawing of a pile of blocks specific to that task, or would it be found to be correlated with abilities in other types of visualization tasks, for example the "surface development" test used by Thurstone or the mental paper folding test studied by Shepard and Feng (1972)? The answers to such a question could be found by analyzing the surface development test and other visualization tests in the manner I have described, and trying to relate the task parameters of these tests to one another. In general, the evidence from factorial studies of spatial abilities tends to indicate that the kind of visualization identified in the block counting test is also required in at least some other types of visualization tasks. If so, visualization can be regarded as a critical element, a component, or a process involved in at least one kind of spatial ability.

A methodology such as I have described in two relatively simple cases can also be applied to identify the critical components and processes in many other kinds of ability. For example, one type of verbal ability appears to relate to the characteristics (frequency of use, familiarity, and semantic complexity) of words whose meanings the individual has a 50% chance of knowing. One type of reasoning ability (often called the Deductive factor) appears to relate to the complexity of the processes involved in following out a line of reasoning such as that required in solving syllogisms, problems with conditionals, and the like. Analysis of verbal ability and reasoning tests with the methodology I have suggested should lead to improved insight into the nature of these abilities.

Most intellectual tests are complex; they can be performed successfully only if the individual has sufficiently high levels in two or more abilities. This will be true, undoubtedly, of many tasks contained in standard intelligence tests. Furthermore, the hierarchical model of intellectual abilities that I have been espousing implies that some abilities are involved in a very broad range of tasks, while others are involved in a much narrower range of tasks. It will be a problem to take account of these possibilities in analyses of tests according to the person characteristic function I have proposed. Nevertheless, this problem merely represents a challenge to be faced and met in a new phase of differential psychology.

Particularly promising is the possibility that the person characteristic function be valuable in interpreting changes in abilities that arise through maturation, training, or age declines. I would suggest that these changes could be indexed in terms of changes in individuals' thresholds of performance mastery along relevant dimensions of task characteristics. For example, if it were found that spatial visualization ability could be improved through practice or training, such improvement would show up as a shifting of the person characteristic function upward along the task difficulty dimension.

I would suggest that the kind of investigation and analysis illustrated here could go far in resolving the difficulties that have been encountered in the definition of intelligence and intellectual abilities. I would like to see it applied to as many as possible of the test defining the several factors of cognitive ability discussed earlier.

COGNITIVE COMPONENTS AND PSYCHOLOGICAL PROCESSES

The topic for this third major section of my paper is undoubtedly the most difficult for me to write. It is farthest from my area of immediate expertise, and my devotion to factor-analytic work in the last several years has precluded my paying any great attention to the veritable welter of discussions of this topic that have come from the minds and pens (or word-processing computers) of such people as E.B. Hunt, James Pellegrino, Michael Posner, Robert Sternberg, and many others. If I am expected to produce some new idea or new twist of thought on this topic, I am not sure that I can do so. I can only adopt a strategy of reviewing some of my past work, pointing out what I have attempted to accomplish and what this work might suggest for the future.

It was more than ten years ago that Lauren Resnick, in organizing a conference on the nature of intelligence, asked me to consider what I might say on this topic - a topic on which I had been largely silent during many years spent on research in language abilities and language functions, particularly in connection with foreign languages. The topic attracted me, however, and it occurred to me to examine the large range of factor tests that had been assembled in the ETS kit then available (French, Ekstrom, & Price, 1963) from the standpoint of the model of cognitive processing that had recently been advanced by Hunt (1971). What struck me forcibly at the time was the fact - not generally recognized previously, I believe - that psychometric tests studied in factor analysis were in nearly all cases examples of "cognitive tasks" of the sort that were being studied in cognitive psychology, and I emphasized this fact in selecting the title for the paper that was eventually published (Carroll, 1976). It seemed to me, consequently, that there was every reason to think that a solid bridge could be built between psychometrics and cognitive psychology. In examining the factor tests in the ETS kit I tried to interpret them rather systematically in terms of putative cognitive processes, cognitive operations and strategies, and different kinds of memory stores. My interpretations were admittedly subjective and speculative, but I tried to reduce subjectivity by seeking to arrive at agreement with the interpretations of one other psychologist (John Frederiksen). As I now peruse the list of cognitive operations, strategies, and memory stores that I postulated in 1974, I cannot see that subsequent empirical work would cause me to modify my list in any substantial way, except possibly to make small revisions and add detail. For example, in discussing the factor Perceptual Speed, I missed the point that a manipulation in the "executive" and STM would be comparison of visual stimuli, a process that has now been much studied in terms of the Posner paradigm.

Another point that struck me, in writing that 1976 article was the fact that the variety of possible "elementary cognitive operations" seemed quite small and finite. Most cognitive operations and strategies appeared to be different combinations and sequences of very basic processes such as "addressing sensory buffers", "searching memory", or "manipulating cognitive representations of stimuli". Further, the variety of individual difference factors appeared to result from the interaction of a small number of elementary processes with different stimulus classes and response modes, different sensory modalities, and with different kinds of memory stores. This, I thought, constituted the true "structure of intellect", and not the simple three-faceted structure that Guilford (1967) had proposed.

As I became more and more fascinated with the idea that links could be made between psychometric findings and those in experimental cognitive psychology, and cognizant of some of the attempts that were being made in that direction, I became concerned with the methodological and theoretical issues that seemed to be arising in current studies; an article published in 1978 was a critical review of some of these issues (Carroll, 1978). In that article, I attempted to point out how factor analysis and other psychometric techniques could be appropriately used to discover relations between psychological processes and individual difference variables.

A monograph issued in 1980 (Carroll, 1980a) was an attempt to review a variety of studies of individual difference relations in psychometric and experimental cognitive tasks, that is, studies concerned with the possibility of measuring important dimensions of human cognitive ability through various types of simple cognitive tasks. In the course of doing my review, it seemed to me necessary to develop a theoretical model of what I called "elementary cognitive tasks" (ECTs), and I proceeded to devise a scheme for classifying ECTs and for analyzing various experimental paradigms in terms of ECTs. I also reviewed 55 studies relevant to individual differences in ECTs, and examined and in many cases reanalyzed through factor analysis 25 pertinent datasets in the literature. I concluded that promising dimensions of individual differences could be found in a number of domains, including basic perceptual processes, reaction and movement times, mental comparison and recognition tasks, retrieval and production of names and other responses from semantic memory, episodic memory tasks, and analogical reasoning and algorithmic manipulation tasks. Individual differences were found in both speed and accuracy dimensions of these tasks; generally, speed and accuracy were found to be unrelated, or to have low intercorrelations. Considerable evidence was found for relations of ECT performances with scores on conventional psychometric tests, but the nature of these relations was seldom clear, chiefly because the components of psychometric test scores had not been adequately identified. I felt also that the relations were complicated by the possible involvement of sex differences and differences in subjects' strategies of performance. Despite all the methodological and other problems that presented themselves in this field, I concluded that the study of individual differences in ECT performances would be an extremely profitable field for further research. Nevertheless I was not optimistic that tests of ECTs could replace more conventional psychometric tests in practical testing situations. I felt that the study of ECTs was more important for theoretical understanding of cognitive ability than for the development of practical testing procedures.

In writing this monograph, it was my hope that some of my suggestions might be taken seriously by workers in this field, and I have some reason to believe that this is the case. Actually, as I have intimated, I have been too much preoccupied with other matters, principally the general survey of factor-analytic literature that I described earlier, to follow in detail what has happened in the field of experimental cognitive psychology since 1980. My impression, however, it that very promising developments have taken place.

For example, Lansman, Donaldson, Hunt, and Yantis (1982) have explored relations between several information processing tasks and certain prominent cognitive ability factors in the Cattell-Horn scheme. They found that mental rotation speed in the Shepard task is a component in several psychometric tests of spatial visualization, that letter matching speed is a component in tests of clerical speed and accuracy, and that sentence verification speed is correlated with tests of Gc and clerical speed. It was striking, however, that none of the information-processing tasks they studied showed significant relations to tests of Gf, fluid intelligence. Possibly this result was simply a consequence of the limited set of information-processing tasks they used.

Similarly, Pellegrino and his colleagues (Mumaw & Pellegrino, 1984; Pellegrino & Goldman, 1983; Pellegrino & Kail, 1982) have been making process analyses of aptitudes in inductive and spatial reasoning. This work is reviewed in Chapter 6, so I will not review it here. I would point out, however, that the methodology being employed seems to be an exemplification of the procedure I was recommending in the second part of this paper, namely, the investigation of probability of successful task performance as a function of relevant task characteristics.

These are only samples of much other work that might be mentioned. My only comment, beyond general approbation and encouragement, is that thus far not much of the total cognitive domain seems to have been covered. Studies have concentrated on the more important portions of this domain - principally in verbal, reasoning and spatial domains - but there are undoubtedly other interesting and important areas that need examination. The list of cognitive factors that I have presented in Table 1 could be a guide to selecting other portions of the cognitive domain that would be amenable to this type of study.

It will be evident that I see psychometric and cognitive psychology (information-processing) approaches as complementary, each assisting the other toward a better understanding of intellectual abilities and intellectual performance. Indeed, it seems now that this combined, cooperative enterprise is now directed toward the development of a more or less all-embracing theory of cognitive behaviour, or perhaps behaviour in general, to the extent that all behaviour is in some sense cognitively directed.

My own contribution to this enterprise can be, I hope, to interpret psychometric findings in such a way as to be useful to those concerned with information-processing approaches. For this purpose, let me return to a further consideration of Table 1, presented earlier.

As stated earlier, it seems fairly clear that my survey of factor-analytic work will support the notion of a very general factor, g, underlying nearly all cognitive tasks, but to varying extents. It is also quite possible that this general factor will turn out to be identical to, or at least very highly correlated with, the factor of what has come to be called "fluid intelligence", or Gf. I have never particularly favoured this term, but I cannot find a better one, so let us accept it. One of the problems in identifying the g factor in factorial studies is that its nature in a particular study depends upon the sample of variables that happen to have been assembled in that study's battery of tests. Frequently a test battery is assembled to study a particular domain, like reasoning, fluency, creativity, or memory. This is true of many of the batteries studied in Guilford's researches. Thus, the "general" factor found in a particular study takes on the general characteristics of tests in that battery, and will not necessarily be exactly comparable with the "general factor" found in a study that concerns a different domain of behaviour. One way out of this difficulty is to study correlations among tests deliberately selected to serve as markers of broad "second-stratum" factors. One of the few such studies I am aware of is that of Hakstian and Cattell (1978). It suggests that the second-stratum factors have varying loadings on a third-order general factor called "Original Fluid Intelligence" by these authors. Gf, Gps (general perceptual speed), and Gm have high loadings, while Gr, Gv, and Gr have low loadings. These findings need replication and further study (for example, other studies show memory abilities to have low loadings on g), but provisionally, we may say that g corresponds to whatever information processes are involved in common over fluid intelligence tasks, perceptual speed tasks, and memory tasks. I suspect that Spearman's original characterizations of g will turn out to be essentially correct, namely, that g involves the ability to educe relations and correlates. Sternberg's (1983) reinterpretation of these abilities in terms of metacomponents and performance components is valuable. I would suggest that a further clarification of g (or of Gf, to the extent that it is the same as g) can come through studying its relation to task difficulty by methods I have outlined earlier.

In Table 1, I have listed the various possible primary or first-order factors under the possible second-order factors, and the second-order factors are arranged in order of their probable loadings on g; thus, Gf is at the head of the list, while Gi (idea production) and Gm (general memory capacity) are at the end of the list. Recall that I believe that the order or stratum at which a factor is assigned is merely an indication of its degree of generality over the domain of possible cognitive tasks, not the degree to which it subsumes lower-order factors. The lower-order factors are arranged under the second-order factors mainly as a matter of convenience, and only partly as a consequence of empirical evidence for such a classification. I do believe, however, that the various factors, at either second- or first-order, will be found to correspond to identifiable information-processing components, skills or domains of the knowledge base, and that the nature of these entities can be discovered through appropriate psychometric analysis of task difficulty and methods of experimental cognitive psychology. I am in fact in hearty agreement with Sternberg's remark in a recent paper (Sternberg, in press) that "on the one hand, it is possible to do factor analyses of identified components of human intelligence; on the other hand, it is also possible to do componential analyses of identified factors of human intelligence".

In Cattell's (1971) theory of intelligence, the status of factors as primary, second-order, or higher order is taken to indicate some correspondence to its status in a taxonomy with three classes: (1) general capacities, (2) provincial organizations having to do with sensory modalities, and (3) agencies. Similarly, Sternberg's (1983) theory implies a tripartite classification of abilities into (1) metacomponents, (2) performance components, and (3) knowledge acquisition components, and one is tempted to perceive a correspondence between Cattell's and Sternberg's taxonomies, also a correspondence with the status of the factors as listed in Table 1. I would urge caution in establishing such correspondences, however, for several reasons. First Cattell's and Sternberg's theories provide criteria for their taxonomic systems that would not necessarily result in identical classifications. Second, the status of a factor in the factorial system is partly an artifact of how variables are selected and treated in factor-analytic studies. Third, a recognized limitation of factor analysis is that it deals with data obtained from groups of individuals. The factorial composition of a variable indicates only that a given portion of test variance is associated with variation over individuals in the use or criticality of a given factor in the performance of a test. It may be that the factor is equally important for all individuals, or it may be that the factor is important for some individuals and not important for others. On the other hand, the fact that it may be important for at least some individuals is a useful guide for further investigation, and certainly in this sense factorial results are valuable for cognitive psychology.

Findings from cognitive psychology should also be valuable for psychometrics, in that clarification of the nature of cognitive processes measured by tests can lead to better test construction and even to the "purer" factor tests that psychometric psychologists have long wished for. I gave an illustration of this in connection with the discussion of the data that I presented from the Block Counting test: a purer block-counting test of visualization could be constructed by emphasizing the feature of the test that requires visualization of "non-visible" blocks, and de-emphasizing the feature whereby answers can be attained by arithmetical processes. I expect that better tests of nearly all of the factors of cognitive ability could be devised in this way; certainly many of the "reference tests" of the ETS kit could be markedly improved through such a procedure. But these reference tests cover only a portion of the total domain of cognitive abilities. More precise cognitive analysis of abilities underlying second- and higher-order factors presents a further possiblity, although this would require some sort of sampling of tasks tapping lower-order abilities to eliminate their effects and allow the remaining variance to capture the higher-order abilities.

I had originally intended to discuss the problems of identifying distinct cognitive processes, but I have decided that this would be too much of a task to undertake here. The componential analysis techniques developed by Sternberg (1977) have much to offer, as do the "cognitive correlates" approaches used for example by Hunt, Davidson, and Lansman (1981) and Jensen (1980). I expect that as time goes on, however, greater convergence between psychometric and information-processing approaches can be attained, in that greater precision and detail will emerge through psychometric examination of information-processing results, and vice versa. For example, I continue to believe that despite the limitations of the data, my factor analysis (Carroll, 1980b) of certain results presented by Sternberg (1977) pointed to interesting and suggestive refinements of Sternberg's analysis of these data. I find it intriguing, also, that some of my predictions about the componential analysis of the letter-matching task were confirmed by Schwartz, Griffin, and Brown's (1983) psychometric study of this matter.

To summarize, I would emphasize the following points:

(1) Factor analysis, if carefully used with adequate attention to how variables are constructed in the light of cognitive theory, can provide a useful guide to the identification and structuring of cognitive abilities;

(2) An important contribution to defining the nature of cognitive abilities can be made by psychometric analysis of task difficulty in relation to ability, through use of the person characteristic function; and

(3) Substantial correspondence can be observed to exist between psychometric findings (particularly those arising in factor analysis) and those emerging from information-processing studies. These two approaches are complementary and can be expected to converge toward a fuller and deeper understanding of cognitive performances.

REFERENCES

Carroll, J.B. (1976). Psychometric tests as cognitive tasks: A new "Structure of Intellect." In L. Resnick (Ed.), The nature of intelligence (pp. 27-56). Hillsdale, NJ: Lawrence Erlbaum Associates.

Carroll, J.B. (1978). How shall we study individual differences in cognitive abilities? - Methodological and theoretical perspectives. Intelligence, 2, 87-115.

Carroll, J.B. (1980a). Individual difference relations in psychometric and experimental cognitive tasks. Chapel Hill: The L.L. Thurstone Psychometric Laboratory, University of North Carolina (Report No. 163. (Document AD-A086 057, National Technical Information Service).

Carroll, J.B. (1980b). Remarks on Sternberg's "Factor theories of intelligence are all right almost." Educational Researcher, 9(8), 14-18.

Carroll, J.B. (1983). The difficulty of a test and its factor composition revisited. In H. Wainer & S. Messick (Eds.), Principals of modern psychological measurement: A Festschrift in honor of Frederick M. Lord (pp. 257-283). Hillsdale, NJ: Lawrence Erlbaum Associates.

Carroll, J.B. (1985) Exploratory factor analysis: A tutorial. In D.K. Detterman (Ed.), Current topics in human intelligence, Vol. 1: Research methodology (pp. 25-58). Norwood, NJ: Ablex.

Cattell, R.B. (1966). The scree test for the number of factors. Multivariate Behavioral Research, 1, 245-276.

Cattell, R.B. (1971). Abilities: Their structure, growth, and action. Boston: Houghton Mifflin.

Cattell, R.B. (1978). The scientific use of factor analysis in behavioral and life sciences. New York: Plenum.

Detterman, D.K. (1982). Does "g" exist? Intelligence, 6, 99-108.

Ekstrom, R.B. (1979). Review of cognitive factors. Multivariate Behavioural Research Monographs, No. 79-2, 7-56.

Ekstrom, R.B., French, J.W., & Harman, H.H. (1976). Manual for kit of factor-referenced cognitive tests. Princeton, NJ: Educational Testing Service.

Eysenck, H.J. (Ed.) (1982). A model for intelligence. Berlin: Springer-Verlag.

French, J.W. (1951). The description of aptitude and achievement tests in terms of rotated factors. Psychometric Monographs, No. 5.

French, J.W., Ekstrom, R.B., & Price, L.A. (1963). Manual and kit of reference tests for cognitive factors. Princeton, NJ: Educational Testing Service.

Guilford, J.P. (1941). The difficulty of a test and its factor composition. Psychometrika, 6, 67-77.

Guilford, J.P. (1967). The nature of human intelligence. New York: McGraw-Hill.

Guilford, J.P. (1979). Intelligence isn't what it used to be: What to do about it. Journal of Research and Development in Education, 12(2), 33-46.

Guilford, J.P. (1981). Higher-order structure-of-intellect abilities. Multivariate Behavioral Research, 16, 411-435.

Guilford, J.P., & Hoepfner, R. (1971). The analysis of intelligence. New York: McGraw-Hill.

Guilford, J.P., & Lacey, J.I. (Eds.) (1947). Printed classification tests. Army Air Force Aviation Psychology Program Research Report, No. 5. Washington, DC: Government Printing Office.

Gustafsson, J-E. (1984). A unifying model for the structure of intellectual abilities. Intelligence, 8, 179-203.

Hakstian, A.R., & Cattell, R.B. (1974). The checking of primary ability structure on a broader basis of performances. British Journal of Educational Psychology, 44, 140-154.

Hakstian, A.R., & Cattell, R.B. (1978). Higher-stratum ability structures on a basis of twenty primary abilities. Journal of Educational Psychology, 70, 657-669.

Holzinger, K.J. (1936). Recent research on unitary mental traits. Character and Personality, 4, 335-343.

Horn, J.L. (1976). Human abilities: A review of research and theory in the early 1970's. Annual Review of Psychology, 27, 437-485.

Horn, J.L. (1978). Human ability systems. In P.B. Baltes (Ed.), Life-span development and behavior, Vol. 1 (pp. 211-256). New York: Academic.

Humphreys, L.G. (1979). The construct of general intelligence. Intelligence, 3, 105-120.

Hunt, E. (1971). What kind of computer is man? Cognitive Psychology, 2, 57-98.

Hunt, E.B., Davidson, J., & Lansman, M. (1981). Individual differences in long-term memory access. Memory & Cognition, 9, 599-608.

Jensen, A.R. (1980). Chronometric analysis of intelligence. Journal of Social & Biological Structures, 3, 103-122.

Jensen, A.R. (1984). Test validity: g versus the specificity doctrine. Journal of Social & Biological Structures, 7, 93-118.

Kelley, H.P. (1964). Memory abilities: A factor analysis. Psychometric Monographs, No. 11.

Kelley, T.L. (1928). Crossroads in the mind of man: A study of differentiable mental abilities.. Stanford, CA: Stanford University Press.

Lansman, M., Donaldson, G., Hunt, E., & Yantis, S. (1982). Ability factors and cognitive processes. Intelligence, 6, 347-386.

Lord, F.M. (1980). Applications of item response theory to practical testing problems. Hillsdale, NJ: Lawrence Erlbaum Associates.

Lumsden, J. (1977). Person reliability. Applied Psychological Measurement, 1, 477-482.

Montanelli, R.G., Jr., & Humphreys, L.G. (1976). Latent roots of random data correlation matrices with squared multiple correlations on the diagonal: A Monte Carlo study. Psychmetrika, 41, 341-348.

Mosier, C.I. (1941). Psychophysics and mental test theory, II. The constant process. Psychological Review, 48, 235-249.

Mumaw, R.J., & Pellegrino, J.W. (1984). Individual differences in complex spatial processing. Journal of Educational Psychology, 76, 920-939.

Pellegrino, J.W., & Goldman, S.. (1983). Developmental and individual differences in verbal and spatial reasoning. In R.F. Dillon & R.R. Schmeck (Eds.), Individual differences in cognition, Vol. 1 (pp. 137-180). New York: Academic.

Pellegrino, J.W., & Kail, R., Jr. (1982). Process analyses of spatial aptitude. In R.J. Sternberg (Ed.), Advances in the psychology of intelligence, Vol. 1 (pp. 311-365). Hillsdale, NJ: Lawrence Erlbaum Associates.

Schmid, J., & Leiman, J.M. (1957). The development of hierarchical factor solutions. Psychometrika, 22, 53-61.

Schwartz, S., Griffin, T.M., & Brown, J. (1983). Power and speed components of individual differences in letter matching.

Intelligence, 7, 369-378.

Shepard, R.N., & Feng, C. (1972). A chromometric study of mental paper folding. Cognitive Psychology, 3, 228-243.

Spearman, C. (1904). "General intelligence", objectively determined and measured. American Journal of Psychology, 15, 291-293.

Spearman, C. (1927). The abilities of man: Their nature and measurement. New York: Macmillan.

Sternberg, R.J. (1977). Intelligence, information processing, and analogical reasoning: The componetial analysis of human abilities. Hillsdale, NJ: Lawrence Erlbaum Associates.

Sternberg, R.J. (1983). Components of human intellignece. Cognition, 15, 1-48.

Sternberg, R.J. (in press). Cognitive approaches to intelligence. In B. Wolman (Ed.), Handbook of intellignece. New York: Wiley.

Thorndike, E.L., Bregman, E.O., Cobb, M.V., Woodyard, E., & the Staff of the Division of Psychology of the Institutue of Educational Research of Teachers College, Columbia University. (1927). The measurement of intelligence. new York: Bureau of Publications, Teachers College, Columbia University.

Thurstone, L.L. (1931). Multiple factor analysis. Psychological Review, 38, 406-427.

Thurstone, L.L. (1938). Primary mental abilities. Psychometric Monographs, No. 1.

Thurstone, L.L. (1947). Multiple factor analysis: A development and expansion of The Vectors of Mind. Chicago: University of Chicago Press.

Trabin, T.E., & Weiss, D.J. (1983). The person response curve: Fit of individuals to item response theory models. In D.J. Weiss (Ed.), New horizons in testing: Latent trait test theory and computerized adaptive testing (pp. 83-108). New York: Academic.

Tucker, L.R., & Finkbeiner, C.T. (1981). Transformation of factors by artificial personal probability functions. Princeton, NJ: Educational Testing Service Research Report RR-81-58.

Underwood, B.J., Boruch, R.J., & Malmi, R.A. (1978). Composition of episodic memory. Journal of Experimental Psychology: General, 107, 393-419.

Vernon, P.E. (1961). The structure of human abilities (2nd edit.) London: Methuen.

Weiss, D.J. (1973). The stratified adaptive computerized ability test (Research Report 73-3). Minneapolis: University of Minnesota, Department of Psychology, Psychometric Methods program.

DIMENSIONS AND COMPONENTS OF INDIVIDUAL DIFFERENCES
IN SPATIAL ABILITIES

DAVID F. LOHMAN

The University of Iowa

JAMES W. PELLEGRINO, DAVID L. ALDERTON, J.W. REGIAN

The University of California, Santa Barbara

INTRODUCTION

The goal of this chapter is to review advances in the study of individual differences in spatial abilities and to consider some of the practical implications of this work. There are many reasons for the study of spatial cognition in general and spatial ability in particular. First, it is of theoretical and practical significance to understand how individuals represent the physical world in which they operate. Evidence exists for a theoretical separation of spatial representations and semantic representations. Second, there is a substantial literature suggesting the existence of several spatial abilities which are differentiable from general ability and from verbal abilities. Third, there appear to be important sex differences in some spatial abilities. Fourth, measures of spatial ability frequently add unique variance to the prediction of performance in certain courses such as engineering design or graphics and occupations such as mechanic, architect, or pilot.

Although our general goal is to review research on spatial cognition and spatial ability, our specific goal is to show how an information processing approach to the study of human cognition can facilitate our understanding of individual differences in spatial ability. We will try to show how such an approach has been fruitful for organizing, analyzing and interpreting an extant body of theory and data on spatial ability. To do so we first review psychometric studies of spatial ability. Such a review traces some of the background and history of the concept of a separate "spatial ability". It also serves the purpose of identifying and clarifying some of the confusion surrounding this ability domain with respect to factors, subfactors, and tests. Using Lohman's (1979a) reanalysis as a framework, we argue for a set of related spatial factors which can be understood in terms of cognitive processing demands. The organizational framework also leads to certain predictions about sources of individual differences which are substantiated in information processing research.

The second section of this chapter is concerned with theories and models of spatial information processing and their application to the analysis of individual differences in spatial cognition. Such theories and models have been developed apart from psychometric theories of spatial ability, with little or no concern for issues of individual differences. Nevertheless, they provide an analytic framework and a methodology for studying tasks, people and the interaction between the two. In this section we briefly consider Kosslyn's (1980, 1981) theory of mental imagery and applications of this type of theorizing to the study of spatial ability. Our primary focus is on studies of individual differences in components of spatial processing and the relationship to ability tests and factors.

Another specific goal of this chapter is to show how an information processing perspective leads us to ask questions about the development and acquisition of spatial ability that would not necessarily follow from a psychometric orientation. In the third major section, we review two types of studies indicating substantial absolute changes in people's ability to manipulate "spatial information". One class of studies focuses on age changes in spatial processing while the other class of studies focuses on within-individual changes as a function of experience and practice. Results from these studies have interesting implications for questions about the modifiability of abilities, the goals of testing, and alternative assessment procedures.

The final section of this chapter is about how the various streams of research can be used to address practical concerns. One such concern is the assessment of human abilities: in particular, improvements in assessment that might come about through the use of modern technology. We argue for three things. First, that information processing research allows one to develop more precise indices for the types of processing associated with typical spatial factors. Second, that such research also leads to the generation of new types of tests. Third, that technology makes possible tests of dynamic spatial processing which can contribute to both theory development and practical assessment. Finally, we consider the implications of information processing research with respect to the purposes and uses of testing.

PSYCHOMETRIC ANALYSIS OF SPATIAL ABILITY

Predictive Validity

Before reviewing the correlational literature on the structure of
spatial abilities, let us briefly emphasize why we might be
interested in this area of intellectual ability. The effective
use of spatial information is one aspect of human cognition that
is manifest in situations ranging from navigating through one's
environment to determining the trajectories of approaching
objects. These skills are also required in intellectual
endeavours ranging from solving problems in engineering and design
to solving problems in physics and mathematics. As stated
earlier, spatial tests have a long history of successful
prediction in a variety of domains. Smith (1964; see also McGee,
1979) provides an extensive review of the predictive validity of
spatial tests. These tests are correlated with success in many
academic courses which are unrelated to general and verbal
intelligence tests. Smith (1948; cited in Smith, 1964)
administered a variety of spatial and intelligence tests to first
and second year secondary school students. The spatial test
battery was predictive of engineering drawing (r = .66) and art (r
= .39) whereas the Otis Intelligence Test produced correlations of
-.07 and .19, respectively. Smith also reports a validity study
by Holzinger and Swineford (1946) which shows that spatial tests
are unrelated to foreign language (.06), biology (.00) but
strongly related to drawing (.69), and shop performance (.46). The
Manual for the Differential Aptitude Test (Bennett, Seashore, &
Wesman, 1974) reports several hundred validity coefficients
between academic achievement and the DAT spatial subtest. The
highest correlations (in the .60's) were obtained with tests of
geometry, math, quantitative thinking and map reading while the
lowest correlations (near .10) were with spelling, writing and
social science.

The validity of spatial tests has also been extensively
demonstrated with technical training and occupational success.
The studies in aviation psychology summarized by Guilford and
Lacey (1947) were directed to evaluate the validity of spatial
tests for predicting the performance of pilots, bombardiers, and
navigators. The validity coefficients for the spatial tests were
among the highest in all three occupations (the values ranged from
near zero to as high as .7). The manual for the Revised Minnesota
Paper Form Board (Likert & Quasha, 1970), an adaptation of one of
the oldest paper and pencil spatial tests, reports over 100
validity coefficients with various technical school courses and
job success. The criteria employed in these studies were quite
diverse, ranging from auto mechanics (.37), baking (.29), detail
drafting grades (.48), electrical circuit design (.52), topography

(.53), dentistry techniques (.24), pharmaceutical packing inspectors (.57), bricklaying performance (.38) and power sewing machine work quality (.32). These results make it quite clear that the abilities assessed by paper and pencil spatial tests are important for successful performance in a variety of occupations and are therefore worthy objects of more detailed research into the cognitive processes which underlie test performance.

Nevertheless, the picture is not entirely unblemished. In spite of massive efforts to develop and validate tests of spatial abilities, such tests are not widely used and often add little to the prediction of criterion performance after general ability has been entered into the regression (McNemar, 1964; Ghiselli; 1973). For this reason, the spatial ability subtest was recently dropped from the Armed Services Vocational Aptitude Battery (ASVAB) that is routinely administered to all U.S. military recruits. Therefore, one of the potentially most important practical contributions of the newer research we reviewed here may be a suggestion for the development of better measures of spatial abilities.

In the first part of this chapter, the results of an extensive review and reanalysis of the major American factor-analytic investigations of spatial ability (Lohman, 1979a), are summarized. There are three reasons for this summary. First, Santayana's admonition about those who do not know history being condemned to repeat it applies to research on individual differences as well. Those who seek to understand spatial abilities in terms of mental processes will find much to ponder in the older literature on human abilities. Second, the original review is long, quite detailed, and available only as a technical report. This chapter provides an accessible summary. Third, previous summaries that review have emphasized the importance of three spatial factors that appeared consistently in the reanalysis. One purpose of this chapter is to describe a much wider array of spatial abilities, to suggest how such abilities might best be measured, and to indicate approximately how factors representing these abilities might be organized in a hierarchical model.

The reanalyses summarized here were performed in order to reinterpret the major American factor analytic studies on spatial ability in terms of a hierarchical model of ability organization. British factorists have, for the most part, interpreted their work from a hierarchical perspective, so no reinterpretation of that work is necessary (see Smith, 1964, for a comprehensive review). There are other reasons, however, for acknowledging but not reanalyzing most of the British work. A major goal of the review was to examine the nature of the minor space factors, to determine how many there are and where they fit into the hierarchical model, and, if possible, to understand the psychological processes which may underlie their differences.   British work, by committment to a broadly-classified hierarchy of factors, has paid scant attention to the subdivisions of the broad group space factor, and so is only marginally related to this concern.

On the other hand, American investigators, using multiple factor methods and following primary factor theories have claimed to have identified a number of _different_ space factors.   Thurstone (1951) claimed three spatial factors (S1, S2, and S3), plus several others such as Closure Speed (Cs), Flexibility of Closure (Cf), Perceptual Speed (Ps), and Kinaesthetic (K) that correlated with the three space factors in varying degrees.   Guilford and Lacey (1947) reported four orthogonal space factors: Visualization (Vz), Spatial Relations (SR or S1), Space 2 (S2), and Space 3 (S3). But there are substantial differences between these factors and those identified by Thurstone. French, Ekstrom, and Price (1963) listed three space factors: Visualization (Vz), Spatial Orientation (SO), and Spatial Scanning (Ss). The Vz factor was essentially the same as that identified by Guilford and Lacey (1947). The SO factor was a combination of Guilford's SR factor and Thurstone's S1, whereas Ss was the same factor Guilford, Fruchter, and Zimmerman (1952) called Planning Speed. Finally, Cattell (1971) placed Vz in the second stratum of the hierarchy under a General Visualization factor labeled Gv (Horn & Cattell, 1966), and later, pv (Cattell, 1971). Gv was defined as a second order factor combining the first order primaries for Flexibility of Closure (Cf), Speed of Closure (Cs), Space (S), Divergent Production of Figural Transformation (DFT), and Visualization (Vz). Further, the primaries that composed Gv were initially placed under Fluid Intelligence (Gf), with Cf and Vz loading strongly. Cattell recognized that complex spatial tests of the Vz and Cf sort measure Gf in part, but forced them under Gv nonetheless (see also Horn, 1976).

In short, there is much confusion in the American work on spatial ability.   Are Cf (Flexibility of Closure) and Vz (Visualization) different abilities?   How do the Thurstone factors map onto the Guilford factors?   What elaborations are requried by Guilford's (1967) later work with the Structure of the Intellect model, which posits thirty separate abilities within the figural content slice of that model?   Finally, where do the replicable factors fit within a hierarchical model?   Are Horn and Cattell correct when they assert that the various spatial primaries form a second order factor that is largely independent of Gf and Gc?

Such questions simply cannot be answered by a typical review of literature.   The labels investigators have attached to their factors are often more misleading than helpful.   Identical tests appear with different names in different studies, and tests with the same name are sometimes quite different. More difficult to detect are the subtle changes in test format and administration that can, and often do, alter the factorial composition of a test. For example, changes in time limit can produce significant changes in the factor structure of many spatial tests. These seemingly minor changes in test format and administration procedures can be as important as differences in the subject populations and range of tests entered into the analysis, primarily because such procedural differences may affect how subjects represent and process information. Most important, however, are the ubiquitous differences in factor extraction and rotation criteria used by different investigators, and even by the same investigator over time (c.f. Carroll, this volume). Perhaps the only way to summarize this incredibly diverse factor analytic literature is to reanalyze studies from a common theoretical perspective. For reasons outlined below reanalyses were guided by a hierarchical model of ability organization. Although some may question the hierarchical model of human abilities, it should be evident that reanalyzing a host of conflicting studies from some common theoretical perspective is a good way to reach meaningful integration.

It was impossible to review every factor analytic study that simply identified a space factor, since most well-designed test batteries include at least a few spatial tests. Rather, the review concentrated on those studies that were specifically designed to clarify the nature of spatial ability (e.g., Michael, Zimmerman & Guilford, 1950), contained a particularly interesting combination of spatial tests (e.g., Thurstone, 1938a), or supported important new models of ability organization (e.g., Horn & Cattell, 1966; Hoffman, Guilford, Hoepfner, & Coherty, 1968). In all, part or all of the data from 35 different studies were reviewed and reanalyzed. Those seeking a broader review of the educational, practical, and personality correlates of spatial ability are referred to Smith (1964) and McGee (1979).

Hierarchical Models

British psychologists have long advocated hierarchical models of ability organization. Spearman's early two factor theory implied a crude hierarchy with g sitting atop a host of uncorrelated specific factors. When group factors were identified they were inserted between g and the specifics. Perhaps the best example of this sort of hierarchy can be found in the later work of Spearman's student Holzinger, using Holzinger's bi-factor method of factor analysis (e.g., Holzinger & Harman, 1938).

Hierarchical theories of ability organization have only recently gained credence in the United States. Shortly after Thurstone introduced his centroid method in the Primary Mental Abilities study (Thurstone, 1938a), multiple-factor theory captured the attention of American theorists. Its popularity has continued to the present; Guilford's facet model of abilities is the most recent attempt to keep all cognitive factors on equal footing (Guilford, 1967).

However, Thurstone himself initiated the first rapproachment between the two systems when he introduced the notion of oblique first-order factors. The matrix of these factor correlations could itself be factored to extract one or more second order factors. Continuing this process should eventually produce a factor akin to Spearman's g. Thurstone's idea was never really pursued because higher order factors were known to be unstable. Factorists were hard pressed to defend the psychological reality of first order factors, never mind factors of factors. Besides, multiple factor theory allowed aspiring students the hope of discovering new factors as important as those already in the catalogue. Thus the number of "primary" factors climbed from Thurstone's seven to Guilford's 120.

One argument for a hierarchical factor theory is parsimony. Early defenders of the theory of parallel abilities had to remember only a handful of factors, and so hierarchical theory was not really simpler or more parsimonious. But French (1951) listed 59 factors in his monograph, and Guilford claimed to have identified 98 (Guilford & Hoepfner, 1971). Parsimony can no longer be deemed irrelevant.

The more recent formulations of Spearman's original hierarchical model place two or more broad group factors between g and the narrow group factors. One such model clusters verbal abilities and educational achievements together in a factor labeled v:ed, while spatial and mechanical abilities are clustered under a factor called k:m. This model was initially proposed by Burt (see Burt, 1949) and was later revised by Vernon (1950).

Another influential ability model was proposed by Cattell (1963), who was a student of Burt, and later modified by Horn (Horn & Cattell, 1966; Horn & Bramble, 1967) and Cattell (1971). The earliest formulation distinguished Fluid Intelligence (Gf) and Crystallized Intelligence (Gc) as two correlated, second order factors derived from first order primaries enumerated by French (1951) and French, Ekstrom, and Price (1963). Fluid ability was represented most strongly by tests highly correlated with Spearman's g, such as Matrices, Classification, Cattell's "culture-fair" tests, and complex spatial tests such as

Thurstone's (1938a) Form Board. It was thought to represent the major measurable outcome of biological factors on intellectual development. Crystallized ability, on the other hand, was defined by the Verbal, Reasoning, and Number primaries. It was thought to represent the crystallization of fluid ability in specific achievement or skill areas, primarily through formal education and cultural experience. More recent formulations of the model have relied heavily on a study by Horn and Cattell (1966) in which three other second order factors were identified: General Visualization (Gv), General Speed (Gs), and General Fluency (Gr). Neither the original Gf-Gc theory, nor its newer versions are truly hierarchical theories. Even though the second order factors are oblique, the theories deny that a third order factor is necessary. Cattell is particularly emphatic about this. However, Horn has referred to g as a combination of second order general factors, particularly Gf and Gc (Horn, 1976). Snow (1981) has also proposed a model of human abilities that relies heavily on the concepts of fluid and crystallized intelligence, but is considerably more explicit about process than the earlier theories of Horn or Cattell. Carroll (this volume) has also proposed a revised version of the hierarchical model.

Hierarchical Factor Methods

Although some American factorists now recognize the utility of hierarchical models, many continue to analyze their data in traditional multiple factor ways. Even those who perform oblique rotations and extract higher order factors rarely transform the series of factor structure matrices into an orthogonal, hierarchical factor matrix. Appropriate procedures were developed some years ago by Schmid and Leiman (1957) and Wherry (1959). In addition to reducing redundancy, a hierarchical transformation allows the investigator to examine the loadings of the tests, not just the loadings of the factors, on the higher order factors.

Several reanalyses summarized in this report were conducted by extracting oblique factors at several levels and then transforming the several factor matrices into an orthogonal, hierarchical factor structure matrix by the Wherry (1959) procedure. However, reanalyzing a large matrix in this way can be time consuming and expensive, so the usual procedure was to scale the correlation matrix using nonmetric multidimensional scaling and then to superimpose on this scaling the clusters obtained from different hierarchical clustering algorithims and first-order oblique factor analyses. Often both hierarchical factor analyses and multidimensional scalings were performed (see also Marshalek, Lohman, & Snow, 1983). The analyses were frankly more exploratory than confirmatory, and appropriately so given the enormous diversity in tests and subject populations among studies. In spite of these differences, however, a remarkably similar set of factors appeared again and again in the reanalyses. These factors are summarized in this review.

Is g sufficient?

Much of the early work on spatial thinking was conducted by British psychologists attempting to demonstrate a group factor common to spatial tests in addition to g. One of the earliest studies in this tradition was reported by McFarlane (1925). Using several wooden construction tests, a cube construction test, and a puzzle test, McFarlane found evidence for a group spatial factor in addition to g for boys but not girls. Foreshadowing later arguments about the cause of sex differences on spatial tests, Spearman (1927) argued that McFarlane's results could be explained by sex differences in experience with construction activities. He preferred to view her "performance" tests as unreliable measures of g. The controversy continued through the early 30's with some investigators finding evidence for a small spatial factor and some finding g sufficient (Smith, 1964).

In 1935, El Koussy administered a battery of 17 figural tests and 9 reference tests to 62 boys aged 11 to 13. He found that although relationships among figural tests were primarily accounted for by a g factor, some residual correlations were significant even after g was removed. El Koussy accounted for this residual covariation by a group factor which he called K.

In these earliest reports we can observe much of the confusion that has plagued subsequent investigations of spatial ability.

1. When using hierarchical factor methods it is often difficult to separate spatial ability from g or Gf, particularly in less able populations and when using complex tests to measure spatial ability.

2. There are sex differences in spatial ability. Interestingly, McFarlane's (1925) failure to find a spatial factor in the female sample indicated a difference in covariance structure, not simply a difference in means. El Koussy's (1935) solution to the problem also foreshadows much later work: one simply excludes females. The vast majority of later studies were conducted on military populations and thus were primarily male.

3. Not all that is figural is spatial. Many early investigators were surprised to discover that skills in reasoning with abstract figures were highly correlated with skills in reasoning with words or numbers. The fact that a test uses figural stimuli is no guarantee that it will require spatial skills. Conversely, some

of the best spatial tests present problems verbally and require a verbal response.

4. Historically, spatial abilities were first measured using concrete materials. The shift to group administered, paper-and-pencil tests was dictated by convenience, not theory. It appears that the measurement of spatial abilities was altered more substantially by this shift from individual tests to group tests than was the measurement of verbal abilities.

5. Spatial or "performance" abilities have often been considered measures of more concrete or lower-level cognitive skills whereas verbal tests have been considered measures of more abstract or higher-level skills. Terman (1921) argued that abstract thinking was impossible without language and was therefore testable only through verbal tests. Further, early investigators found spatial tests more useful than verbal tests for predicting success in technical schools, which fostered the notion that spatial skills depended less on higher intellectual processes than did verbal skills (Smith, 1964).

The proliferation of spatial factors

In 1938, Thurstone reported the results of the first large-scale attempt to apply the new methods of factor extraction and rotation he had developed seven years earlier (Thurstone, 1931). The study set the agenda for all future factorial investigations of spatial ability. There were four reasons for this.

First, the tests Thurstone constructed and adapted for his battery were used extensively in subsequent research on spatial abilities.

Second, although Thurstone (1938a) reported only one spatial factor in this study, a subsequent reanalysis by Zimmerman (1953) found two spatial factors. Zimmerman called the factors Spatial Relations (SR) and Visualization (Vz). These are the two spatial factors most commonly reported in the literature (Lohman, 1979a).

Third, in this study, Thurstone showed that the computational economies of the centroid method of factor extraction made it possible to factor analyze very large test batteries. In the PMA study, 13 factors were extracted from the correlation matrix for 56 tests. Even Thurstone's critics marveled at the size and comprehensiveness of the test battery (see, e.g. Spearman, 1939).

Fourth, and most important, however, was Thurstone's method for rotating factor axes toward a criterion of simple structure. The proliferation of spatial factors that occurred in subsequent years would never have been possible without his model of parallel abilities. Further, factorially complex tests tended to be eliminated and factorially "pure" tests retained as markers in subsequent studies. Thus, the criterion of simple structure not only served as a guide for the rotation of factor axes, but also served as a guide for selection of tests to be included as markers for factors in subsequent studies. But since factorially pure tests tended to be much simpler than factorially complex tests, new spatial factors tended to be defined by increasingly simpler and specific tests.

Spatial Factors

The major spatial factors identified in the years since Thurstone's (1938a) PMA study that also emerged in the reanalyses using a hierarchical model of human abilities are listed in Table 1. The table contains a brief description of each factor and tests that might be used to estimate the factor. This list is not exhaustive; there are, potentially at least, an infinite number of spatial factors. And we suggest later that attempting to catalogue the factors in a domain is not the most profitable way to understand the correlational literature. Nevertheless, Table 1 provides a brief glimpse of the type of spatial skills that have been studied correlationally. For more extensive treatment, see Lohman (1979a), Guilford (1967), Smith (1964), Eliot and Smith (1983), Ekstrom, French, and Harman (1976), McGee (1979), and Seibert and Snow (1965).

General Visualization (Gv or Vz). This factor is listed first because it is the most general spatial factor. However, it is not always the easiest factor to identify, since the tests that define it usually have high loadings on the g or Gf factors as well. Indeed, Thurstone (1938a) did not label this factor axis in the PMA study since the factor did not exhibit simple structure, i.e., many different tests - even some nonspatial tests - had high loadings on the factor. The factor was first identified in the Army Air Force (AAF) work (Guilford & Lacey, 1947) and was usually defined by complex spatial and mechanical comprehension tests. However, the factor was often difficult to separate from the Reasoning (or Gf) factor (Zimmerman in Guilford & Lacey, 1947). With the hindsight of the AAF work and Thurstone's later studies (Thurstone, 1944, 1951), Zimmerman (1953) showed that additional rotation of factor axes also revealed the factor in Thurstone's (1938a) PMA study.

One important characteristic of tests that define on the General Visualization factor is their complexity. Tests that load on this factor are quite diverse in other respects. Some require the rotation, reflection, or folding of complex figures, others

TABLE 1

Major Spatial Factors

Factor Label	Factor Name	Tests that Often Define the Factor	Chapter in Eliot & Smith (1983)[1]
Vz or Gv	Visualization or General Visualization	Paper Folding, Paper Form Board, Surface Development, Block Design, Shepard-Metzler Mental Rotations, Mechanical Principles	6, 8, 9, 11
SO	Spatial Orientation	Aerial Orientation, Chair-Window Test	12
Cf	Flexibility of Closure	Embedded Figures Test	4
SR	Spatial Relations	Cards, Flags, Figures	7
Ss	Spatial Scanning	Maze Tracing, Choosing a Path	3
Ps	Perceptual Speed	Identical Forms	
SI	Serial Integration	Successive Perception III, Picture Identification (Siebert & Snow, 1965)	
Cs	Closure Speed	Street Gestalt, Harshman Figures, Close Ups (Hoffman et al., 1968)	5
Vm	Visual Memory	Memory for Designs	
K	Kinesthetic	Hands (Thurstone, 1938)	

[1]See referenced chapter in Eliot and Smith (1983) for example items, additional tests, and sources for all tests without a specific reference.

require that figures be combined, some require multiple transformations, others require no transformations. Particular transformations (e.g., rotation) may be important only because they are most easily performed on a particular type of mental representation. This argument is supported by the fact that skill in drawing a briefly-presented geometric design from memory loads on this factor only when drawings are scored for maintaining correct proportion among elements in the figure (Lohman, 1979b; Smith, 1964).

Spatial Orientation (SO). Tests that load on this factor require the examinee to determine how an object or scene will appear when viewed from a new perspective. Some tests require a left-right discrimination from the imagined perspective. Tests are similar in intent to Piaget and Inhelder's (1967) perspective problem but are conducted entirely from the line-drawings. The factor is difficult to separate from the Vz factor, probably because these tasks can require considerable reasoning skill and because subjects can often solve items by mentally rotating the array rather than moving an image of the self to the desired perspective (Barratt, 1953). High correlations between SO and Vz tests may also mean that skill in rotating a complex stimulus or array differs only in detail from rotating an image of, the self. Future work on these skills must attend closely to subjects' solution strategies. Using real stimuli instead of paper-and-pencil tests would also seem desirable since the graphics on many of the paper-and-pencil tests are difficult to decipher. For some particularly clever tests of this skill see Hoffman, Guilford, Hoepfner, and Doherty (1968), Barratt (1953), and the reanalyses of both studies in Lohman (1979a).

Flexibility of Closure (Cf). This is the first of the two closure factors identified by Thurstone (1944). tests that load on this factor seem to require that the examinee break one gestalt and form another. Tests sometimes use geometric stimuli such as Internally Consistent Figures (Hoffman et al., 1968) or Gottschaldt Figures A (Thurstone, 1944), sometimes present more natural scenes in which animals or objects are concealed, such as Penetration of Camouflage (Hoffman et al., 1968) or Hidden Pictures (Thurstone, 1944) although these tests sometimes load highly on the Closure Speed factor as well (e.g., Botzum, 1951; Pemberton, 1952). Tests such as Two-Hand Coordination and Color-Form Memory that defined the factor in the original Thurstone (1944) study seemed to require the examinee to do two things at once. However, later investigations by Pemberton (1952) and Witkin et al. (1962) emphasized the Gottschaldt Figures type of test (see also Messick & French, 1975). However, when the factor is measured by this sort of test (e.g., the Embedded Figures Test of Witkin et al., 1971 or especially the more difficult Hidden Figure Test of French et al., 1963), then the factor is virtually indistinguishable from Gf or Vz. The "real" flexibility of closure factor is defined by tests that use simpler stimuli, require a more rapid response, and are not heavily dependent on figural reasoning.

Closure Speed (Cs). The Closure Speed factor appears to represent the ability to identify quickly an incomplete or distorted picture. The factor is usually estimated by one or more variations on the Street Gestalt test. It is noteworthy, however, that a test called "Closeups" had the second highest loading on this factor in a reanalysis of the Hoffman et al. (1968) study (see Lohman, 1979a). In Closeups, the examinee is shown a close-up picture of part of a common object and is required to identify that object. Picture completion tests (e.g., Wechsler, 1955) sometimes show significant loading on the factor. Tests presenting distorted or reverse printed words are also sometimes to be used to estimate the ability, but appear to be poor choices since they are often factorially complex. Finally, paper-and-pencil versions of the better markers such as the Street Figures or Closeups may be poor measures unless items are presented individually. Tests that require rapid identification of the stimuli appear to involve somewhat different skills than tests that permit a prolonged period of hypothesis testing.

Serial Integration (SI). This factor appears to measure the ability to integrate temporally spaced visual stimuli. It was identified in research on dynamic visual abilities (Seibert & Snow, 1965). In Successive Perception III, one of the marker tests for this factor, the examinee must identify a still photograph of a common object. However, different portions of the picture are obscured by a series of eight overlay mats. Each mat is composed of a 16x16 grid from which 32 cells have been randomly deleted. Mats change every 42 msecs and so the examinee never sees the complete photograph, but all details of the picture appear three times every second. Although typical closure speed tests show only weak loadings on the factor, another marker for the factor called Picture Identification presented still photographs of common objects partially obscured by overlay strip mats. Item exposure was limited to 20 seconds per item. Thus, the integration of information over time may be less important here than the integration of information in a limited time, much as in Thurstone's (1944) initial measurement of Closure Speed. In any event, this sort of skill appears to have important relationships with other short-term visual memory tasks and possibly would have more substantial relationships with carefully administered Closure Speed tests.

Spatial Relations (SR). A better name for this factor would be speeded rotation or reflection. We keep the traditional label only for continuity with previous factorial work. This factor has usually been defined by the Cards, Flags, and Figures tests developed by Thurstone (1938a) and Thurstone and Thurstone (1941). All three tests require the examinee to determine whether a given stimulus is a rotated version of the target or is a rotated and reflected version of the target. Many subjects solve such problems by mentally rotating and reflecting the stimuli although some subjects use other strategies. Thus, the factor appears to represent the ability to solve simple rotation problems quickly, by whatever means. More difficult rotation tests usually show stronger loadings on the Gv factor than on the SR factor.

Spatial Scanning (Ss). This factor is sometimes called "Planning Speed", since it was initially identified in the AAF investigations of planning abilities. Ekstrom et al. (1976) call it Spatial Scanning since "the level of planning required by the tests seems to be simple willingness to find a correct path visually before wasting time marking the paper" (p.155). The factor appears only if two or more simple maze-tracing or path-finding tests are included in a battery, and even then shows a substantial correlation with the Perceptual Speed factor (see Lohman, 1979a, p.53). Thus, the Ss factor probably does not capture a unique type of spatial skill, but, like many minor factors, may be more influenced by method variance than by unique psychological processes.

Perceptual Speed (Ps). Tests that define this factor require subjects to match visual stimuli rapidly. Although numeric or verbal stimuli are sometimes used, there is a tendency for tests to cluster on the basis of content, with the verbal-numerical matching tests defining a Clerical Speed factor and the figural matching tests defining the Perceptual Speed factor. In a sense, this is the simplest or degenerate version of several other factors. Thus, although complex form board tests load on the Vz factor, exceedingly simple form board tests will load primarily on the Ps factor (see, e.g., the Pattern Assembly test in Guilford, Fruchter, & Zimmerman, 1952). Similarly, complex figural disembedding tasks such as Hidden Figures (French et al., 1963) load primarily on the Vz factor, disembedding tasks of intermediate complexity such as Gottschaldt Figures A (see Thurstone, 1944) load on the Cf factor, and very simple disembedding tasks such as Designs (see Thurstone, 1951) load on the Ps factor (see Lohman, 1979a, p.48, and Zimmerman, 1954). Such simplexes reveal the importance of the complexity dimension in individual differences in spatial task performance.

Visual Memory (Vm). These tests usually require the examinee to recognize a previously presented picture or geometric form (see, e.g., Thurstone, 1951). Although there is some evidence that memory for position, color, detail, and form are distinguishable facets of visual memory (Conry & Lohman, 1976; Christal, 1958; Seibert & Snow, 1965), other task facets such as duration of stimulus exposure, study-test delay interval, and artificiality of the display, and subject characteristics such as prior experience with the figures and memorization strategy are probably more important determinants of test clustering (see Lohman, 1979a, p.113). Recall tests in which examinees must actually draw their responses load on this factor only if the drawings are scored in the most superficial way. Scoring such drawings for correct proportions produces much higher correlations with Vz-type tests (Smith, 1964; Lohman, 1979b). Christal (1958) appears to have been the first to note that memory for geometric forms showed higher correlations with tests of spatial ability than with other tests of visual memory.

Kinaesthetic (K). This factor represents the ability to make rapid left-right discriminations. It represents, then, the ability to orient oneself in space. The K1 factor appears to be an essential component of more complex SO tests and of some mechanical comprehension tests. It may also be involved in discriminating a standard from a reflected version of a pattern, as in the Flags or Lozenges tests (see Thurstone, 1951).

Underlying Dimensions

These, then, are some of the more important spatial factors that have been identified in the correlational literature. The list is by no means complete since there exist a virtually unlimited number of spatial factors that can be defined by including two or three usually speeded, highly similar tests in a particular analysis. Guilford's insight here seems to be essentially correct even though the reanalyses of his data did not support all of the distinctions he would make (see also Cronbach & Snow, 1977, p.97ff). Facet models such as those proposed by Guilford (1967) and Eysenck (1967) can help guide the search for important clusters of tests in this seemingly limitless universe. And facet models can be coordinated with hierarchical models (Humphreys, 1962) and with Guttman's (1954) radex model (Marshalek, Lohman, & Snow, 1983).

Although there are (potentially at least) an infinite number of different factors, most of these factors would be only weakly differentiated from each other. Further, practice on a particular type of problem (say, mazes or circuit tracing in schematic diagrams) generally leads to stronger differentiation of the

particular skills used in solving the practiced task from general
visualization abilities, and, for that matter, from general fluid
ability. This differentiation of skills occurs in spite of the
fact that, after training, some subjects show strong transfer
effects to related but nonidentical spatial tests (Alderton,
Pellegrino, & Lydiatt, 1984; Kyllonen, Lohman, & Snow, 1984).
Thus, architecture students (such as those studied by Hoffman et
al., 1968) should show greater differentiation of spatial
abilities than a group of aspiring novelists. Nevertheless, a
strong general visualization factor can be defined even in groups
showing a great differentiation of spatial abilities (Lohman,
1979a, p.99). Thus, the fact that many different spatial skills
can be identified should not obscure the fact that such skills are
usually more or less hierarchically ordered. However, this
hierarchy is not well represented in a two-dimensional drawing.
Many of the distortions introduced in the typical two-dimensional
rendition of the hierarchical model may be eliminated by imagining
that factors subdivide from g like roots from the trunk of a
tree. Compressing this tangled, three-dimensional model into a
neat, two-dimensional picture obscures much, especially at the
lower levels.

Correlational studies of spatial ability are perhaps more
interesting for what they tell us spatial ability is not than for
what they tell us it is. For example, there is no clear
separation of two-dimensional from three-dimensional tasks, nor do
the various transformations (rotation, folding, synthesis) seem to
depend on radically different skills. Further, complex spatial
tests are highly correlated with figural reasoning tests, such as
Progressive Matrices (Raven, 1962) and geometric analogy tests.

Perhaps the most important influence spatial skills can exert on
thinking is through analogy. The essence of a spatial image is
that it is a relation-preserving cognitive structure. Many
complex relationships among elements are contained in a line
drawing or in a spatial image. Relationships among a complex set
of ideas can be maintained as a single chunk in working memory in
a single image, thereby substantially increasing the amount of
organized information that can be maintained in an active state at
a given moment. Thus, when used analogically, spatial images can
substantially improve our ability to think about and to
communicate complex ideas.

Speed and Level

Complex spatial tests tend to correlate highly with other complex
spatial tests and, to a slightly lesser degree, with tests of

reasoning or fluid ability (Gf). Simple spatial tests usually correlate only with one or two other simple, highly similar tests. Complex tests are scored for number correct on tests with liberal time limits. There are many errors of commission, and items that subjects attempt but cannot solve. Simple tests are also scored for number correct. However, time limits are rigid, errors of commission are few, and so total scores are highly correlated with number of problems attempted. Thus, test speededness is confounded with test complexity. Further, the location of spatial factors within a hierarchical model is directly related to the complexity of the tests that define the factor. Complex tests cluster together in a single factor (Gv or Vz) near the top of the hierarchy, whereas the simplest tests are fractionated into a dozen specific factors at the base. Individual differences in latencies on error-free spatial tasks are more likely to correlate with a single factor near the bottom of the hierarchy than with factors near the top.

Further, factors in the lower branches of the hierarchical model are quite sensitive to even minor changes in test format or content. In the extreme, some of these factors are defined by what amounts to a parallel forms reliability coefficient. Factors near the top of the hierarchy are not nearly so sensitive to method variance. Indeed, the Gv or Vz factor is defined by a veritable hodgepodge of complex tests. The implication, of course, is that latency-based parameters from relatively simple information processing tasks will be quite sensitive to even minor variations in experimental method (cf. Glushko & Cooper, 1978). Further, since tests that define factors low in the hierarchical model correlate poorly both with tests loading on factors above them in the model and with tests loading other factors at their own level, speed of error-free processing on simple spatial tasks is likely to be quite task-specific and to explain little of the variance in the sort of spatial abilities defined by complex tasks (Lohman, 1979b). Nevertheless, systematic combinations of such measures using multiple regression or other multivariate techniques may prove more successful, especially if some process measures estimate limits of performance (i.e., errors).

Solution Strategy

One of the major problems with spatial tests is that subjects often solve items on such tests using a variety of strategies (see Lohman & Kyllonen, 1983, for a review). This simple fact complicates enormously the interpretation of both correlational studies and information processing studies of spatial ability. As Thurstone (1938b) noted, routine interpretations of test scores presume that all subjects solved tests using the same strategy. Radically different factor patterns can be obtained if factor analyses are performed on strategy-heterogeneous groups than on strategy-homogeneous groups (French, 1965; Lohman & Kyllonen, 1983). Diversity in solution strategy also means that spatial tests are sometimes poor measures of spatial ability. Evidence for variability in solution strategy comes from studies in which subjects are separated into strategy-homogeneous groups on the basis of self-reported solution strategy (e.g., Barratt, 1953; French, 1965) from records of subjects' eye fixations while solving spatial test items, (e.g., Snow, 1980; Just & Carpenter, 1985), and from componential analyses of performance on complex spatial tasks (Kyllonen, Lohman, & Woltz, 1984). Since this issue is most clearly documented in the process research, we discuss it in greater detail in the next section.

Spatial Ability and Visual Memory

Spatial ability is not simply "good visual memory". Recognition memory for random shapes has virtually no correlation with spatial ability (Seibert & Snow, 1965), nor does the ability to select a tachistoscopically presented rectangle from a set of distractors (Seibert & Snow, 1965). Recall of systematic shapes (such as those used in the Memory for Designs test) shows an intermediate correlation with others spatial tests (Lohman, 1979b; Thurstone, 1944, 1951). Yet memory for the relationships among all elements in a complex figure often shows high correlations with other spatial tasks. The key, then, is not simply memory, but memory for spatial relationships in spatially regular (i.e., symmetric, redundant, nonrandom) forms. Transformations (such as rotation) may be important because they place extraordinary demands on the relation-preserving aspects of the representation.

Spatial Ability and Visual Imagery

The reported vividness of one's visual imagery as assessed by various imagery questionnaires shows no relationship with performance on spatial tests. Smith (1964) suggests that the relationship may be negative, that is, extremely vivid imagery is associated with poor spatial problem solving skills. One possible explanation is that many spatial tasks require one to transform visual images. This may be difficult if the image is vivid since it would be difficult to imagine that the image is "not there". Most spatial tests require abstract, figural problem solving skills. We probably come closer to understanding performance on most spatial tests by understanding reasoning and problem solving than by estimating the vividness of one's visual imagery. However, it is difficult to interpret these findings since self-reports of vividness of visual imagery are of questionable value. The relationship between spatial abilities and information processing theories of imagery abilities (such as Kosslyn's theory) may be more substantial. We explore this issue in the next section.

Hypotheses about Processes

A key important issue we address in this chapter is the relationship between psychological processes and factors. The review and reanalyses of the correlational literature suggest several important hypotheses about individual differences in spatial information processing that we will examine in the next section. Here we merely attempt to summarize some of the more important implications of the correlational literature for process theories of spatial abilities. The major spatial factors we have discussed may be schematically arrayed in three-dimensional space as in Figure 1.

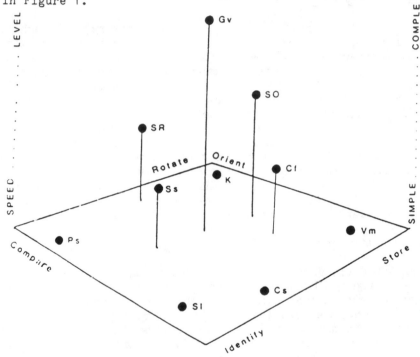

Figure 1   Hypothetical three-dimensional model showing relationships between factors in the spatial branch of the hierarchical model, task speededness, task complexity complexity, and mental process.

Note that this figure could also be drawn as a three-dimensional hierarchy with Gv at the top. If compressed into two dimensions, (i.e., viewed from above), Gb would be at the center. Inclusion of verbal and numerical tests would substantially alter relationships in this two dimensional space. In particular Gv would be pushed away from the center and the configuration would look more like a three- dimensional version of Guttman's radex, with g at the centre and three content regions (verbal, numerical-symbolic, and spatial) (see Marshalek et al., 1983).

Although the number of potentially identifiable spatial factors is quite large (perhaps even unbounded), the number of distinct psychological processes required by spatial tasks appears to be much smaller. At the most elementary level, visual stimuli must be held in sensory memory while encoding processes (or pattern matching productions) operate to identify all or parts of the stimuli. The Serial Integration factor and, perhaps, the Closure Speed factor, appear to represent the speed with which these processes occur (Seibert & Snow, 1965, Snow, 1980). Siebert and Snow (1965) used a film adaptation of the Averbach and Coriell (1961) experiments on visual masking in iconic memory. They presented eight-letter arrays tachistocopically with varying delays between presentation of the array and circular marker that appeared around the target letter. Individual differences in the ability to identify the target letter were substantially correlated with scores on the Perceptual Integration factor only when the circle marker appeared less than 94 ms after the array. Longer delays produced less masking and higher correlations with other factors. Thus, SI is at least correlated with the ability to identify stimuli rapidly.

Other factors represent the ability to construct an image in working memory, to retain a relatively novel image for a short duration, to compare two stimuli, to compare a stimulus with an image in working memory, to determine the orientation of a stimulus, especially after some transformation of the image or of one's perspective, and, finally, to transform the image in some way, either by combining it with other images, by decomposing it or by enlarging or shrinking it. All told, then, we have six basic categories of processes: pattern matching, image construction, storage (iconic to LTM), retrieval, comparison, and transformation.

Transformations are of two general varieties: synthesis and movement. The synthesis transformation is most evident on those tasks in which the subject must mentally combine separate images, usually reorganizing them in some way to reproduce a new image with properties not contained in the separate parts (see, e.g., Kyllonen, Lohman, & Woltz, 1984). Mental movement includes transformations such as reflecting, rotating, folding, or transposing stimuli. Of course, many complex spatial tests require more than one transformation. Thus, Form Board (Ekstrom et al., 1976) requires synthesis, transposition, and rotation.

Conclusions

This first section summarizes the results of an attempt to reanalyze some of the major American studies of spatial ability from the perspective of a hierarchical model of human abilities. In all, ten factors were described: General Visualization, Spatial Orientation, Spatial Scanning, Spatial Relations, Flexibility of Closure, Speed of Closure, Serial Integration, Perceptual Speed, Visual Memory, and Kinasthetic. Tests that define these factors differ in the complexity or speededness of the items, in the type of mental operations required, and in susceptibility of the task to alternative solution strategies. Two major types of transformation were noted: movement and synthesis. However, it was suggested that spatial ability may not consist so much in the ability to transform an image as in the ability to create the type of abstract, relation-preserving structure on which these sorts of transformations may be most easily and successfully performed. Differences between spatial ability and visual imagery and between spatial ability and visual memory were also noted. Finally, it was argued that in addition to providing a rich source of hypotheses for research on spatial thinking, this older research on individual differences defines many problems that the newer research must also confront.

INFORMATION PROCESSING AND INDIVIDUAL DIFFERENCES

Given the importance of spatial ability as a major aspect of intellectual ability, and the wide variation among individuals, how might we understand this aspect of cognition? By understanding we mean being able to describe the mechanisms associated with individual differences, the changes in processing associated with experience or practice, and finally, the modifiability of such skills. To address these issues we must look to another well-developed body of research and theory on spatial cognition.

A Theory of Spatial Cognition

Cognitive psychologists have vigorously pursued issues in spatial information processing. As a result of these efforts we now have reasonably well-developed theories of cognitive structures and processes that underlie the solution of a wide range of spatial problems including those found on standardized tests of spatial ability. For purposes of discussion, we will briefly focus on the elaborate theory developed by Kosslyn (1981). His theory evolved from an extensive program of research on the processing of mental images. Although it is conceived as a theory of mental imagery, it is also applicable to the processing of visual stimuli. A central aspect of this theory is the idea that the human mind creates and operates on analogical representations that preserve spatial properties of visual stimuli. The theory distinguishes between __structures__ and __processes__. There are two types of structures. One is a visual buffer or short-term memory. This medium mimics a coordinate space and supports data structures that depict information. Regions of the buffer are activated and these regions correspond to portions of depicted objects. Relations among activated portions mirror actual physical relations of the object or objects depicted. The visual image or representation resides in the visual buffer and such a representation is derived either from actual visual input or from information stored in long term memory. Important properties of this medium include resolution and spatial extent. The other major structures in the theory are the types of information stored in long-term memory. This includes both propositional information about their relations, and information about the literal appearance of any object.

Kosslyn postulates a set of processes that operate on the various structures just described. For present purposes, we focus on those processes that operate on the visual buffer. One major process is __regenerate__ which refreshes or reactivates the representation that fades over time, thereby permitting other processes to operate on the representation. Of particular significance are the processes for operating on visual representations for the purpose of transforming them. Several specific transformation processes are postulated and these include rotate, scan, pan, zoom, and translate. Each of these processes involves some manipulation of the representation resulting in a modification of the representation in the visual buffer. Finally, there are processes that inspect and classify patterns depicted in the representation. These include a Find and Resolution Process.

The structures and processes in Kosslyn's theory work together and their interaction is modelled within a computer simulation program. The purpose of the simulation is to test the sufficiency of these assumptions for mimicking results obtained in a variety of studies on the processing of visual images. Suffice it to say Kosslyn has been successful in simulating a wide range of empirical results. He has also used his theory to derive additional predictions about human performance that were subsequently verified.

Applicability of the Theory

Kosslyn's theory is an attempt to address one of the major issues raised earlier in this section, specifically, what are the mechanisms underlying specific intellectual performances? The performances of interest are the manipulation of simple and complex visual representations for the purposes of making decisions or solving problems. There are several ways in which we can use his theory to discuss issues about this domain of intellectual ability. First, it emphasizes the fact that the processing of visual-spatial information is composed of several basic processes that interact with information representations. Second, tasks or performances can vary on several dimensions. One such dimension is the number of processes that must be executed to achieve a given result. Another dimension represents the types of processes necessary to achieve that result. Third, individuals can vary in their performance depending upon how well they execute certain processes and the extent to which they use particular processes for solving different types of problems.

Any theory of spatial information processing must not only address issues concerning the mechanisms underlying this class of intellectual performance, but it must also provide a basis for understanding individual differences within this domain. Kosslyn's theory provides a framework for simultaneously analyzing differences among individuals and tasks and for understanding psychometric data on spatial ability. We now examine methods of assessing these individual differences.

There are three ways in which information processing theories and models have been used to study issues of individual differences in visual-spatial processing. One way is initially to ignore psychometric tests and to examine individual differences entirely within the context of the Kosslyn theory of mental imagery. In this approach, the theory is not really used to study issues of individual differences, rather, individual differences are used to test implications of the theory. Kosslyn, Brunn, Cave and Wallach (1983) conducted a study representing such an effort. It was designed to do two things: (1) determine if imagery ability was general and "undifferentiated" or, as suggested by his theory, a collection of separate abilities which can vary independently, and (2) to use an individual differences approach to verify the psychological validity of the components specified in the theory. They used a series of imagery tasks designed to tap various components in this theory. For each task, they postulated an information processing model representing the specific processes required for performing that task. The tasks included image rotation, image generation, image inspection, and image reorganization. A total of eight tasks were used and eleven performance measures were derived from these eight tasks. The tasks were administered to a random sample of 50 adults ranging in age from 17 to 48 years old.

The results of this study supported two conclusions. First, imagery ability is not general and undifferentiated but rather is composed of several elements corresponding to components of the imagery theory. Correlations among performance measures varied substantially and the pattern was generally consistent with assumptions about the imagery components contributing to a particular performance measure. Second, the theory appeared to predict at least some of the correlations among task performance measures and thereby provided a framework for interpreting the results of cluster and factor analyses.

The Kosslyn et al. (1983) study is one example of linking information processing theories to issues concerning individual differences. It supports the idea that individuals vary in their specific abilities and that tasks vary in the extent to which they typically call upon these abilities. What Kosslyn et al. (1983) have not done is to provide a link between their theory and traditional measures of spatial ability such as those described earlier.

A second way of linking an information processing theory with the analysis of individual differences is to go one step beyond the Kosslyn et al. (1983) study and show how the components of the imagery theory are related to each other and to traditional measures of spatial ability. Such an effort was pursued by Poltrock and Brown (1984). The starting point for their study is Kosslyn's theory of the structures and processes associated with imagery. The theory suggests that potential sources of individual differences can be the properties of the visual buffer and the efficiency of the processes that operate on information contained in this medium. Poltrock and Brown used several imagery and spatial processing tasks designed to tap various processing capacities. The tasks were administered to a group of 77 adults who varied in spatial ability as measured by reference ability tests.

Poltrock and Brown derived nine measures of imagery or spatial processing ability. Each measure corresponded to one or more functions in the Kosslyn imagery theory. In addition to obtaining measures of imagery functions, Poltrock and Brown administered a battery of eight spatial ability tests. Confirmatory factor techniques were then used to test the hypothesis that the visualization factor was defined by a linear combination of the various imagery measures. Although six of the nine coefficients or paths between imagery measures and the visualization factor were significant, only one coefficient exceeded .30. This coefficient related accuracy in rotating three-dimensional figures from the Shepard-Metzler (1971) task to the visualization factor. Although Poltrock and Brown interpreted this accuracy score as a measure of buffer accuracy, accuracy in rotating complex figures may reflect other processes as well.

In spite of these limitations, the Poltrock and Brown study represents an important attempt to link information processing theories to psychometric test data. Like Kosslyn et al. (1983) it supports several assumptions. First, that imagery and spatial processing involve separable components, second, that individuals vary in these component functions, and third, that tasks vary in the functions necessary for performance. However, Poltrock and Brown have also shown that these separate functions combine to capture some of the variance in the ability construct referred to as spatial visualization that is assessed by a wide range of standardized tests.

The research described thus far leads us to a better understanding of one complicated aspect of human cognition and the ways in which individuals may vary in their capacities to solve spatial problems. What we have yet to demonstrate is how differences in specific information processing capacities are manifest in actual measures of spatial ability. We have an indirect link between cognitive processing measures and performance on tests representing spatial ability.

The third way of linking an information processing theory to psychometric tasks and data is to use it as a basis for rational and empirical task analysis. This is sometimes referred to as a cognitive components approach to the analysis of individual differences (Pellegrino & Glaser, 1979; Sternberg, 1977). The essential elements of this approach are as follows. First, a task or set of tasks denoting a specific ability is analyzed from an information processing perspective. This analysis involves specifying one or more information processing models for task performance. The processes specified within the model are derived from a general theory, of which Kosslyn's imagery theory is one example. Systematic problems are designed to provide an empirical test of the model. The model testing also provides mechanisms for deriving estimates of the time and/or accuracy of executing individual processes. These estimates can then be used to examine the component processes contributing to individual differences in the task or tasks of interest.

Earlier, we indicated that spatial ability can be decomposed into several separate factors and these factors seem to vary on a speed-power or complexity dimension and on several process dimensions. We can treat these dimensions as hypotheses about what we would expect to find as the major sources of individual differences in tasks sampled from these continua. More specifically, we would expect that individual differences in perceptual speed and simple spatial relations tasks would be primarily associated with measures of processing speed while individual differences in complex spatial orientation and spatial visualization tasks would reflect an increasing contribution of processing accuracy. Similarly, we would expect that models for describing task performance would reflect a larger number of component operations and/or more executions of individual processes.

These predictions will be easier to understand if we briefly reconsider particular spatial factors and their associated tasks. Perceptual speed tests have the following generic characteristics: (1) the stimuli are simple, consisting of alphanumerics or simple geometric figures, and (2) there is either a comparison of stimuli to determine if they physically match or a search through an array for the presence of a physical target. Speed of making comparisons rather than accuracy is the basis of differentiation given the brief time limits and the simplicity of the stimuli. In information processing terms, only encoding, comparison and response components are required for problem solution. Spatial relations tests have the following generic characteristics: (1) the stimuli are unfamiliar two- or three-dimensional shapes or structures and (2) there is a comparison of stimuli in different orientations to determine if they physically match. Individual differences can be a function of both speed and accuracy of process execution and this will vary with properties of the stimuli such as complexity and dimensionality. These latter affect the certainty of difference detection and also interact with structural characteristics such as capacity and quality of representation. In information-processing terms, basic encoding, comparison and response processes are required for problem solution as well as rotation or transformation processes. Spatial visualization tasks are far more heterogeneous. They do, however, have the following characteristics: (1) the stimuli are multiple element two- or three-dimensional shapes and (2) there is a comparison of the physical match of folded and unfolded objects or completed objects and sets of pieces. Individual differences are more likely to be associated with accuracy rather than speed since multiple processes need to be executed and coordinated, with these operations performed on complex representations that tax representational capacity. There is also a possibility of strategic differences in problem solution. The processes required for solution include encoding, comparison, response, search, rotation, and other transformations.

The correlations between performance on tasks representing the
same or different factors should be a product of the common
aspects of the processes required for problem solution, the
relative significance of each process to overall solution, the
type and amount of "data" submitted to the process, and process
interactions with structural capacity and strategies. On this
basis, one expects tests of perceptual speed to correlate more
highly with simple spatial relations tests than spatial
visualization tests. Spatial relations tests should have moderate
correlations with both perceptual speed and spatial visualization
tests. We and others have found this to be the case and it
emphasizes the idea that the dividing line between "spatial"
factors must always be somewhat arbitrary since how performance
correlate will depend on the cognitive processes, structures and
strategies contributing to the performances, not the factors
From an empirical and theoretical standpoint, we can use this typ
of approach to analyze (1) relationships among spatial processin
tasks, as was done by Kosslyn et al. (1983), and/or (2) source
of individual differences in performance on tasks associated wit
various spatial factors. In the following brief sections we
review the results of studies focusing on sources of individua
differences in perceptual speed, spatial relations, and spatia
visualization tasks.

Perceptual Speed

In the preceding section we noted that tests of perceptual spee
can be characterized as requiring three basic cognitive processes
encoding, comparison and response. We do not know how and ho
much each of these processes contributes to overall individua
differences on standarized instruments. To address this issue tw
tasks can be constructed that permit a systematic decomposition c
performance. In one task, the individual is presented pairs c
matrices contraining 3, 5, 7 or 9 alphanumerics. The task is t
determine if the matrices are the same or different. By varyin
the number of elements in the matrices and the degree c
difference (1, 2 or all mismatching elements) we can test variou
models of performance while simultaneously estimating thre
components of processing: (a) time for a single encoding a
comparison, (b) motor response time, and (c) additional time for
"different" response. The second task is visual search for a
unfamiliar symbol in an array of fifteen symbols. On each tria
the individual is presented a target stimulus for a brief interv
and then shown the array. The task is to make one response whe
the target is found in the array and another response if it is n
present. Response time is a linear function of target positio
and thus we estimate two components of processing: (a) time for
single encoding and comparison and (b) motor response time.

These tasks were administered to two separate groups of individuals (N=60 in each group) who varied in several cognitive abilities as determined by a battery of reference ability tests. In each study, the processing components were estimated for each individual and correlated with reference ability scores. In the matrix comparison task, the measure of encoding and comparison speed correlated -.48 (p < .001) with perceptual speed scores whereas the measure of response speed correlated only -.32(p<.05) with perceptual speed. The time to respond "different" was uncorrelated with perceptual speed. None of the measures were correlated with the other reference abilities. In the visual search task only the measure of encoding and comparison speed had a significant simple correlation (r= -.32 p<.05) with perceptual speed. However, a multiple regression analysis indicated that both measures of processing speed significantly contributed to the prediction of perceptual speed with encoding and comparison speed the more important predictor. Thus, in both tasks, results were obtained supportive of the hypothesis that measures of perceptual speed can be decomposed into processing components and that individual differences are a function of the speed of executing encoding-comparison operations as well as motor responses. The latter, however, is less important that the former.

Spatial Relations

We and others have also analyzed sources of individual differences in spatial relations ability. In one study, we focused on spatial relations ability as measured by Thurstone's Primary Mental Abilities (PMA) space test (Mumaw, Pellegrino, Kail & Carter, in press). The PMA test contains two-dimensional stimuli and each problem requires identification of stimuli that are identical to a standard following rotation in the picture plane. To study performance in this type of task we drew upon the information processing model developed by Cooper and Shepard (1973). Pairs of stimuli which were either familiar alphanumerics or unfamiliar characters drawn from the PMA test were presented on individual trials. When problems such as these are presented, the typical result is a linear relationship between overall solution time and the angular disparity between the two stimuli in the pair. The model for performance includes several processes. Measures of the speed of executing these processes are derived from the linear function relating reaction time to angular disparity. The slope of the linear function reflects rotation rate and the intercept reflects the time for encoding, comparison and response processes. A large number of young adults were tested on problems of this type. For each individual, four measures of performance were derived: two intercept measures and two slope measures reflecting performance on each class of stimuli. Figure 2 shows data for the intercept measures as a function of spatial ability

scores on the Primary Mental Abilities test. As can be seen in
this figure, there are minimal ability differences in the speed of
encoding, comparing and responding to familiar alphanumeric
stimuli. There are, however, ability differences in encoding and
comparing unfamiliar stimuli. This figure also shows data for the
two slope measures, again plotted with respect to spatial
ability. There are substantial ability differences in the speed
of performing the rotation process and these differences are
larger for the unfamiliar stimuli. We failed to observe any
substantial ability differences in the accuracy of solving such
problems. Correlational analyses confirmed that individual
differences in reference test performance were predicted only by
differences in the speed of process execution.

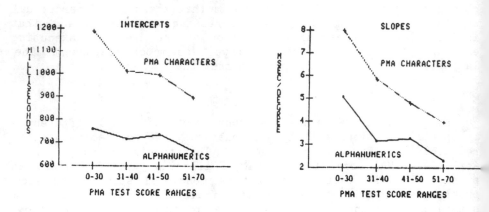

Figure 2   Ability differences in latency patterns
of mental rotation

In another study (Pellegrino & Mumaw, 1980), we pursued a simila
analysis of individual differences in spatial relation
performance with more complex stimuli involving three-dimensiona
mental rotation. Differences in the speed of solving two- versu
three-dimensional mental rotation problems are usuall
substantial. Both types of stimuli produce linear reaction tim

functions but the slopes and intercepts are considerably higher for the three-dimensional rotation problems. In addition, individuals tend to be more error-prone in solving three-dimensional rotation problems. In this study, we presented a large number of problems to individuals varying in spatial ability as determined by a reference test requiring complex mental rotation. Again, we derived various measures of processing speed and accuracy. The left panel of Figure 3 shows intercept data contrasting individuals in the top and bottom quartiles of ability on the reference test. There are substantial ability differences, particularly with respect to the speed of making different judgments.

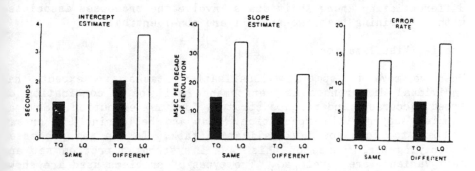

Figure 3   Ability differences in parameters of complex
mental rotation separately for same and
different judgements. Key: TQ is Top Quartile,
LQ is Lower Quartile

e center panel of this figure shows similar data for the slope asures. Both slope measures show substantial ability fferences in the speed of executing processes associated with e rotation of three-dimensional objects. The right panel of the gure shows similar data for solution accuracy. Unlike o-dimensional rotation problems there are   ability fferences in the accuracy of solving these problems. Further,

accuracy scores on three-dimensional rotation problems often show
stronger relationships with visualization tests than with spatial
relations tests.

Before discussing similar analyses of spatial visualization tasks,
we should summmarize the results described thus far. On simple
spatial relations tasks, the results are consistent in showing
substantial speed differences in (a) the encoding and comparison
of unfamiliar stimuli; and (b) the execution of a mental rotation
or transformation process that operates on the internal stimulus
representation. The differences in encoding, comparison and
rotation processes that exist for simple spatial relations tasks
are even greater in complex spatial relations tasks (see also
Egan, 1978; Just & Carpenter, 1985; Lansman, 1981). The complexity
of stimuli such as the Shepard and Metzler block figures leads to
substantial errors on these problems; and error rates also
correlate with individual differences in spatial test
performance. The particular errors that seem most important for
differentiating among individuals involve the processes associated
with determining that two stimuli are non-identical.

Spatial Visualization

When we move to spatial visualization tasks, we expect that
individual differences in performance will be a combination of
speed, accuracy, and perhaps strategy for task execution. Several
studies support this expectation. Mumaw and Pellegrino (in press)
studied the Form Board visualization task. To map the processes
underlying performance on this task a systematic problem set and
task variant were developed. The types of problems used are shown
in Figure 4 and they systematically vary in process complexity.
Problems such as these were used to test an information processing
model as well as to reveal individual differences in process
execution. As shown in the top panel of Figure 5, the time for
problem solution increases as more processes are required and as
each required process must be re-executed for each new problem
element. Not only does solution time increase with problem
complexity but errors also show a similar increase. As shown in
this figure, there were also systematic latency differences
between high and low ability individuals. The top two panels show
performance on problems where the individual pieces corresponded
to the completed puzzle. As problem complexity increased, ability
differences in solution time also increased. This was also
reflected in correlations based on measures of processing speed
derived form fitting the information processing model to the data
of individual subjects. The bottom two panels show performance
differences on problems where there was a total mismatch between
the completed puzzle and the individual pieces. High ability
individuals were very fast in detecting these mismatches while low

ability individuals were exceedingly slow. Not only did
individuals differ in the speed of detecting differences but they
differed substantially in the accuracy of doing so. Individual
differences in this visualization task were predicted by a
combination of both speed of processing and accuracy of processing
measures. However, the accuracy measures made a more substantial
contribution to the prediction of individual differences in
ability level.

Figure 4   Experimental Form Board problem types.   From Mumaw
           & Pellegrino (in press)

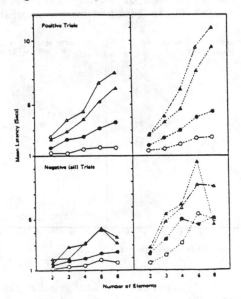

Figure 5   Ability differences in Form Board performance.

The second visualization task we will discuss is generally known as surface development. In the Alderton and Pellegrino (1984) variant of this task, the individual is presented a flat, unfolded representation of a cube with two or three surfaces shaded. The task is to determine the relationships among the shaded surfaces when the cube is constructed. We can specify a general model for this type of task and demonstrate that the time to determine the relationships among the shaded surfaces is a function of the minimum number of folds necessary to establish their relative positions (Shepard & Feng, 1972). We have used problems of this type to analyze individual differences in spatial visualization ability (Alderton & Pellegrino, 1984). Ability differences were not associated with speed of solving these problems, in fact the correlation between mean response latency and reference test scores was practically zero. Ability differences were associated with the accuracy of solving problems and high ability individuals could solve problems involving more complex folding sequences. A closer look at our latency data revealed an interesting difference between our high and low ability individuals and helped explain why mean solution time was unrelated to ability. Figure 6 shows the relationship between problem solution time and problem complexity. The high ability individuals showed a very systematic latency pattern. Problem solution time increased with each additional surface to be manipulated for final solution. In contrast, the low ability individuals showed a much less systematic latency pattern suggesting an erratic solution procedure and/or a breakdown in the ability to coordinate the image beyond a certain level of complexity. The erratic latency pattern coincides with their lower overall accuracy of solution.

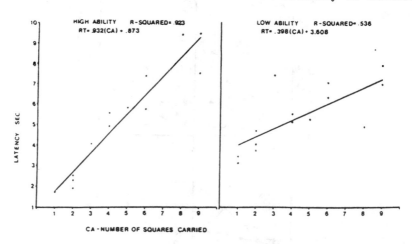

Figure 6   Ability differences in Surface Development
performance

Another test commonly used as a marker for the Visualization factor is the paper-folding test. In this test, subjects are shown a series of line drawings, each representing a square sheet of paper in various folded states. A hole is punched on the last line drawing, which represents the completely folded paper. The subject's tasks is to imagine how the paper would appear if it were completely unfolded. The subject responds either by drawing holes in their proper locations in a square that represents the unfolded paper, or more commonly, selects an alternative from several choices provided (Ekstrom, French and Harman, 1976).

Kyllonen (1984) has proposed a three-phase model of the paper-folding test and then used this model to predict subjects' errors on paper-folding items in which they were required to draw their answers. The model divides the solution process into three phases: folding, unfolding, and response. During folding, the model proposes that subjects attempt to understand, and then remember, what kind of fold is represented at each folding step. This is accomplished through the application of four pattern-recognition rules for folds. The rules vary in complexity, suggesting that sometimes recognizing the fold - that is, deciphering the line drawing - is a nontrivial task. The output of this encoding phase is a structural description of each fold. In the unfolding phase, the subject must first imagine the holes in their proper locations and then must reflect the holes (or patterns of holes) about the axis defined by the folds. The reflection process is modeled by three production rules. Finally, in the response phase, the subject must construct an answer or select an alternative, depending on the nature of the task.

Using this model, Kyllonen (1984) was able to account for over 95% of the errors made by 56 subjects on 32 paper-folding items on which subjects were required to draw their responses. The most common errors were: substituting incorrect folds for folds actually made (30% of all errors), forgetting particular folds or holes together (20%), miscoding the location of the punched hole or reflection axis (9%), and "buggy" transformations in which a pattern of holes was transformed incorrectly (9%). When compared with subjects low in spatial ability, subjects high in spatial ability made fewer errors that could be attributed to forgetting, replacing, or adding structures. However, spatial ability was not significantly related to positioning errors, buggy transformations, whole pattern changes, or order errors. Verbal ability was significantly related to the frequency of buggy transformations, with high verbals making fewer of these errors. Males made significantly fewer of the forgetting-structure errors than did females. Thus, Kyllonen argues that the major individual difference variable might be considered the probability...of forgetting something about the item" (p. 242).

Strategy Differences

Subjects often report using different strategies to solve different items on spatial tests (Barratt, 1953; Lucas, 1953). Variation in reported solution strategy is usually greater for complex spatial tasks than for simple spatial tasks. Further, within-person variability in reported solution strategy is often substantially greater than between-person variability in reported solution strategy. In other words, individual subjects are often not easily classified according to preferred solution strategy; rather, subjects vary their strategies to meet the demands of particular items (see Lohman & Kyllonen, 1983 for a review of this literature). Detailed studies of subjects' eye-fixations while solving spatial tests (Just & Carpenter, 1985; Lohman, 1977; Snow 1980) and modeling of solution latencies on complex spatial tasks (Kyllonen, Lohman, & Snow, 1984; Kyllonen, Lohman, & Woltz, 1984) support these retrospective reports.

Kyllonen, Lohman, and Woltz (1984) developed an extension of Sternberg's (1977) procedures for componential analysis that allowed them to compare various single strategy and strategy-shift models for subjects' performance on the synthesis trials of the visualization task developed by Lohman (1979b). Sample items are shown in columns 4 through 7 in Figure 7 below.

On each trial, subjects were required to encode and remember the first stimulus, to add one or two additional stimuli to this image, and them to compare the synthesized image with a probe. Although total errors on the task were highly correlated with a reference Visualization factor (r = .66). Componential analyses suggested that, on each of the three task steps, different subjects used different strategies. For encoding, some subjects appeared to memorize the initial stimulus figure by representing the figure in memory as a set of basic features. Other subjects appeared to decompose the figure into more elementary units such as rectangle and triangles before representing the basic features of these elementary units in memory. Still other subjects appeared to label some of the figures and decompose others, shifting strategy according to the comparative difficulty of labeling or decomposing the figure.

For synthesis, the analyses suggested that some subjects either consistently synthesized figures and stored the resulting product or consistently failed to synthesize figures and instead stored the three figures as separate units. However, most subjects appeared to shift back and forth between these two strategies or between one or both of these and a strategy of combining only two of the figures, depending on the complexity of the final image.

For the comparison step, the analyses suggested that some subjects compared their mental image of the set of figures with the test probe one feature at a time; some subjects compared the two in larger units, one chunk at a time; and still others shifted back and forth between the feature- and unit-comparison strategies, depending on the relative difficulty of the two methods. A small subset of the subjects appeared to compare their image with the probe by the feature-comparison technique, except on items in which the image and probe differed radically. When the image-probe discrepancy was great, these subjects quickly responded that the two were different and avoided the more time-consuming feature-comparison strategy.

In two of the three task steps, some of the strategies appeared to be better than others in that subjects who used them made fewer errors or performed the task step more quickly. For the encoding step, those who consistently used the decomposition strategy made fewer errors and encoded faster than subjects in the other strategy groups. Feature analysis was shown to be an accurate strategy but one that resulted in slow encoding. Decomposition-labeling shifting was a quick strategy, but it led to more errors, possibly because labeling resulted in a poor description of the figure. In the synthesis step, the strategy that led to fewest errors was a shift strategy that required subjects continually to synthesize figures and evaluate their product until an optimal combination was obtained. The poorest strategy for this step was one in which subjects worked backward from the available stimuli to the previously presented one. Kyllonen et al. (1984) argued that subjects using backward synthesis were forced into this strategy because they simply could not remember the figure that was out of view.

Further, strategies were systematically related to ability factors. For the encoding step, for example, those who selected the decomposition strategy tended to score higher on measures of Visualization (Gv) and Closure Speed (Cs). It may be that the skills represented by these factors are necessary to execute the decomposition strategy. For synthesis, the subjects who selected the most demanding shift strategy which required constant synthesis and evaluation processes, tended to score well on all ability tests. Here aptitude may have played a restricting role in strategy selection: The most demanding strategy may have required the greatest amount of skill.

Strategy shifts can be noise or substance. They can be noise if the goal is to estimate a particular set of process parameters (e.g., rate of rotation) from a sample of items. They can be substance if, at some point, higher levels of skill mean having a flexible approach to problem solving. In either case, in

interpreting research on spatial abilities, we cannot presume that
all problems are solved in the same way or that subjects differ
only parametrically, that is, in the speed or power with which
they execute a common set of processes. The spatial abilities
measured by Visualization-factor tests appear to be more complex
than this. Such tests are often more like figural reasoning tasks
with a spatial component than pure tests of some combination of
spatial skills.

A faceted test of several spatial abilities

We have argued that the various spatial factors differ in terms of
the information-processing requirements of the tests which define
them. If this is true, then it should be possible to measure
different spatial factors by systematically manipulating the
complexity of processing required by a single task. This
hypothesis led to the development of a faceted spatial task in
which items varied systematically in presumed processing
complexity in order to represent the sort of items typically
observed in marker tests for various spatial factors, from simple
Perceptual Speed and Closure Speed tests through Spatial Relations
tests to complex Visualization tests. Subjects were required to
memorize, synthesize, rotate, and match various polygons.
Ememplary items from this task are shown in Figure 7.

The first column in Figure 7 shows the sequence of events for the
simplest item; simple 90 and 180 degree rotation trials are shown
in columns 6 and 7. The plus sign indicates the location of the
synthesis, and, on two-piece additions, subjects were instructed
to work from left to right (e.g., columns 5 and 7). Stimulus
complexity of both the stimulus pieces and to-be-constructed
stimulus was varied systematically. Complex pieces could combine
to form either a simple or a complex product image, and simple
pieces could do the same. Finally, all types of addition could be
followed by rotation, as shown in columns 8 and 9. The three
levels of construction (zero, one, or two additions), three levels
of rotation (9, 90, or 180), three levels of stimulus complexity
(low, medium, or high), and two types of discriminative response
(correct or incorrect) were fully crossed. Additionally, location
of addition (left or right) and complexity of the
to-be-constructed image were crossed with each other and all other
design facets for construction items. In addition to correctness
and confidence, two or four latencies were recorded for each item:
encoding (time to memorize the first figure), synthesis (time to
synthesize the separate stimuli), rotation (time to rotate
stimuli), and comparison (time to accept or reject the test
probe).

A stratified random sample of 30 high school and college males
selected to represent the full range of verbal and spatial
abilities in a much larger sample of high school students and

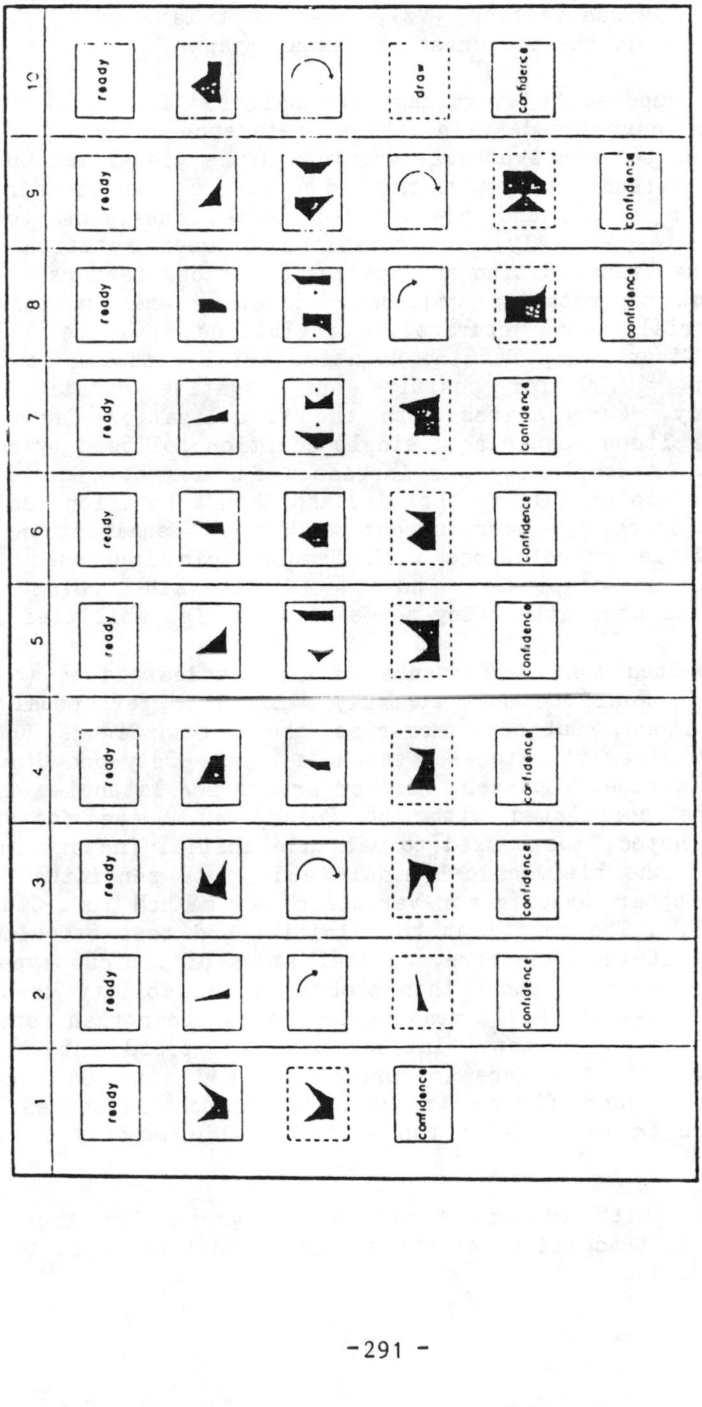

Figure 7 Examples of trials in the faceted spatial task.
From Lohman, 1979b.

university undergraduates solved the 216 items in this task. All subjects had previously taken a large battery of reference aptitude tests including measures of verbal ability (V), fluid ability (Gf), memory span (Ms), Perceptual Speed (Ps), Closure Speed (Cs), Visualization (Vz), Spatial Relations (SR), and a questionnaire on the vividness of visual imagery.

Subscores computed by averaging over selected facets of the task were then correlated with these reference ability factors. Correlations between synthesis trials and the visualization factor increased systematically with number synthesis operations required ($r = .21$, $r = .43$, and $r = .55$ for zero-, one-, and two-piece additions, respectively). Correlations between rotation trials and both the Visualization and Spatial Relations factors increased with amount of rotation required. However, when positive and negative trials were separated, correlations with the SR factor were significant only for the negative trial rotation items ($r = .04$ and $r = .37$ for positive and negative rotation items, respectively. Correlations with the Visualization factor were highest for items requiring a single addition followed by rotation ($r = .67$). As complexity was increased further by requiring the addition of two stimuli to the base and then a rotation (columns 8 and 9 in Figure 7), correlations with the Visualization factor declined while correlations with Memory Span increased. Thus, increases in complexity beyond a certain point become disfunctional when attempting to measure spatial abilities.

It was expected that performance on the simplest items (column 1 in Figure 7) would be most strongly related to perceptual speed. On these items, subjects memorize the first figure and then determine whether it matches a second figure. Only one figure was visible at a time. However, neither errors nor latencies on these trials were correlated with the Perceptual Speed factor. As previously noted, tests used to estimate spatial factors in lower branches of the hierarchical model tend to be sensitive to what sometimes appear to be minor variations in method (cf. Glushko & Cooper, 1978). The fact that both initial and test stimulus were not visible at the same time, or that items of various types were randomly intermixed rather than blocked as on ability tests, may have caused these items to measure abilities other than perceptual speed. Indeed, when total latency was decomposed into time to memorize the first figure (memorization) and time to accept or reject the second figure (match), the match latencies showed correlations in the 0.4-0.5 range with a wide variety of spatial tests.

Correlations with Closure Speed were highest for those items requiring right additions of three stimuli that combined to make a simple new image.

Finally, correlations between errors and latencies showed that speed of solving simplest items offered no prediction of number of errors on complex problems.

Facet tests can provide much information. Here, the facet design helped demonstrate the fact that various spatial factors are arbitrary points in a continuous, but multidimensional space. Further, loadings of scores for different item-types on reference ability factors were systematically altered by manipulating the information processing requirements of the items.

Conclusions

We can summarize the implications of these studies of perceptual speed, spatial relations, and visualization performance and the relationship to Kosslyn's and Poltrock and Brown's research. Individual differences data obtained from several simple and complex spatial processing tasks can be considered together to formulate a preliminary answer to the question of what constitutes spatial ability. By looking across tasks, one might initially conclude that spatial ability is a function of several capacities including the ability to establish precise and stable representations of unfamiliar visual stimuli. Such representations can then be operated on or transformed with minimal information loss or degradation. It appears that individuals high in spatial ability are faster representing unfamiliar visual stimuli and in constructing representations that are more precise. Differences in the quality of representation may also give rise to other speed differences such as the superior rotation and search rates observed in different tasks. Problems of representation are most apparent in the more complex tasks that require the representation and manipulation of stimuli having several interrelated elements. If we assume that stimulus representation and processing involve a visual short term memory or buffer, then skill differences may also be a function of capacity and resolution within this system. Differences between spatial relations and visualization tasks may partially reflect a difference in the importance of coding versus transformation processes within this system. Another difference between the two factors appears to involve single versus multiple transformations and the coordination and monitoring of the latter. Complex spatial tasks also can require general reasoning and problem-solving skills.

These illustrations of linking information processing research with individual differences emphasize the importance of trying to relate dimensions of variation in human performance with theories and models of the mechanisms underlying a given intellectual performance. Our understanding of intellectual ability, and spatial ability in particular, is enhanced by considering simultaneously the dimensions of variation in solving spatial problems and the mechanisms responsible for performance and performance variation

Acquisition of Spatial Processing Skill

We know that there are reliable individual differences in spatial ability. We also know that such differences are partially attributable to the speed and accuracy of executing specific mental processes. It is not uncommon to view such aptitude differences as relatively stable characteristics of individuals and populations. Standard testing procedures tell us that if we re-administer ability tests then the test-retest correlations will be high, 0.75 or above for any respectable test. In addition, absolute scores will not change greatly. An individual's scores may go up or down by a few points reflecting practice or regression to the mean. Such data are often interpreted as an indication that ability differences represent immutable characteristics of individuals and that they are relatively fixed.

Another basis for the belief in the stability of intellectual abilities comes from longitudinal research projects in which individuals are administered tests for several years in succession. In these cases, one can compute correlations between intelligence as an adult and intelligence at various points earlier in development. In fact, test scores obtained from infancy typically are poorly correlated with adult intelligence. However, beginning in the preschool years the correlations are statistically significant and by the elementary school years they are quite large.

Ignored here is the fact that stability and change can have two meanings. One meaning refers to the relative level of performance and the other refers to absolute level of performance. The correlation between performance at two points in time ignores absolute changes and instead reflects only shifts in individual deviations from one group mean from time 1 to time 2. Thus, a preoccupation with correlations obscures the fact that all abilities show substantial growth, often into the mid-twenties and beyond.

Our view of intellectual abilities may be distorted by correlations that show only relative stability yet are erroneously interpreted to mean absolute stability of such abilities. A different view of intellectual abilities is suggested by research combining developmental and information processing approaches. Anyone who has been involved in developmental research, or who has been a parent, knows the changing capabilities of children at different ages. These developing capabilities can be documented for specific intellectual functions such as those associated with spatial information processing. Figure 8 is an illustration of developmental changes in one aspect of spatial processing. These data are from a study conducted by Rob Kail on the development of rotation speed (Kail, 1983). Rate of rotation changes substantially and reaches adult-like levels in early adolescence. Like many other physical and mental characteristics, the growth curve is best captured by a logistic function. These data illustrate the point that there are substantial absolute changes in specific mental functions that are associated with maturation. These data also argue that components of spatial ability are not fixed even if there is relative stability or ordering of the individuals within and across ages. Similarly, anyone who has tested individuals in a laboratory information processing task can tell you that the ubiquitous law of practice operates. Individuals show substantial practice effects in tasks such as mental rotation. These practice effects occur within testing sessions that last an hour and over multiple testing sessions occurring on different days. However, most ability tests are administered in time intervals ranging from three to thirty minutes. The typical aptitude testing situation does not permit much in the way of adaptation to task demands. Thus, it is not too surprising that differences in test performance, both relative and absolute, remain moderately stable over testing situations.

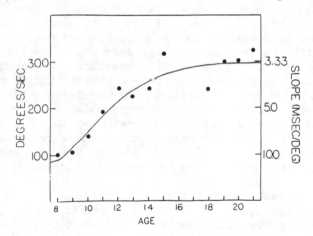

Figure 8   Developmental changes in rate of mental rotation.
          From Kail, 1983.

Typical aptitude tests tell us how an individual performs at a given point in time. Information processing analyses tell us what mechanisms are responsible for those individual differences. What tests and process analyses do not tell us is how well an individual might ultimately perform given sufficient practice, training or exposure to the cognitive performance domain. We have been exploring this issue in a series of studies that follow from our process-oriented approach to the analysis of individual differences in spatial aptitude.

We will briefly describe two such studies, the first of which had several different purposes (Alderton, Pellegrino, & Lydiatt, 1984). The first purpose was to examine changes in components of spatial processing as a function of practice. The second purpose was to examine such changes for high and low ability individuals in the context of two different spatial processing tasks. One task represented spatial relations ability and the other represented spatial visualization ability. The third purpose of the study was to examine changes in reference ability scores as a function of extended practice on laboratory spatial processing tasks. Specifically, we were concerned with the effect that extended practice in spatial tasks might have on measured ability levels. The fourth major purpose of this study was to examine reference ability scores and components of spatial processing after a long delay interval.

Initially the individuals were administered a battery of reference tests assessing various spatial factors including perceptual speed, spatial relations, and spatial visualization. We then selected 36 high and 36 low ability individuals for extended testing on two processing tasks. Subjects were familiarized with each task during an initial practice session. They then received eight sessions of testing with four sessions on each processing task. The two tasks were mental rotation and form board solution. At the end of testing, the reference battery was re-administered. Finally, two to three months after the study was completed, many of the individuals returned for two additional sessions. The first delayed session was used to re-administer the reference test battery while the second session was used to collect performance data on the two spatial processing tasks.

Data from both tasks showed that practice leads to substantial improvement in the speed of executing specific mental processes. Figure 9 contains one such example. It shows data on the speed of mental rotation as a function of both testing session and pre-experimental measures of spatial ability. Two things are apparent. On the initial testing session there are substantial differences among individuals in the speed of rotation and the ordering of groups is consistent with the reference ability scores obtained prior to the experiment. However, the low ability individuals are capable of achieving highly speeded performance as a function of practice. Their initial inferiority relative to high ability individuals is not completely eliminated by providing practice, although they do achieve processing speeds equivalent to the levels exhibited by the highest ability individuals at the start of testing. The question then is what effect all this practice has on the performance of both high and low ability individuals when we remove them from the laboratory task situation and retest them with standard measures of spatial ability.

Figure 10 contains three panels representing performance on three different spatial factors. In each panel, pretest, posttest and delayed-test data are presented for our high and low ability groups. Data are presented as percentiles based on external norms. In the left hand panel, there is a substantial pretest to posttest gain in performance for two different perceptual speed measures. In the center panel, the low ability individuals show substantial gains in performance for two different spatial relations measures. In the right hand panel, the low ability individuals show a substantial gain in performance for the spatial visualization measure. The performance changes exhibited in this figure exceed normal test-retest effects and can not be attributed solely to regression toward the mean.

One might wish to assume that the effects of extended practice on reference ability measures are situation specific and ephemeral. There are three arguments against this conclusion. First, the effects observed in test score performance following extended practice were not limited to a single test. Instead, they generalized to other tests including measures of perceptual speed and other measures of spatial relations using very different types of visual stimuli. Second, the laboratory tasks are different in format and content from the reference tests they were modeled after. Third, for every reference test, performance in the delayed testing session following extended practice. A similar pattern of results was obtained for performance measures from the laboratory spatial processing tasks.

The data from this extended practice study can be discussed in several ways. First, they replicate previous results showing speed and accuracy differences in specific components of spatial processing. There are replicable differences between high and low ability individuals in various components of spatial processing. Second, the data indicate that many low ability individuals are capable of substantial improvement in various components of spatial information processing. By the end of four sessions of testing, we have not transformed our low ability individuals into our high ability individuals. We have, however, reduced some of the differences between ability groups. The changes in spatial processing ability are still evident after a delay of several months.

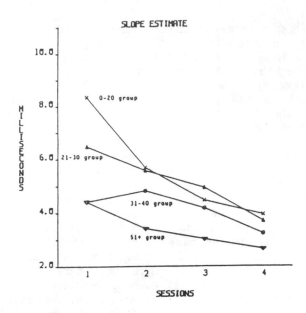

Figure 9   Practice effects in the rate of mental
           rotation separately for PMA Space test
           raw score groups.

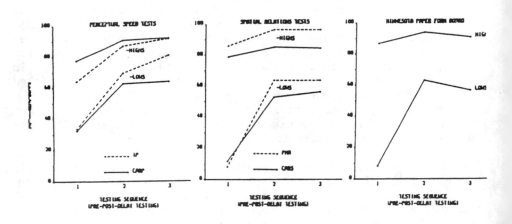

Figure 10   Test score changes following extended
            practice separately for high and low
            ability groups.

A second study illustrates an attempt to further examine the effects of extended practice on mental rotation processing parameters and psychometric indices (Regian & Pellegrino, 1984). The previous study demonstrated that practice on laboratory spatial processing tasks can influence performance on subsequently administered psychometric tests. The design of the present study permitted an investigation of the hypothesis that extended practice at mental rotation might translate to a specific pattern of enhanced performance on tests varying in content and factor identification. Previous research on mental rotation has also demonstrated practice effects for both the slope and the intercept of the rotation function. What is not clear is if either or both of these are general processing effects and/or stimulus specific processing effects. The present design permitted the discrimination of practice effects due to increased efficiency of specific processing components and practice effects due to stimulus familiarity.

Thirty-seven individuals were tested on a battery of spatial tests consisting of two perceptual speed tasks, two spatial relations tasks, and one spatial visualization task. They were then given five sessions of mental rotation practice followed by a readministration of the spatial test battery. The sessions varied with respect to the presence or absence of specific sets of "equivalent" stimuli. Stimulus set X was presented in five sessions and provides a baseline for comparing practice effects. Stimulus set Y occurred in sessions one, two, and five, while stimulus set Z occurred in sessions three, four, and five. As individuals became increasingly practiced at mental rotation it was possible to compare stimulus sets with varying degrees of familiarity to observe general and item specific effects. Session three provides key comparisons of interest since individuals were highly familiar with one set of stimuli but unfamiliar with the other set of stimuli. In all sessions, the stimulus sets were not separated but were randomly intermingled. All stimuli consisted of random polygons similar to those found on the Card Rotation Test.

Practice related changes in the intercept of the rotation function were substantial and primarily complete by session three. In addition, these effects fully generalized to the new stimulus set. Changes in the slope were also substantial and continued over the course of the experiment. More importantly, these effects did not generalize to the new stimulus set in session three. The slope for the unfamiliar stimulus set in session three was equivalent to the slope for the stimulus sets in session one. Thus, the intercept reduction was independent of stimulus familiarity while the slope reduction was not. Figure 11 shows that both of these practice effect patterns were present for high

and low ability individuals. In addition, the figure shows that
ability differences exist for both components of processing at the
beginning of practice and are reduced by the end of practice.

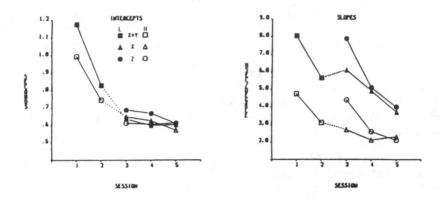

Figure 11   Ability differences in practice effects for
            parameters of mental rotations. Filled symbols
            for low ability.

As in our previous study, practice had an impact on ability tests
with individuals showing systematic increases on all five tests.
These increases were beyond what would be expected in a
test-retest situation without intervening practice. Since each
test is scaled differently, it is useful to express the pretest to
posttest changes in a standardized format. By dividing each
absolute change by the maximum possible change we obtain the
percent increase in performance relative to the maximum possible.
Of the two perceptual speed tests, there was a mean increase of
52% on the cards Rotation Test and 42% on the Primary Mental
Abilities space test. Again, the stimuli for the cards tests are
more similar to the stimuli in the practice study than are the
stimuli from the PMA space test. The spatial visualization tasks
showed an increase of 28%. A smaller increase on this task would
be expected since spatial visualization tasks involve processing
components of perceptual speed and spatial relations tasks, but

also require higher order processing components as well. Finally, we should note that in most cases, low ability individuals achieved performance on the posttest comparable to high ability individuals on the corresponding pretest.

Conclusions

We think that our data on the relationships among practice effects, ability levels and test scores provide a strong argument for the need to combine psychometric, information processing, and developmental or learning approaches to the study of intellectual ability. Certainly, the data indicate that ability differences manifest on standard reference tests are interpretable in terms of theories and models of spatial information processing. However, our data on practice effects, as well as developmental data, also seem to argue that differences obtained in a five to 25 minute testing session are not the whole picture with respect to an individual's abilities in the spatial domain. Like many other cognitive activities, spatial processing is subject to substantial developmental change and practice effects. Our low ability individuals show this to be the case. What we have not shown are data on individual subjects. These data reveal that the practice effects obtained in the experimental tasks and the score changes on the reference tests are highly variable over individuals. Some low ability individuals show substantial improvements in spatial processing while others do not. Other experimental attempts to improve subjects' performance on visualization tasks using different interventions also show that different subjects profit most readily from different types of treatments (Kyllonen, Lohman, & Snow, 1984). Typical testing procedures are incapable of detecting such differences and provide little or no information about the level of performance or skill that an individual could achieve.

IMPLICATIONS FOR ASSESSMENT

Questions about intellectual ability, including the development of a comprehensive theory of intellectual ability, can be better pursued when psychometric, information processing, and developmental approaches are integrated. We have tried to illustrate this by reviewing efforts of this type focusing on spatial cognition. Similar illustrations could be provided for other areas of cognition such as verbal ability and reasoning. For many years, psychometricians have known about individual differences in spatial cognition and they have developed many instruments that assess this aspect of intellectual ability. These instruments predict performance in certain academic and technical courses. By linking information processing theories and methods of analysis with psychometric data we have begun to

understand better individual differences in spatial ability. By
introducing an individual differences approach into information
processing theory we have also begun to tap a powerful method for
testing certain basic assumptions of this theoretical
perspective. More specifically, individual differences are what
Underwood (1975) termed "a crucible in theory construction"
providing tests of assumptions such as separability of processes
and process invariance over situations. By combining information
processing and developmental or learning approaches we can better
understand the qualitative and quantitative performance changes
that occur with development, experience, and practice. Such a
combination of perspectives also enhances our understanding of the
evolution of cognitive structures, processes, and knowledge. All
of the preceding represent enhancements to theory.

There are also benefits to be gained relative to the technology of
ability assessment. Elsewhere, it has been argued that modern
computer technology, in combination with extant psychometric
procedures and information processing models, can contribute to
new forms of ability assessment (Hunt & Pellegrino, in press).
This can come about in two general ways. The first is by
permitting a more refined measurement of performance for tasks and
factors currently in use. The second is by permitting the
measurement of performance on tasks that it would be impossible to
present without modern technology.

In the first case, enhanced assessment may be accomplished by
decomposing performance on perceptual speed, spatial relations, or
spatial visualization tasks into sets of measures reflecting
cognitive processes and capacities. Rather than just an overall
performance score, we also derive measures of variables such as
encoding speed, rotation speed, and transformation accuracy. The
faceted synthesis and rotation task shown in Figure 7 represents a
preliminary step in this direction. The tasks and measures used
come from existing tests and theories. At present, it is possible
to construct a battery of computer-administered tasks preserving
the general factor structure we have referred to throughout this
paper while at the same time providing detailed diagnostic
information about specific cognitive functions. To do so would
require two things: (1) systematic problem sets like those used in
process analyses of individual differences, and (2) computers for
the presentation of problems and the monitoring of response
latency and accuracy. This can be done now for many
perceptual-spatial processing components by simply drawing upon
information processing studies such as those described earlier.
We could also enhance such a battery by including tasks that do
not currently appear in paper and pencil batteries but which
assess certain imagery and spatial functions postulated in
Kosslyn's theory. Some of the tasks could be drawn from the work

of Kosslyn et al. (1983) and Poltrock and Brown (1984). It should
be noted that one contribution of information processing research
to the construction of such an assessment battery is a framework
and method for decomposition of existing measures while a second
contribution is the generation of new tasks and measures.
Further, careful process analyses of existing tests may suggest
ways in which such tasks could be altered in order to make them
more dependable indicators of the constructs they purport to
measure. All of the foregoing deal with the processing of static
displays of stimuli.

The second case that must be considered with respect to spatial
cognition is the processing of dynamic rather than static spatial
relations. Our intuitive sense of "spatial ability" is that it
extends beyond dealing with static images and is frequently
exercised in a world of objects moving in relation to each other
and individuals moving in relation to objects. Given two or more
objects on a display moving with a certain speed and on a certain
trajectory, how well can we predict and infer what will happen?
Will they collide? Which one will reach a certain point first?
When will an object reach a certain point? The processing of
dynamic spatial relations is of interest both in terms of
psychological theories of spatial cognition and in terms of the
psychometric assessment of human spatial abilities. Furthermore,
research on dynamic visual abilities using film tests suggests
that some dynamic spatial abilities may be identified that are at
least partially independent of spatial abilities measured by
paper-and-pencil tests (Seibert & Snow, 1965). Theory-based
measures of dynamic spatial abilities would probably show even
greater uniqueness. Computer technology permits the development,
implementation and evaluation of dynamic spatial reasoning tasks
that are otherwise not possible even with film. Such tasks might
constitute an important part of the assessment of spatial
ability. Should we just go ahead and develop such tasks or should
we do so within a theoretical context? Asked in another way, do
we want to do more than just simply report correlations between
new instruments and old ones? We believe that the answer is
obvious. The solution is to develop tasks and analyze
relationships within an information processing framework. By
doing so we can enhance both theory and practice at the same
time.

We need to consider the benefits of such modified assessment in
light of another practical issue, one that has been at the center
of much controversey. The issue concerns the goals and purposes
of assessing intellectual ability and the uses of mental tests.
For some time there has been consensus among psychometricians that
the predictive level of mental tests is probably about as high as
one can expect to achieve, given the typical constraints of the

testing situation. The historical emphasis on predictability stems from two sources, the first being the use of tests for selection purposes. Implicit in this use, however, is a view that abilities are relatively stable. That is, the assumption underlying traditional mental testing is that some mental entity, call it g, or Gc, Gf, or Gv, or v:ed or k:m determines success in school and similar intellectual endeavors. By measuring this accurately, one can then predict a person's success in such endeavors. From cognitive and developmental perspectives it seems more reasonable to start with the point of view that intellectual skills are malleable rather than fixed. With a malleable intelligence as the starting point, the predictive value of tests is no longer a prime concern. If we believe that intelligence is malleable, then what educators need to know are those experiences that will be most likely to assist a student to achieve particular educational goals. Believing that intelligence is malleable, the value of tests lies in their ability to provide some of the information needed to design instruction appropriate for an individual. Thus, the important criterion for evaluating a test becomes its diagnostic value. Mental tests derived from the predictive tradition in psychometrics are not terribly useful in this regard. The outcome of almost any mental test is a score that simply indicates a person's standing relative to a normative sample. However, such information is insufficient for the design of appropriate instruction. In this regard, mental tests are not unlike a thermometer as a measure of physical health. They provide a rough index as to whether a person is healthy or not but provide precious little in the way of specific diagnostic information. One could hope then that by combining the focus on process exemplified in information processing and developmental approaches with existing psychometric measures, it would be possible to devise instruments and testing situations that, although they may be no more predictive than their predecessors, will provide more extensive diagnostic information regarding an individual's cognitive assets and liabilities. This would include testing situations sufficiently extended so that changes in performance could be observed, including the capacity to adapt to novel situations and automate performance (Sternberg, 1984 and Chapter 3, this volume).

In summary, whether considering practical issues of the uses and misuses of tests or the more theoretical facets of intelligence and intellectual ability, the conclusion is much the same. Psychometric theory and practice, though it has long held center stage, is necessary but not sufficient to address the theoretical and applied issues associated with intellectual ability. Information processing theory is a relative newcomer and it alone or in combination with developmental theory is also insufficient to address these issues. An integration of perspectives and disciplines is needed to achieve progress in understanding many of the theoretical and pragmatic issues associated with the constructs of intellectual ability in general, and of spatial ability in particular.

REFERENCES

Alderton, D.L. & Pellegrino, J.W. (1984). Analysis of mental paper-folding. Unpublished manuscript, University of California, Santa Barbara, Ca.

Alderton, D.L., Pellegrino, J.W., & Lydiatt, S. (1984). Effects of extended practice on spatial processing ability. Unpublished manuscript, University of California, Santa Barbara, Ca.

Averbach, E., & Coriell, A.S. (1961). Short-term memory in vision. Bell System Technical Journal, 40, 309-328.

Barratt, E.S. (1953). An analysis of verbal reports of solving spatial problems as an aid in defining spatial factors. Journal of Psychology, 36, 17-25.

Bennett, G.K. , Seashore, H.G & Wesman, A.G. (1974). Manual for the Differential Aptitude Test (5th ed.). New York: The Psychological Corporation.

Botzum, W.A. (1951). A factorial study of reasoning and closure factors. Psychometrika, 16, 361-386.

Burt, C. (1949). The structure of the mind: A review of the results of factor analysis. British Journal of Educational Psychology, 19, 100-114.

Carroll, J.B. (1976). Psychometric tests as cognitive tasks: A new "structure of intellect". In L.B. Resnick (Ed.), The nature of intelligence (pp. 27-56). Hillsdale, NJ: Erlbaum.

Cattell, R.B. (1963). Theory of fluid and crystallized intelligence: A criticial experiment. Journal of Educational Psychology, 54, 1-22.

Cattell, R.B. (1971). Abilities: Their structure, growth, and action. Boston: Houghton Mifflin.

Christal, R.E. (1958). Factor analytic study of visual memory. Psychological Monographs, 72 (13, Whole No. 466).

Conroy, R., & Lohman, D.F. (1976). Characteristics of a facet-designed measure of memory for pictures. Paper presented at the annual meeting of the American Educational Research Association, New York.

Cooper, L.A., & Shepard, R.N. (1973). Chronometric studies of the rotation of mental images. In W.G. Chase (Ed.), Visual information processing (pp. 75-176). New York: Academic Press.

Cronbach, L.J., & Snow, R.E. (1977). Aptitudes and instructional methods: A handbook for research on interactions. New York: Irvington.

Egan, D.E. (1978). Characterizing spatial ability: Different mental processes reflected in accuracy and latency scores. Unpublished manuscript, Bell Laboratories, Murray Hill, NJ.

Ekstrom, R.B., French, J.W., & Harman, H.H. (1976). Kit of factor-referenced cognitive tests. Princeton, NJ: Educational Testing Service.

Eliot, J.C., & Smith, I.M. (1983). An international directory of spatial tests. Windsor, England: NFER-Nelson.

Eysenck, H.J. (1967). Intellectual assessment: A theoretical and experimental approach. British Journal of Educational Psychology, 37, 81-98.

French, J.W. (1951). The description of aptitude and achievement tests in terms of rotated factors. Psychometric Monographs, 5.

French, J.W. (1965). The relationship of problem-solving styles to the factor composition of tests. Educational and Psychological Measurement, 25, 9-28.

French, J.W., Ekstrom, R.B., & Price, L.A. (1963). Kit of reference tests for cognitive factors. Princeton, NJ: Educational Testing Service.

Ghiselli, E.E. (1973). The validity of aptitude tests in personnel selection. Personnel Psychology, 26, 461-477.

Glushko, R.J., & Cooper, L.A. (1978). Spatial comprehension and comparison processes in verification tasks. Cognitive Psychology, 10, 391-421.

Guilford, J.P. (1967). The nature of human intelligence. New York: McGraw-Hill.

Guilford, J.P., Fruchter, B., & Zimmerman, W.S. (1952). Factor analysis of the Army Air Forces Shepard Field battery of experimental aptitude tests. Psychometrika, 17, 45-68.

Guilford, J.P., & Hoepfner, R. (1971). The analysis of intelligence. New York: McGraw-Hill.

Guilford, J.P., & Lacey, J.I. (Eds.) (1947). Printed classification tests. AAF aviation psychology research program reports (No. 5). Washington, DC: GPO.

Guttman, L. (1954). A new approach to factor analysis: The radex. In P.F. Lazarfield (Ed.), Mathematical thinking in the social sciences, 216-257. Glencoe, IL: Free Press.

Hoffman, K.I., Guilford, J.P., Hoepfner, R., & Doherty, W.J. (1968). A factor analysis of the figural-cognition and figural-evaluation abilities (Rep. No. 40). Psychological Laboratory, University of Southern California, Los Angeles.

Holzinger, K.J., & Harman, H.H. (1938). Comparison of two factorial analyses. Psychometrika, 3, 45-60.

Horn, J.L. (1976). Human abilities: A review of research and theory in the early 1970's. Annual Review of Psychology, 27, 437-485.

Horn, J.L., & Bramble, W.J. (1967). Second-order ability structure revealed in right and wrongs scores. Journal of Educational Psychology, 58, 115-122.

Horn, J.L., & Cattell, R.B. (1966). Refinement and test of the theory of fluid and crystallized general intelligences. Journal of Educational Psychology, 57, 253-270.

Humphreys, L.G. (1962). The organization of human abilities. American Psychologist, 17, 475-483.

Hunt, E. & Pellegrino, J.W. (in press). Expanding intelligence testing with interactive computer terminals: A critique and prospectus. Intelligence.

Just, M.A., & Carpenter, P.A. (1985). Cognitive coordinate systems: Accounts of mental rotation and individual differences in spatial ability. Psychological Review, 92, 137-172.

Kail, R. (1983). Growth functions for information processing parameters. Paper presented at the annual meeting of the Psychonomic Society, San Diego, Ca.

Kosslyn, S.M. (1980). Image and Mind. Cambridge, MA: Harvard University Press.

Kosslyn, S.M. (1981). The medium and the message in mental imagery: A theory. Psychological Review, 88, 46-66.

Kosslyn, S.M., Brunn, J.L., Cave, C.R. & Wallach, R.W. (1983). Components of mental imagery representation (Technical Report No. 1). Waltham, MA: Brandeis University.

Koussy, A.A.H. El (1935). The visual perception of space. British Journal of Psychology, 20. (Monograph supplement)

Kyllonen, P.C. (1984). Information processing analysis of spatial ability. Unpublished Doctoral Dissertation, Stanford University.

Kyllonen, P.C., Lohman, D.F., & Snow, R.E. (1984). Effects of aptitudes, strategy training, and task facets on spatial task performance. Journal of Educational Psychology, 76, 130-145.

Kyllonen, P.C., Lohman, D.F., & Woltz, D.J. (1984). Componential modeling of alternative strategies for performing spatial tasks. Journal of Educational Psychology, 76, 1325-1345.

Lansman, M. (1981). Ability factors and the speed of information processing. In M.P. Friedman, J.P. Das and N. O'Connor (Eds.), Intelligence and learning (pp. 441-457). New York: Plenum Press.

Likert, R. & Quasha, W.H. (1970). Manual for the revised Minnesota paper form board test. New York: The Psychological Corporation.

Lohman, D.F. (1979a). Spatial ability: A review and reanalysis of the correlational literature (Tech. Rep. No. 8). Stanford, CA: Stanford University, Aptitude Research Project, School of Education. (NTIS NO. AD-A075 972)

Lohman, D.F. (1979b). Spatial ability: Individual differences in speed and level (Tech. Rep. No. 9). Stanford, CA: Stanford University, Aptitude Research Project, School of Education. (NTIS NO. AD-A075 973)

Lohman, D.F. (1977). Eye movement differences reflecting aptitude
    processes. Paper presented at the meeting of the American
    Psychological Association, San Framcisco.

Lohman, D.F., & Kyllonen, P.C. (1983). Individual differences in
    solution strategy on spatial tasks. In R.F. Dillon & R.R.
    Schmeck (Eds.), Individual Differences in cognition, 1,
    105-135. New York: Academic Press.

Lucas, C.M. (1953). Analysis of the Relative Movement test by a
    method of individual interviews (ETS RM 53-08). Princeton,
    NJ: Educational Testing Service.

Marshalek, B., Lohman, D.F., & Snow, R.E. (1983). The complexity
    continuum   in   the   radex   and   hierarchical   models   of
    intelligence. Intelligence, 7, 107-128.

McFarlane, M. (1925). A study of practical ability. British
    Journal of Psychology, 8. (Monograph supplement)

McGree, M.G. (1979). Human spatial abilities: Environmental,
    genetic, hormonal, and neuroligcal influences. Psychological
    Bulletin, 86, 889-918.

McGree, M. (1979). Human spatial abilities: Sources of sex
    differences . New York: Praeger.

McNemar, Q. (1964). Lost: Our intelligence? Why? American
    Psychologist , 19, 871-882.

Messick, S., & French, J.W. (1975). Dimensions of cognitive
    closure. Multivariate Behavioral Research, 1, 3-16.

Michael, W.B., Zimmerman, W.S., & Guilford, J.P. (1950). An
    investigation of two hypotheses regarding the nature of the
    spatial relations and visualization factors. Educational and
    Psychological Measurement, 10, 187-243.

Mumaw, R.J. & Pellegrino, W.J. (in press). Individual differences
    in complex spatial processing. Journal of Educational
    Psychology.

Mumaw, R.J., Pellegrino, J.W., Kail, R.V. & Carter, P. (in
    press). Different slopes for different folks: Process
    analysis of spatial aptitude. Memory and Cognition.

Pellegrino, J.W. & Glaser, R. (1979). Cognitive correlates and
    components in the analysis of individual differences.
    Intelligence, 3, 187-214.

Pellegrino, J.W. & Mumaw, R.J. (1980). Multicomponent models of spatial ability. Unpublished manuscript, University of California, Santa Barbara, CA.

Pemberton, C. (1952). The closure factors related to other cognitive processes. Psychometrika, 17, 267-288.

Piaget, J., & Inhelder, B. (1967). The child's conception of space. NY: Norton.

Poltrock, S.E. & Brown, P. (1984). Individual differences in visual imagery and spatial ability. Intelligence, 8, 93-138.

Regian, J.W. & Pellegrino, J.W. (1984). Practice and transfer effects in two-dimensional mental rotation.. Unpublished manuscript, University of California, Santa Barbara, CA.

Raven, T.C (1962). Progressive matrices. London: Lewis.

Schmid, J., & Leiman, J. (1957). The development of hierarchical factor solutions. Psychometrika, 22, 53-61.

Seibert, W.F., & Snow, R.E. (1965). Studies in cine-psychometry I: Preliminary factor analysis of visual cognition and memory. Audio Visual Center, Purdue University, Lafayette, Indiana.

Shepard, R.N. & Feng, C. (1972). A chronometric study of mental paper folding. Cognitive Psychology, 3, 228-243.

Shepard, R.N. & Metzler, J. (1971). Mental Rotation of three-dimensional objects. Science, 171, 701-703.

Smith, I.M. (1964). Spatial ability. San Diego: Knapp.

Snow, R.E. (1980). Aptitude processes. In R.E. Snow, P.A. Rederico, & W.E. Montague (Eds.), Aptitude, Learning and Instruction, 1, Cognitive process analyses of aptitude, 27-64. Hillsdale, NJ: Erlbaum.

Snow, R.E. (1981). Toward a theory of aptitude for learning: Fluid and crystallized abilities and their correlates. In M.P. Friedman, J.P. Das, & N. O'Connor (Eds.), Intelligence and Learning, 345-362. New York: Plenum.

Spearman, C. (1927). The abilities of man. London: MacMillan.

Spearman, C. (1939). Thurstone's work re-worked. Journal of Educational Psychology, 30, 1-16.

Sternberg, R.J. (1977). Intelligence, information processing, and analogical reasoning: The componential analysis of human abilities. Hillsdale, NJ: Lawrence Erlbaum Associates.

Sternberg, R.J. (1984). Toward a triarchic theory of human intelligence. Behavioral and Brain Sciences, 7, 269-315.

Terman, L. (1921). Symposium on intelligence and its measurement. Journal of Educational Psychology, 12, 127-133.

Thurstone, L.L. (1931). Multiple factor analysis. Psychological Review, 38, 406-427.

Thurstone, L.L. (1938a). Primary mental abilities. Psychometric Monographs, 1.

Thurstone, L.L. (1938b). The perceptual factor. Psychometrika, 3, 1-12.

Thurstone, L.L. (1944). A factorial study of perception. Chicago: University of Chicago Press.

Thurstone, L.L. (1951). Analysis of mechanical aptitude (Rep. No. 62). Psychometric Laboratory, University of Chiacago, Chicago, Il.

Thurstone, L.L., & Thurstone, T.G. (1941). Factorial studies of intelligence. Psychometric Monographs, 2.

Underwood, B.J. (1975). Individual differences as a crucible in theory construction. American Psychologist, 30, 128-134.

Vernon, P.E. (1950). The structure of human abilities. London: Methuen.

Wechsler, D. (1955). Wechsler adult intelligence scale. New York: Psychological Corporation.

Wherry, R.J. (1959). Hierarchical factor solutions without rotation. Psychometrika, 24, 45-51.

Witkin, H.A., Dyk, R.B., Faterson, H.G., Goodenough, D.R., & Karp, S.A. (1962). Psychological differentation. New York: Erlbaum.

Witkin, H.A., Oltman, P.K., Raskin, E., & Karp, S.A. (1971). Embedded figures test. Palo Alto, CA: Consulting Psychologists Press.

Zimmerman, W.S. (1953). A revised orthogonal rotation solution for Thurstone's original primary mental abilities test battery. Psychometrika, 18, 77-93.

Zimmerman, W.S. (1954). The influence of item complexity upon the factor composition of a spatial visualization test. Educational and Psychological Measurement, 14, 106-119.

CHAPTER 7

A FOCAL REVIEW OF RESEARCH ON THE LURIA-DAS MODEL OF COGNITIVE PROCESSING

L.Z. KLICH

University of New England, Australia

INTRODUCTION

It is now a decade since the simultaneous-successive model of cognitive abilities, derived from the work of A.R. Luria, was publicised in Psychological Bulletin, (Das, Kirby & Jarman, 1975). More recently, the Kaufman Assessment Battery for Children (Kaufman & Kaufman, 1983), which is explicitly based on Luria's theory of functional organisation in the human brain and incorporates extensive measures of simultaneous and successive information processing, has attracted a great deal of attention, and reviews of it (Sewell, 1983; Sternberg, 1983) have raised relevant questions about the validity of Luria's theory.

Sternberg (1983) has argued that the empirical literature supporting Luria's theory is rather sparse, that the bulk of research on simultaneous and successive processing factors has come from one source i.e., the work of J.P. Das and his colleagues, and that "most other psychologists studying intelligence, who are not believers in this theory, have not isolated factors even remotely resembling the simultaneous and successive ones" (p. 202). It seems apposite therefore at this time to consider in closer detail how and in what contexts Luria's theory has come to be operationalised in the research literature, to critically examine the analytical procedures used, to evaluate how the resulting data have been utilised as evidence in support of the theory, and thus identify any major areas of methodological or interpretative concern.

After a short introduction to Luria's theory, and a brief survey of the evidence relating to simultaneous and successive processing, this review will focus on two areas considered problematical in the literature: a) research with different cultural groups which has been cited in support of the Luria-Das model, and b) associated methodological procedures.

LURIA'S THEORY

Luria's theory of functional organisation in the human brain was concerned with the cerebral bases of psychological processes, or how intellectual functions relate to cortical and subcortical neurological components. Luria was an eclectic scholar and prolific researcher (Cole, 1977; Pribram, 1978), who consistently acknowledged his indebtedness to the ideas of his mentor and colleague, Vygotsky, and emphasized that valid pychological theories needed to be constructed from a sound physiology of brain activities (Cole, 1979).

The need to develop scientifically-based techniques for the restitution of damaged human brain mechanisms after the Second World War led to Luria's most prodigious research, the major practical tasks of which were to study the nature of functional change following brain lesions, to identify the factors underlying disturbance amongst groups of cognitive tasks, and finally, where possible to encourage rehabilitation of brain-injured patients by devising programmes to restore impaired functions. What came to be known as Luria's neuropsychological method, or syndrome analysis (Christensen, 1975), was evolved from such clinical investigations of human behaviour and Luria himself likened the procedures to qualitative "factor analyses in individual subjects" (1970, p. 72).

An adequate conceptualisation of the brain's functional organisation was clearly necessary in order to direct the restoration of cognitive operations through system reorganisation, and so the nature of cortical and sub-cortical components in the coordination of mental activities came to be painstakingly inferred from persistent observations of brain-behaviour relationships. Innumerable such "individual factor analyses", gathered over many years of research and involving many different localised lesions, enabled Luria to gradually build a comprehensive though succinct neuropsychological theory of functional organisation in the human brain (Luria, 1970; 1973; 1979).

Luria stated that higher mental functions are complex, organised functional systems which operate as the result of interactions between differentiated brain structures. This dynamic localisation of functional cognitive systems relies on elements represented in different areas of the brain which may be integrated according to the demands of a processing task. Luria (1971) stressed that such functional systems of conjointly working cortical zones are not predetermined structures, but are formed during the course of each individual's development in response to environmental and social influences. The theory therefore appears to have potentially extensive applications in cross-cultural psychology.

According to Luria, the functional organisation of the brain can be understood in terms of three basic units. The first unit is responsible for regulating the energy level and tone of the cortex (i.e. for optimal arousal), and is located in the brain stem and reticular formation. The second unit is highly specialised for the analysis, coding and storage of information, and Luria considered that it operated through two forms of integrative activity: <u>simultaneous synthesis</u>, or the integration of stimuli into maintained spatial groupings, and <u>successive</u> or <u>sequential synthesis</u>, where serially perceived stimuli are temporally ordered such that each element exists only as part of a retraceable sequence. The occipito-parietal zones are responsible for simultaneous synthesis, and the temporal and frontotemporal regions for successive synthesis.

Both forms of synthesis operate at the <u>perceptual</u> level (in the course of direct perception), at the <u>mnestic</u> level (during the process of memorising previous experience), and at the <u>intellectual</u> level as part of the performance of complex higher cognitive functions such as the syntactic structure of narrative speech (successive) or comprehension of interrelated mathematical concepts (simultaneous). The third unit of the brain, comprising the frontal lobes, is involved in the orgnisation of conscious activity through the programming, regulation and verification of behaviour i.e., planning and monitoring functions.

Luria's theory provided a provocative fusion of original findings and reinterpretations of evidence long-established in the field of neurology, and was soon applied in developing the new discipline of neuropsychology. Thus, Jakobson (1971), a linguist, utilised Luria's model in tackling the problems of linguistic aphasia, and considered that "among the contributions of neurologists, psychiatrists and psychologists to the study of aphasia, Luria's work seems to be the most instructive" (p. 98), particularly the way in which the two forms of synthesis explained basic language disorders. Joint research between Jakobson, Pribram and Luria went on to postulate two major neurolinguistic axes underlying problems with the variety of language uses (Pribram, 1971, p. 359).

Luria's influence can also be seen in the work of Bruner and his colleagues on cognitive growth, and their "line of enquiry about the relation of serial and simultaneous orgnisation in perception and behaviour" (Bruner, Olver and Greenfield, 1967, p. 18). Bruner's transposition was probably the first attempt to apply Luria's ideas beyond the clinical pale and into the realm of Western individual differences psychology. Luria's theory was based on data from 'individualised factor analyses' carried out with very atypical individuals. Recent attempts to examine

- 315 -

simultaneous and successive syntheses as dimensions of individual differences in more normal samples have relied heavily on factor-analytic studies in the psychometric tradition.

SIMULTANEOUS-SUCCESSIVE PROCESSING

The introduction of Luria's model of simultaneous and successive syntheses into psychometric studies of individual differences came about through the apparent incapacity of a well-documented North American model of cognitive 'abilities' to explain the results of a study comparing patterns of cognitive functioning amongst atypical and 'normal' children.

Das (1972) administered six tasks to samples of mildly retarded and non-retarded Canadian children in order to examine whether Jensen's model of Level 1 and Level 2 abilities would explain any differences found between the two samples. In brief, Jensen (1970) had argued that intellectual performance depended on the combination of two abilities: Level 1 was simple association and memory, while Level 2 involved reasoning and conceptual learning. The two were also hierarchically arranged such that memory was considered necessary although not sufficient for reasoning, but not the converse.

The six tasks were: Raven's Coloured Progressive Matrices, widely acknowledged as a measure of reasoning and often thought to reflect general intelligence; Graham-Kendall's Memory for Designs, a popular test for assessment of brain-damage which required children to reproduce visually displayed designs from memory; Cross-modal Coding, where children listened to patterns of sound after which they were asked to identify one of three dot patterns as resembling the original auditory stimulus; Visual Short-term Memory, in which a five-digit grid arranged in the shape of a cross was presented, and following a delay with a colour-naming filler task, children were asked to reproduce the digits on an empty grid; and finally Auditory Short-term Memory, which consisted of four-word lists. Twelve lists had words that were semantically similar, another twelve lists had words that were acoustically similar, and a further twelve lists had unrelated or 'neutral' words. The child was required to recall each list orally immediately after its presentation, and two separate scores were noted, one for items correctly recalled <u>serially</u>, and the other for total number of items correct, i.e., <u>free recall</u>.

Results for the two samples were separately subjected to principal components analysis, and for each group two factors clearly emerged after orthogonal rotation. For both groups Raven's Matrices loaded highly on factor 1 but minimally on factor 2, and the reverse applied to Auditory Serial Recall and Auditory Free

Recall. The other three variables however showed a different pattern of loadings between the groups on the two factors (see Table 1).

Table 1

Principal components with varimax rotation for
retarded and nonretarded children: from Das (1972), p. 10

Test	Nonretarded		Retarded	
	1 (Sim)	2 (Succ)	1 (Sim)	2 (Succ)
Raven's Progressive Matrices	792	161	786	007
Memory for Designs	269	579	830	-061
IQ Score	492	176	529	326
Cross-modal coding	742	020	546	482
Visual Short-term Memory	693	294	533	481
Short-term Memory (auditory)	154	683	048	855
Short-term Memory (free recall)	023	757	043	856

N.B.   Decimal points omitted.

The starkest contrast was provided by Memory for Designs, which loaded highly on factor 1 (with Raven's Matrices) for the retarded sample, but in exactly the opposite way for the non-retarded group (i.e. with Auditory Serial and Free Recall). Cross-modal Coding and Visual Short-term Memory for the retarded group had medium loadings split across both factors, but both loaded highly only on factor 1 (with Raven's Matrices) for the non-retarded group.

Das's interpretation inferred processing differences between the two groups on the three variables with disparate loadings, and argued that the hierarchical memory-reasoning distinction did not provide a coherent explanation of these results. Borrowing Bruner's terminology to propose that enactive as against iconic modes for transforming information differentiated between the non-retarded and retarded children seemed to provide a more reasonable explanation of results on some tasks. However, Luria's non-hierarchical model of simultaneous and successive syntheses appeared to most cogently describe the two factors, suggesting a different use of these integrative processes by the two groups of children on particular tasks e.g., Memory for Designs:

> "...in producing the designs, the non-retarded child, is defining the task operationally as a sequence of pencil movements which he remembers, and this guides his reproduction. The retarded child, on the other hand, has to remember it as a total picture ... What we are suggesting here is that Jensen's Level I and Level II may be limiting instances of successive and simultaneous modes of processing information." (Das, 1972, p. 11).

In subsequent investigation Das, his students, and colleagues from the University of Alberta extended and refined the battery of tests employed to operationally define simultaneous and successive syntheses (Das, 1973a, 1973c; Das, Kirby and Jarman, 1975, 1979; Das and Molloy, 1975; Kirby and Das, 1978). Utilising principal components analysis, factors representing the two modes of information integration across the range of tasks have been identified in different age-groups (Das and Molloy, 1975; Jarman 1979), in children of different socio-economic backgrounds (Das et al., 1975; Molloy and Das, 1979), in children assessed as having low, average, and high I.Q. levels (Jarman and Das, 1977), and in further groups of mentally retarded children (Cummins and Das, 1980; Das and Cummins, 1978).

Later studies have sought to validate Luria's predictive statements about the involvement of Unit 2 functions in specific intellectual tasks. As a result simultaneous and successive processes have been implicated in a variety of learning disabilities (Das, Leong, and Williams, 1978), in specific problems associated with achieving reading proficiency and the registration, coding and integration of linguistic information (Cummins and Das, 1977, 1978; Das and Cummins 1978; Das, Cummins, Kirby and Jarman, 1979; Kirby, 1978, 1980; Kirby and Das, 1977; Kirby, Moore and Cousins, 1978; Leong, 1976, 1977, 1980a, 1980b; Ryckman, 1981), in the developmental shift from syntagmatic to paradigmatic word association (Cummins and Das, 1978; Jarman, 1980a), in narrative speech (Cummins and Mulcahy, 1979), in cross-modal and intra-modal functions (Jarman, 1978c, 1980b), in the Uznadze haptic illusion (Cummins, 1976), the Muller-Lyer visual illusion (Jarman, 1979), and in the use of alphabetic mnemonics to recall labelled pictures (Jarman, 1978d). The two forms of synthesis have also been related to performance on test batteries of traditional primary mental abilities (Das, Cummins,

Kirby and Jarman, 1979; Kirby and Das, 1978), and on the old and revised Wechsler Intelligence Scale for Children (Cummins and Das, 1980; Das and Cummins, 1978; Kaufman, 1981).

Further confirmation of Unit 2 functions in Luria's model has come from researchers who have examined real-life behaviours such as intentional-incidental learning (Hunt, 1980) and card-playing (Davidson, 1979). Some efforts have also more recently been made to extend the factor analytic model to encompass Unit 1 and 3 functions such as attention (Hunt, 1980), and planning (Das, 1980; 1984).

Other studies, while making no attempts to directly operationalise the two modes of processing have nevertheless called upon interpretations of them in research areas as diverse as university students' study processes (Biggs, 1978), the syndrome of dyspraxia in deaf children (Van Uden, 1981), dyslexia in schoolchildren (Aaron, 1978), the ability of young children to infer another person's thinking, or 'cognitive perspective taking' (Kurdek, 1977, 1980), optometric treatment (Solan, 1981), and feature interactions in consumer judgements of product design (Holbrook and Moore, 1981).

A reappraisal with modifications of the Das battery was undertaken by Jarman (1978a) who tried to replicate Das's original (1972) investigation with a sample of retarded children only. Commenting on the consistency with which simultaneous and successive cognitive processing factors had been found in a variety of populations Jarman stated that "the initial study of retarded and non-retarded children represents the only circumstance in which clearly discrepant patterns of abilities have been found" (Jarman, 1978a, p. 344). This is in fact incorrect, since, as will be established later, studies by Das (1973b) and Krywaniuk (Krywaniuk and Das, 1976; Das, Kirby and Jarman, 1979) showed differences in the patterns of loadings on the same variables for culturally-different groups. The simultaneous marker tests used by Jarman were Raven's Coloured Progressive Matrices, Memory for Designs, and Figure Copying (Ilg and Ames, 1964), which replaced Das's Cross-Modal Coding. Figure Copying consists of geometric figures that are presented consecutively for reproduction while each is in full view. The successive marker tests were Serial Recall (a different label but the same test as Das's Auditory Short-term Memory scored for correct serial order in recall), Visual Short-term Memory, and Digit Span Forward from the Wechsler Intelligence Scale for Children, in which a child is asked to recall series of digits gradually increasing in difficulty from three digit span to nine digits. Digit Span replaced Das's Free

Recall, which had simply been Auditory Short-Term Memory rescored for total number of correct items recalled irrespective of their serial position.

The results for Jarman's retarded sample yielded a factor matrix virtually identical to those found for other groups with the same tests (see Table 2): the two processing factors were clearly defined by their respective marker tests. Jarman therefore considered that the inclusion of Figure Copying and Digit Span provided a clearer operational definition of the two modes of integration by lending stability to the simultaneous and successive factors.

Table 2

Principal components with varimax rotation for retarded children in Jarman (1978a), and comparisons with Das (1972): from Jarman (1978a), p. 347, and Das (1972), p. 10

Test	Jarman (retarded)		Das (retarded)		Das (nonretarded)	
	Sim.	Succ.	Sim.	Succ.	Sim.	Succ.
Raven's Matrices	943	076	786	007	792	161
Figure Copying	865	-159	-	-	-	-
Memory for Designs	-894	183	830	-061	269	579
IQ score	-	-	529	326	492	176
Cross-modal coding	-	-	546	482	742	-020
Visual Short-Term Memory	060	977	533	481	693	294
Serial recall	198	879	048	855	154	683
Free recall	-	-	043	856	023	757
Digit-Span Forward	033	809	-	-	-	-

N.B. Decimal points omitted. Not all tests were administered in each study.

In attempting to explain the difference between Das's original results and his own, Jarman contended that the marker tests in his study were "homogeneous" measures of each process requiring unambiguous information integration:

"...the particular set of tests used here measures the same cognitive processes in subjects from many different environments and with many different inherited traits; i.e., these tests measure basic processes and are not amenable to wide variations in strategic behaviour." (Jarman, 1978a, p. 348).

While this appears a plausible explanation in relation to Cross-Modal Coding, which had split medium loadings in Das's study and could therefore be considered as 'heterogeneous' i.e., allowing differential coding or processing of information, it seems to be a contradiction in relation to Memory for Designs (see Table 2). In one case it is classified as 'homogeneous' (one of Jarman's simultaneous marker tests), in the other clearly 'heretogeneous' (in Das's original study it loaded highly on the successive factor for the non-retarded group and on the simultaneous factor for the retarded group, and Das himself specifically argued for differential strategies employed by the two groups in Memory for Designs performance). Indeed, it is ironic to record (as Das et al., 1979, have done) that, where Memory for Designs is concerned, the results for Das's retarded group can therefore be considered as more consistent with the extensive subsequent findings across many other samples than the results for the non-retarded group. A similar problem exists with Visual Short-Term Memory: it loaded exclusively on the successive factor in Jarman's study, had split loadings in Das's retarded group, and loaded predominantly on the simultaneous factor in Das's non-retarded sample. Although such minor interpretative problems concerning specific variables occur in the literature, the remarkable overall consistency of factor-analytic results identifying Unit 2 functions in studies by Das and his colleagues is nevertheless impressive.

Cross-validations of simultaneous and successive factors with very different tasks have been reported by Naglieri, Kaufman, Kaufman and Kamphaus (1981) and Richman and Lindgren (1980). Only a handful of studies however have directly attempted to seek validation of simultaneous and successive syntheses with culturally different samples, due no doubt to the difficulties associated with cross-cultural psychometric research. (Cronbach & Drenth, 1972; Irvine & Carroll, 1980).

CROSS-CULTURAL RESEARCH

While not specifically employing a factor-analytic design, Farnham-Diggory (1970) was the first to apply Luria's descriptions of Unit 2 processing functions in a cross-cultural context. Starting with Jensen's (1969) statement that changes in methods of presenting individual I.Q. items may produce very different

ability rankings within the same group of subjects,
Farnham-Diggory postulated that Negro and white North American
children might respond differentially to complex thinking tasks
requiring different modes of information integration. Three tasks
were assembled exemplifying verbal, spatial and quantitative
cognitive abilities.

The verbal synthesis task required children to learn symbols
(logographs) for words they were already familiar with, to read
two or three-word sentences from those symbols, and finally to act
out the meaning of the sentences they had read. In the maplike
spatial task four cards, each with a simple line pattern, were
placed for the student. A straight horizontal line was called a
"road", two parallel horizontal lines were a "river", two diagonal
lines crossing in the shape of the letter X were called a
"crossroad", and three lines (two short uprights with a horizontal
longer line across the top of them in the shape of a soccer goal)
were called a "bridge". The student was initially asked to
reconstruct each symbol in turn from a pile of correct length
strings. Once this performance check was completed, the scored
task required the child to "make a bridge, going across a river,
with a road on each side".

The mathematical task tested ability to match order in one set of
materials with order in a different set of materials (small,
medium and large plywood squares were to be matched with cards
containing one, two or three black dots). Farnham-Diggory
considered that the mathematical task resembled the maplike task
more than it did the verbal task, but all three were measures of
symbolic thinking. Using Luria's theoretical framework she argued
moreover that the verbal task involved successive synthesis
whereas the other two tasks illustrated simultaneous synthesis.

Performance on the verbal task by Negro and white children in
grades 1 to 4 showed no significant difference between the two
groups although Negro scores tended to be higher. However,
significant differences favouring the whites were found on both
the maplike and mathematical tasks. Farnham-Diggory's explanation
of these results opted for specific perceptual defects amongst
Negroes as the underlying cause, citing Pollack's (1969) theory
concerning the role of retinal pigmentation in perceptual
development i.e., Negro children suffer initially from greater
retinal insensitivity associated with dark-skinned groups, and
this is cumulatively compounded by cultural influence which may
deprive the children of situations necessary for the development
of complex perceptual coordination. Such an interpretation falls
clearly into the centricultural tradition of viewing a cultural
difference in performance as being due to an intellectual, or in
this case perceptual, deficit.

Five factor analyses of data from non-European cultures have been presented in the literature, and will now be considered in detail. Two were conducted with children from India (Table 3), and on closer examination it appears that the last three were from the one study with Canadian Indian children (Table 4).

Das (1973a, 1983c; Das et al., 1976; Das and Singha, 1975) has reported research with ninety high-caste (Brahmin) children from Orissa, India, using six tasks. Four are normally considered measures of simultaneous processing (Raven's Matrices, Figure Copying, Memory for Designs, and Cross-modal Coding), one of successive processing (Visual Short-term Memory), and a separate measure of processing speed was also added: Word Reading, also later called Word Naming, which is based on one of the three tests developed by Stroop (1935) as measures of cognitive speed.

The rationale for including speed of integration within a design based on Luria's theoretical framework was not made explicit. Das (1973c) stated that "Speed appeared as a factor along with simultaneous and successive integration in one of the previous factor analyses (Das, 1972)" (Das, 1973c, p. 104). An inspection of Das (1972) (the study with retarded and non-retarded groups reviewed earlier) reveals no mention or evidence of a speed factor. However, Das (1973c) goes on to clarify that the Word Reading test had been included in the earlier (1972) study and had loaded on a distinct speed factor, suggesting that "speed of information integration may be a factor in many cognitive tests" (Das, 1973, p. 105).

Analysis of the results with the High-caste Orissa children (see Table 3a) indeed produced three factors. Figure Copying and Memory for Designs defined a simultaneous factor. Raven's Matrices had a dominant loading on the same factor as well as a substantial loading on the successive factor defined by Visual Short-term Memory. Cross-modal Coding acted like a marker for speed processing, loading highly on a separate factor with Word Reading. The implications were clear: assumptions made about processing demands on a task within one culture may not necessarily transfer automatically to another culture.

Das et al. (1979) also reported a subsequent study with 48 school children from aboriginal tribes of Souther Orissa, India (see Table 3b). This time Colour Naming, another Stroop-based task, was included with Word Reading to indicate processing speed, alongside the same four simultaneous markers, with Visual Short-term Memory and Digit Span as successive processing measures.

Two factors emerged from the analysis: the one defined predominantly by Visual Short-term Memory, Digit Span, and Word

Table 3

a)   Principal components with varimax rotation for
90 high-caste children from Orissa (India):
from Das (1973a), p. 47

Test	1 (Sim)	2 (Speed)	3 (Succ)
Word Reading	-011	830	032
Raven's Matrices	624	253	433
Figure Copying	800	-278	-112.
Memory for Designs	-809	111	-037
Cross-Modal Coding	206	-640	233
Short-Term Memory (Visual)	-013	175	918

b)   Principal components with varimax rotation for
48 Aboriginal children from Orissa (India):
from Das et al. (1979), p. 124

Test	Successive and speed	Simultaneous
Raven's Matrices	548	527
Figure Copying	083	682
Visual Short-Term Memory	830	028
Memory-for-Designs (errors)	-452	-523
Cross-modal Coding	134	577
Digit Span	750	088
Color Naming	-450	616
Word Reading	-743	-140

N.B.   Decimal points omitted.

Reading was labelled "successive and speed", the other, defined by
Figure Copying and Cross-modal Coding was called "simultaneous".
Three supposed marker tests had split loadings: Raven's Matrices,
Memory for Designs, and Colour Naming. The inclusion of speed
measures and speed in the factor-name appears to have added little
to the clarity of the solution. It may well have been more
circumspect to simply label the two factors as successive and
simultaneous while acknowledging that many of the these tasks may
be 'heterogeneous' measures of synthesis in non-European cultures,
no matter how invariably they may elicit a particular form of
synthesis in individuals from European cultural groups.

It is of some interest to note here that a study by Jarman and Das
(1977) indicated that cognitive speed processes involved in the
Stroop tasks may be primarily of a successive variety. A further
study by Jarman and Krywaniuk (1978) attempted to remedy the
situation that "there is little information available from
existing studies of simultaneous and successive syntheses on the
possible nature of the cognitive processes in many other varieties
of tasks which use speed as a criterion measure" (p. 1167). They
factor-analysed eleven measures of cognitive speed, and summarised
their results by suggesting that "speed of information processing
may be described as essentially two varieties: simultaneous and
successive" (p. 1172). One wonders therefore why separate measures
of speed intended to define a distinct cognitive processing speed
factor continue to be included in the Das battery (Das et al.,
1979). As also occurred in the Jarman discussion of task
'homogeneity', there appears to be little interchange or
application of intracultural findings to cross-cultural research,
or vice-versa.

Research by Krywaniuk (Krywaniuk and Das, 1976; Das et al., 1979)
with Canadian Indian children has further confirmed that the same
task may elicit different Unit 2 functions in individuals with
different cultural backgrounds, thus emphasising the need for
considerable care to be exercised in the selection of tasks to
define simultaneous and successive cognitive processes in
cross-cultural research. Unfortunately reports of this
potentially valuable study have been plagued with
inconsistencies.

Krywaniuk and Das (1976) presented two factor analyses (Table 4)
carried out with 40 Canadian Indian children. The design of the
study dictated that a battery of baseline tests was initially
administered, followed by an intervention programme intended to
provide remedial experience to compensate for inefficient use of
successive processing strategies. Finally the same battery of
baseline tests was re-administered after the intervention
programme to assess its effects.

Table 4

a)   Principal components with varimax rotation
for 40 Canadian native children,
before intervention:
from Kryweniuk and Das, (1976), p. 277

Test	I Successive	II Speed	III Simultaneous
WISC Verbal	479	639	-029
Performance	431	574	235
Raven's Matrices	678	-047	458
Figure Copying	330	-165	743
Memory for Designs	074	-287	-801
Stroop Word Reading	-056	-717	112
Visual STM	065	707	435
Cross-modal Coding	584	037	162
Serial Recall	840	287	-066
Free Recall	787	352	000

b)   As for a) above, following i. ervention:
from Kryweniuk and Das (1976), p. 278

Test	I Successive	II Speed	III Simultaneous
WISC Verbal	347	665	364
Performance	515	547	391
Raven's Matrices	253	276	544
Figure Copying	-034	-227	848
Memory for Designs	-232	-110	-720
Stroop Word Reading	036	-833	136
Visual STM	401	303	499
Cross-modal Coding	749	252	-062
Serial Recall	881	026	317
Free Recall	892	022	293

c)   Principal components with varimax rotation
for 38 Canadian native children:
from Das et al. (1979), p. 129

Test	I Successive	II Speed	III Simultaneous
Raven's Matrices	688	072	379
Cross-modal Coding	585	-126	125
Figure Copying	341	036	711
Memory-for-Designs (errors)	-002	080	-831
Visual Short-Term Memory	-067	-424	481
Serial Recall	863	-139	-004
Free Recall	852	-184	-007
Word Reading	-126	856	135
Color Naming	-243	(missing)	-069

N.B.   Decimal points omitted.

The test battery consisted of the usual four simultaneous markers, Visual Short-term Memory and Serial Recall (also rescored for Free Recall) as successive markers, Word Reading as a speed marker as well as the Wechsler Intelligence Scale for Children (WISC) and the Schonell Graded Readiness Vocabulary Test. A table of means was then provided (Krywaniuk and Das, 1976, p. 273) which unfortunately omitted to report mean scores for Visual Short-term Memory and Stroop Word Reading.

Based on an inspection of these means it was concluded that since WISC Performance scores were higher than the WISC Verbal scores and that scores on Raven's Matrices were in the normal range (slightly more than half the group were reported as being above the fiftieth percentile) the children had adequately developed spatial abilities but had difficulties in the verbal area. Without any further clarification the assumption was made that "these findings indicate good simultaneous strategies but poor successive strategies in cognitive operations" (p. 273), (thus clearly equating 'spatial ability' with simultaneous processing and 'verbal ability' with successive processing) and a remedial programme for successive processing was designed and implemented.

Later in the same report a factor analysis of the initial data i.e., before intervention, is presented (Table 4a), and the information in this appears to make questionable the rationale for a successive processing remedial programme. We were told that the children did well on Raven's Matrices, considered a measure of simultaneous processing in previous studies with European children. An inspection of the factor pattern with this group of Canadian Indians, however, shows that the <u>dominant</u> loading for Raven's Matrices was on the <u>successive</u> factor. We were told that the children did well on the WISC Performance Scale, indicating good simultaneous coding skills: the lowest loading of WISC performance is on the simultaneous factor. Clearly the decision to assume successive processing deficits was determined by some previously established nonspecified criteria, not by the cognitive patterns evident in the data from these children.

Other features of the factor pattern are worthy of comment. Visual Short-term Memory, usually a successive marker, had its major loading on the speed factor, a minor loading on simultaneous, and a totally insignificant loading on the successive factor. Cross-modal Coding, a simultaneous marker, loaded almost exclusively on the successive factor. The cumulative evidence for cross-cultural 'heterogeneity' of these measures is compelling.

Krywaniuk and Das then report (with the unremarked omission of Memory for Designs and Word Reading data) that after the

intervention programme significant improvements in performance
were recorded for Schonell, Visual Short-term Memory, and Serial
Learning. The last of these appears from the factor analysis to
have been a measure of successive synthesis, and thus far it is
feasible to argue with Krywaniuk and Das's assessment that the
remedial programme was a success. However, the Schonell test for
no stated reason was omitted form the reported factor analyses,
and Visual Short-term Memory most emphatically was <u>not</u> a
successive processing measure for this sample.

The difficulty of assessing the effects of the intervention
programme is further compounded by an inspection of the factor
analysis reported after the completion of remediation (Table
4.4.b). A major effect of the programme (designed to remedy
supposed defects is successive processing) as evidenced by a
comparison of the two factor patterns appears to be that a measure
with a <u>high successive</u> loading before intervention (Raven's
Matrices) now had a <u>high simultaneous</u> loading after intervention.

The account of Krywaniuk's work in Das et al. (1979) does little
to clarify the imprecisions of the report by Krywaniuk and Das
(1976), indeed it is difficult at times to ascertain whether the
same study is being referred to. Das et al. for example, give
n=38 in their report, and state that after intervention complete
data were available only for 35 children, whereas Krywaniuk and
Das give n=40 for the factor analyses before and after
intervention. Das et al. state that for the remedial programme
children were randomly divided into two groups, whereas Krywaniuk
and Das say that the sample was divided into two groups of
subjects matched on the WISC scales.

Sample descriptions suggest that the same children were involved,
as do the equivalent tables of mean scores (with minor
discrepancies) although some data were omitted in the Krywaniuk
and Das report, and Colour Naming has been added to the list of
variables in the Das et al. account. One assumes that a
typographical or positional error is responsible for the
suggestion in the figures provided by Das et al. (1979, p. 127)
that the mean Verbal WISC score for the Canadian Native children
was about the same as their Performance score, and higher than
that of a comparable white group (the text and figures do not
agree). Again there are missing data: a table in Das et al.
(1979, p. 164) concerning pre- and post-intervention differences
lists Word Reading but provides no figures, and in the factor
analysis of the data on p. 129 the loading for Colour Naming on
the second (speed) factor has been omitted (one assumes it may
have been important, since the other two loadings provided are
minimal, see Table 4c).

The Krywaniuk and Das (1976) report was clearly so confusing that Das et al. (1979) have chosen not to provide any references to it at all, preferring instead to refer to the original unpublished dissertation. However, a closer scrutiny of the factor analysis they provide reveals a pattern that differs little from the Krywaniuk and Das (1976) pre-intervention result: it appears essentially to be an analysis of the same data omitting WISC scores and with the addition of Colour Naming, albeit incomplete (Tables 4a and 4c).

In relation to the categorisation of Canadian Indian children by Krywaniuk and Das (1976) as deficient in successive coding strategies, it is interesting to note the results of a study by Das, Manos and Kanungo (1975). Some of the tests of Unit 2 functions in the Das battery were administered as part of a larger investigation seeking to predict intelligence test performance and school achievement from personological characteristics of parents and from measures of personality and cognitive processes among Canadian Indian children, and white children of high and low socio-economic status. Although the sample sizes were small and no factor analysis was reported, no differences were found on tests otherwise assumed to be measures of successive processing, and results were mixed on simultaneous processing tasks.

While it was stated earlier that the consistency of factor-analytic results identifying simultaneous and successive syntheses in studies by Das and his colleagues has been impressive, results from their studies conducted with culturally different samples are not included in that evaluation. Not only have cross-cultural studies of Luria's Unit 2 functions been remarkably sparse but their results, as reviewed above, can be fairly described as inconsistent.

METHODOLOGICAL CRITICISM

Attempts to operationalise the Luria model in the study of individual differences by Das and his colleagues have met with a number of critical reactions. These can be generally sub-divided into those that query theoretical postulates of the model, and those concerned primarily with alleged weaknesses in the methodology and analytical procedures.

Paivio (1975) claimed that Das et al. (1975) had failed to recognise that the simultaneous-successive processing distinction (which he preferred to call synchronous and sequential organisation) had already been "theoreticlaly coordinated with the verbal- nonverbal dichotomy" (p. 151) in Paivio's own dual-coding theory. This distinguished between imaginal processing assumed to be specialised for handling nonverbal information stored in the form of images, and verbal processing which deals with discrete units of sequentially ordered linguistic information. The verbal system is described as an abstract and logical mode of thinking in opposition to the concrete, analogical imaginal mode, and Paivio (1974) has linked the verbal-nonverbal coding dimensions with the left and right halves of the brain.

Kirby and Das (1976), Das et al. (1979), and Kirby (1980) have responded by arguing that, as was evident in Luria's original research, it is an unacceptable oversimplification to equate a verbal-nonverbal dichotomy, relying on the contradistinction of left versus right brain hemisphere activities, with Luria's descriptions of simultaneous and successive cognitive processes, which essentially distinguish between fronto-temporal and parieto-occipital functions. Furthermore this simple equation obscures the difference between the type of information to be coded and the actual coding operations that may be carried out. As Wittrock commented "It is not only the verbal or spatial mode of the information but more importantly the type of orgnisation or transformation performed upon it that characterises its contructed and remembered meaning" (1978, p. 65). Luria had of course illustrated how, for example, simultaneous processing in verbal and nonverbal contexts could be impaired by lesions in both the left and right hemispheres of the brain, and similarly, how successive processing was involved in the syntactic structure of narrative speech while the decoding of logico-grammatical relationships in language use depended on simultaneous synthesis.

Despite these convincing responses however, one point made by Paivio (1976) remains critical: although within the framework of the Luria theory it is incorrect to simply equate verbal-nonverbal coding with simultaneous and successive processing, a close examination of the actual measures used by Das et al. (1975) clearly demonstrated a confounding of the two. Thus "successive processing was consistently defined by serial and verbal recall of short lists of words presented auditorily", and "all of the tests which consistently load highly on the factor identified with simultaneous synthesis involve visual spatial processing and are generally nonverbal" (Paivio, 1976, p. 70). Future studies of the two integrative processes would obviously benefit from a selection of variables designed to avoid any potential confounding by association with modal specificity and verbal-nonverbal materials.

Vernon, Ryba and Lang (1978) reviewed the early Das studies, and their evaluation suggested that the way in which the successive factor had been operationalised left Das's interpretations of it vulnerable to criticism. Two measures had been consistently used to define a successive factor, Free Recall and Serial Recall.

These were both scores from the one administration of series of words, and Vernon et al. considered that "it is unfortunate that the two tests were so nearly identical, since this inevitably tends to yield a spurious factor in a principal components analysis" (p. 4). This is an important point, and confirmation of it may be found in Korth (1975), who emphasizes that scores to be used in a principal components analysis should be experimentally independent of each other: "each measure must be in some way primary rather than derived from any other scores in the analysis" (p. 129). In addition, and perhaps ironically in view of Das's original rejection of Jensen's theory, the factor defined by those two tests could be equally well interpreted as rote recall of Jensen's Level I associative memory instead of successive synthesis. They also pointed out that although Das had produced logical explanations for why some marker tests had on occasions produced very incongruent loadings on the two integrative factors, such explanations had always been ex post facto and on no occasion were the alterations predicted beforehand.

Vernon et al. further argued that Das's analyses were based on a numerically limited set of cognitive measures, and that the factor pattern for a larger group of variables might differ by splitting up into the traditional hierarchical clusters of abilities. They therefore conducted a study of their own, including the Das battery along with other measures assumed by them to require either simultaneous or successive processing. Altogether there were 6 simultaneous measures and 8 measures of successive processing, and the tests were administered to a group of 91 undergraduates. Six factors were extracted from a principal-factor solution: 3 were clearly comprised of successive measures, 2 of simultaneous, and 1 factor called "perceptual reasoning" was defined by Raven's Progressive Matrices and the Trail-making Test.

A second analysis was conducted using only 8 of the tests, including 6 of the Das measures, and this restricted set yielded 3 factors: one was clearly made up of simultaneous measures, the other two consisted of the successive processing tasks. Vernon et al. concluded that with a small number of tests, this solution provided partial support for the Luria model, but the earlier analysis had shown that when further variables were added, an interpretation favouring a hierarchical taxonomy of mental abilities was more appropriate. In their view, the model "has appeared rather consistently in most of Das's studies, partly because too few variables were factored, and partly because a strong successive factor was produced by using two nearly identical tests of Serial and Word Learning" (Vernon et al., 1978, p. 12).

One criticism of the Vernon et al. study itself is that whereas the problematical element in the early Das studies was perhaps an inappropriate operationalisation of Luria's integrative construct although the theoretical basis was sound, Vernon et al. failed to provide an adequate conceptualisation of Luria's theory. As a result successive synthesis was equated with rote memorising, and their extended battery was questionably subdivided into supposed measures of the two modes of integration, although many of the tasks were demonstrably ambiguous with respect to the processing operations involved.

There have been two procedurally-critical reactions to specific findings. Balla (1973) considered that the original Das (1972) study had ignored the distinction between organic and familial retardation both conceptually in the rationale and more importantly in the selection of subjects, so that the sample had a high probability of containing many organically impaired children. This, together with the use of tasks that had been traditionally used as indicators of organic brain damage in non-retarded individuals made it likely that the tests had simply done their job of differentiating between organically damaged and non-brain-damaged children. Das's response argued that there was no evidence of organic impairment in the sample, and moreover that an insistence on demonstrating beyond doubt that any of the subjects were not impaired was to require a logically-absurd proof of the null hypothesis. He reiterated forcefully that "all the tests used in my study can be described adequately by two orthogonal factors, simultaneous and successive processing" (Das, 1973b, p. 75).

Humphreys (1978), in what could be described as an exercise in fastidious statistical ratiocination, castigated Kirby and Das (1977) for their use of a double median split on simultaneous and successive factor scores to assign subjects to groups which were then used in analyses of variance computed for four dependent achievement variables. His critique elaborates on two basic points: a measure of individual differences is not an independent variable, and the power of the appropriate statistical procedures is reduced when a continuous or quasi-continuous measure is converted to a small number of categories. A subsequent reanalysis of the data using composite correlations instead of analysis of variance showed the calculated effects to be even stronger than had been found in the original study.

As Das and Kirby (1978) were quick to point out in their rejoinder, the reanalysis undoubtedly proved Humphreys right in terms of statistical power, but changed nothing in relation to the findings of the study or their interpretation. They defended the use of individual differences measures as classification variables in analyses of variance, and cited the influential work of Eysenck (1975) and McLaughlin and Eysenck (1967) on introversion and neuroticism as a powerful example of the usefulness of the 'double median split followed by analysis of variance' research design. Their response competently emphasized that the procedure provides essentially a conservative test of the data.

Carroll (1978) conducted a major review of methodological and theoretical issues involved in the study of individual differences in cognition, and in a section devoted to cataloguing "the major statistical sins that can be committed" (p. 103) chose a study by Jarman and Das (1977) to illustrate some of the many problems that may be associated with factor analytic methodology. Jarman and Das (1977) had administered 7 cognitive tasks to 3 groups of children categorised as of high, normal and low intelligence on the basis of their I.Q. scores, and then compared group differences in levels of performance as well as the factor patterns of the three groups. The principal finding of the study was considered to be "that simultaneous and successive syntheses are two major dimensions along which individual differences in intelligence may be identified" (p. 167). Carroll's assessment was less favourable: "Their results concerning differential use of such simultaneous and successive processes in groups at different IQ levels are almost completely unconvincing because of limitations in their methodology" (Carroll, 1978, p. 105).

Some of Carroll's criticisms were largely matters of stylistic preference intended to aid clarity of presentation e.g., failure to reflect variables, and factors. Some were specific to that particular study, e.g., separate factor analyses in range-restricted ability strata, and have been competently dealt with in Jarman's (1980c) reply. Those criticisms however that addressed the question of techniques in factor analysis, and the problem of selecting the appropriate factor model in particular, apply equally to most of the other studies of simultaneous and successive processing completed to date, and thus warrant more detailed consideration.

Carroll, while acknowledging that no consensus of expert opinion exists on the issue of which factoring method to employ, nevertheless stresses that principal components analysis tends to produce factor loadings that are considerably inflated over those of common factor analysis leading to overgenerous interpretations, and states a preference for "some form of common factor analysis that avoids the intrusion of variance uniquely associated with each variable into the common factor space" (Carroll, 1978, p. 95). Empirical confirmation of Carroll's judgement exists in the form of a study by Elkins and Sultmann (1979), who used common factor analysis to reanalyse the data from a principal components analysis included in Kirby and Das's (1978) examination of the relationship between the Das battery of processing measures and 6 tests of primary mental abilities. The common factor analysis confirmed the results presented by Kirby and Das: a similar pattern of the factor emerged within each set of variables and when all measures were factored together, and the factor loadings were indeed smaller.

Factor analysis is a general label for a number of analytical techniques that seek to identify and interpret the underlying structure of a number of original observed variables by representing them in terms of a smaller number of "factors": Bennett and Bowers (1976) present the main aim of factor analysis as parsimony of description. In simplified terms, the common factor model seeks to explain only the common or shared variance amongst the original variables and acknowledges that each variable may be influenced by unique sources independent of the other variables. The proportion of the variance of each variable excluding the variance attributed to the common factor is called the variable's uniqueness(U). Since "all theories of measurement postulate the presence of error in the measurements taken to obtain scores on variables" (Mulaik, 1972, p. 132), this unique part of the variance may be due to unreliability (error) of measurement as well as to any sources specific to that variable e.g., systematic distortions or bias in the scores, or legitimate causal influences which do not affect other variables (Gorsuch, 1974).

The component analysis model, on the other hand, takes no account of unique variance (in other words the total variance of each variable is assumed to be shared variance) and principal components analysis attempts to explain the total variance of all variables in the whole set with as small a number of components as possible. Detailed comparisons of the two techniques, their assumptions and their appropriate mathematical derivations are presented in Gorsuch (1974), Harman (1976), Kim and Mueller (1978), Korth (1975), Mulaik (1972) and Rummel (1970).

Gorsuch (1974), like Carroll (1978), expressed a preference for the common factor extraction procedure and produced a detailed rationale to justify it. Gorsuch made the case that in the social sciences generally there are few research studies where it may be assumed that measurement has been free of error. Perhaps his most forceful argument was that common factor analysis will produce a component analysis if the latter is indeed appropriate: "a common factor analysis is more likely to result in an actual component analysis when that is the best model than vice versa" (Gorsuch, 1974 p. 124). Furthermore, substantial differences between the products of the two methods were most likely when the number of variables was small (less than 20), component analysis produced higher loadings, and on occasions "the loadings may be sufficiently inflated to be misleading" (p. 121). Carroll in his critique had also pointed to the small number of variables and the small sample size as weaknesses in the Jarman and Das (1977) research, and similar reservations must apply to the Krywaniuk and Das (1976) cross-cultural study (10 variables and 40 subjects).

McNemar (1951) reported a number of criticisms of the earlier factor analytic research of that period and these were later classified as "errors by factor analysts" (Gorsuch, 1974, p. 328). One of the major "errors" was the inclusion in principal component analysis of measures with low relaiability. Principal component analysis has been the primary analytic tool used in the psychometric modelling of Luria's theory, particularly by the Das group, yes not one of the published studied reviewed earlier that utilised principal component analysis provided any data on the reliablity of the instruments employed.

In similar fashion Gorsuch augments his arguments in favour of the common factor model by clarifying that in analyses where the number of variables is less than 20 (and that applies to all the Luria-modelling studies reviewed in this chapter) the results of a component model can only be accepted if the resulting communalities turn out to be high. While some published studies have been meticulous in reporting communalities (e.g., Cummins, 1976; Cummins and Das, 1978; Kirby and Das, 1977, 1978a, 1978b), many have completely omitted any mention of them (Das, 1972, 1973a; Das and Molloy, 1975; Das and Singh, 1975; Jarman, 1978a, 1978c; Jarman and Das, 1977; Krywaniuk and Das, 1976; Molloy and Das, 1979). None of the studies with culturally different groups have provided any information on instrument reliability or the communalities following component analysis.

Das and his colleagues are certainly not insensitive to the different assumptions behind the use of the two analytic models (Das et al., 1979, p. 57), but state that the use of common factor analysis has produced results that differ minimally from their component analyses. Elkins and Sultmann's reanalysis certainly adds substance to that claim, and Leong (1974), who set out to achieve 'method independent' results by using both principal components and alpha factor analysis, found little difference in the 'factors' produced, although this evidence would be more convincing if both methods were not variants of component analysis (McDonald, 1970; Mulaik, 1972). The consistency of the factor analytic results found by Das with North American samples of European origins is perhaps in itself an eloquent argument.

It is a pertinent consideration, however, to examine in what circumstances that consistency has faltered, and whether an alternative analytical technique may then be more appropriate. It was argued earlier that research on simultaneous and successive processes with samples from non-European groups had produced very unpredictable results. In psychometric studies of cognition with culturally different groups, among whom the degree of test-taking sophistication may vary considerably between individuals and groups, and for whom the tasks themselves may be quite unrepresentative of any familiar cognitive demands, it seems indefensible to assume no error of measurement. It may perhaps be more defensible to presuppose perfect instrument reliability for measures that have been refined time and again with samples from the same culture, but most measurement theorists, as Mulaik suggested, would still argue otherwise.

Attention to other aspects of methodological imprecision evident in the literature to date would also enhance confidence in the findings of future studies concerned with the cross-cultural applications of Luria's theory. Most studies of the Luria model, particularly those concerned with Unit 2 functions, have been designed "to show that simultaneous and successive processing emerge as relatively stable factors across cultural groups, age groups, achievement levels, and socioeconomic strata" (Das et al., 1975, p. 91). As such this is a fairly straightforward task of comparing factor structures across a number of groups i.e., once the factors have been identified in exploratory research using a carefully selected group of variables with initial samples, the task is then to "confirm" that similar factor structures can be found in other samples, and confirmatory (as opposed to exploratory) factor analytic techniques are available to do explicitly that. However, although Das et al. (1975, 1979) state specifically that their use of the factor analysis is intended to be confirmatory, they have nevertheless persisted with the use of an exploratory method of analysis.

This is not simply a question of proselytising the merits of one analytic technique over another per se, but rather a matter of using the correct analytic tool designed to perform a required function. Exploratory factor analysis is appropriate when "a researcher enters a new domain with very little knowledge of what to expect" (Mulaik, 1975). If however prior substantive theory (often as the result of exploratory analyses) dictates the search for predefined structure allowing the formation of a priori expectations about which factors will be related to particular variables, then confirmatory factor analysis exists to explicitly test how well the theoretical model fits the data (Mulaik, 1975). Detailed comparative accounts of the two methodological techniques, their aims, and their mathematical derivations may be found in Gorsuch (1974), Kim and Mueller (1978), and Mulaik (1972, 1975).

Kim and Mueller, for example, direct attention to the potential use of confirmatory factor analysis for examining the invariance of factors across many different groups, and Brislin et al. (1973) have specifically advocated its cross-cultural applications. Since confirmatory factor analysis allows the testing of hypotheses derived from theory or from the results of previous exploratory analyses, its use would also go some way towards mollifying Vernon et al.'s stricture that only ex post facto rationalisation has been used to explain unexpected findings - the same practice has been described in cross-cultural methodology as "armchair speculation" (Brislin, Bochner, and Lonner, 1975). Similar concerns about the subjective interpretation of factor analytic results have been expressed by Armstrong (1967), and particularly by Gorsuch (1974): "The widely followed practice of regarding interpretations of a factor as confirmed solely because the post hoc analysis 'makes sense' is to be deplored. Factor interpretations can only be considered hypotheses for another study" (p. 188). It appears to be professionally lax, at best, and a methodological indictment at worst, that during more than a decade of research on the psychometric modelling of Luria's theory it appears that only one cross-cultural study in the published literature (Klich & Davidson, 1984) has employed confirmatory factor analysis.

One final but by no means trivial methodological procedure needs to be questioned, especially in relation to the results of cross-cultural studies, and this is the almost automatic practice of comparing mean levels of performance between groups on the same measure. The interpretation of test scores between different cultural groups has become a controversial topic, and forms a major issue in the methodology of cross-cultural research (Adler, 1977; Berry and Dasen, 1974; Brislin, 1976; Brislin et al., 1973; Cole and Bruner, 1971; Cole and Scribner, 1974; Irvine, 1969, 1973, 1979; Irvine and Carroll, 1980; Segall, 1979; Sheehan, 1976).

While it is neither advisable nor possible to summarize that literature here, all of these sources agree that no meaning can be assigned to mean scores on the same variable from two or more cultural groups without comprehensive checks to maximise confidence that the interactions between task materials and individuals have been similar within each group, since of course performance on any measure may be due to a number of sources other than the skills which the test was designed to measure. The minimal checks would appear to be a comparison of the separate reliabilities on each measure for each group, and a check for factorial invariance among the whole set of measures between the groups. Even so, "If one then wants to move from these checks to a comparison of mean levels of performance within each test or factor score, one may proceed, it seems, at one's peril...it should be underlined that factor analysis supports the assumption of similar interaction between stimuli and subjects. It does not prove it: it is not certain what constitutes proof of such an assumption" (Irvine and Carroll, 1980, p. 219).

Das et al. (1979, pp. 128/129) present a "comparison of means of low-achieving white and native children" on a simultaneous and successive battery, as well as the principal components analysis for each group. Although no tests for factorial invariance are reported, it is reasonably evident from the pattern of factor loadings that there are disparities between the groups (Progressive Matrices, for example, loads predominantly on very different factors for the two groups). While these disparities may well form the basis for specific hypotheses in subsequent studies, it should be clear that they mitigate against any direct comparison of the two groups on those measures, for if the interactions with the stimuli for the two groups have been different, then a simple comparison of means involves the researcher in committing that recurrent methodological lemon of juxtaposing apples and oranges.

CONCLUSION

Cross-cultural cognitive psychology aims to search intensively within cultural systems for sources of cognitive variation, and across cultural systems for universal characteristics of cognitive functioning (Berry and Dasen, 1974), and it has proven to be a particularly rigorous disciplinary area for exposing flaws in Western psychological theory and methods (Irvine and Carroll, 1980; Sheehan, 1976). Psychometric cross-cultural applications of theories, such as that of Luria, and of the models derived from them, cannot afford the inappropriate methodological procedures discussed in this papaer if they intend to make a serious contribution to the fulfillment of such aims. Cross-cultural examination of Luria's theory therefore continues to remain an important research priority for its validation, as the evidence gleaned so far is certainly less than compelling.

REFERENCES

Aaron, P.G. (1978). Dyslexia, an imbalance in cerebral information processing strategies. Perceptual and Motor Skills, 47, 699-706.

Armstrong, J.S. (1967). Derivation of theory by means of factor analysis, or Tom Swift and his electric factor analysis machine. American Statistician, 2, (5), 17.

Balla, D. (1973). Comment on Das' "Patterns of Cognitive Ability in Nonretarded and Retarded Children". American Journal of Mental Deficiency, 77, 748-749.

Bennett, S., and Bowers, D. (1976). An Introduction to Multivariate Techniques for Social and Behavioural Sciences. London: MacMillan.

Berry, J.W., and Dasen, P.R. (1974). Culture and Cognition : Readings in cross-cultural psychology. London: Methuen.

Biggs, J.B. (1978). Individual and group differences in study processes. British Journal of Educational Psychology, 48, 266-279.

Brislin, R. (1976). Comparative research methodology: cross-cultural studies. International Journal of Psychology, 11, 3.

Brislin, R.W., Bochner, S., and Lonner, W.J. (Eds.) (1975). Cross-cultural Perspectives on Learning. New York: Wiley.

Brislin, R., Lonner, W., and Thorndike, R. (1973). Cross-cultural research methods. New York: Wiley.

Bruner, J.S., Olver, R., and Greenfield, P. (1966). Studies in Cognitive Growth. New York: Wiley.

Carroll, J.B. (1978). How shall we study individual differences in cognitive abilities? - Methodological and theoretical perspectives. Intelligence, 2, 87-115.

Christensen, A.L. (1975). Luria's Neuropsychological Investigation. Copenhagen, Denmark: Munksgaard.

Cole, M. (1977). Alexander Romanovich Luria: 1902-1977 (Obituary). American Psychologist, 32(ii), 969-971.

Cole, M. (1979). A portrait of Luria. In Luria, A.R. The Making of Mind. Cambridge, U.S.A.: Harvard University Press.

Cole, M., and Scribner, S. (1974). Culture and Thought: A Psychological Introduction. New York: Wiley.

Cronbach, L.J., and Drenth, P.J.D. (Eds.) (1972). Mental tests and cultural adaptation. The Hague: Mouton.

Cummins, J.C. (1977). The cognitive basis of the Uznadze illusion. International Journal of Psychology, 11, 89-100.

Cummins, J., and Das, J.P. (1977). Cognitive processing, academic achievement, and WISC-R Performance in EMR children. Journal of Consulting and Clinical Psychology, 48, 777-779.

Cummins, J.P., and Das, J.P. (1978). Simultaneous and successive syntheses and linguistic processes. International Journal of Psychology, 13, 129-138.

Cummins, J., and Mulcahy, R. (1979). Simultaneous and successive processing and narrative speech. Canadian Journal of Behavioral Science, 111, 64-71.

Das, J.P. (1972). Patterns of cognitive ability in nonretarded and retarded children. American Journal of Mental Deficiency, 77, 6-12.

Das, J.P. (1973a). Cultural deprivation and cognitive competence. In N.R. Ellis (Ed), International Review of Research in Mental Retardation (Vol. 6). New York: Academic Press.

Das, J.P. (1973b). The uses of attention. Alberta Journal of Educational Research, 19, 99-108.

Das, J.P. (1980). Planning: Theoretical considerations and empirical evidence. Psychological Research, 41, 141-151.

Das, J.P. (1984). Aspects of planning. In J.R. Kirby, (Ed.) Cognitive Strategies and Educational Performance. New York: Academic Press.

Das, J.P., and Cummins J.P. (1978). Academic performance and cognitive processes in EMR Children. American Journal of Mental Deficiency, 83, 2, 197-199.

Das, J.P., and Kirby, J.R. (1978). the case of the wrong exemplar: a reply to Humphreys. Journal of Educational Psychology, 70, 877-879.

Das, J.P., and Molloy, G.N. (1975). Varieties of simultaneous and successive processing in children. Journal of Educational Psychology, 67, 213-220.

Das, J.P., and Singha, P.S. (1975). Caste, class and cognitive competence. Indian Educational Review, 10, 1-18.

Das, J.P., Kirby, J., and Jarman, R.F. (1975). Simultaneous and successive syntheses: An alternative model for cognitive abilities. Psychological Bulletin, 82, 87-103.

Das, J., Kirby, J., and Jarman, R. (1979). Simultaneous and Successive Cognitive Processes. New York: Academic Press.

Das, J.P., Leong, C.K., and Williams, N.H. (1978). The relationship between learning disability and simultaneous-successive processing. Journal of Learning Disabilities, 11, 16-23.

Das, J.P., Manos, J., and Kanungo, R.N. (1975). Performance of Candian Native, Black and White children on some cognitive and personality tasks. Alberta Journal of Educational Research, 21, 183-195.

Das, J.P., Cummins, J., Kirby, J.R., and Jarman, R.F. (1979). Simultaneous and successive processes, language and mental abilities. Canadian Psychological Review, 20, 1-11.

Davidson, G.R., (1979). An ethnographic psychology of Aboriginal cognitive ability. Oceania, XLIX, 4, 270-294.

Elkins, J., and Sultmann, W.F. (1979). Simultaneous and successive processing: a reanalysis of Kirby and Das's data. Paper presented at the Annual Conference of the Australian Association for Research in Education, Melbourne, Australia.

Eysenck, H.J. (1957). The dynamics of anxiety and hysteria. London: Routledge & Kegan Paul.

Farnham-Diggory, S. (1970). Cognitive synthesis in negro and white children. Monographs of the Society for Research in Child Development, Whole No. 135, Vol. 35.

Gorsuch, R.L. (1974). Factor Analysis. Toronto: Saunders.

Harman, H.H. (1976). Modern Factor Analysis. Chicago: University of Chicago Press.

Holbrook, M.B., and Moore, W.L. (1981). Feature interactions in consumer judgements of verbal versus pictorial presentations. Journal of Consumer Research, 8, 103-113.

Humphreys, L.G. (1978). Doing research the hard way: substituting analysis of variance for a problem in correlational analysis. Journal of Educational Psychology, 70, 873-876.

Hunt, D., (1980). Intentional-incidental learning and simultaneous-successive processing. Canadian Journal of Behavioural Science, 12, 4, 373-383.

Irvine, S.H., (1969). Factor analysis of African abilities and attainments: constructs across cultures. Psychological Bulletin, 71, 20-32.

Irvine, S.H., (1973). Tests as inadvertent sources of discrimination in personnel decisions. In P. Watson (Ed.), Psychology and Race. London: Penguin books.

Irvine, S.H., (1979). The place of factor analysis in cross-cultural methodology and its contribution to cognitive theory. In Eckensberger, L. (Ed.). Cross-cultural Contributions to Psychology. Lisse, Netherlands: Swets and Zeitlinger.

Irvine, S., and Carroll, W., (1980). Testing and assessment across cultures: issues in methodology and theory. In H.C. Triandis and J.W. Berry, Handbook of Cross-Cultural Psychology, Vol.2, Boston: Allyn and Bacon.

Jakobson, R., (1971). Studies on child language and aphasia. The Hague: Mouton.

Jarman, R.F., (1977). Patterns of cross-modal and intramodal matching among intelligence groups. In P. Mittler (Ed.), Research to practice in mental retardation, (Vol.11). Baltimore, Md.: University Park Press.

Jarman, R.F., (1978a). Patterns of cognitive ability in retarded children: A re-examination. Amerian Journal of Mental Deficiency, 82, 344-348.

Jarman, R.F., (1978b). Level I and II abilities: Some theoretical reinterpretations. British Journal of Psychology, 69, 257-269.

Jarman, R.F., (1978c). Cross-modal and intramodal matching: Relationships to simultaneous and successive syntheses and level of performance among three intelligence groups. Alberta Journal of Educational Research, 24, 100-112.

Jarman, R.F., (1978d). Successive cognitive processes in the alphabetic recall of labelled pictures. The Journal of Psychology, 98, 109-115.

Jarman, R.F., (1979). Simultaneous and successive cognitive processing in the Mueller-Lyer illusion. Journal of Genetic Psychology, 134, 23-32.

Jarman, R.F., (1980a). Cognitive processes and syntactical structure: Analyses of paradigmatic and syntagmatic associations. Psychological Research, 41, 153-167.

Jarman, R.F., (1980b). Modality-specific information processing and intellectual ability. Intelligence, 4, 210-216.

Jarman, R.F., (1980c). Comments on John B. Carroll's "How Shall We Study Individual Differences in Cognitive Ability? - Methodological and Theoretical Perspectives". Intelligence, 4, 73-82.

Jarman, R.F., and Das, J.P., (1977). Simultaneous and successive syntheses and intelligence. Intelligence, 1, 151-169.

Jarman, R.F., and Krywaniuk, L.W., (1978). Simultaneous and successive syntheses: a factor analysis of speed of information processing. Perceptual and Motor Skills, 46, 1167-1172.

Jensen, A.R., (1969). How much can we boost IQ and scholastic achievement? Harvard Educational Review, 39, 1-123.

Jensen, A.R., (1970). Hierarchical theories of mental ability. In B. Dockerell (Ed.). On Intelligence. Toronto: Ontario Institute for Studies in Education.

Kaufman, A.S., (1981). The WISC-R and Learning Disabilities Assessment. Journal of Learning Disabilities, 14, 520-526.

Kaufman, A.S., and Kaufman, N.L., (1983). Kaufman Assessment Battery for Children. Circle Pines, MN: American Guidance Serivce.

Kim, J.A., and Mueller, C.W., (1978). Factor Analysis: Statistical Methods and Practical Issues. London: Sage University Papers.

Kirby, J.R., (1980). Individual differences and cognitive processes: Instructional application and methodological difficulties. In J.R. Kirby and J.B. Biggs (Eds.). Cognition, Development and Instruction. Academic Press, New York.

Kirby, J.R., and Das, J.P., (1976). Comments on Paivio's imagery theory. Canadian Psychological Review, 17, 66-68.

Kirby, J.R., and Das, J.P., (1977). Reading achievement, IQ and simultaneous-successive processing. Journal of Educational Psychology, 69, 564-570.

Kirby, J.R., and Das, J.P., (1978). Information processing and human abilities. Journal of Educational Psychology, 70, 58-66.

Klich, L.Z., and Davidson, G.R., (1984). Toward a recognition of Australian Aboriginal cognitive competence. In J.R. Kirby (Ed.), Cognitive Strategies and Educational Performance. New York: Academic Press.

Korth, B., (1975). Exploratory factor analysis. In D.J. Amick and H.J. Walberg, (Eds.). Introductory Multivariate Analysis. California: McCutchan.

Krywaniuk, L.W., and Das, J.P., (1976). Cognitive strategies in native children: analysis and intervention. Alberta Journal of Educational Research, 22, 271-280.

Kurdek, L.A., (1977). Structural components and intellectual correlates of cognitive perspective taking in first through fourth-grade children. Child Development, 48, 1503-1511.

Kurdek, L.A., (1980). Development relations among children's perspective taking, moral judgement and parent-rated behaviours. Merril-Palmer Quarterly, 26, 103, 121.

Leong, C.K., (1976). Lateralisation in severely disabled reachers in relation to functional cerebral development and synthesis of information. In R.M. Knights and D.J. Bakker, (Eds.), The Neuropsychology of Learning Disorders. Baltimore: University Park Press.

Leong, C.K. (1977). Spatial-temporal information processing in children with specific reading disability. Reading Research Quarterly, 2, 204-215.

Leong, C.K., (1980a). Cognitive patterns of retarded and below average readers. Contemporary Educational Psychology, 5, 101-117,

Leong, C.K., (1980b). Laterality and reading proficiency in children. Reading Research Quarterly, 2, 185-202.

Luria, A.R., (1966a). Human brain and psychological processes. New York: Harper & Row.

Luria, A.R., (1966b). Higher cortical functions in man. New York: Basic Books.

Luria, A.R., (1970). The functional organization of the brain. Scientific American, 222, 3, 66-78.

Luria, A.R., (1971). Towards the problem of the historical nature of psychological processes. International Journal of Psychology, 6, 259-272.

Luria, A.R., (1973). The working brain. Harmondsworth: Penguin.

Luria, A.R., (1979). Neuropsychology of complex forms of human memory. In L.G. Nilsson, (ed.), Perspectives on Memory Research. New York: Halstead Press.

McLaughlin, R.J., and Eysenck, H.J., (1967). Extraversion, neuroticism and paired-associated learning. Journal of Experimental Research in Personality, 128-132.

McNemar, Q. (1951). The factors in factoring behaviour. Psychometrika, 16, 353.

Molloy, G.N., and Das, J.P., (1979). Intellectual abilities and processes. Australian Journal of Education, 23, 83-92.

Mulaik, S.A., (1972). The foundations of factor analysis. New York: McGraw-Hill.

Mulaik, S.A., (1975). Confirmatory factor analysis. In D.J. Amick and H.J. Walberg (eds.). Introductory multivariate analysis. Berkeley: McCutchan.

Naglieri, J.A., Kaufman, A.S., Kaufman, N.L., and Kamphaus, R.W., (1981). Cross-validation of Das' simultaneous and successive processes with novel tasks. Alberta Journal of Educational Research, 27, 264-271.

Paivio, A., (1974). Language and knowledge of the world. Educational Research, 3, 5-12.

Paivio, A., (1975). Imagery and synchronic thinking. Canadian Psychological Review, 16, 147-163.

Paivio,   A.,   (1976). Concerning   dual-coding   and
    simultaneous-successive processing. <u>Canadian Psychological
    Review</u>, <u>17</u>, 69-72.

Pollack, R.H., (1969). Some implications of ontogenetic changes in
    perception. In D. Elkind and J.H. Flavell (Eds.), <u>Studies in
    cognitive development</u>, New York: Oxford University Press,
    365-408.

Pribram, K. (1971). <u>Languages of the brain</u>. Englewood Cliffs,
    N.J.: Prentice-Hall.

Pribram, K., (1978). Obituary in memory of Alexander Romanovitsch
    Luria. <u>Neuropsychologia</u>, <u>16</u>, 137-139.

Richman,   L.C.,   and   Lindgren,   S.D.,   (1980). Patterns   of
    intellectual   ability   in   children   with   verbal   deficits.
    <u>Journal of Abnormal Child Psychology</u>, <u>8</u> (1), 65-81.

Rummel,   R.J. (1970). <u>Applied   Factor   Analysis</u>. Evanston:
    Northwestern University Press.

Ryckman,   D.B. (1981). Reading   achievement,   I.Q.,   and
    simultaneous-successive   processing   among   normal   and
    learning-disabled children. <u>Alberta Journal of Educational
    Research</u>, <u>27</u>, 74-83.

Sewell, T.E., (1983). New thinking cast in an old mold: the K-ABC.
    <u>Contemporary Education Review</u>, <u>2</u> (3), 209-214.

Sheehan,   P.W. (1976). The   methodology   of   cross-cultural
    psychology.   In G.E. Kearney   and   D.W. McElwain,   (Eds.).
    <u>Aboriginal Cognition</u>. Canberra: A.I.A.S.

Solan, H.A., (1981). A rationale for the optometric treatment and
    management of children with learning disabilities. <u>Journal
    of Learning Disabilities</u>, <u>14</u>, 586-572.

Sternberg, R.J., (1983). Should K comes before A, B and C? A
    review of the Kaufman Assessment Battery for Children.
    <u>Contemporary Education Review</u>, <u>2</u> (3), 1199-1207.

Stroop, J.R., (1935). Studies of interference in serial verbal
    reactions. <u>Journal of Experimental Psychology</u>, <u>18</u>, 643-662.

Van Uden, A.M. (1981). Early diagnosis of those multiple handicaps
    in prelingually profoundly deaf children which endanger an
    education according to the purely oral way. <u>Journal of the
    British Association for Teachers of the Deaf</u>, <u>5</u>, 112-127.

Vernon, P.E., Ryba, K.A., and Lang, R.J., (1978). Simultaneous and successive processing: An attempt at replication. <u>Canadian Journal of Behavioural Science</u>, <u>10</u>, 2-15.

Wittrook, M.C. (1978). Education and the cognitive processes of the brain. In J.S. Chall and A.F. Mirsky (Eds.), <u>Education and the brain</u>. Chicago: University of Chicago Press.

CHAPTER 8

A GENERAL SYSTEMS APPROACH TO THE MEASUREMENT OF
INTELLIGENCE AND PERSONALITY

H. J. EYSENCK

Institute of Psychiatry, London

INTRODUCTION

In recent years, general systems theory has become widely accepted
and used, particularly in the biological sciences. Bertalanffy
(1972) has pointed out "that order or organization of a whole or
system, transcending its parts when these are considered in
isolation, is nothing metaphysical, not an anthropomorphic
superstition or a philosophical speculation; it is a fact of
observation encountered whenever we look at a living system, a
social group, or even an atom." (p.23.) He contrasts this new
development with the Galilean or 'resolutive" method, that is, the
resolution and reduction of complex phenomena into elementary
parts and processes. "Reductionism" would thus be considered the
opposite of general systems theory.

As Bertalanffy (1952) has also pointed out: "The properties and
modes of action of higher levels are not explicable by the
summation of the properties and modes of action of their components
taken in isolation. If, however, we know the ensemble of the
components and the relations existing between them, then the
higher levels are derivable from the components." (p.148.)
Unfortunately, as he also points out, normal science, in the sense
of Thomas Kuhn, was little adapted to deal with "relations"
systems. Weaver (1948) had already stressed that classical
science was concerned with one-way causality or relations between
two variables, such as the attraction of the sun and a planet, but
even the three-body problem of mechanics, and the corresponding
problems in atomic physics, permits no close solution by the
analytic method of classical mechanics. It was to deal with
problems of this kind that general systems theory was developed
(Bertalanffy, 1968; Klir, 1972; Zadeh and Polak, 1969), and
applied to social systems (Berrien, 1968), behavioural sciences
(Buckley, 1968), and psychiatry (Gray, Rizzo, and Duhl, 1969),

with obvious extensions to control system theory (Elgerd, 1967). Bertalanffy, as a practising biologist, was particularly interested in developing the theory of "open systems", that is, systems exchanging matter with environment as every "living" system does.

General systems theory may be subdivided into three major sets of topics. The first is system science, or mathematical system theory. This involves the scientific exploration and theory of "systems" and the various sciences, and general systems theory as a doctrine of principles applying to all systems. Second there is systems technology, that is, the treatment of the problems arising in modern technology and society. The third, finally, is systems philosophy, that is, the reorientation of thought and world view following the introduction of "system" as a new scientific paradigm, contrasted with the analytic, mechanistic, linear-causal paradigm of classical science.

It will be obvious that personality, like the concept of the organism, is a clear example of a biological system where it would be idle to look for single cause-effect mechanisms. Organisms always function as wholes, traditionally greater than their parts, and are understandable only in terms of the systematic relations between the parts. Much the same may be said of personality, which for the purpose of this chapter may be subdivided into <u>temperament</u>, the non-cognitive aspects of personality, and <u>intelligence</u>, or the cognitive side of personality, embracing the many different types of abilities. One obvious example of the need for a systems approach is the definition of man as a biosocial organism (Eysenck, 1983b). While paying lip service to this doctrine, most psychologists adopt the strictly environmental point of view, disregarding biological facts and determinants, while sociobiologists tend to disregard environmental influences and concentrate on biological ones. Integration between the two approaches is seldom found, and instead of working towards a proper systems theory we find, rather, a polarisation of attitudes contrasting sociophiles and biophiles. Personality is a crucial concept related equally strongly to biological and social determinants, and for that reason a paradigm of personality structure has seemed such an important <u>desideratum</u> in the construction of a scientific psychology (Eysenck, 1983a, b).

In constructing such a system (Eysenck and Eysenck, 1984), it is essential to distinguish between three major meanings and connotations of terms like intelligence, personality, temperament etc. It may be useful to establish the use of these terms by reference to intelligence. Hebb (1949) and Vernon (1970) have referred to intelligence A as a basic potentiality of the organism to learn and to adapt to its environment. Intelligence A is determined by the genes but is mediated mainly by the complexity and plasticity of the central nervous system. It is, as it were, the biological substratum which is essential for the development of cognitive abilities; but these, of course, can only be developed through the action of environmental determinants of one kind or another.

Intelligence B is defined as the level of ability that a person shows in his behaviour, in his adaptation to the environment, his reasoning, his judgement, his problem-solving ability, his capacity for learning, comprehension, memory, information processing, and the adoption of suitable strategies. This distinction is similar to that made by geneticists between genotype and phenotype.

As a third conception (Intelligence C) we have that of the IQ, i.e. the quantification of intelligence in terms of standardised problems, chosen in such a way as to minimise the influence of educational, cultural and socio-economic factors. One can show the relative inclusivity of intelligence A, IQ, and intelligence B. Most fundamental is intelligence A, but IQ to some extent, and intelligence B to a much larger extent, are affected also by other variables, such as personality, education, socio-economic status, parental upbringing, cultural factors and many more. IQ itself is not unitary, but can be divided into mental speed, error checking and continuance or persistence (Eysenck, 1982); we will not here be concerned with this particular breakdown.

Psychologists have always alternated in their concepts and definitons between intelligence A and intelligence B, and many rather useless disagreements and controversies have arisen because of their failure to realise that they were taking about quite different concepts hidden under the same terms used by both parties. It may be useful here to use the term biological intelligence for intelligence A, social intelligence, for intelligence B, and psychometric intelligence for intelligence C. In that way it will be clear just what is being discussed, and no problem should arise through misunderstanding of the concepts involved.

Some sociophiles (e.g. Kamin, in Eysenck and Kamin, 1981) deny the existence of biological and genetic determinants of intelligence, and would hence reduce the term completely to the concept of social intelligence; the evidence against this view is so overwhelming (Eysenck, 1979; Vernon, 1979) that little needs to be said here. Strands of evidence from MZ twins brought up in isolation, from comparisons between MZ and DZ twins, from studies of adopted children, from intra-familial correlations, from work on inbreeding depression and on heterosis, as well as the phenomena of genetic regression to the mean, agree conspicuously in suggesting a strong influence of genetic factors, involving both additive genetic variance, dominance, and assortative mating. Estimates of uncorrected broad heritability vary from 50% to 70%, but the precise value is irrelevant for this discussion. In any case, heritability is a population statistic, and hence may differ within limits between one population and another, and from one time interval to another. What is important is the fact that it would be difficult now to deny the biological reality we represented by intelligence A; biological intelligence is too central and important a concept to be thrown over in the service of ideological and political dogma.

There is, however, another argument which separates the advocates of biological intelligence and social intelligence. The argument in question is quite central in any discussion of intelligence, and arose right from the beginning in the contrasting doctrines of Sir Francis Galton and Alfred Binet. Galton, representing the biological view of intelligence, conceived of intelligence as a general factor underlying all cognitive abilities and performance, central to the abilities which made human beings learn, memorise, adapt to the environment and generally succeed in problem solving tasks of all kinds. Binet, on the other hand, really did not believe in intelligence as a meaningful concept at all; he preferred to think in terms of a large variety of different intellectual capacities, unrelated to each other, and generating "intelligence" only through averaging, i.e. as a kind of statistical artifact. Some of his postulated abilities were similar to those later on discovered through factorial analysis by Burt, Spearman, Thurstone and others; others strike us now as rather odd and not truly belonging to this company, such as suggestibility. The work of Guilford (1967), which postulated 120 or more independent " intelligences", is a reductio ad absurdum of this multiple-factor approach; psychometrically it has been found that all these different abilities are in fact highly correlated, and define a general concept of "intelligence", and in addition a few special abilities of the kind already recognised by Thurstone and Burt (Eysenck, 1979). Binet was right in asserting the importance of special abilities, such as verbal, numerical, visual spatial etc., in addition to general intelligence, but he was wrong in denying the meaningful postulation of biological intelligence, and in assuming that intelligence was only a statistical artifact.

This deep division between the followers of Galton, stressing the importance of biological intelligence, and the followers of Binet, stressing the importance of social intelligence, becomes particularly apparent in their respective answers to the questions of how intelligence is to be measured? (For Binet there is of course a paradox, in that he attempted to measure intelligence while believing it to be a statistical artifact. It is clear from his writings that he was feeling his way, and that his thought lacked a consistency which according to the proverb characterises little minds. Nevertheless, if we conceive of "intelligence" as the average of a number of disparate cognitive abilities, it would obviously follow that any measurement we undertake should embrace as many of these abilities as possible. Interestingly enough, therefore, Binet's approach coincides with that of Spearman (1927), who, as a follower of Galton, used factor analysis to establish the existence of a general factor of intelligence (g) which would represent Galton's biological intelligence. In doing so he advocated the use of as many widely different types of test as possible, on the grounds that too-similar tests would create artificial correlations between those specific factors which related to each test separately, and were not in common between tests of different abilities. The fact that psychometric work along these lines did succeed in establishing a very powerful general factor is ample evidence that Binet's assumptions were unjustified, and that intelligence is more than a statistical artifact.)

For Galton, the obvious way of measuring intelligence was by reference to the biological substrate of cognitive ability; in the absence of EEG and other modern methods of investigating the actual functioning of the central nervous system at the cortex, he suggested, among other things, using reaction time as a measure of intelligence. Binet, on the other hand, in line with his conception of social intelligence, suggested tests involving learning, following instructions, memory, problem-solving, etc. Inevitably the Binet tests were contaminated, as Galton's would not have been, by educational, cultural and other environmental factors which could not be eliminated easily from the final score. In this battle, as is well known, Binet was victorious. Practically all modern IQ tests are modelled upon the ones originally produced by Binet, and share the disadvantages as well as the advantages of his work. The disadvantages are related to the intrusion of environmental factors which contaminate the measurement of biological intelligence; the advantages are concerned with the relative closeness of IQ measures of this kind to social intelligence. From the technological point of view the advantages predominate; IQ tests have been found extremely useful in relation to educational selection and prediction, in relation to industrial selection for work and training, and in relation to many other practical purposes of one kind or another (Eysenck, 1979). Under suitable conditions very high predictive accuracy can be achieved, as when IQ tests given at the age of 5 are used to predict IQ and scholastic achievement at age 16 (Yule, Gold and Busch, 1982). This advantage is based on the congruence of factors of a non-cognitive type promoting success on IQ tests and in educational and other life situations. Such factors may be related to personality, socio-economic status, to parental influence, or to many other factors irrelevant to the scientific measurement of intelligence A.

It is with respect to the scientific analysis of intelligence that the Galtonian suggestion would seem to have a better claim to our attention. Given that biological intelligence is fundamental to the more complex and highly contaminated notions of IQ and social intelligence, clearly the task of scientific research should have been to try and carry out Galton's prescription and measure biological intelligence in as pure a form as possible. We may compare the situation with that obtaining in physics, say in the measurement of heat. Here too we may talk of heat A (physical heat), in contrast to social heat (to coin a phrase), i.e. the heat experienced by a given individual. This is of course largely determined by the actual physical heat, i.e. the speed of movements of molecules in the air, but it is also affected by a variety of factors which are not directly related to physical heat. Among these are the so-called chill factor, i.e. the amount of air movement present, the amount of food the individual has eaten recently, the amount of alcohol in the blood stream, the amount of exercise he has taken, the amount of fat on his bodily frame, and many others of a similar kind. Given an identical amount of physical heat, some people will apply the term "cold" to it, others the term "warm", and even the same person may at one time call an identical temperature "cold" or "warm". There is a well known psychological experiment to illustrate the point. The subject puts his left hand in a basin full of hot water, his right hand in a basin full of cold water; after a few minutes, he transfers both hands to a bowl of lukewarm water, which now feels cold to the left hand, hot to the right hand. Clearly physical cold, i.e. the temperature of the water, is quite different to "social heat", i.e. the temperature as experienced.

In addition, of course, we have heat C, i.e. heat as measured. As there are different methods of measuring intelligence, so there are many different methods of measuring heat. There is the mercury-in-glass thermometer, depending on the change in volume of the mercury with increase in heat; the constant-volume gas thermometer, depending on the reactants of the welded junction of two fine wires; resistance thermometers, depending on the relation between resistance and temperature; thermocouples, depending on the setting up of currents by a pair of metals with their junctions at different temperatures; etc. Nelkon and Parker (1968), in their Advanced Level Physics, point out that temperature scales differ from one another, "that no one of them is any more "true" than any other, and that our choice of which to

adopt is arbitary, so it may be decided by convenience." (p.186.)
Thus when the mercury-in-glass thermometer reads 300° C, the
platinum-resistance thermometer in the same place and at the same
time will read 291°C There is no meaning attached to the question
of which of these two values is "correct", just as little as there
would be to the question of whether an IQ given by the Wechsler or
by the Binet scale is more "correct". There is thus a perfectly
homologous relation between the theory and measurement of heat,
and the theory and the measurement of intelligence, an application
of systems theory already previously suggested (Eysenck, 1979).

It is interesting to note, from the point of view of the history
of science, why Galton's suggestion of using reaction times as a
measure of intelligence was rejected by psychologists, almost
unanimously, until recently. Clark Wissler (1901), on the basis
of a badly planned, badly executed and badly analysed study
concluded that there was no correlation between intelligence and
reaction time, and although much better studies, such as that of
Peak and Boring (1926) gave very positive results, it was not
until recently that the Zeitgeist permitted a resurrection of
Galton's theory. Rehabilitation of reaction time as a measure of
intelligence was due to Roth (1964), who based himself on the work
of Hick (1952) and his demonstration that multiple choice RT
increases as a linear function of the increase in amount of
information in the stimulus array, when information is measured in
bits, that is the logarithm (to the base 2) of the number of
choices. The slope of this function can be interpreted as a
measure of the speed or rate of information processing, expressed
as the number of milliseconds per bit of information. The
reciprocal of the slope (x1000) expresses the rate of information
processing in terms of number of bits per second. The general
results of Roth's work are shown in Eysenck (in press), and verify
his proposition that the slope is steeper for dull subjects than
for bright ones, i.e. that the rate of information processing is
quicker for high IQ subjects than for low IQ subjects. This study
gave rise to the so-called Erlangen school in Germany (Lehrl,
1983; Frank, 1971). Eysenck (in press) has given an outline of the
work of this school, and the resulting general systems theory.
Figure 1 shows a diagrammatic model of the theory. Information
about changes in the outer world or in the body reaches the cortex
by way of the sense organs and the sensory nerves, resulting in
the transmission of between 10^9 and 10^{11} bits per second. Only a
small portion of this information can be received by the cortex,
and this flow of information (C_k) amounts to between 15 and 16
bits per second in the average adult. This capacity forms the
upper limit of the amount of information used in cognitive
activities, such as changes or combinations of items of
information through thinking or creative activity, as in
problem-solving. Part of the information finds a place in

long-term memory, where it can be stored and can be accessed at any time.

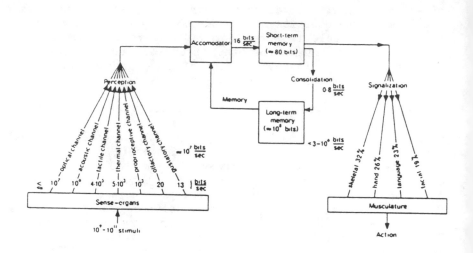

Figure 1   Diagrammatic model of Frank and Lehrl's theory

In addition to the speed of information-processing, Frank and Lehrl considered the duration of short-term memory (T_R) as a vital part of biological intelligence. This corresponds to the time during which information is readily accessible before either being forgotten or being transferred through a consolidation process to long-term memory. On the average, T_R amounts to between 5 and 6 seconds, and information offered during the period of this duration would be available to the person concerned without effort.

It is the product of T_R and T_K which is identified as a cause of differences in phenotypic intelligence, i.e. IQ scores. The great advantage of this new way of looking at the problem of individual differences in intelligence is that all the values entering into the equation can be measured directly in terms of objective and absolute units (bits and seconds), rather than, as in the case of IQ measurements, in terms of relative values and percentiles.

Jensen (1982a, b) also starts with a major axiom, namely that the conscious brain acts as a single channel or a limited capacity information-processing system. Like Frank and Lehr, he posited that the brain can deal simultaneously only with a very limited amount of information, and this limited capacity also restricts the number of operations that can be performed simultaneously on the information that enters the system, either from external stimuli, or from retrieval of information stores in short-term or long-term memory. It follows that speed of mental processing is advantageous in that more operations per unit of time can be executed without overloading the system. This, of course, is the basis of Lehrl's attempt to provide an absolute or physical system of measurement for intelligence.

Jensen also points out that there is a rapid decay of stimulus traces of information, suggesting that there is an advantage to speed of any operations that must be performed on the information while it is still available, i.e. in the short-term memory store. Last but not least, to compensate for limited capacity and rapid decay of incoming information, the individual resorts to rehearsal and storage of the information into intermediate or long-term memory, which has relatively unlimited capacity. The process of storing information in long-term memory, however, also takes time (consolidation), and therefore uses channel capacity by giving a trade-off between the storage and the processing of information. The more complex the information and the operations required on it, the more time will be required and consequently the greater will be the advantage of speed in all the elemental processes involved.

Jensen also introduces the concept of short-term memory into his system, but his discussion of this feature is relatively distinct from that of reaction time. Jensen postulates two relatively distinct types of ability, called Level 1 and Level 2 ability. Level 1 ability is essentially the capacity to receive or register stimuli, to store them and later recognise or recall the material with a high degree of fidelity. Digit span is a good measure of this ability. Level 2, on the other hand, is characterised by transformation and manipulation of the stimulus prior to making the response. It is a set of mechanisms which made generalisation beyond primary stimulus generalisation possible. Spearman's (1927) characterisation of g as an eduction of relations and correlates corresponds to Level 2. While thus recognising the importance of Level 1 ability as a basic contribution to Level 2 manipulation, Jensen has never, unlike the Erlangen School, tried to combine both these concepts into a single system.

The available evidence from many studies now supports the view that RT and IQ are quite closely related. IQ has been shown to be correlated with simple RT, more highly with choice RT, with the Hick slope, and particularly with the variability of an individual's RT scores - the smaller the variability, the higher the IQ. Actual correlations reported differ according to methods of measurement, type of IQ test used, range of ability in the population studied, etc., but for normally distributed samples of subjects on reliable and valid IQ tests correlations of between .5 and .6 can be expected, and have been found in our own work (unpublished). It is well known that day to day fluctuations in RT occur, so that corrections for attenuation, taking this factor into account, would raise the observed correlations markedly. There seems to be no doubt that Galton was right, and his detractors were wrong; RT is intimately connected with IQ, and hence the theories of the Erlangen School and of Jensen, attempting a systems approach to the definition and measurement of biological intelligence, acquire a considerable degree of importance.

An even more direct biological measure of intelligence A is furnished by the recent work on the averaged evoked potential (AEP), reviewed by Eysenck and Barrett (1984). The AEP has been studied for many years, with particular attention devoted to the amplitude and latency of the wave forms resulting from the administration of a visual or auditory stimulus, and relatively low correlations of between .2 and .3 have been observed with both latency (negative) and amplitude (positive). Both of these measures are related to the variability of response; the greater the variability, the longer the latency and the smaller the amplitude, for obvious reasons (Callaway, 1975). The original reasons for looking at evoked potentials as possible measures of IQ were similar to those which persuaded Binet to include certain types of tests in his battery, namely a change in scoring rate with age. Older children, as compared with younger ones, have higher scores on the typical Binet test item, and similarly older children have _shorter_ latencies and _greater_ amplitude in the evoked potential.

This early, relatively unsystematic and purely pragmatic approach has been succeeded in recent years by attempts to formulate specific theories, deduce novel measures from these theories, and validate these measures against established IQ tests. There are three major paradigms in the field. The first is that of A.E. Hendrickson (1982) and D.E. Hendrickson (1982). This represents a truly general systems approach, starting out with a biological theory of the processing of information through the cortex, and ending up with a measure of biological intelligence. The theory is much too complex to be discussed here, even in outline, but the

essential link is provided by the postulation that individuals
differ in the number of errors that occur in the processing of
information through the cortex, presumably at the synapse, and
that error-free processing of information leads to high IQ scores,
error-prone transmission to low IQ scores. Errors in transmission
are indexed in terms of high variability and low complexity of -the
trace, and remarkably high correlations have been reported between
these variables (often combined into a single measure) and IQ. In
the largest study so far published (D.E. Hendrickson, 1982), a
correlation of .83 was found between this combined AEP measure and
Wechsler IQ on 219 15-year old children. Several replications
(e.g. Blinkhorn and Hendrickson, 1982; Haier et al., 1983) have
shown that the results are essentially reproducible, although many
unsolved questions remain. Clearly this is a most important
validation of Galton's concept, and one that deserves to be
followed up and extended. Typical results are shown in Figure 2.

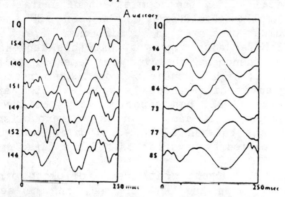

Figure 2a   Evoked potential waveforms for six high and six low
            IQ subjects. Auditory stimulation.

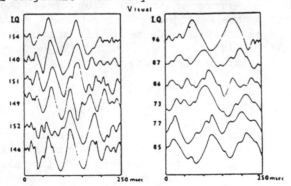

Figure 2b   Evoked potential waveforms for six high and six low
            IQ subjects. Visual stimulation.

The second model is Schafer's (1982) neural adaptability theory.
It is well known that selective attention has an influence on the
amplitude of AEP's, demonstrating a cognitive modulation of EEG

activity. This modulation is manifested as a tendency for unexpected or "attended" stimuli to produce AEP's of larger overall amplitudes than in those generated using stimuli whose nature and timing is known by the individual (Eysenck and Barrett, 1984.) Schafer has extended the scope of this empirical phenomenon by hypothesizing that individual differences in the modulation of amplitude (cognitive neural adaptability) will relate to individual differences in intelligence. The physiological basis mediating this relationship is hypothesized to be neural energy as defined by the number of neurons firing in response to a stimulus. A functionally efficient brain will use fewer neurons to process a fore-known stimulus, whereas for a novel, unexpected stimulus, the brain will commit large numbers of neurons. Given the relationship between individual neuron firing patterns and observed cortical AEP's, the committment of neural energy will be observed as amplitude differences between AEP's elicited from various stimulus presentation conditions, i.e. expected and unexpected. Schafer also suggests that this tendency is related to habituation phenomena observed in repeated stimulation with identical stimuli; high IQ subjects would show greater habituation as well as greater differences between expected and unexpected stimuli. Schafer (1982) has reported very positive results for tests of his hypothesis, and in an as yet unpublished study has found correlations between IQ and habituation of about the same size as that reported by Hendrickson for his paradigm.

It is possible to suggest that the Hendrickson paradigm may be more fundamental than the Schafer one, in the sense that the findings of the latter can be deduced from the theories of the former. Habituation is dependent on the identity of repeated stimuli, and when errors of transmission occur the identity of stimuli is not preserved; hence error-prone transmission would lead to reduced habituation effects. This hypothesis is of course highly speculative, but in a new field where very little evidence is available speculation may become imperative.

The third model is that of Robinson (1982a, b). This also has generated a model accounting for individual differences both in personality and intelligence, and this model deals with physiological events in a more gross manner than that of Hendrickson, without having recourse to hypotheses concerning individual neuron function. Robinson has taken a more conservative approach, postulating physiological events generally in line with current established evidence. No new physiological mechanisms are proposed within his model; rather he has used Pavlovian typology and general systems theory as his framework, and generated a very precise model. Subsequently, he tested the parameters of his model with some startling success.

Robinson, starting out with Pavlov's notions of excitatory and inhibitory processes, and the balance between them, suggested that certain neurophysiological sub-systems corresponded to Pavlov's hypothetical processes. Robinson suggested that the diffuse thalamocortical system could be used as a mediator of Pavlovian excitation, and he also identified the inhibitory process with distinct thalamic neurons,. Given the reciprocal axonal connection between these neurons in addition to evidence demonstrating that both sets of neurons may be activated by the same conditioned stimulus, concordance with Pavlov's speculation is thus maintained.

It would take us too far to discuss the rather complex details of Robinson's model, but he has provided evidence from an empirical study to show that relationships postulated by him between excitation and inhibition variables as measured by the evoked potential, on the one hand, and both personality and intelligence variables, on the other, can indeed be demonstrated to exist, and to reach a high degree of statistical significance. So far no replication of the study is available, but the model is perhaps closer to orthodox neurophysiology than that of Hendrickson, and deserves to be followed up.

Detailed reviews and criticisms of these three models are available elsewhere (Eysenck and Barrett, 1984); here let us merely note the deliberate efforts of these authors to construct models of biological intelligence along the lines of modern system theory, and note also the startling success of all three models in relating the electrophysiological variables generated by these models to IQ measures. Figure 3 shows the kind of relationship postulated in the theories between biological intelligence (here identified as error-free transmission), IQ, and the great variety of cognitive processes identified in intelligence B, and sometimes used to define social intelligence (Eysenck, 1982). This figure illustrates the kind of system which requires analysis before we can come to any agreed conclusions about human intelligence; clearly the distinction between biological intelligence and social intelligence is a vital one, as is the relationship between these two, and between them and psychometric intelligence (IQ). A recognition of the complexity of the system, and of the need to recognise the precise type of "intelligence" one is arguing about, must be a precursor to any agreed formulation of both the problem and the solution of the puzzle presented to science by human intelligence.

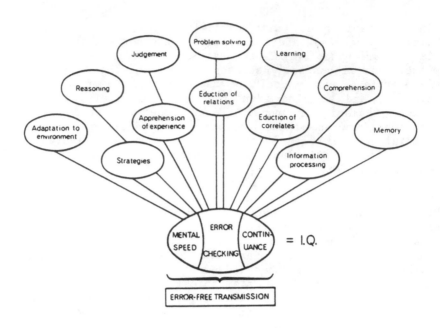

Figure 3   Relation between different kinds of intelligence.

Whatever may be one's estimate of the demonstrated relationship between psychometric intelligence (IQ), on the one hand, and RT and AEP measurement on the other (to which could be added work on inspection time, e.g. Brand and Deary, (1982)), there is little doubt that it constitutes a Kuhnian revolution in the field of intelligence theory. Current social intelligence theories (Sternberg, 1982) are quite incapable of digesting the facts as outlined, namely the very close relationship between psychometric intelligence and biological intelligence, and while much "normal science" puzzle-solving activity will be necessary to establish the biological intelligence model more firmly, it is already clear that some form of general systems approach will be required to unify the different aspects and areas loosely grouped under the general heading of "intelligence". Only in this way will we be able to make firm assertions about the relationships between biological intelligence, psychometric intelligence and social intelligence.

The position in the field of temperament is very similar to that in the field of intelligence. Here too we may speak of personality A, personality B and personality C, i.e. biological personality (sometimes denoted by the term "temperament" - Strelau, 1983), social personality, i.e. the manifestation of biological personality in everday life behaviour, and personality C, i.e. the measurement of personality by means of questionnaires and other devices (Eysenck and Eysenck, 1984.) For many years, the notion of a biological basis for personality was abjured by psychologists, largely due to a Zeitgeist which was as hostile to genetic and other biological influences here as it had proved to be in the field of intelligence. The early twin studies of Newman, Freeman and Holzinger (1937) suggested that heredity played little part in the genesis of differences between individuals, as far as personality was concerned, but his work was full of methodological and statistical errors, as pointed out by Eysenck (1967); and many recent studies, using better methods and better statistics, notably the model-fitting approach to genetic analysis pioneered by the biometrical genetical Birmingham School, have shown conclusively that genetic factors are as active in the field of temperament as they are in the field of intelligence (Fulker, 1981).

Modern developments have the following advantages over previous work. (1) We now have available refined methods of analysis which go well beyond making simple statements about heritability, but enable us to look at the whole architecture of hereditary and environmental influences, and separate out total phenotypic variance into additive genetic variance, dominance, epistasis, and assortative mating, while also partitioning environmental variance into a between-families and within-families portion. In addition, it enables an analysis to be made of the interaction between heredity and environment (Eaves and Eysenck, 1985). (2) In the second place, the number of subjects taking part in genetic experiments has now increased dramatically, in order to make possible the more refined analysis outlined above. Where previously MZ and DZ twins taking part in a study might number a few dozen, we now have samples of 10,000 or 12,000 being used. The formulae of biometrical genetical analysis make it possible to indicate the numbers required for any degree of refinement in the analysis, and such large numbers have been found necessary in order to achieve any kind of precision. (3) While Newman, Freeman and Holzinger had little in the way of reliable and valid tests in the personality field, and nothing in the way of theory, we now have both good theories and well established tests to use in genetic analyses (Eysenck and Eysenck, 1984). Thus the conclusions to be formulated presently are based on a much firmer grounding than was possible even a few years ago.

The major findings in this field are as follows: (1) For almost all personality traits and dimensions studied, between one-half and two-thirds of the phenotypic variance is due to genetic factors. (2) The genetic part of the variance is almost entirely of the additive kind; there is little in the way of evidence for epistasis, dominance, or assortative mating. There is some slight evidence for dominance as far as extraversion is concerned, but none for the other factors analysed. (3) Most if not all of the environmental variance is of the <u>within-family</u> kind; there is no evidence for <u>between-family</u> environmental variance. This seems to disconfirm most of the currently widespread psycho-analytic and other "dynamic" theories which rely on factors, such as child upbringing, weaning and potty-training, which would come under the heading of between-family environmental variance. These findings would seem to establish the necessity of postulating biological personality as a fundamental concept within this general field (Eysenck, 1967).

The model of personality here discussed has been claimed to constitute a paradigm in this field (Eysenck, 1983; Eysenck and Eysenck, 1984) and we will now briefly consider the reasons why this claim may not be entirely unjustified. Before doing so, however it may be useful briefly to set out the descriptive system involved. Essentially this is based on a factor analytic hierarchical model, which through large numbers of empirical investigations has thrown up three major dimensions of personality or superfactors (Royce and Powell, 1983). These are given different names by various authors, but will here be referred to as psychoticism (P), extraversion (E) and neuroticism (N). Figure 4 shows the traits, the intercorrelations between which generate the super-factors, P, E and N, and are the empirical basis for the postulation of these dimensions.

In order to demonstrate the paradigmatic status of these factors, it would have to be demonstrated (1) that they occur whenever analyses are carried out of the intercorrelations between large numbers of traits, such as appear in the MMPI, the 16PF, the CPI and many other well known scales. This has been shown to be so; the same major dimensions of personality appear whenever these scales are subjected to factorial analysis (Royce and Powell, 1983; Eysenck and Eysenck, 1984). (2) As a second requirement, the same dimensions should appear in cross-cultural studies, i.e. they should not be confined to American and European populations. Barrett and Eysenck (in press), have carried out such analyses for 25 different nationalities, and have shown very high indices of factor comparison, demonstrating that identical factors are involved in all these different countries and nations, ranging

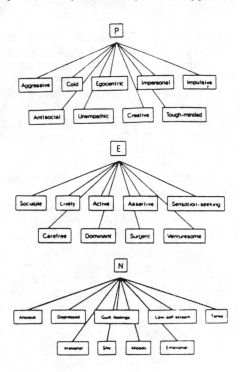

Figure 4   Traits defining Psychoticism.   (Eysenck & Eysenck, 1984)

from African states like Uganda and Nigeria, to Asian populations like Japanese and Mainland Chinese, and from Communist countries, like Yugoslavia and Hungary, through South American countries like Brazil, and Asian countries like Bangla Desh and Sri Lanka, to the usual European and North American countries. Thus these dimensions appear to be <u>universal</u> among present-day cultures and nations.

Given that these descriptive variables are hypothesized to have a biological foundation, it would be expected (3) that dimensions similar to P, E and N would be found in the animal world too. This is indeed so; Chamove, Eysenck, and Harlow (1972), have shown that long-continued observation of social behaviour in rhesus monkeys discloses three major personality features which are analogous to these three factors, namely aggression, sociability and fearful behaviour. Similarly, Garcia i Sevilla (1984) has demonstrated similar behaviour patterns in rats. A more detailed account of these and similar investigations will be found in Eysenck and Eysenck (1984).

Given the hypothesis of a biological and genetic basis for personality, one would expect (4) <u>longitudinal consistency</u> of these behaviour patterns over time. There is a good deal of evidence, extending to follow-ups continued over 50 years, and the evidence certainly suggests a great deal of consistency for personality traits, particularly P, E and N, almost reaching the same level as intelligence. Conley (1984) has recently surveyed this field, and has verified the existence of a high degree of consistency. Using the formula:

$$C = Rs^n$$

where C is the observed retest coefficient, R is the internal consistency or period-free reliability of the measuring instrument, s the annual stability and n the interval in years in which the coefficient is calculated, he found annual stabilities of intelligence and personality traits of .99 and .98, respectively.

We thus find that the personality concepts of P, E and N are found regardless of type of measuring instruments and personality theories held by the investigator; occur universally in all the countries and cultures where studies have been carried out; give rise to behaviour patterns in animals similar to those observed in humans; and have very strong longitudinal consistency over time. It seems reasonable, therefore to regard these dimensions of personality as firmly established and approaching the status of a paradigm. Objections and criticisms have been considered by Eysenck and Eysenck (1984), and have been shown to be largely irrelevant.

It might be thought that if personality variables are so universal, powerful and biologically determined, (5) they would be related to important differences in social behaviour. This indeed has been found to be so. The personality variables in question have been related to neurosis (Eysenck, 1977a), criminal behaviour (Eysenck, 1977b), sexual behaviour (Eysenck, 1976), and many others listed by Wilson (1981), such as affiliation, birth order, group interaction and social skills, speech patterns, expressive behaviour and person perception, expressive control, field dependence, suggestibility, conflict handling, attraction, attitudes and values, recreational interests, occupational choice, industrial performance, academic aptitude and achievement, drug use and abuse, and many others. The literature leaves little doubt that personality indeed is very influential in determining people's social behaviour in many different ways, and has many important consequences.

Much work has been done in recent years to formulate causal theories of a biological kind to account for the observed differences in personality, e.g. Mangan, (1982), Prentsky (1979),

Zuckerman, Ballinger and Post (1984) and many others, beginning
with the well known studies in physique of Kretchmer and Sheldon.
Much of this interest began with the publication of The Biological
Basis of Personality (Eysenck, 1967), which postulated that
individual differences in extraversion-introversion were produced
by the habitual arousal level and the arousability of the cortex,
in the sense that introverts are characterised by high levels of
arousal, extraverts by low levels, with ambiverts intermediate.
This   hypothesis   has   been   widely   tested   along   its
psychophysiological   parameters,   and   a   good   review   of   the
literature is provided by Stelmack (1981). On the whole, the
evidence is confirmatory, although it appears to be fairly
dependent on the choice of correct parameter values in the testing
conditions and stimulus selection.

A recent review by Zuckerman, Ballinger and Post (1984) also
discusses   in   great   detail   the   literature   on   arousal   and
arousability,   but   also   shows   that   there   are   biochemical
differences between extraverts and introverts which are of
considerable interest. To take but one example, there is an
interesting negative correlation between monoamine oxidase (MAO),
on the one hand, and extraversion and sensation-seeking on the
other. This enzyme is present in tissues including the brain,
with the highest brain concentration in the hypothalamus. Studies
of humans have relied largely on measurement of MAO from blood
platelets, which has an uncertain relation to brain MAO, but has
been found to be powerfully related to personality. Measurement
over time is reliable and Zuckerman et al. list a series of
studies, both with humans and animals, indicating extraverted
behaviour patterns in low MAO subjects, introverted behaviour
patterns in high MAO subjects. The relationship between MAO and
cortical arousal has not been studied in detail yet, although such
a relationship   would   be   predicted,   and   would   add   to   our
understanding   of   the   biological   causes   of
extraversion-introversion.

Many detailed predictions have been made from the arousal theory
on to a great variety of psychological variables testable in the
laboratory, such as Pavlovian conditioning, memory retrieval,
learning,   pain   tolerance   for   sensory   deprivation,   stimulus
intensity   modulation,   sensory   thresholds,   flicker   fusion,
kinesthetics. figural after-effects, vigilance, and many others
(Eysenck, 1976). The great majority of the predictions made have
been verified, and the results have served to establish more
firmly the theory as probably pointing in the right direction,
although clearly much work remains to be done to work out precise
parameter relations in all these different physiological and
psychological areas.

As far as neuroticism is concerned, there is an obvious connection with the limbic system and the autonomic nervous system, differences in the activation of which can account for differences in the personality variable. There has been much less work in trying to establish the precise relationships here, and the work of Myrtek (1980) and Fahrenberg et al. (1984) has shown that much remains to be done before we can regard this relationship as established. It would certainly not be true to say that high N scorers show greater reactivity to physical stimuli; Saltz (1970) has shown that stimuli such as electric shocks produce quite different effects in anxiety-prone subjects than do socially threatening variables and situations. Choice of the correct stimulus is therefore an obviously vital part of any proper programme of investigation. It may be that duration of physiological effects is more important than intensity of reaction, which in any case is difficult to measure due to threshold and ceiling effects. The possibility should also be considered that hormonal secretions, e.g. adrenaline, may show more powerful relationships with personality than do psychophysiological reactions; possibly this is because it is the hormones that determine to some extent the duration of the evoked response. There are many unsolved problems in this area which require investigation. Recent work by Kelley (in press) has shown an involvement of ACTH (Adrenocorticotropic hormone) in the extinction of conditioned fear responses, in the sense that an injection of ACTH considerably <u>delays</u> extinction; this is important in view of the relevance of extinction or incubation of anxiety to modern theories of neurosis (Eysenck, 1982b). According to this theory, neurotic disorders are produced by Pavlovian conditioning, and are eliminated through Pavlovian extinction. The extinction process is consequently a vital one for any consideration of psychotherapeutic or behaviour therapy effects, and the postulation that it is affected powerfully by personality factors, particularly introversion and neuroticism, is strongly supported by the relationship between extinction and ACTH, which in turn is related to these personality variables.

Psychoticism, too, has been related to basic biological variables, particularly the sex hormones; P is powerfully related to masculinity, in the sense that males have much higher P scores on the average than do females, and there has been some evidence that testosterone, the male hormone, is correlated with P (Eysenck and Eysenck, 1976). There are biological correlates of P also, such as HLA B-27, a leucocyte antigen which is found significantly more frequently in schizophrenics than in normals. It has been shown that when comparing normal high P with normal low P scorers, or psychotic high P with psychotic low P scorers, the high P scorers in each case show a higher level of HLA B-27 than do the low scorers (Gattaz, 1981; Gattaz and Seitz, in press). In a similar way, Claridge (1981) in a series of studies found that acute, untreated schizophrenics show a paradoxical inversion of the usual relationship between two-flash threshold and skin conductance, and that normal high P scorers showed the same inversion as compared to normal low P scorers The work of Claridge is a particularly clear example of the importance of a systems theory approach; it is not individual relationships between variables such as two-flash threshold or electro-dermal response, on the one hand, and schizophrenia on the other, which give meaningful and replicable results, but rather the <u>systematic interactions</u> of these variables, which differ between schizophrenics and normals, or between high and low P scorers.

This chapter contains a very brief and incomplete account of the writer's system theory approach to the study of personality, both in its cognitive and non-cognitive aspects. Much fuller accounts are available elsewhere (Eysenck, 1981, 1982; Eysenck and Eysenck, 1984). It is hoped, nevertheless, that the main outlines of the type of research advocated have emerged from this presentation. The proper study of personality has to be inclusive, rather than exclusive; it must look at genetic factors, biochemical determinants, electrophysiological influences, constitutional factors, as well as social influences of various kinds, educational, cultural, socioeconomic etc. It must then try to weave these into an interactional network, possibly along the lines of path analysis, with as many quantitative indices as possible to facilitate causal analaysis. It will be obvious that much of this work is still in tho future; only a beginning has been made because of the general tendency among psychologists to adopt a very one-sided approach, e.g. biophile or sociophile, rather than to treat man as a biosocial animal, which is the only possible way of approaching the subject. System theory does not suggest specific answers, but merely a way of approaching the subject; it tells us to avoid looking for a "resolutive" method, and look instead for nomological networks more appropriate to the study of organisms. The analytic method works very well in science when we can <u>decompose</u> the subject of investigation into elementary parts, but the study of organisms by definition requires the organism to remain intact, with all its parts interacting in a systematic fashion which requires to be unravelled before we can claim to have an answer to any of our problems concerning that organism. This does not prevent us from recognising parts and sub-parts, but it imposes on us the duty to analyse their inter-relations in detail.

It will be clear, for instance, that while statistically P, E and N are independent from each other, as well as from g, nevertheless from the point of view of the functioning of the total organism their interaction is extremely important. A high E - high N individual who is high on P and g will differ profoundly in his actions and behaviours from a high E - high N individual who is low on P and low on g. The former may turn out to be a fascinating psychopath specialising in computer frauds; the latter is more likely to turn out to be a broken-down drunkard living by occasional thieving and spivving. it is likely that the most important next step in the study of personality will be the investigation of the interaction of P, E, N, and g; very little empirical work has in fact been done along these lines. Without such knowledge, however, it can hardly be claimed that we have done more than taken the first few, faltering steps in the scientific study of personality.

REFERENCES

Barrett, P., & Eysenck, S.B.G. (in press). The assessment of personality factors across 25 countries. Personality and Individual Differences.

Berrien, F.K. (1968). General and Social Systems. New Brunswick: Rutgers University Press.

Bertalanffy, L. (1952). Problems of Life. New York: Wiley.

Bertalanffy, L. (1972). The history and status of general systems theory. In G.J. Klir (Ed.), Trends in General Systems Theory, pp. 21-41. London: Wiley.

Blinkhorn, S.F., & Hendrickson, D.E. (1982). Averaged evoked response and psychometric intelligence. Nature, 295, 596-597.

Buckley, W. (Ed.) (1968). Modern Systems Research for the Behavioural Scientist. Chicago: Aldine.

Callaway, E. (1975). Brain Electrical Potential and Individual Psychological Differences. London: Grune & Stratton.

Chamove, A.S., Eysenck, H.J., & Harlow, H.F. (1972). Personality in monkeys: Factor analysis of rhesus social behaviour. Quarterly Journal of Experimental Psychology, 24, 496-504.

Claridge, G. (1981). Psychoticism. In: R. Lynn (Ed.), Dimensions of Personality. Pp. 79-109. London: Pergamon Press.

Conley, J.J. (1984). The hierarchy of consistency: a review and model of longitudional findings on adult individual differences in intelligence, personality and self-opinion. Personality and Individual Differences, 5, 11-26.

Eaves, L. & Eysenck, H.J. (1985). The Genetics of Personality. New York: Cambridge University Press.

Elgerd, O.I. (1967). Control Systems Theory. London: McGraw-Hill.

Eysenck, H.J. (1967). The Biological Basis of Personality. Springfield: C.C. Thomas.

Eysenck, H.J. (1976a). Sex and Personality. London: Open Books.

Eysenck, H.J. (1976b). The Measurement of Personality. Lancaster: MTP.

Eysenck, H.J. (1977a) You and Neurosis. London: Maurice Temple Smith.

Eysenck, H.J. (1977b) Crime and Personality. London: Routledge & Kegan Paul.

Eysenck, H.J. (1979). The Structure and Measurement of Intelligence. New York: Springer.

Eysenck, H.J. (1980a). The biosocial nature of man. Journal of Social and Biological Structure, 3, 125-134.

Eysenck, H.J. (1980b). Man as a Biosocial Animal: Comments on the sociobiology debate. Political Psychology, 2, 45-51.

Eysenck, H.J. (1981). Model for Personality. New York: Springer.

Eysenck, H.J. (1982a) A Model for Intelligence. New York: Springer.

Eysenck, H.J. (1982b) Neobehavioristic (S-R) theory. In: G.T. Wilson & C.R. Franks (Eds.), Contemporary Behaviour Therapy. Pp. 205-276. New York: Guilford Press.

Eysenck, H.J. (1983a) Is there a paradigm in personality research? Journal of Research in Personality, 17, 369-397.

Eysenck, H.J. (1983b) Personality as a fundamental concept in scientific psychology. Australian Jounral of Psychology, 35 289-304.

Eysenck, H.J. (in press). The theory of intelligence and the psychophysiology of cognition. In: R.J. Sternberg (Ed.),

Advances in Research in Intelligence, Vol. 3. Hillsdale: Erblaum.

Eysenck, H.J., & Barrett, P. (1984). Psychophysiology and the Measurement of Intelligence. In: C.R. Reynolds & V. Wilson (Eds.), Methodological and Statistical Advances in the Study of Individual Differences. New York: Plenum Press.

Eysenck, H.J., & Eysenck, M.W. (1984). Personality and Individual Differences. New York: Plenum Press.

Eysenck, H.J., & Eysenck, S.B.G. (1976). Psychoticism as a Dimension of Personality. London: Hodder & Stougton.

Eysenck, H.J., & Kamin, L. (1981). The Intelligence Controversy. New York: Wiley.

Fahrenberg, J., Foerster, F., Schneider, H.J., Muller, W., & Myrtek, M. (1984). Aktivierungsforschung im Labor-Feld-Vergleich. Munchen: Minerva.

Frank, H. (1971). Kybernetische Grundlagen der Padagogie. Stuttgart: Kohlhammer.

Fulker, D.W., (1981). The genetic and environmental architecture of psychoticism, extraversion and neuroticism. In: H.J. Eysenck (Ed.), A Model for Personality. Pp. 88-122. New York: Springer.

Garcia i Sevilla, L. (1984). Extraversion and neuroticism in rats. Personality and Individual Differences, 5, 511-532.

Gattaz, W.F. (1981) HLA-B27 as a possible genetic marker of psychoticism. Personality and Individual Differences, 2, 57-60.

Gattaz, W.F., & Satz, M. (1984). A possible association between HLA-B27 and the vulnerability to schizophrenia. Personality and Individual Differences.

Gray, W., Rizzo, N.D. & Duhl, F. J. (1969). General Systems Theory and Psychiatry. Boston: Little, Brown & Co.

Guilford, J.P. (1967). The Nature of Human Intelligence. New York: McGraw-Hill.

Haier, R.J., Robinson, D.L., Braden, W., & Williams, D. (1983). Electrical potentials of the cerebral cortex and psychometric intelligence. Personality and Individual Differences, 4, 591-599.

Hebb, D.O. (1949). The Organization of Behaviour. New York: Wiley.

Hendrickson, A.E. (1982). The biological basis of intelligence: Part 1. Theory. In: H.J. Eysenck (Ed.), A Model for Intelligence. Pp 151-196.

Hendrickson, D.E. (1982). The biological basis of intelligence: Part 2. Measurement. In: H.J. Eysenck (Ed.), A Model for Intelligence. Pp. 197-228. New York:Springer.

Hick, W. (1952). On the rate of gain of informaiton. Quarterly Journal of Experimental Psychology, 4, 11-26.

Jensen, A.R. (1982a). Reaction time and psychometric g. In: J.J. Eysenck (Ed.), A Model for Intelligence. Pp. 93-132. New York: Springer.

Jensen, A.R. (1982b). The chronometry of intelligence. In: R.J. Sternberg (Ed.), Advances in Research in Intelligence pp. 242-267. Hillsdale: Erlbaum.

Klir, G.J. (Ed.) (1972). Trends in General Systems Theory. London: Wiley.

Lehrl, G. (1983). Intelligenz: Informationspsychologische Grundlagen. Enzyklopadie der Naturwissenschaft und Technik. Landsberg: Moderne Industrie.

Mangan, G. (1982). The Biology of Human Conduct. London: Pergamon Press.

Myrtek, M. (1980). Psychophysiologische Konstitutionsforschung. Gottingen: Hogrefe.

Newman, H.H., Freeman, F.N. & Holzinger, K.J. (1937). Twins. A Study of Heredity and Environment. Chicago: University of Chicago Press.

Peak, H., & Boring, E.G. (1926). The factor of speed in intelligence. Journal of Experimental Psychology, 9, 71-94.

Prentsky, R.S., (1979). The Biological Aspects of Normal Personality. Lancaster: MTP.

Robinson, D.L. (1982a). Properties of the diffuse thalamocortical system and human personality: A direct test of Pavlovian/Eysenckian theory. Personality and Individual Differences, 3, 1-16.

Robinson, D.L. (1982b). Properties of the diffuse thalamocortical system, human intelligence and differentiated interpreted modes of learning. Personality and Individual Differences, 3, 393-405.

Roth, E. (1964). Die Geschwindigkeit der Verarbeitung von Information und ihr Zusammenhang mit Intelligenz. Zeitschrift fur experimentelle und angewandte Psychologie, 11, 616-622.

Royce, J.R., & Powell, S. (1983). Theory of Personality and Individual Differences: Factor, Systems and Processes. Englewood Cliffs, N.J.: Prentice-Hall.

Saltz, E. (1970). Manifest anxiety: Have we misread the data? Psychological Review, 77, 568-573.

Schafer, E.W.P. (1982). Neural adaptability: a biological determinant of behavioral intelligence. International Journal of Neuroscience, 17, 183-191.

Spearman, C. (1927). The Abilities of Man. London: Macmillan.

Stelmack, R.N. (1981). The psychophysiology of extraversion and neuroticism. In: H.J. Eysenck (Ed.), A Model for Personality. Pp. 38-69. New York: Springer.

Sternberg, R.J. (1982). Handbook of Human Intelligence. London: Cambridge University Press.

Strelau, J. (1983). Temperament, Personality, Activity. London: Academic Press.

Vernon, P.E. (1979). Intelligence: Heredity and Environment. San Francisco: W.H. Freeman.

Weaver, W. (1948). Science and complexity. American Scientist, 36, 536-544.

Wilson, G.D. Personality and social behaviour. In: H.J. Eysenck (Ed.), A Model for Personality. Pp. 210-245. New York: Springer.

Wissler, C. (1901). The correlation of mental and physical tests. Psychological Review Monograph, 3.

Yule, W., Gold, R.D., & Busch, C. (1982). Long-term predictive validity of the WPPSI: An 11-year follow-up study. Personality and Individual Differences, 3, 65-71

Zadeh, L.A., & Rolak, E. (Eds.) (1969). System Theory. New York: McGraw-Hill.

Zuckerman, M., Ballenger, J.C., & Post, R.N. (1984). The neurobiology of some dimensions of personality. International Review of Neurobiology, 25, 391-436.

COGNITIVE AND MOTIVATIONAL DIFFERENCES BETWEEN ASIAN AND OTHER SOCIETIES

PHILIP E. VERNON

University of Calgary, Alberta

INTRODUCTION

Numerous writers, including Jahoda and Berry, have pointed out that contemporary psychology is largely based on work with American college students, or with white rats; and though young children are often studied, they are mostly drawn from restricted samples of middle class Western cultures. Thus cross-cultural research should be able to provide a much broader perspective on mental functioning, and thereby improve the external validity of our findings. For example, by sampling a wider data base it should help to illumine the nature and development of cognitive abilities such as intelligence. But before proceeding, I intend to define intelligence as "the complexity and efficiency of the higher mental processes of members of any given cultural group". Specifically, I want to know what genetic constitutional and environmental factors, and what child-rearing practices are chiefly involved in such mental growth.

Over the past 25 years, on and off, I have carried out field work with groups of 11-year boys in several contrasted ethnic groups - English, Gaelic, Jamaican, Ugandan, and Canadian native Indian and Eskimo. My wife, Dorothy, and I have applied an extensive battery of tests including verbal, nonverbal reasoning, number, spatial, memory, imaginative, and Piaget-type tests of conceptual abilities (Vernon, 1969). These were mostly given individually by ourselves, with some help from local assistants, in order to get them across to children with little English, and to explore some of their major cultural differences. Several Ph.D. students of mine, such as the late Russ MacArthur, Alan Bowd and Ian Brooks, have been involved in more detailed studies, mainly of Canadian indigenes. More recently (Vernon, 1982) I have been particularly interested in Asian cultures - Chinese, Japanese and East Indians, both in their own countries and as emigrants and their descendants abroad. Though I have done little field work with these, I have surveyed rather thoroughly the available literature on their abilities, achievements, and their child development. I would like to spend a little time describing the characteristics of these Asian societies before going on to more general topics such as methodology in cross-cultural research.

Arthur Jensen first drew my attention to the remarkable cultural phenomenon of orientals in North America who, despite discrimination and persecution by the white majority - quite comparable to the treatment of negroes by American whites - have survived and flourished both educationally and occupationally. Even in the 1920s when Chinese and Japanese in California, British Columbia and Hawaii were living in extreme poverty, and largely retained their own highly distinctive languages in their homes, they were scoring equal to, or above, white norms on tests of nonverbal reasoning, visuospatial and some memorizing abilities, though often considerably handicapped on verbal tests and English usage. With greater acculturation, and acceptance by white society after the Second World War, they made remarkable progress. Currently they obtain about two and a half times as many doctoral degrees in American universities (relative to their numbers in the population) as do Caucasians (McCarthy & Wolfle, 1975); also the same proportional excess in professional employment (Weyl, 1969). Thus they contradict any simplistic theory that environmental hardship, discrimination, and linguistic handicap, account by themselves for the below average intelligence and achievement of most ethnic minority groups. Since they originated in the 19th and early 20th centuries from poor peasant stock, it is improbable that they are genetically superior to Caucasians in general intellectual potentialities. (Though there is some evidence of greater temperamental placidity and less excitability in oriental infants than in Caucasian (Freedman, 1974)). The more likely explanation of their success lies in their home upbringing, in child-rearing practices that instil docility to social norms, acceptance of traditional values, and strong motivation to achievement.

It is not only those orientals who reside, and are educated in Western societies who show such remarkable abilities. Large groups of Chinese are found in Hong Kong, Singapore and Taiwan; and their average performance on figural tests such as Raven's Matrices and Cattell Culture-Fair are quite comparable to English and American norms (Rodd, 1959; Chan, 1974). M.W. Stevenson (1982), Stigler (1982) and their colleagues have developed reading and arithmetic tests at primary school level which have been carefully equated for difficulty in Taiwan, Japan and the U.S. In arithmetic both oriental groups were considerably ahead of American children, despite their being taught in school classes of

about twice the size of those in the U.S. (i.e. 40+ as against
20). In reading, however, all 3 groups obtained much the same
means, though one might have expected the Chinese and Japanese
idiographic scripts to be considerably more complex and difficult
to read and write than Roman alphabetic script. The technological
achievements of modern Japan are well known to be as advanced as
those of the U.S. You may have read the recent claims by Richard
Lynn (1977) that the Japanese are genetically superior to the
white average on WAIS, WISC and WPPSI scales. I do not accept
these claims since comparisons between these ethnic groups are
possible only on the performance, or apparatus tests and Digit
Span, and, as I mentioned earlier, orientals characteristically
show higher nonverbal than verbal scores. Flynn (1982) has drawn
attention to other methodological weaknesses in Lynn's
comparisons.

While Japan is obviously the most technologically advanced country
in Asia, Indians and Chinese are among the least advanced, and
have some of the lowest standards of living. Twenty-five percent
of Japanese are classified as rural dwellers, as against 80% of
Indians and mainland Chinese. The chequered history of China, with
its continual warfare, widespread malnutrition, extreme poverty,
political instability, and extermination of many intellectuals,
must mean that its educational standards are very low; though, for
obvious reasons, we have no evidence of their scores on
standardized tests. In India, the country has been less affected
by wars, but its use of a considerable number of different
languages in different areas adversely affects communication and
education. Also the rigid caste system, although officially
banned, still prevents many of the brighter Untouchables from
achieving as they should. The most extensive cross-national
surveys of educational achievements are those carried out by the
IEA (International Educational Achievement) project; especially
Husen's (1967) volume on mathematics, Comber & Keeves (1973) on
science, and Thorndike (1973) on reading comprehension. In these
studies the same tests, suitably translated, were given to as
representative samples of students as possible, in anywhere from a
dozen to twenty different countries. I have extracted some of the
means for 10 yr. or 13 yr. samples in Table 1. It may be seen
that the average level of achievement in underdeveloped countries
is deplorably low. Indeed it would be lower still had really
representative samples been available. About one third of the
child population in these three countries had to be omitted
because they did not attend school, or could not attempt the tests
at all. Nevertheless, despite the near illiteracy of a large
proportion of the Indian children, one should remember that an
appreciable number do survive the educational system (possibly by
attending private schools), reach university and achieve Bachelor
or higher degrees, though usually at a rather low level. And they

have produced a considerable number of internationally known mathematicians, psychologists, and artists. Of greater interest is the finding that children of immigrant Indians in the U.K., attending British schools, appear to catch up rather quickly and, in 3 to 6 years, reach much the same examination marks and scores on a variety of cognitive tests, as English children of the same age. Incidentally they seem to catch up more successfully in British schools than do West Indian immigrant children, which may suggest - though obviously does not prove - genetic differences. Four researches with East Indians in Britain (Sharma, 1971; Ghuman, 1975) have shown similar results, and their authors did try to provide control groups either of Indians still living in India, or of newly arrived immigrants. But it is difficult to ensure that the good achievers were not mainly children of immigrant parents with above average education and drive. At least these investigations suggest that scholastic achievement is low in India, partly because of inadequate health provisions and nutrition, and largely because of the ineffectiveness of the Indian educational system. The same would be true of mainland China, since its emigrants in Taiwan, Hong Kong or America are quite comparable in achievement to Caucasians. I find it a rather chilling prospect that the one billion inhabitants of China are potentially as able as the Japanese and, with improved medical, educational and economic conditions, are capable of the same level of technology; though obviously this will not happen in our life time.

Table 1

Achievement Test Scores of 10 or 13-year Children in Selected Countries (I.E.A.)

Reading Comprehension 10 yr.		Science 10 yr.		Mathematics 13 yr.	
Sweden	21.5	Japan	21.7	Japan	31.2
U.K.	18.5	U.K.	15.7	U.K.	19.3
U.S.A.	16.8	U.S.A.	17.7	U.S.A.	16.2
Chile	9.1	Chile	9.1		-
India	8.5	India	8.5		-
Iran	3.7	Iran	4.1		-
Approximate S.D.s	10.0		8.5		15.0

I expect several of you have already condemned my application of tests constructed in the U.S. or other Western countries to Asians, Africans, etc. as being outmoded, ethnocentric, or even racist. I do not think that would be fair since I have repeatedly declared my acceptance of Hebb's view that intelligence and other abilities result from the interaction between genetic determinants and environmental stimulation. This implies that, by definition, intelligence is not a universal entity, but is relative to each different culture. In my 1969 book I pointed out, also, that any test scores are greatly affected by the familiarity of the subjects with the particular types of test items, and by their attitudes to the strange social situation of being tested by a foreigner or an interpreter. I referred to these as extrinsic conditions affecting test scores. But in so far as any two cultures show much the same cultural values and concepts, it is legitimate, given no statistical bias in the items, to compare them on the same test (translated if necessary). Japan and U.S.A. have very similar technological civilizations, and similar educational systems. Hence the test scores of Japanese and Americans can be compared, even though there are many differences in their values and child-upbringing. Whereas it would be quite absurd to give the translated Binet, let us say, to mainland Chinese peasant children, even it one could get permission to do so.

This raises the issue of 'emic' vs. 'etic' research. Admittedly my work has been mainly etic, though I have always tried to soak myself, as it were, in the culture of any non-Caucasian group I was studying, with a view to getting a better understanding of that group's test scores, and to allow for the likely biases in my tests. Actually much of John Berry's (1976) work was also etic, when he compared native Indian, African, or other groups on field independence and perceptual tests; though he did also assess such relevant variables as ecology, socialization, acculturation and acculturational stress.

It seems to me that the emic-etic distinction has much wider ramifications. For example it is closely related to the ideographic vs. nomothetic approaches to the study of personality, described by Gordon Allport (1937) in the 1930s. He argued that we can obtain useful knowledge of people's common traits like neuroticism, introversion, etc. by applying personality tests, but also insisted that we cannot understand a person except by studying him or her as a unique structure, as advocated by German Verstehen psychologists, or by clinical and psychodynamic psychologists generally. My own sympathy with idiographic approaches was also demonstrated when I got into a public controversy with Ray Cattell in 1937. As a disciple of Spearman he believed that abilities should be assessed by tests of known factor content, given under standard, controlled conditions; whereas I argued that the Stanford-Binet test, given in a more flexible way so as to suit the individual child, yields a better understanding of the child's strengths and weaknesses and prognosis, although this involves subjective judgements.

There seems to be a noteworthy trend in comtemporary developmental and social psychology to take more account of the overall background of the persons studied, or what Kurt Lewin called the field, or the life-space in which an individual operates. Two good examples come to mind - first Bronfenbrenner's 1979 book, The Ecology of Child Development, where he brings out differences in children's abilities and personalities resulting from different family climates, or the social system in which they grow up. Secondly Michael Rutter's Fifteen Thousand Hours (1979) - a study of Junior High Schools in England where differences in teachers' attitudes, and in the ethic, or morale of the schools brought about differences in school achievements, delinquency rates, etc. In statistical terminology there are significant interactions between attitudes or motivation, and cognitive factors, in determining mental and personality growth. Many earlier writers have, of course, studied environmental variables, but mostly global ones likes socioeconomic status; whereas Bronfenbrenner, Rutter and many others seem to be applying the emic approach of cross-cultural psychology to subgroups within a Western culture. At the same time there are innumerable etic type investigations of subgroup differences in abilities and achievements, which are still regarded as entirely legitimate.

I hope that this rather lengthy digression justifies the kind of psychometric cross-cultural research in which I am interested. But I would have to agree that the work is weakened by being conducted on samples of convenience, rather than, as in Berry's investigations, on samples chosen to exemplify particular hypotheses. Also I admit to being somewhat ethnocentric in assuming that some cultures are more advanced, others more backward in so far as they approximate more, or less, closely to Western technology and values, and develop concepts and thinking skills similar to those of Caucasians. But I would willingly add that other abilities than Western-type intelligence are of greater importance for survival and progress in many groups - particularly those which have to cope with unusually adverse ecological conditions, for example Eskimos, Kalahari bushmen, or Australian aboriginals. I am also struck by the fact that even in countries like Japan and India which do have trained psychologists, they rely almost exclusively on adaptations of Western tests, and have not attempted to analyze the major attributes of higher mental processing in their own cultures, nor to develop their own tests to measure these. Nevertheless some attempts to aim at local conceptions of intelligence have occurred in Africa, e.g. by Wober (1972). Also work such as that of Irvine and Reuning (1984) on Perceptual Speed, or other ability factors across cultures, is helping to legitimize etic comparisons.

Now Berry (1976) urges that cross-cultural psychology should avoid value-laden terms such as general intelligence, or civilized, progressive, modernistic vs. primitive, traditionalistic, etc. Actually he does report differences among native Indian groups in acculturation, which is defined by adoption of a Western-type educational system, having wage-earning employment, and degree of urbanization. But he is much more interested in the dimension of psychological differentiation - the term derived from Witkin's (1962) theory of field independent vs. dependent cognitive styles. Witkin found that a number of visuospatial tests intercorrelated consistently, either among children or adults, to support the notion of a psychological dimension basically distinct from general intelligence. These included the Rod and Frame (RFT), Embedded Figures (EFT), Kohs Blocks, and Draw-a-Man scored for sophistication of body concepts. However these tests are very much the same as those which make up the British K-factor, Thurstone's S or spatial factor, his Flexibility of Closure, and Guilford's Visualization factor. At the same time the correlations of such batteries with verbal ability tests are positive but quite low. Now in 1959, Barry, Child and Bacon contrasted two main types of cultures, namely hunting-gathering peoples vs. sedentary-agricultural peoples. The former tend to stress independence and resourcefulness in rearing their children, while the latter more strongly emphasize conformity with the group norms, and use strict socialization practices. At about the same time, in the early 60's John Dawson, Berry and I, working independently, all applied visuospatial tests to cultural groups which differed in their resourcefulness vs. conformity, and we confirmed that such groups differ on field-independence tests as Witkin had claimed (Dawson, 1967; Berry, 1966; Vernon, 1965). In 1960 I was working in Jamaica and Trinidad on their methods· of selecting bright primary school children for secondary education, and I hoped to improve on the conventional verbal group intelligence tests then being used. But the nonverbal test which I constructed actually showed Jamaican children to score even lower relative to English children than on the verbal and standardized achievement tests. Since the negro cultures in the West Indies and Africa are mainly agricultural, and are highly conformist, I hypothesized that Canadian Inuit and Indian children would score relatively better on visuospatial tests, and so it turned out in 1965. Figure 1 summarizes the mean scores I obtained on verbal, nonverbal intelligence, and spatial tests for Jamaican, native Indian, Eskimo, Ugandan, and Chinese children, in terms of white means of 100 on each dimensions, and Standard Deviation 15.

The Chinese, of course, are not hunting-gathering but, as mentioned earlier, they score much above average on nonverbal and spatial tests. Berry (1976) reported findings from 17 very varied samples of children, mostly Canadian Indian or Inuit, but also African and Australasian, which confirmed the high correlation between tests of psychological differentiation or field indepedence, and ecological or sociocultural differences. But he believes that this relationship holds only among peoples living in subsistence economies. Thus it would not be expected to appear in a society like the Japanese, who raise their children with a strong emphasis on social conformity and dependence on the mother, the family and the work group. But they also get high scores on Witkin's and other spatial tests. It would seem, though, that the Chinese are anomalous, since they are likewise dependent and conformist, and the immense majority are sedentary-agricultural, living at subsistence level; yet they too are highly field-independent.

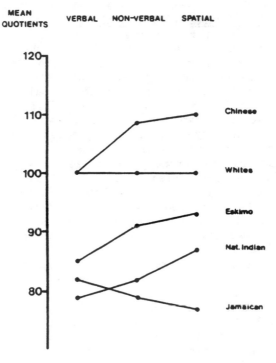

Figure 1   Mean Quotients of Children in 5 Cultural Groups
          on 3 Ability Measures

Several other researches indicate the complexity of the relations between field independence ability and type of culture. Thus

Witkin and Berry (1975) tested samples of 10yr. and 13 yr. boys and girls in Mexico, Holland, and Italy. In each country, two groups were chosen, one which was noted for severe discipline and rigid religious beliefs, the other being more permissive and open-minded. All of the samples could be called agricultural, though they were also mostly wage-earning. In each country the more open community scored more highly on spatial tests. Likewise Dershowitz (1971) compared two groups of Jewish boys in New York, one reared in highly orthodox families, the other in more emancipated and Americanized families. Also a control group of white Protestant boys was tested. The differences on spatial and other tests were often small, and not always statistically significant. But there was a clear tendency for the Protestants to score most highly on spatial tests, then the nontraditional Jews, and the traditional Jews lowest in independence. Note that all these samples live in an urban, wage-earning environment.

It is interesting that all of the groups of Mongoloid origin that I have studied, including Chinese in Taiwan, Hong Kong, Hawaii, U.S. and Canada, Japanese at home or abroad, Eskimo and native Indian, show this tendency to score more highly on nonverbal and spatial than on verbal tests. The objection that all groups tested in English were handicapped by lack of familiarity with the English language, is contradicted by the fact that many Japanese and Chinese in America or Canada have been living in English-speaking environments for several generations, and mostly speak English at home, at school, or in their jobs. But although they have caught up to about the white average on verbal tests, they are still about 10 IQ points better on spatial tests. Now I would hesitate to claim that there is a common genetic spatial ability factor running through all these groups, which include both hunting and agricultural societies; though it is interesting to speculate that there might be some differences in lateralization of brain functions between Mongoloids and Caucasians. Witkin's description of field-independence emphasizes it as analytical rather than global, which one would expect to depend on left rather than right brain functions. So theorizing along these lines appears to be a dead end.

I would like to spend a bit more time on North American native Indians since, along with many psychologists, educationists and politicians, I tend to talk of them as if they all have the same cultural characteristics. This of course is untrue; for although the majority of Indian bands are low in educational and occupational achievements, yet they differ in beliefs and customs just as they do in their numerous languages or dialects. Many of the Eastern tribes were largely sedentary-agricultural before the

white man arrived, though often combining this livelihood with
some hunting, fishing and gathering, and with fighting one
another. It was the Plains Indians who suffered most, since their
livelihood was centred around the buffalo. When white immigrants
came, they killed a large number of Indians with their guns, still
more with their diseases like smallpox, and with alcohol; and they
virtually exterminated the buffalo. The remnants of the tribes
were herded onto reservations, mainly consisting of poor quality
land. They were forced to sign treaties, and their affairs were
administered, and their children educated, by white officials and
teachers, who not only knew nothing about their cultures and
languages, but set out to suppress them. The result was complete
demoralization and alienation. Naturally they are still resentful
and suspicious even of whites who genuinely want to help them. By
the age of 13 or so adolescent Indians begin to realise how little
life holds for them, when the unemployment rate often exceeds 60%,
and when they are stereotyped by whites as being shiftless and
untrustworthy. However in the past 20 years or so, many tribes
have begun to show more initiative in demanding civil rights, the
running of their own educational systems, and now the right to
govern themselves. They are at last rebuilding their own
self-respect, and several bands have set up local industries on
the reserves which are self-supporting. According to a recent
Department of Indian Affairs report, some 72% of children are now
staying on at school up to 9th grade. Even more remarkably,
industrial, commercial and agricultural enterprises are
flourishing in numerous American Indian tribes.

The Pacific west coast tribes fared rather better than those on
the Plains, since they were able to retain their traditional
economies based on fishing. However their social organization
broke down badly with the abolition of potlatch, and of their
rigid social stratification into nobles, commoners, and slaves.
The tribes living closest to Vancouver, such as Kwakiutl, Nootka
and Haida, number less than a quarter as many as they did in the
early 1800s, and they may even be dying out.

However the Tsimshian tribes further north, which have had fewer
contacts with whites, seem to be more prosperous; and they have
relatively stable economies based on fishing (mainly salmon),
hunting and gathering, and a little agriculture. Berry found his
two samples of Tsimshian to be among the most acculturated of his
Indian groups, and they showed the least acculturational stress.
Particularly noteworthy are the Nishga. This band, which borders
on Alaska, is a large, self-sufficient community. Every member,
including women, and children when out of school, has his or her
own job, in which they take great pride, and there is a strong
tribal spirit. They are one of the few bands to have taken over
their education completely; they have built a large school, and

teach the tribal language as well as English. Their drop-out rate
is much below that usually found elsewhere, and their suicide rate
is very low. Also they have little trouble with drunkenness. I
attempted to get permission to test the intelligence and
achievements of Nishga children, as I believe that they would be
close to white standards. Unfortunately I was refused on the
quite reasonable grounds that they dislike becoming a show place,
and want to get on with their own lives without publicity.

Clearly we need a lot more comparative studies of Indian groups.
But those that are available seem to support the view that
motivational factors, positive social attitudes and morale are
major factors underlying the differences in educational and
occupational achievements, and the differences in intelligence
test scores. In addition it is probable that the quite inadequate
health provisions available to most bands, and the widespread
malnutrition on the reserves, are also involved in their generally
low educational standards.

Since I included the term motivational in my title, I must admit
that I have no quantitative data on motivational differences
comparable to that on abilities, only some subjective ratings, and
qualitative observations. Various personality and attitude scales
have been given to native Indian groups, others to Japanese. but
the responses seem so susceptible to faking or bias that I would
regard them as of quite limited value. However when we study
cognitive development and achievement across cultures,
motivational factors become much more obvious. Thus the misery
and helplessness of underdeveloped countries, and most minority
groups, compared with the optimism, and confidence in the efficacy
of modern technology in developed countries, outweigh any other
factors one can think of.

It might appear from my paper that I have deserted the ranks of
psychologists who support - at least in part - Jensen's views on
the influence of genetic factors in intelligence. Actually my
support was always rather guarded; and well before Burt's
fabrications were unveiled, I suggested that heritability variance
was nearer 50 or 60% than Burt's, Jensen's and Eysenck's 80%
upwards. But in addition it has been pointed out by Jensen
himself and other writers that the heritability figure is not an
absolute quantity - not an attribute of intelligence regardless of
cultural differences. It is a statistical rather than a
biological entity. It is in fact inversely related to the amount
of environmental variance in the population being studied. If all
members of the population were brought up under almost identical
environmental conditions, most of the measured differences in the
IQs would have to be ascribed to the genes; whereas the greater
the environmental heterogeneity, the less important heredity

becomes. Now despite the obvious variations within Western cultures in standards of living, health care and nutrition, schooling and intellectual stimulation at home, there is considerable homogeneity in their environments, languages, access to health care, schooling and television; and this applies - though to lesser degree - to ethnic minorities such as blacks, Indians and Hispanics in the U.S., not only to whites. But of course there is far greater environmental variance between Caucasians, East Indians and Chinese in their own countries, and Australian or other aboriginal peoples. Hence any genetic differences, even if we were able to measure them without bias, would be obfuscated by environmental differences.

At the same time, I believe we should take seriously Jensen's criticisms of environmental theorists, namely that they list a lot of likely environmental differences between, say, blacks and whites. If any or all of these are put to the test and turn out to be inconsequential, the authors merely put forward some other hypothetical differences. Jensen calls these 'X-factors', since obviously they can explain anything, and therefore explain nothing. I accept this criticism myself, but suggest that environmental influences are so complex that any single difference may fail to show statistically significant effects. Rather it is the overall pattern of environments between whites and blacks, or other cultures, which affect mental growth. And we have been unable so far to define such patterns sufficiently precisely to prove their effects. But, as I said earlier, when mentioning Bronfenbrenner's and Rutter's books, we are making progress in analysing the crucial features of environmental contexts.

The physiological bases of intelligence which Jensen and Eysenck (1983) have brought to our notice have always been publicised widely, particularly those that are said to be assessed by so-called "Simple" tasks. Like several other writers I am doubtful of the stability of the correlations claimed between "elementary" measures of cognitive speed or accuracy, and IQ. The figures seem to vary so much under slight variations in experimental conditions; also the representativeness of the samples so far tested is not convincing. I would accept the existence of correlations up to about .5, which would mean that reaction time, inspection time, and evoked potentials might cover some 25 to 30% of variance in intelligence test performance. This amount of variance would allow for the greater g-variance of tests of more complex information processing. Also I would not be surprised if the mean values of these simple measures differed between racial-ethnic groups, e.g. if Japanese were top, followed by Caucasians, then native American Indians, East Indians and Chinese, and Aboriginals the lowest. But, as an interactionist, I see no reason why the causal direction should always be one-way.

It need not follow from the correlations that neural attributes always precede and underly complex psychological attributes. As early as 1969, I pointed out that the growth of Intelligence B might bring about changes in the neurones and brain mechanisms. Indeed Krech, Rosenzweig and Bennett in 1962 showed that the stimulation of baby rats by handling them frequently, not only improved their later maze learning, but also brought about anatomical and biochemical changes in the brain. The ratio of brain weight to body weight and the thicknesses of the cerebral cortex increased. Thus a fairly high correlation between neural measures and IQ would be at least partly explicable by the influence of learning on neurological as well as mental growth.

After this highly discursive survey, I come back to my starting point, hoping to have shown that cross-cultural comparisons can be considerably more fruitful than comparisons of subgroups within one culture in broadening our conceptions of cognitive development.

REFERENCES

Allport, G.W. (1937). Personality - A psychological interpretation. New York: Holt.

Ashby, B., Morrison, A. & Butcher, H.J. (1970). The abilities and attainments of immigrant children. Research in Education, No. 4, 73-80.

Darry, H., Child, I. & Bacon, M.K. (1959). Relation of child training to subsistence economy. American Anthropologist, 61, 51-63.

Berry, J.W. (1966). Temne and Eskimo perceptual skills. International Journal of Psychology, 1, 207-229.

Berry, J.W. (1976). Human ecology and cognitive styles: Comparative studies in cultural and psychological adaptation. New York: Wiley.

Bronfenbrenner, U. (1979). The ecology of child development. Cambridge, Mass.: Harvard University Press.

Cattell, R.B. (1937). Measurement versus intuition in applied psychology. Character and Personality, 6, 114-131.

Chan, J. (1964). Intelligence and intelligence tests in Hong Kong. New Horizons in Education, 15, 82-88.

Comber, L.C. & Keeves, J.P. (1973). Science education in nineteen countries. Stockholm: Almquist & Wiksell.

Cox, M.V., Bryant, D.C. & Agnihotri, R.K. (1982). A cross-cultural study of spatial ability in children. Educational Psychology, 2, 37-46.

Dawson, J.L.M. (1967). Cultural and physiological influences upon spatial-perceptual processes in West Africa. International Journal of Psychology, 2, 115-128; 171-185.

Dershowitz, Z. (1971). Jewish subcultural patterns and psychological differentiation. International Journal of Psychology, 6, 223-231.

Eysenck, H.J. (ed.) (1983). A model for intelligence. Berlin: Springer.

Flynn, J.R. (1982). Lynn, the Japanese, and environmentalism. Bulletin of The British Psychological Society, 35, 409-413.

Freedman, D.G. (1974). Human infancy: An evolutionary perspective. New York: Wiley.

Ghuman, P.A.A. (1975). The cultural context of thinking: A comparative study of Punjabi and English boys. Slough: National Foundation for Educational Research.

Husen, T. (1967). International study of achievement in mathematics. Stockholm: Almquist & Wiksell.

Irvine, S.H. & Reuning, H. (1984). "Perceptual speed" and cognitive controls. Journal of Cross-cultural Psychology, 12, 425-444.

Krech, D., Rosenzweig, M.R. & Bennett, E.L. (1962). Relations between brain chemistry and problem-solving among rats reared in enriched and impoverished environments. Journal of Comparative and Physiological Psychology, 55, 801-807.

Lynn, R. (1977). The intelligence of the Japanese. Bulletin of the British Psychological Society, 30, 69-72.

McCarthy, J.L. & Wolfle, D. (1975). Doctorates granted to women and minority groups members. Science, 189, 856-859.

Rodd, W.G. (1959). A cross-cultural study of Taiwan's schools. Journal of Social Psychology, 50, 3-36.

Rutter, M., Maughan, B., Mortimore, P. & Ouston, J. (1979) Fifteen Thousand Hours. London: Open Books.

Sharma, R. (1971). The measured intelligence of children from the Indian subcontinent. PhD Thesis, University of London.

Stevenson, H.W., Stigler, J.W., Lucker, G.W. et al. (1982). Reading disabilities: the case of Chinese, Japanese and English. Child Development, 53, 1164-1181.

Stigler, J.W., Lee, S., Lucker, G.W. & Stevenson, H.W. (1982) Curriculum and achievement in mathematics: A study of elementary school children in Japan, Taiwan, and the United States. Journal of Educational Psychology, 74, 315-322.

Thorndike, R.L. (1973). Reading comprehension in fifteen countries: An empirical study. New York: Wiley.

Vernon, P.E. (1937). The Stanford-Binet test as a psychometric method. Character and Personality, 6, 99-113.

Vernon, P.E. (1969). Intelligence and cultural environment. London: Methuen.

Vernon, P.E. (1982). The abilities and achievements of orientals in North America. New York: Academic Press.

Weyl, N. (1969). Some comparative performance indexes of American ethnic minorities. Mankind Quarterly, 9, 106-119.

Witkin, H. & Berry, J.W. (1975). Psychological differentiation in cross-cultural perspective. Journal of Cross-cultural Psychology, 6, 4-87.

Witkin, H., Dyk, R., Faterson, W., Goodenough, D. & Karp, E. (1962). Psychological differentiation. New York: Wiley.

Wober, M. (1972). Culture and the concept of intelligence: A case in Uganda. Journal of Cross-cultural Psychology, 3, 327-328.

CHAPTER 10

THE COMPARATIVE STUDY OF COGNITIVE ABILITIES

JOHN W. BERRY

Queen's university

INTRODUCTION AND PRELIMINARY FRAMEWORK

The conceptualization and assessment of cognitive abilities across
human populations is a research area of longstanding difficulty
and debate (see Berry & Dasen, 1974; Cole & Scribner, 1974;
Cronbach & Drenth, 1972; Irvine & Carroll, 1980). This chapter
attempts to identify the issues, to place them in both historical
and contemporary terms, and then to present a set of proposals
which can guide the further study of, and perhaps the resolution
of, some of the disputes in this area. A preliminary framework
provides some common terms, so that the balance of the chapter may
be understood within a common conceptual framework.

Before this presentation, it is appropriate to justify the title
of the chapter. Those familiar with the general field will know
that two alternative approaches have been established which
represent differing perspectives on the issues. My own approach
is that of cross-cultural psychology, a tradition which tends to
emphasize the cultural (i.e. individually-learned, and
socially-transmitted) contribution to the development of cognitive
abilities; others in this tradition might have called the chapter
"Cross-Cultural Studies of Cognitive Abilities". An alternative
position is held by those who have advocated the biological
(genetic, and related) contributions to these pheonomena; a
chapter from that position might have been termed "Racial
Differences in Intelligence". As will be evident from the
preliminary framework, my general position (Berry, 1976) is that
human populations adapt to the context in which they operate using
both the mechanisms available to them: the cultural and the
biological. As I have argued previously (Berry 1981, 1984), most
attention has been paid to cultural adaptation and transmission
because they are much more readily researchable in the field:
cultural characteristics and the processes of enculturation
(socialization) can be (and have been) studied for a century or

more, and are clearly to be associated with variations in psychological characteristics (at both group- and individual-difference levels of analysis). In contrast, the field use of biological variables is more problematic (see also Thompson, 1980) and hence less well-developed in general, and in particular in psychological studies (note 1). The crude classification of individuals into "races" on the basis of a few superficial or extraneous characteristics, and the use of such category names as explanatory variables is outmoded; its analogue (the use of cultural group category names as explanations) stopped long ago in cross-cultural psychology.

Despite these practical difficulties, I believe that any conceptual framework needs to make room for all potential contributors to our understanding of human variation, even though limited techniques and little data are available at the present time to speak to them. Thus, no mention of culture (to the exclusion of biology) is made in the title, and in Figure 1 variables which are broadly cultural and biological are both incorporated.

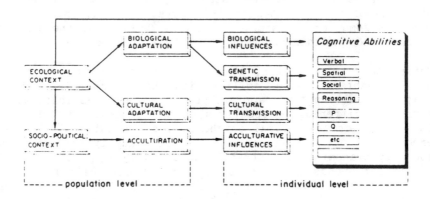

Figure 1   Framework for identifying possible sources of
influence on cognitive abilities in cross-cultural
work.

In Figure 1 are illustrated the major concepts, variables and relationships which will be addressed in this chapter. It is an elaboration of my ecocultural model (Berry, 1976) and makes more explicit the presence of biological and socio-political variables, and the action of transmission variables; these extensions have been stimulated by the work of Cavallisforza & Feldman (1981), and of Boyd & Richerson (1985), and by discussions with many Third World researchers who decry the absence of political variables in understanding group differences.

The flow of the framework is from left to right, with exogenous (input) variables on the left, and with resultant cognitive abilities on the right; the left half deals with populations, while the right half deals with individuals. The two middle groups of variables represent the point of transmission or influence from population variables to individuals; cultural and biological features of the population, and those due to acculturation are related to individual behaviour (in this case cognitive abilities) by way of cultural and genetic transmission, and biological and acculturative influence.

At this point I do not wish to elaborate in any detail on the variables or their relationships; the basic presentation of the constituent elements of each block, and arguments for their inter-relationships have appeared and been reviewed in numerous recent publications. Instead, I wish to provide a single illustrative example here, and will return in later sections to various details.

To exemplify the framework we may take the example of spatial ability (or the 'k' factor). Evidence has been accumulated (e.g. Berry, 1966, 1976) that hunting and gathering populations engage their ecological context by moving through it, lifting resources (both fauna and flora) in a symbiotic fashion. Certain abilities (including spatial, disembedding, and navigational abilities) may be learned by direct ecological engagement (illustrated by the over-riding arrow from ecological context to cognitive abilities). However, it is known that some particular cultural practices tend to be most common in nomadic hunter-gatherer populations, including minimal social stratification, and socialization for independence. These practices have been linked, both within Western societies and cross-culturally (Witkin & Berry, 1975) to a pattern of abilities (the field-independent cognitive style) which includes the particular abilities listed above. Thus, it is possible to argue that these cultural characteristics tend to develop in a way that permits a population to deal effectively with their ecological context; this view of culture as a uniquely human form of adaptation is a hallmark of the anthropological school of cultural ecology. Further, there is evidence of deliberate cultural transmission of such abilities in hunter-gatherer populations (Berry 1966; Berry et al, in press). In sum, cognitive abilities may be directly learned, or be mediated by adaptive forms of culture and cultural transmission; in either case, one should be able to predict cognitive abilities by moving from left to right across the ecocultural line of the framework.

For the biological line of transmission, traditional Darwinian arguments would lead us to conclude that selection processes are adaptive in the sense that the gene pool in the population will evolve in the direction of genes which may underlie those abilities which are of survival value in the group; spatial abilities are obvious candidates in hunter-gatherer populations, and a genetic basis has been claimed (e.g. Bock and Kolakowski, 1973). In parallel form for biological influences, Dawson (1966) has argued that protein deficiency, commonly found in agricultural populations, may suppress the development of spatial abilities, such protein deficiency is relatively rare in hunter-gatherer populations. Thus, there is clear evidence that biological adaptation (both via genetic transmission and non-genetic influences) may be predictive of the development (or not) of particular cognitive abilities. This "dual inheritance" is consistent with recent proposals (e.g. Boyd and Richerson, 1985) regarding the distribution of population characteristics.

Finally, the socio-political context of a population will be an important factor in the degree to which it is subjected to acculturation (culture learning from outside). This portion of the framework is necessary because during the historical period of colonialism, and continuing undiminished to the present time, there can obviously be important influences on human abilities which are not under the influence of the original ecological context of the population. Some abilities will be diminished (due to cultural or biological destruction and loss), while others may be introduced, due to formal schooling, to interbreeding, and other demands (such as industrialization). The importance of these factors in altering the ability pattern has been reviewed frequently (e.g. Scribner and Cole, 1973, and Rogoff, 1981) and while major changes can be documented, the "depth" has been questioned: are there basic additions and losses, increases or decreases in ability , or does acculturation only affect the test-sophistication of individuals, contributing to altered test performance?

The arrow between the two input variables indicates that there are known relationships between them: in one relationship groups living in certain ecological contexts (e.g., prime areas for agricultural development or mineral exploitation) have been colonized more than peoples in less desirable areas; in the other direction, socio-political intrusion from the outside has led to changes in the ecological context (e.g., forest habitat reduction in Central Africa, and game reduction in the Arctic following the introduction of the rifle). Thus while conceptually distinct, the interactions between the two factors need to be monitored in research on the origins of cognitive abilities.

With this framework as a guide we now turn to a consideration of a number of specific issues, beginning with an attempt to identify in the historical literature many of those that continue to confront us to this day.

HISTORICAL OVERVIEW: A LEGACY

It is fair to say that the issues being addressed today were all identified around the turn of the century by a handful of scholars who worked simultaneously, and at ease, in the two emerging disciplines of Anthropology and Psychology. The list includes Rivers, MCDougall, Myers, and Seligmann, of Torres Straits Expedition fame (1899), Boas (1911) with his Mind of Primitive Man, Wundt (1916) in the Elements of Folk Psychology, and Levy-Bruhl (1910 and 1923) in his two books How Natives Think and Primitive Mentality. There is no need here to document the contribution of each, since it has been done elsewhere (see Klineberg, 1980, for a general account; Berry and Dasen, 1974, for one focussed on cognition; and Berry, 1983, for one specifically concerned with the contribution of Wundt). From this early work, five issues may be identified.

Evolution

Scratch a human being (even a psychologist) today and one is likely to find not too subtle notions of "progress", over time, of the species. These beliefs are likely to pertain both to group cultural qualities ("primitive culture" to "civilization"), and to individual psychological qualities in the cognitive ("backward" to "intelligent") and other domains: cultures and their members have become "better" over the course of human history. A century ago, these beliefs may have been even more common than today (perhaps a function of the very evolution postulated); however, Boas and others maintained that such judgements likely reflect our lack of awareness and understanding of what other people do with their lives, rather than their being any lower form of life. Indeed, since the work of Summer (1908), the evidence has been available to show that virtually all peoples view themselves as the best, the epitome of cultural and psychological development. Armed with this knowledge, it is not difficult to accept the obvious alternative, that such judgements are entirely dependent on context: we must always ask, better for what? Related to this issue is that of ontogenetic change; the child and the savage have been identified with one another historically, and this linkage can be found still in the contemporary literature. We will return in the next section to this issue, in our discussion of ethnocentrism, relativism and universalism in the study of cognition.

Process and Performance

Clearly people in different cultures do different things with their lives; does this mean that they function differently psychologically? Such a question was grappled with by Boas (1911, p.102). He stated:

"We recognize that there are two possible explanations of the different manifestation of the mind of man. It may be that the minds of different races show differences of organisation; that is to say, the laws of mental activity may not be the same for all minds. But it may also be that the organisation of mind is practically identical among all races of man; that is, that mental activity follows the same laws everywhere, but that its manifestations depend upon the character of individual experience that is subjected to the action of these laws."

Today we refer to the process-performance distinction: "organization of mind" and "laws of mental activity" may be identified with the notion of the underlying processes; and "manifestations of the mind" refer to the actual outcome or performance.

Clearly, the latter is all we have to work with in psychology; products, whether behavioural or physiological, can be the only basis for empirical examination and comparison. Given the large variation in input (experience, socialization, nutrition, etc.), variation in output may be examined for its co-variation with input. Current researchers tend to look for, and find, substantial relationships between input and output, and on this basis frequently do not consider the other possiblility, that processes may actually differ. Scientifically this view fits the data best (see Cole et al, 1971); this is particularly true since we have clear evidence for input-output correlations, and no data at all regarding process variation. This view (communality in process) also fits the current emphasis on universals in cross-cultural psychology - those psychological phenomena which tend to be characteristic, species-wide, features.

Universals

In cognate disciplines, there is ample evidence for universals (Lonner, 1980). Biology provides us with a list of needs and drives shared by all, Anthropology a set of cultural phenomena (social organization, language, technology, etc.) present in all human societies, and Linguistics and Sociology provide others. The conclusion is frequently drawn that, with so many universals in other domains, can they be absent as species-wide characteristics in the psychological domain? Indeed, the presence of such universals, it is argued by cross-cultural methodologists (e.g., Frijda and Jahoda, (1966), is necessary before comparison is sensible: "dimensional identity" needs to exist before comparing the differing positions of individuals or groups on that dimension.

In contemporary cross-cultural work, the "universal process" position as espoused by Boas seems to be widely accepted (see Cole and Scribner, 1974), and we will adopt this here, in the absence of evidence to the contrary.

Organization

Do cognitive performances cohere in a constant pattern independently of culture; do performances remain resolutely unrelated to each other in any culture; or do they cohere in various ways depending on the cultural context? The old debate (one intelligence or many?, a general factor or specific ones?) remains in full force in cross-cultural psychology. Of course, the how will always depend on the what; relationships will be a function of which abilities are measured, and the degree to which they are an important feature of the daily functions of the population. These three alternatives will be examined in detail in the later section on the organization of abilities.

Sources

At the beginning of the divergence between Anthropology and Psychology there were already signs that each discipline would rely on different sources of evidence: Anthropology on naturalistic observation and normative information from a few knowledgeable informants, Psychology on material from a sample of individuals using standardized instruments in more artifical situations (Jahoda, 1982). This divergence became extreme, so that at its height, IQ testers and ethnographers could barely communicate, even if they wanted to. On the one hand, peoples all over the world were obviously carrying out lives in a competent manner, possessing language underlaid by complex grammar, and a detailed and sophisticated knowledge of their social and environmental relationships; on the other hand, cognitive tests were yielding evidence of stupidity. The break in this impasse came with the realization that one source was providing evidence about what was there, and the other was doing the same for what was not there. The current rapprochement, very much in full swing, is to employ both methodological approaches: one starts with observations and analyses of "what gets done well around here", then moves to operationalizing these abilities in standard test or task format, and finally to their validation back against the original evidence of competence in daily life (Berry and Irvine, 1985).

THREE CONTEMPORARY POSITIONS

These five issues come together, in various combinations, to form three general positions which can be used to represent contemporary thinking about cognition across groups: ethnocentrism, relativism, and universalism.

Ethnocentrism

While more easily identified with early thinking, there is substantial evidence to indicate that this general point of view is still widely held. For many, perhaps most, psychologists practicing today, there is no serious questioning of the evidence that on standardized cognitive tests those of Euro-American background do "better" than those of other origins. My impression is that there is a very close parallelism between popular beliefs (stereotypes and ethnic attitudes) about the "place" or "value" of a group in a world hierarchy (note 2), and the means of their scores on cognitive tests. One can take this observation as an indication of convergent validity, or as a warning signal that our science is not independent of our ideology. The latter has been the interpetation by scholars in Anthropology for decades, and in History (e.g., Preiswerk and Perrot, 1978) more recently. We in Psychology risk being known as the "ethnocentric science" unless we attend, both in our theory and in our research, to these obvious linkages between our prejudices and our practices.

The initial goal of cross-cultural psychology is, in fact, to reduce the ethnocentrism of our discipline: we are now obliged to understand the cultural roots of what we do as a science, and to examine the possible cultural roots of what our subjects give us as data. Without good evidence, to remain fixed in the view that our tests tap cognitive abilities well, for other peoples in other places, is to do bad science. Many of us may deny that we are ethnocentric, and this may be the case; but I would argue that most of our academic colleagues, our graduate students, and professional psychologists in practice either do hold these views or, just as importantly, act as if they do, in their use of cognitive tests.

Relativism

An alternative to ethnocentrism is to avoid viewing differences in a predetermined hierarchy with one's own group at the top, and to consider each group in its own terms, exhibiting a unique set of cognitive phenomena which should be understood in relation to its own particular context; in essence it is anti-comparativist. This position of relativism arose partly in reaction to ethnocentrism, and partly as one facet of a general functionalist movement in 20th Century science (which includes, in addition to functionalist schools in the social sciences, the more specific positions of cultural ecology, ecological psychology, situationism, etc.).

In Anthropology, Herskovits (1948), and in Psychology, Segall et al. (1966) have articulated the position well:
"...the ethnographer attempts to describe the behaviour of the people he studies without the evaluation that his own culture would ethnocentrically dictate. He attempts to see the culture in terms of its own evaluative system. He tries to remain aware of the fact that his judgements are based upon his own experience and reflect his own deep-seated enculturation to a limited and specific culture. He reminds himself that his original culture provides no Olympian vantage from which to view objectively any other culture" (Segall et al. 1966; p.17).

Pursuit of this relativist point of view not only entails the avoidance of ethnocentrism, but also the <u>practice</u> of certain research strategies. First is to attempt to discover, using ethnographic and ecological techniques (see later section) what is happening in the group being studied. For cognitive studies this would include finding out <u>what</u> cognitive abilities are valued locally, <u>how</u> they are conceptualized, <u>who</u> displays them, <u>why</u> people think so, and <u>how</u> they are acquired (Berry, 1972). This scientific thrashing around within a group can be very rewarding, as well as very threatening: one may discover a lot, but what one discovers may be challenging to one's established beliefs and practices.

Universalism

An obvious goal of all sciences is to say something in general about a set of phenomena; bits and pieces of knowledge can only be valuable in the long run when they form the basis of laws, generalizations and theories. While the position of ethnocentrism met this general requirement, it has other flaws; and while relativism attempts to address these flaws, it lacks generality, and indeed retreats into an infinite particularism. A resolution of this problem is the third position,, that of universalism: here the eventual goal is to achieve generalizations about the cognitive abilities of human beings, by way of the comparative method (Poortinga, 1983), but employing the rich context-related data supplied from the relativist research strategy, and avoiding hierarchies based upon the ethnocentric view of human variation. How this might be achieved in practice is outlined in a later section on cognitive universals. For the time being, we may simply identify the position and its intent, and indicate that the position of universalism is based on the demonstrated existence of biological and cultural universals; these are employed as common dimensions along which individuals and groups can vary, according to their functional adaptation to local context, rather than according to absolute hierarchies of superiority.

ORGANIZATION OF ABILITIES

At the present time one may discern at least three general positions with respect to the organization of cognitive abilities: general intelligence, specific abilities and cognitive styles. In certain respects, these three conceptualizations parallel the three positions outlined in the last section; however, they are not linked so strongly that one could claim that all those working from a position of ethnocentrism also subscribe to a general intelligence position, or that relativism and specific abilities, and universalism and cognitive styles are perfectly linked.

In Figure 2 are depicted these three current views on the organization of performances on tests of cognitive abilities (Berry, 1979); depicted as well are parallel views about the organization of cultural contexts, of the organism (processor), and of relationships across the three parts of the model.

Particular elements (of context, process and performance) are indicated by small circles; larger organizations (if any) are indicated by a solid oval (if fixed) or dotted oval (if variable); and relationships are indicated by arrows.

General Intelligence

The classical approach to the study of cognitive differences across populations has been to take existing general intelligence tests and to administer them to different populations . Of course, there has been a recognition that the test may not get any response at all until a translation has been made. Typically the only modifications or additions undertaken were those necessary to obtain data; modifications to match the test to the cognitive life

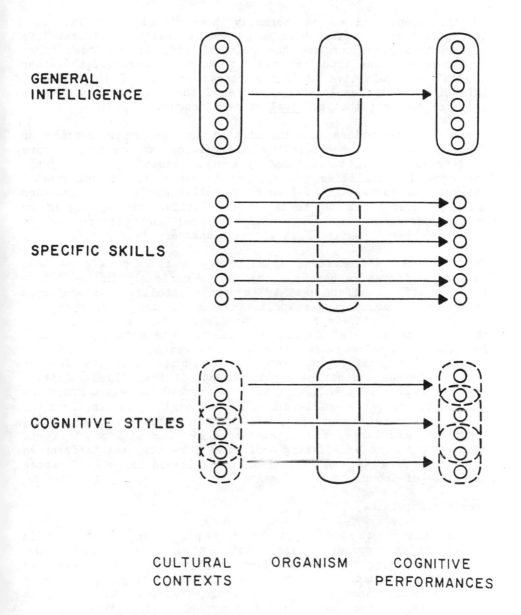

GENERAL
INTELLIGENCE

SPECIFIC SKILLS

COGNITIVE STYLES

CULTURAL   ORGANISM   COGNITIVE
CONTEXTS   PERFORMANCES

Figure 2   Framework for Identifying Possible Sources of Influence on
           Cognitive Abilities in Cross-Cultural Work

of the people have not normally been done. That is, two assumptions have usually been made: one is that the cultural life of the test developer and the cultural life of the test taker differ in only one important respect, that of language, the other is that the cognitive abilities characteristic of the cultural life of the test developer and those of the test taker differ in only one respect; that of <u>level</u> of development.

These two assumptions are illustrated in the upper portion of Figure 2. First, elements in the cultural context are treated more or less as a unit (solid boundary around elements), and, second, the cognitive abilities are assumed to be a single universally interrelated package (i.e. "general intelligence"). Both are then usually interpreted in terms of populations having bigger or smaller packages: those with small cultural packages are thought to be "deprived", while those with big ones are 'enriched".

With respect to the first assumption, it is clear to me that cultural differences have not been taken seriously in the debate on population differences in general intelligence; cultures obviously differ in many respects, beyond the languages they use. And with respect to the second assumption, little attempt has been made to find out what cognitive abilities are actually in place locally, and how they are structured. Given these two errors of omission, the great logical error of commission is then performed: if the cultures are not really different, if the valued abilities are not really different, then the differences in test performance must be due to different levels of development. However, from the point of view of relativism, if cultural differences are real, important, and large, and if abilities develop differentially in adaptation to these differing ecological contexts, the differences in test performance cannot logically be claimed to be differences in levels of amount of development.

Specific abilities

An alternative to this approach is that taken by workers in "cognitive anthropology" (e.g., Cole et al., 1971). From their perspective, single features of the context (such as a specific role or a particular experience) are linked to a single performance (such as performance on a categorization task, or accuracy on a test of quantity estimation); this approach is illustrated in the mid portion of Figure 2. They contrast their notion of culture-specific skills with general ability theory which often asserts that in some cultures, cognitive development is pushed further than in some other cultures. Assuming that cognitive processes are universal (Cole and Scribner, 1974, p. 193), they argue that "cultural differences in cognition reside more in the situations to which particular cognitive processes are applied than in the existence of a process in one cultural group and its absence in another" (Cole et al., 1971, p. 233). This emphasis on the particular, and culturally relative, nature of cognitive abilities has meant that Cole and his coworkers have not usually searched for patterns of intertask relationships in their data. Generally, they are not much concerned whether cognitive performance 1 correlated with performance 2, or whether cultural element 1 tends to be experienced along with cultural element 2 by individuals in their studies. Unlike intelligence testers, they do not assume any universal pattern of structure in their ability data, nor have they examined their data for such patterns. And finally, they avoid explicit cross-cultural comparisons as being inconsistent with their local relativistic (emic) emphasis.

Cognitive styles

The two approaches thus far considered have differed in their acceptance of relativism, in their interest in systematic relationships, and in their use of comparisons. The approach taken by intelligence testers ignored relativism, assumed a universal structure in test to test relationships, and readily made cross-cultural comparisons; the approach taken by those interested in specific abilities assumed the position of cultural relativism, but ignored systematic relationships and avoided cross-cultural comparisons. The approach taken by researchers into cognitive styles also assumes the position of relativism, but in addition, searches for systematic relationships among abilities, and engages in cross-cultural comparisons (see lower part of Figure 2).

One basis for this approach is in the work of Ferguson (1954, 1956) who argued that "cultural factors prescribe what shall be learned and at what age; consequently different cultural environments lead to the development of different patterns of ability" (1956, p. 121). Further, he argued that through over-learning and transfer these patterns of cognitive abilities became stabilized for individuals in a particular culture. Both the perspective of cultural relativism and the existence of systematic relationships are thus implicated in this approach, and these have been adopted in much of the work on cognitive style.

A recent review of the research on various cognitive styles (Goldstein and Backman, 1978) makes it clear that while sharing a general approach, there are many important differences among the numerous cognitive style research traditions. This need not be a problem here, for only one has received any substantial treatment in the cross-cultural field, that of field dependence-field independence (Witkin et al., 1962; Witkin and Goodenough, 1981).

This cross-cultural work (see e.g., Berry, 1976; Witkin and Berry, 1975) is characterized by analysis of the local cultural context (termed "ecological demands" and "cultural supports" by Berry, 1966), by attempts to assess the cognitive performances of individuals in a number of groups, and by a search for systematic relationships among performances (the "style"), and between performances and cultural contexts. No interpretation is made about levels of development, given that no assumptions are made about the absolute value of a particular style; indeed, work within this ecological tradition assumes that differing positions on a cognitive style dimension will best meet the requirements of living in differing ecological and cultural contexts (Berry, 1976). Finally, while a search is made for systematic relationships among performances to discover whether they will remain constant or vary with cultural context, there is no assumption or requirement that they should. Similarily, while a search is made for systematic relationships among elements comprising the cultural contexts, there is no predetermined pattern which is related to Western culture.

ECOLOGICAL CONTEXT

A concern with ecological context was introduced in Figure 1, where it was argued that both biological and cultural adaptation to context is a process of importance, and that the outcome is crucial for understanding the kinds of cognitive abilities that are likely to be distributed in a population. Again in Figure 2, the context (this time focussing on cultural context) was argued to be an important input to the development of cognitive abilities, no matter which pattern or organization was being advocated. We have also identified context as an important notion in our discussion of sources of data (where Anthropologists tend to rely on performances on their full, natural contexts), and in the presentation of relativism (where, it was argued, that each custom or behaviour can only be understood as a unique, local phenomenon if it is viewed in its particular functional context).

Following the arguments of Brunswik (1955, p.237) who argued persuasively that there is a need to "balance psychology in the molar and molecular realm", and Whiting (1976) who argued that we need to "unpackage" our cultural variables, an ecological model has been developed (Berry, 1980) which attempts to analyse ecological and cultural contexts into their operative components (i.e., unpackaging) while seeking to maintain both the holistic (molar) and particularistic (molecular) features of the contexts in which we develop and perform cognitively. The model is an attempt to solve the dilemma caused by the prescription that we accept in psychology the natural cultural environment as the context of behaviour and that we week to discover those

independent variables which are operative. The solution is not to
control the variables experimentally (for this would not only
unwrap the package, but would also destroy the texture); rather it
is to analyse (both conceptually and statistically) the
constituent elements in the habitat. How to do this is the focus
of the balance of this section.

From one point of view (the experimental-reductionist), the
contexts are a nuisance; but from the ecological point of view,
they constitute a wealth of information concerning the habitat of
a psychological phenomenon. To transform a nuisance into an
asset, we need to be able to analyse, assess, interpret and relate
these variables to each other and to the psychological phenomena
being studied.

In Figure 3 there are illustrated four environmental (ecological
and cultural) contexts and four effects related through a human
organism. The structure of the diagram places the various
contexts at the left and the various effects at the right. Toward
the top are natural and holistic contexts and effects, while at
the bottom they are more controlled and reductionistic.

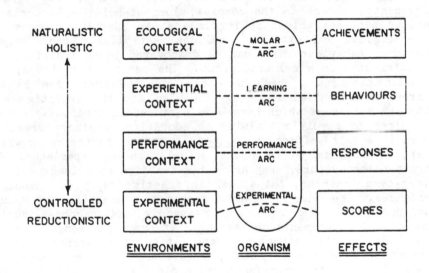

Figure 3 Framework showing Four Levels of Relationships
          Between Environments and Effects

Looking in more detail at the environmental contexts, the ecological context is the "natural-cultural habitat" of Brunswik, the "physical world" of Lewin, and the "preperceptual world" of Barker. It consists of all the relatively permanent characteristics which provide the context for human action. Nested in this ecological context are two levels of the "life space" or "psychological world" of Lewin. The first, the "experiential context" is that pattern of recurrent experiences which provide a basis for learning; it is essentially the set of independent variables which cross-cultural psychology tries to spot as being operative in a particular habitat in the development of behavioural characteristics. The other, the performance context, is the limited set of environmental circumstances which may be observed to account for particular behaviours; these are immediate in space and time. The fourth context, the experimental context, represents those environmental characteristics which are designed by the psychologist to elicit a particular response or test score. The experimental context may or may not be nested in the first three contexts; the degree to which it is nested represents the ecological validity of the task.

Paralleling these four contexts are four effects. The first, achievements, refers to the complex, long-standing and developed behaviour patterns which are in place as an adaptive response to the ecological context. It includes established and shared patterns of behaviour which can be discovered in an individual or are distributed in a cultural group. The second, behaviours, are the molar behaviours which have been learned over time in the recurrent experiential context. Included are the abilities and traits and attitudes which have been nurtured in particular roles, or acquired by specific training or education, whether formal or informal. A third effect, responses, are those performances which appear in response to immediate stimulation or experience. In contrast to behaviours, they are not a function of role experience or long-term training, but appear in fleeting reply to immediate experiences. The fourth effect, scores, is comprised of those behaviours which are observed, measured, and recorded during psychological experiments or testing. If the experimental context is nested in the other contexts, then the scores may be representative of the responses, behaviours and achievements of the organism. If the experiment has ecological validity, then the scores will have behavioural validity.

Relationships can be traced between the elements across the model. The molar arc ("E-O-E arc" in Brunswik's terms) operates across the top of the model. It is concerned with the life situation (in physical, environmental and cultural terms) of an organism and its accomplishments. At the second level, the learning arc is concerned with tying together recurrent independent variables in the experience of an individual with his characteristic behaviours. The third level, that of the performance arc, is interested in more specific acts as a function of immediate and current experience. And at the fourth level, the experimental arc is devoted to the laboratory or other systematic study of relationships between experimental problems and test scores. These latter relationships are known to be variable, depending on the other contexts in the model (e.g. Irvine, 1983).

A recurrent problem for general experimental psychology, in these terms, is to say anything of value about causal relationships (at the two middle levels) while working almost exclusively with the experimental arc. And to this Brunswik would add the further problem of saying anything meaningful on this basis about the molar arc as well. The problem facing cross-cultural psychology tends to be the reverse: rather than failing to ascend the reductionistic-holistic dimension to achieve ecological validity, cross-cultural psychology has failed to descend the dimension to achieve a specification of experiential performance and experimental context variables which are responsible for task performance and behavioural variation across natural habitats. In Campbell's (1957) terms there has been insufficient concern in these two branches of psychology for "external" and "internal" validity respectively.

BRICOLAGE

In the section on "sources", which contrasted the anthropological and psychological approaches, and again in the last section which laid out a set of contrasts between the naturalistic, holistic and molar point of view on the one hand, and the controlled, reductionistic and molecular one, we have seen that positions vary dramatically regarding the "level" at which cognitive performances many be studied. Because of the general familiarity among psychologists with the "experimental arc", it is useful here to highlight the "molar arc" in this separate section. It has been termed bricolage to emphasize the exhibition of cognitive abilities in the daily lives of people, wherever they are, and whatever they do. In a recent review (Berry and Irvine, 1985), the idea of the bricoleur (handyman, jack-of-all-trades) is used to introduce the psychological study of cognitive abilities in their practical mundane (non-test, non-school) guise.

The concept, of course, was first introduced by the anthropologist Levi-Strauss (1962/1966) to contrast the "savage mind" with that of the contemporary scientist: "cash-crop agriculture is hardly to be confused with the science of the botanist" (Levi-Strauss, 1966, p. 3). Levi-Strauss is not promoting the idea that there are two distinct varieties of cognition: magic and science are "two parallel modes of acquiring knowledge", both requiring "the same sort of mental operations, and they differ not so much in kind as in the different types of phenomena to which they are applied" (1966, p. 13). Nevertheless, he quite clearly considers bricolage to be a "lesser" form of cognitive life.

A parallel set of ideas may be discerned in the work of Vernon (1969). With respect to developed intelligence, Vernon (1969, p. 23) argued that "we should expect people like the Eskimos or Australian aboriginals to be handicapped in using the symbols, or acquiring the mental skills, which western culture has evolved. On the other hand we should not claim that they are intelligent in a different way just because they are better than us at survival in the snows or in the desert. These are traditional, lower-level skills, built up over generations and possessing little transferability".

It is my position that the close study of these day-to-day cognitive abilities is likely to give us a more accurate picture of what cognitive development has actually achieved. In contrast, continued formal testing with imported standard instruments is likely to tell us only, and over and over again, that their performance is different, and from our ethnocentric position, deficient.

At the collective level, where anthropologists usually work, there are obvious domains of competence ("achievements" in Figure 3, across the molar arc). At the individual level, psychologists can work (still fairly naturalistically) across the learning arc (in Figure 3) to discover exactly what particular individuals are able to do in their daily lives. The review by Berry and Irvine (1985) recounts such work in a variety of domains: botanical and pharmaceutical knowledge (Mott, 1979); hunting techniques (Bahuchet, 1978); animal behaviour (Blurton-Jones and Konner, 1976); map-making (Bagrow, 1948); navigational techniques (Gladwin, 1970); and rules of land tenure (Hutchins, 1980). Many such examples now exist in the literature, and serve as important models for the study of cognitive abilities. It should be clear that, to me, bricolage should not be viewed as a set of "lower level skills" but as abilities exhibited at the level appropriate for cognitive functioning in particular contexts; judgements of "lower" or "higher" can only be made relative to some absolute criterion, and to my knowledge no such criterion has yet been demonstrated.

DEVELOPMENT OF ABILITIES

That cognitive abilities develop from birth to adulthood is not an issue in the cross-cultural literature. Whether they develop to the same <u>extent</u>, or in the same <u>direction</u> in all peoples, however, are substantial issues. By extent is usually meant power and/or speed, or more generally, competence; by direction, is meant the cultural goals or cognitive values which are shared by the group and transmitted across generations. These two aspects of development are illustrated in Figure 4 in three hypothetical cultural groups (A,B and C); three tests of cognitive abilities are also shown (1,2 and 3).

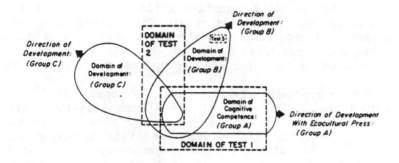

Figure 4 Framework for Conceptualizing Differing Directions of Cognitive Development, and Domains of Cognitive Competence in Varying Ecocultural Contexts Showing Unequal Validity of Three Tests, for Three Groups

In Culture A, cognitive development takes place in the direction of those abilities which are adaptive to the ecocultural context of Group A; a domain of cognitive competence is achieved (oblong form, solid line). A test battery (rectangle marked Test 1, dotted line) is developed by psychologists in Culture A to assess this developed competence, and there is a reasonably good fit between the cognitive domain and the test (note 3). Some aspects of the test go beyond the competence, and some abilities are not sampled by the test; however, Test 1 matches the competence domain of Group A with a substantial validity.

In Culture B, other demands are placed on developing individuals, and a fairly distinct domain of competence is achieved. Some overlap exists between the competence of individuals in Culture B and Culture A, but not enough for them to share more than a portion of their developed abilities. It should be obvious that Test 1 if used in Culture B would not adequately sample the abilities of these people, and has little chance of attaining validity. Similarly, for Culture C, with an even greater difference in the goals of cognitive development, Test 1 would sample much less of their abilities.

Test 2 represents another test battery, perhaps created in Culture A to provide cognitive assessment for "others". It clearly attempts to assess other cognitive abilities than those in Test 1, but misses the mark by a wide margin for Cultures B and C as well as A. Test 3, in contrast, illustrates a test of a single ability which has been identified as being of great value in Culture B, and appears to be valid for that group, but not for others.

Seeds of this approach were first sown by Goodenough (1936, p. 5) who argued that we must "be sure that the test-items from which the total trait is to be judged are representative and valid samples of the ability in question as it is displayed within the particular culture with which we are concerned". Similarly Berry (1966, 1972, 1984) has argued that indigenous conceptions of cognitive ability need to be represented in tests, and Wober (1969) has argued that no assessment of "their tricks" can be accomplished with tests of "our tricks". This point of view is just as valid for ethnic groups within plural societies as it is across cultures (Samuda, 1983).

The general argument should by now be clear. We propose that cognitive abilities develop and display themselves in different ways in different cultures according to the adaptive requirements in those ecocultural contexts. The assessment of these varying domains of cognitive competence requires knowledge on the part of the researcher regarding the cognitive values (toward which development takes place) of the culture in which he is working, including the collective achievements (across the molar arc), the individual cognitive behaviours which are culturally transmitted and carried out in day-to-day activity (across the learning arc), and the conditions under which such cognitive performances may be displayed (the performance arc), all before attempting to assess individual cognitive competence (across the experimental arc). If this programme of research is not attempted and achieved, then the extent of development can never be ascertained, because unidentified variation in direction will always stand in the way, and remain as an alternative description of the data obtained.

TOWARD COGNITIVE UNIVERSALS

The foregoing argument clearly represents a position of
relativism. However, most researchers probably accept that there
are some species-wide cognitive characteristics to be discovered;
the bases for expecting such universals were outlined earlier in
this paper, and in factor analytic work by Irvine (1979) and
Carroll (1983). The problem is how to pursue these cognitive
universals without destroying the context-related arguments and
research strategy just described. In Figure 5 is illustrated a
framework for pursuing a universal psychology of cognitive
competence. Down the left hand side are the areas of cognitive
competence which may be identified in particular cultures, such as
reasoning, spatial, vocabularly, social; the list is extendable
until all culturally-identified and valued cognitive activities
are included, representing the first part of our prescription -
the emic inclusion strategy. Across the top of Figure 5 is a
dimension which provides a rationale for comparing individuals in
cultures on that particular cognitive ability, such as the
language basis for vocabulary ability, or the ecological basis for
spatial ability; along this dimension, societies may be sampled to
provide a good cross-cultural representation of cultural variation
in, for example, linguistic families (not all Indo-European) or
ecological engagement (not all agriculturalists).

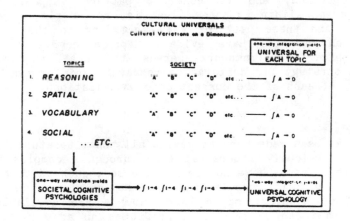

Figure 5 Framework For Pursuing a Universal
         Cognitive Psychology

Empirical studies guided by the framework may proceed in a variety of ways. If one wishes to search for a universal in a particular cognitive function, one would work across a single line, across cultures; integrating these findings would say something about the universality of, for example, reasoning ability. If one wishes to understand the cognitive abilities of people in a particular culture, one would work down a single column; integrating these findings would say something about the "societal psychology" of cognitive ability in a particular culture.

It should be obvious that only by working both across, and down, can one be in a position to achieve anything close to a universal psychology of cognitive competence. Such a two-way integration is demonstrably different, in this framework, from what has been so far achieved (a single societal psychology for Western, Euro-American cognitive competence), and from what is being attempted occasionally (the tracing of a particular cognitive ability across a few cultures).

If, in the end, all information in the framework can be neatly integrated in the lower right-hand corner, then we will have evidence for a universal general cognitive ability (all abilities cohere similarly in all cultures); if integration is not possible in either direction (no cross-cultural pattern, nor intra-cultural pattern), then we will have evidence to support a specific abilities approach; and if coherent patterns appear across competence areas within cultures (that is, not a single general competence), and these patterns vary according to the cultural context, then we will have evidence for a cognitive styles approach. Thus, the framework serves the dual purpose of outlining a strategy for comparative research, and for evaluating the validity of each of the current conceptualizations.

CONCLUSIONS

No attempt has been made here to review all the literature in this field; it is obviously a personal tour through a complex field. Major technical issues have not been addressed, such as test bias, heritability within populations, and problems of test administration; however, major recent works are available for these issues and can be read with profit as an adjunct to this chapter. Rather, I have chosen to address those issues which are not likely to be well-known outside the cross-cultural literature; in a sense, I have taken the opportunity to "rub your noses" in these new materials rather than rehash the well-known ones.

It seems to me that no case can be made for ethnocentric cognitive psychology. One cannot forever follow a strategy of attempting to measure <u>what is not there</u>, mistaking population performance differences to lie on a vertical dimension (us "higher"; them "lower") when the more plausible alternative is that they lie on a horizontal dimension (we assess "here"; they operate "there"). As psychologists, we have answered the question "their incompetence or ours?" in both an unscientific and ethnocentric way: we have failed to consider alternatives, and we have derogated others while elevating ourselves.

It may not be that the pursuit of cognitive universals will succeed, in the sense that we will find all of them. However, ecological analyses, indigenous test development, and comparative research (as advocated here) will succeed in the sense that we will rescue our science from ethnocentrism, and we may even discover something more general about cognitive abilities.

FOOTNOTES

1. Some techniques, such as blood-grouping, are possible under some field conditions, but even this is expensive or very difficult in remote areas. However, there is no known link between such data and psychological characteristics. In contrast, a particular custom (such as independence training in children) may be both readily measureable and have some plausible connection to the particular psychological characteristic being examined.

2. Regional hierarchies also seem to exist, with parallels between the attitudes and the test scores across groups within plural nations (e.g. the U.S.) and across nations within continents (e.g. Europe).

3. The elements of this diagram may be compared to the distinctions between Intelligence A,B, and C of Vernon (1969).

REFERENCES

Bagrow, L. (1948). Eskimo maps. *Imago Mundi*, 5, 92-93.

Bahuchet, S. (1973). Contraintes ecologiques en foret tropicale humide: l'exemple des Pygmees Aka de la Lobaye. *Journal d'Agriculture Topicale et Botanique Appliquee*, 25, 257-285.

Berry, J.W. (1966). Temne and Eskimo perceptual skills. *International Journal of Psychology*, 1, 207-229.

Berry, J.W. (1972). Radical cultural relativism and the concept of intelligence. In L.J. Cronbach and P. Drenth (Eds.) Mental tests and cultural adaptation. Mouton: The Hague.

Berry, J.W. (1976). Human ecology and cognitive style: Comparative studies in cultural and psychological adaptation. New York: Sage-Halsted.

Berry, J.W. (1979). Cultural systems and cognitive styles. In M.P. Friedman, J.P. Das, and N. O'Connor (Eds.) Intelligence and Learning. New York: Plenum.

Berry, J.W. (1980). Ecological analyses for cross-cultural psychology. In N.Warren (Ed.) Studies in cross-cultural psychology, Vol. 2. London: Academic Press.

Berry, J.W. (1981). Developmental issues in the comparative study of psychological differentiation. In R. Munroe, R. Munroe & B.B. Whiting (Eds.) Handbook of cross-cultural human development. New York: Garland Press.

Berry, J.W. (1983). Wundt's Volkerpsychologie and the comparative study of human behaviour. In G. Eckardt & L. Sprung (Eds.) Advances in historiography of psychology. Berlin, D.D.R.: Deutscher Verlag der Wissenschaften.

Berry, J.W. (1984). Towards a universal psychology of cognitive competence. International Journal of Psychology, 19, 27-54.

Berry, J.W. & Dasen, P.R. (Eds.) (1974). Culture and cognition. London: Methuen.

Berry, J.W. & Irvine, S. (1985). Bricolage: Savages do it daily. In R. Sternberg & R. Wagner (Eds.) Practical intelligence: Origins of competence in the everyday world. New York: Cambridge University Press.

Berry, J.W., van de Koppel, J., Senechal, C., Annis, R., Bahuchet, S., Cavallisforza, L.L. & Witkin, H.A. On the edge of the forest: Cultural adaptation and cognitive development in Central Africa. (In press).

Blurton Jones, N. & Konner, M. (1976). Kung knowledge of animal behavior. In R.B. Lee, & I. DeVore. (Eds.) Kalahari hunter-gatherers. Cambridge: Harvard University Press.

Boas, F. (1911). The mind of primitive man. New York: Macmillan.

Bock, R. & Kolakowski, D. (1973). Further evidence of sex-linked major gene influence on human spatial visualizing ability. American Journal of Human Genetics, 25, 1-14.

Boyd, R. & Richerson, P.J. (1985). Culture and the evolutionary process. Chicago: University of Chicago Press.

Brunswick, E. (1955). In defense of probabalistic functionalism: A reply. Psychological Review, 62, 236-242.

Campbell, D.T. (1957). Factors relevant to the validity of experiments in social settings. Psychological Bulletin, 54, 297-312.

Carroll, J.B. (1983). Studying individual differences in cognitive abilities: Implications for cross-cultural studies. In S.H. Irvine, & J.W. Berry, (Eds.) Human assessment and cultural factors. New York: Plenum.

Cavalli-Sforza, L.L. & Feldman, M. (1981). Cultural transmission and evolution: A quantitative approach. Princeton: Princeton University Press.

Cole, M., Gay, J., Glick, J. & Sharp, D. (1971). The cultural context of learning and thinking. New York: Basic Books.

Cole, M. & Scribner, S. (1974). Culture and thought. New York: Wiley.

Cronbach, L.J. & Drenth, P. (Eds.) (1972). Mental tests and cultural adaptation. The Hague: Mouton

Dawson, J.L.M. (1966). Kwashiorkor, gynacomastia and feminization processes. Journal of Tropical Medicine and Hygiene, 67, 87-98.

Ferguson, G. (1954). On learning and human ability. Canadian Journal of Psychology, 8, 95-112.

Ferguson, G. (1956). On transfer and the abilities of man. Canadian Journal of Psychology, 10, 121-131.

Frijda, N. & Jahoda, G. (1976). On the scope and methods of cross-cultural psychology. International Journal of Psychology, 1, 110-127.

Gladwin, T. (1970). East is a big bird: Navigation and logic on Puluwat atoll. Cambridge: Harvard University Press.

Goldstein, K. & Backman, S. (1978). Cognitive style: Five
    approaches and relevant research. New York: Wiley.

Goodenough, F. (1936). The measurement of mental functions in
    primitive groups. American Anthropologist, 38, 1-11.

Herskovits, M.J. (1948). Man and his works. New York: Knopf.

Hutchins, E. (1980). Culture and inference: A Trobriand case
    study. Cambridge: Harvard University Press.

Irvine, S.H. (1979). The place for factor analysis in
    cross-cultural methodology and its contribution to cognitive
    theory. In L. Eckensberger, Y. Poortinga & W. Lonner (Eds.)
    Cross-cultural contributions to psychology. Amsterdam: Swets
    and Zeitlinger.

Irvine, S.H. (1983. Testing in Africa and America: the search for
    routes. In S.H. Irvine & J.W. Berry (Eds.) Human assessment
    and cultural factors. New York: Plenum.

Irvine, S.H. & Carroll, W.I. (1980). Testing and assessment across
    cultures: Issues in methodology and theory. In H.C. Triandis
    and J.W. Berry (Eds.) Handbook of cross-cultural psychology,
    Vol. 2, Methodology. Boston: Allyn and Bacon.

Jahoda, G. (1982). Psychology and anthropology: A psychological
    perspective. London: Academic Press.

Klineberg, Otto (1980). Historical perspectives: Cross-cultural
    psychology before 1960. In H.C. Triandis and W.W. Lamberg
    (Eds.) Handbook of cross-cultural psychology, Vol. 1,
    Perspectives. Boston: Allyn & Bacon.

Levi-Strauss, C. (1962/1966). The savage mind. London: Weidenfeld
    and Nicholson.

Levy-Bruhl, L. (1910/1926). How natives think. London: Allen and
    Unwin.

Lonner, W.J. (1980). The search for psychological universals. In
    H.C. Triandis & W.W. Lambert (Eds.) Handbook of
    cross-cultural psychology, Vol. 1, Perspectives. Boston:
    Allyn and Bacon.

Motte, E. (1979). Therapeutique chez les Pygmees Aka de Mongoumba.
    In S. Bahuchet (Ed.) Pygmees de Centrafrique. Paris: SELAF.

Poortinga, Y. (1983). Psychometric approaches to intergroup
    comparison: The problem of equivalence. In S.H. Irvine &
    J.W. Berry (Eds.) Human assessment and cultural factors. New
    York: Plenum.

Preiswerk, R.& Perrot, D. (1978). Ethnocentrism and history. New
    York: NOK Publishers.

Rogoff, B. (1981). Schooling and the development of cognitive
    skills. In H.C. Triandis & A. Heron (Eds.) Handbook of
    cross-cultural psychology, Vol. 4, Development. Boston: Allyn
    and Bacon.

Samuda, R. (1983). Cross-cultural testing within a multicultural
    society. In S.H. Irvine & J.W. Berry (Eds.) Human assessment
    and cultural factors. New York: Plenum.

Scribner, S. & Cole, M. (1973). Cognitive consequences of formal
    and informal education. Science, 182, 553-559.

Segall, M., Campbell, D.T. & Herskovits, M.J. (1966). The
    influence of culture on visual perception. Indianapolis:
    Bobbs-Merrill.

Sumner, W.G. (1908). Folkways. New York:

Thompson, W.R. (1980). Cross-cultural uses of biological data and
    perspectives. In H.C. Traindis & W.W. Lambert (Eds.)
    Handbook of cross-cultural psychology, Vol. 1, Perspectives.
    Boston: Allyn and Bacon.

Vernon, P.E. (1969). Intelligence and cultural environment.
    London: Methuen.

Whiting, B.B. (1976). The problem of the packaged variable. In K.
    Riegel & J. Meachan (Eds.) The developing individual in a
    changing world. The Hague: Mouton.

Witkin, H.A. & Berry, J.W. (1975). Psychological differentiation
    in cross-cultural perspective. Journal of Cross-cultural
    psychology, 6, 4-87.

Witkin, H.A., Dyk, R.B., Faterson, H.F., Goodenough, D.R. & Karp,
    S. (1962). Psychological differentiation. New York: Wiley.

Witkin, H.A. & Goodenough, D.R. (1981). Cognitive styles: Essence
    and origins. New York: International Universities Press.

Wober,   M. (1969). Distinguishing   centri-cultural   from cross-cultural tests and research. Perceptual and Motor Skills, 28, 488.

Wundt, W. (1916). Elements of folk psychology. London: Allen and Unwin.

CHAPTER 11

PERFORMANCE, MOTIVATION AND ANXIETY: THE CONSTRUCT OF
"EFFORT" FROM A CONTROL THEORY PERSPECTIVE

MICHAEL E. HYLAND

Plymouth Polytechnic

INTRODUCTION

The testing of ability has been an important part of psychology
from the early days of psychology (as will be evident from reading
previous chapters in this book). This is not accidental. Ability
testing has important practical implications for people working in
a number of environments. Ability testing is part of the
important exercise of selecting people who are suitable for
certain sorts of task, that is, people who perform well on certain
skills relevant to activities in the "real world".

However, it is very easy on reading this book to lose sight of the
fact that ability is just one factor which affects performance.
Vroom (1964, p. 203) suggests that performance is determined by
ability and motivation, and he expresses this by the formula:

Performance = f(ability x motivation)

The importance of motivation to performance is recognised in many
practical contexts. For example, it is an adage amongst teachers
that a pupil's performance reflects (a) his intelligence and (b)
something which is loosely called "the teacher's estimate." This
second factor relates to all those personality/motivational
characteristics which determine whether and how the pupil applies
him/herself to work. Every educator knows that there are some
students who are bright but lazy, and some who are less able but
industrious.

So, if we accept that the practical objective of ability testing
is to predict performance in real life settings, then it is also
important to know how motivational factors can affect
performance. Motivation is a very broad area of theory and

research, and in this chapter I shall focus on just one aspect of motivation: The construct of effort. First, I will examine the effort-performance relationship in terms of traditional accounts of motivation. Second, I will show how control theory provides a new approach to the effort-performance relationship.

HISTORICAL OVERVIEW

A useful starting point for modern motivation theory is a book by Murray (1938) entitled Personality. Murray suggested that there were some thirty or so different needs which were shared by all individuals and which gave rise to goal directed behaviour. Murray suggested that needs were aroused by specific features of the environment, which he labelled "environmental presses". By "press" Murray meant some description of the environment in goal-opportunity terms and he used this word specifically to distance himself from the word "stimulus" which was used by the associationist movement current amongst neobehaviourists. Individuals differ in the arousability of needs in the presence of environmental presses. For example, an individual high in the need for achievement is an individual whose achievement need is easily aroused in achievement oriented contexts.

Murray used this differential arousability of motives in two quite distinct ways. First, the arousability of a motive can be used to explain the proportion of time people spend in different goal oriented activities. For example, individuals with an easily aroused need for achievement will spend more time engaged in achievement oriented activity than individuals with a less easily aroused need for achievement. Arousability of motives thus provides a motivational description of personality in terms of choice behaviour.

Second, the arousability of a motive is one factor determining what Murray called the intensity of goal seeking behaviour, with the assumption that intensity improves performance. The effect of environmental press is to arouse a need, and the aroused level of need, or motivation level, explains the intensity of goal striving. To the extent that intensity of goal striving corresponds to effort, motivation level explains effort.

Murray's ideas and particularly the need for achievement became the basis of later motivational research. Here I shall briefly mention only two strands in this research, Atkinson's motivational theory (Atkinson, 1957, 1981; Atkinson & Birch, 1973) and Weiner's (Weiner, 1980; Weiner & Kukla, 1970) attributional reformulation of motivation theory.

Atkinson's Motivational Theory

Empirical studies by Atkinson and his colleagues (reviewed in Atkinson & Birch, 1978) established that the motive for achievement was too crude a construct to explain achievement-oriented behaviour. Instead, two different achievement needs were distinguished, the need for success and the need to avoid failure. Atkinson (1957) assumed that the need for success and fear of failure motives were additive in their effect on achievement behaviour. Consequently, the important difference was between subjects high in need for success and low in fear of failure, and those low in need for success and high in fear of failure. The former or success-oriented subjects were defined as high in "resultant achievement tendency" (which is the difference between the need for success and fear of failure) , whereas the latter, or failure-oriented subjects were defined as low in resultant achievement tendency.

Atkinson (1957) proposed a mathematical model of achievement behaviour which allowed the calculation of motivation level under different conditions of expectancy of success. The details of the theory need not concern us here, but it provided predictions about choice preference for achievement tasks of varying levels of difficulty. According to the theory, success-oriented individuals should prefer moderately difficult tasks (i.e., with a probability of success of about .5), whereas subjects low in resultant achievement tendency should prefer tasks which are either very easy or very difficult. Empirical research supported these claims.

Murray's original formulation also suggested that motivation level should correspond to the intensity of behaviour. Following on from this idea, Atkinson suggested that performance should improve with motivation level. However, very high levels of motivation are associated with performance deficits, and so Atkinson suggested a curvilinear relationship between motivation and performance (Atkinson, 1974). Atkinson did not commit himself to a mechanism responsible for performance deficits associated with high levels of motivation, but he did explore the possibility that it was related to high levels of arousal.

In summary, Atkinson's theory follows the pattern set down by Murray where the construct explaining the intensity of goal oriented activity is the same as that explaining choice of goal. Within limits, you try hard to do the things which you like.

Weiner's Attributional Reformulation of Achievement Motivation

Weiner's theory (Weiner, 1980; Weiner & Kukla, 1970) is based on
the assumption that people choose tasks which have some
combination of (a) high expectancy of success and (b) positive
affective consequence of success. Put colloquially, people choose
tasks where the likely result is something nice happening.

Individual differences in choice of different tasks are explained
in terms of individual differences in attributional style.
Attributional style is a description of the way people
characteristically attribute causes to events. Some sorts of
attributional style are conducive to people engaging in
achievement behaviour whereas other sorts of attributional style
are not. For example, people who attribute the cause of failure
to some external factor (such as bad luck) are more likely to
persist in a situation of failure than individuals who attribute
their failure internally (for example, to their own stupidity).
Thus, a student's own perceptions of his or her ability will
affect subsequent choice behaviour and subsequent opportunity to
succeed. To the extent that persistence is an indicator of effort
(but see Weiner, 1983) the theory also explains effort and hence
performance.

In many ways the predictions of Weiner's theory are similar to the
predictions of Atkinson's. Indeed, Atkinson's distinction between
success-oriented and failure-oriented people correlates with the
attributional style dimensions proposed by Weiner. Weiner and
Atkinson are consistent with the approach taken by Murray (1938)
where the construct explaining choice is used as the basis for an
explanation of effort or performance.

Neither type of theory, however, spells out in any detail how
effort actually affects performance. This particular area of
concern has been the focus of some recent accounts within the
motivational framework.

CONTROL THEORY

Effort

Humphreys and Revelle (1984, p. 158) define "effort" as the
"motivational state commonly understood to mean trying hard or
being involved in a task." They go on to distinguish on-task
effort, which is the effort put into a particular task, from
off-task effort, which is the effort being invested in non-task
activities.

Humphreys and Revelle suggest that the motivational construct of effort can affect performance through a mechanism called **allocation**, a mechanism based on an assumption about human cognition taken from Navon and Gopher (1979, p. 233)

"The human system is probably not a single-channel mechanism but rather a complicated system with many units, channels, and facilities. Each may have its own capacity (which is, roughly, the limit on the amount of information that can be stored, transmitted, or processed by the channel at a unit of time). Each specific capacity can be shared by several concurrent processes; thus it constitutes a distributable resource."

The basis of Humphreys and Revelle's theory is that effort can alter the allocation of processing capacity between the different channels. For example, in a multi-task situation, the individual can allocate more resources to one task than to another.

Humphreys and Revelle suggest also that allocation can affect performance on a single task in three different ways. (a) First, the subject can trade off one component of the task against another. For example, speed can be traded against accuracy. (b) Second, the subject can trade off allocation of resources between the experimenter-defined task and a subject-defined task (such as day-dreaming). I believe this to be an important aspect of allocation, and I shall develop it further within a control theory framework. Note meanwhile that the experimenter-defined task corresponds to on-task effort whereas the subject-defined task corresponds to off-task effort. (c) Third, there may be a "cost" of allocation, so that when allocation is high, additional allocation produces little or no improvement in performance.

In addition, Humphreys and Revelle suggest that the **availability** of processing capacity can be increased through a second motivational construct of arousal. I shall, however, restrict my discussion to a consideration of effort and its effect on cognitive processing capacity.

Overview of Control Theory

The basic unit of control theory is the negative feedback loop (see figure 1). A **reference criterion** is compared with a **perceptual input** and the difference or **detected error** generates behaviour which reduces the detected error.

The negative feedback loop is familiar to many psychologists in the form of a homeostatic device. However, there are three ways

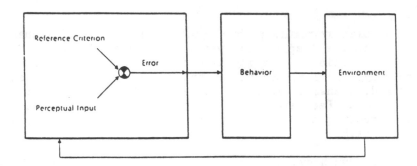

Figure 1   Components which make up a negative feedback
           loop are shown. The reference criterion and
           perceptual input are compared, and the difference
           generates behavior. The relationship between
           level or error and intensity of behavior is called
           error sensitivity.

in which control theory differs from what is normally understood
by homeostasis. First, in homeostasis the reference criterion or
"set point" is fixed; in control theory the reference criterion
can vary over time. In control theory, the reference criterion
represents the system's "goal" and goals can change from moment to
moment (Ashby, 1952; Boden, 1972; Powers, 1973, 1978; Wiener,
1948).

The second difference is that in homeostasis it is normal to use
only one feedback loop. In control theory, control loops are
arranged hierarchically (Carver & Scheier, 1981, 1982; Powers,
1973) so that the detected error for a high level loop causes
reference criteria at lower level loops to activate (see figure
2). That is, high level control loops reduce detected error by
activating control loops at lower levels which then produce
appropriate behaviour.

This hierarchical organization of control loops can be
conceptualized as the relation between goals which are ends in

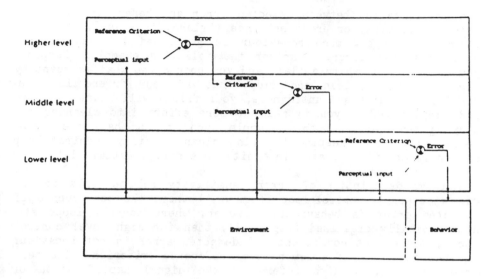

Figure 2 An illustration of how three control loops may be
related in a hierarchy of control loops.
Reproduced with permission from Hyland (in press),
Copyright APA.

themselves and goals which are means to ends. In order to achieve
ends, it is often necessary to set up subgoals, or means. The
subgoals act "in the service of" the higher level goals. For
example, a high level goal such as positive self-esteem can be
attained by setting up a lower level goal, such as passing exams,
which itself can be achieved though a yet lower level goal, such
as spending time revising for exams.

There is a third way in which control theory differs from a common
sense understanding of homeostasis. In control theory, the signal
amplification round the control loop plays an important role in how
the loop functions (Porter, 1969; Ogata, 1970). Amplification
between the detected error in one loop and either a reference
criterion in a lower loop or behaviour (see figure 1) is relevant

to, though not identical with, the construct of effort.

The amplification between detected error and behaviour is called error sensitivity or error salience (Hyland, in press). That is, it represents how much behaviour is generated to counteract a given detected error. Consider the following example. Suppose you and a friend share a flat, and you both agree what is meant by the flat being clean and tidy. But if your friend is more sensitive to dirt and untidyness, your friend will start cleaning and tidying before you do and put more effort into cleaning and tidying than you. In this example, your friend has more error sensitivity on a 'keeping the flat clean and tidy' control loop and so reacts with greater intensity to a dirty, untidy flat.

The above description of error sensitivity relates only to the case of a single control loop (figure 1) where the consequence of detected error is behaviour. However, where control loops are hierarchically organized (figure 2), then for high level control loops, the direct consequence of detected error is not behaviour but the causation of a lower level reference criterion. The term error sensitivity also refers to the signal amplification of detected error in one of these higher level control loops. Here, error sensitivity affects the type of goal which is caused at the lower level. So, error sensitivity either describes the amount of behaviour generated to counteract a particular level of detected error, or it describes the type of causal relationship between a higher and lower level control loop.

According to the control theory of motivation, effort is defined as a function of error sensitivity and detected error. The relation is likely to be multiplicative and so we can write

Effort = f(detected error x error sensitivity)

The above formula describes a process which is distal to that described by Humphreys and Revelle (1984) in their information processing account of effort. Putting the two processes together implies the following: Error sensitivity and detected error are determinants of effort, and effort is a determinant of allocation of cognitive processing capacity. Therefore, error sensitivity and detected error can both affect the allocation of cognitive processing capacity.

As noted above, the hierarchical organization of control loops (or hierarchical organization of goals) is an important feature of the control theory account of motivation. Carver and Scheier (1982) suggest that error sensitivity (or, as they call it, salience) can differ at different levels of the hierarchy. Moreover, the error sensitivity at any one level may vary between people and can be changed by situational manipulations. For example, error sensitivity for self-referent control loops can be increased by self-focussing manipulations such as the presence of a mirror, the presence of an audience, or the presence of a video camera. Thus, error sensitivity is a variable at each level in the hierarchy.

The theoretical consequence of there being different amounts of error sensitivity at different levels in the hierarchy is that there will be different types of effort corresponding to the different levels in the control hierarchy. If there are different types of effort, then they may have different functions in the allocation of cognitive processing capacity.

On-task and Higher-than-task Effort

As described above, Humphreys and Revelle distinguish on-task effort from off-task effort. Their arguments are based on the assumption that on-task effort is relevant to performance but off-task effort is not. The hierarchical organization of control loops leads to the conclusion that at least some aspects of off-task effort may be relevant to performance on a task, specifically, effort relating to control loops which are higher in the hierarchy but causally related to the task control loop.

In control theory terms, on-task effort is defined as the effort relating to the control loop whose reference criterion is to carry out the task. That is, on-task effort is a function of error sensitivity and detected error of the task control loop.

Higher-than-task effort is defined as the effort relating to control loops which are placed higher in the control hierarchy than the task loop. There may be many higher-than-task control loops and so there will be more than one type of higher-than-task effort.

Let us suppose that performance on a task is determined by the allocation of cognitive processing capacity to that task. Allocation of cognitive processing, I have already said, is determined by effort which is determined, in part, by error sensitivity. Therefore, performance is determined directly only by on-task effort. However, higher-than-task effort may affect on-task effort and thereby have an indirect effect on performance. I suggest that there are two ways in which higher-than-task effort can affect performance; one way improves performance and the other way results in a performance decrement.

First, error sensitivity at a higher level control loop can have a causal relationship with error sensitivity at a lower level control loop. Such causal relations of error sensitivity, I assume, occur in instances only where there is a causal relation between the detected   of a higher level loop and the reference criterion of the lower level loop. (Note that the causal relation between high level and low level error sensitivity may be only one determinant of low level error sensitivity.)

This causal relation between error sensitivities of different loops corresponds to a common sense understanding of the relationship between goals which are ends and goals which are means to ends. If one student has high error sensitivity to success on an exam, then that student should work harder for the exam than a student who finds the exam less salient. In general, we would expect that the more salient the end goal, the more salient are the goals which are means to the end.

A second way in which higher-than-task error sensitivity can affect performance obtains if we assume that there is a <u>limited error sensitivity capacity</u>. That is, there is a limited amount of error sensitivity which can be distributed amongst the different control loops. If there is a limited errror sensitivity capacity, then an increase in higher-than-task error sensitivity may "rob" error sensitivity from the task control loop. As a result, high levels of higher-than-task error sensitivity may actually produce a performance decrement as cognitive processing capacity is being taken from the task to some non-task activity. To take our previous example of a student studying for an exam, if the student is overly concerned about the exam he may spend so much time thinking about doing well on the exam that he spends little time revising.

A demonstration that higher-than-task error sensitivity can either improve or harm performance is provided by Hyland, Coates, Curtis, Hancocks, Mean and Ogden (1986) who used an attentional focus manipulation (presence or absence of mirror) and a motivational manipulation (ego-aroused and ego-relaxed instructions).

In the absence of a mirror, the ego-relaxed instruction reduced on-task error sensitivity relative to the ego-arousing instruction. However, the ego-arousing instruction did not appear to increase higher-than-task effort (a result confirmed in two experiments).

In the presence of a mirror, on the other hand, there was a substantial increase in higher-than-task error sensitivity for ego-arousing instruction when compared with ego-relaxed instructions. Moreover, there was now less on-task error sensitivity for the ego-arousing instructions when compared with the ego-relaxed instructions.

This interaction between attentional and motivational manipulations can be interpreted as follows. Under most circumstances, the ego-arousing instruction "this task measures ability and intelligence" has a causal effect on on-task error sensitivity. Consequently people devote more effort to the task and, thus, do better when given motivating instructions.

However, when the ego-arousing instruction occurs in the presence of a self-focussing stimulus, then there is a much greater increase in higher-than-task error sensitivity. The consequence of this increase in higher-than-task error sensitivity is that error sensitivity is deflected from the task control loop. Colloquially put, the subject is so concerned about the ego-arousing instructions that less resource allocation is made to the task.

These findings and this theory explain what to many students is a paradox in the literature. On the one hand achievement motivation theory suggests that external rewards increase task performance; data confirm these predictions. On the other hand, intrinsic motivation theory suggests that external rewards decrease task performance; data confirms these predictions..

According to the control theory view, external rewards (e.g., money, praise, status) are usually at a higher-than-task level. Whether the external rewards result in performance improvement or decrement depends on (a) whether the higher-than-task error sensitivity has a causal effect on the on-task sensitivity thereby improving performance, or (b) whether the higher-than-task sensitivity subtracts error sensitivity from the task loop due to limited error sensitivity capacity.

Anxiety

That test anxiety produces test performance decrements is well known. The most common way of explaining these decrements is in terms of the construct of arousal (e.g., Humphreys & Revelle, 1984). That is, high level of arousal disrupts performance. Control theory offers an alternative though not incompatible explanation for such performance decrements in terms of the construct of effort.

According to the control theory viewpoint, high levels of anxiety are associated with high levels of error sensitivity on higher-than-task goals. That is, the high test anxious subject is particularly concerned about the outcome of the test. This concern, or error sensitivity, about the outcome of the test means that processing capacity is deflected from the test itself. According to this viewpoint, amelioration of the debilitating effect of anxiety could be brought about by attentional focus, and by encouraging the subject to think less about the consequences of the test.

To the extent that test anxiety is a generic (i.e., not situation specific) form of reacting to test situations, high anxiety subjects may be characterised as individuals who are particularly prone to performance decrements arising out of a limited error sensitivity capacity. The reason for this style of reacting to test situations may be due to one or a combination of two factors. It may be that high anxiety subjects are prone to greater amounts of error sensitivity in high level loops compared with low anxiety subjects. Alternatively, it may be that high anxiety subjects have a smaller total error sensitivity capacity for distribution amongst the different loops when compared with low anxiety subjects. Whatever mechanism is involved, it would seem that the distribution of error sensitivity within the hierarchy is a useful starting point for further research.

CONCLUSIONS

Control theory provides a significant departure from the traditional motivational account of effort. In traditional motivation theory, the construct determining choice is the same as that determining intensity. That is, for any action, there is just one quantitative person variable used to explain the intensity of that action.

In control theory, on the other hand, the introduction of a causal hierarchy of goals means that there are many different sorts of effort which may be relevant to the intensity of a particular action. By including an information processsing approach within the control theory framework, I have shown that the allocation of processing resources to a particular task is a direct consequence of effort to engage in that task. But that effort to engage in a task is also a function of the effort to achieve goals higher in the hierarchy. That is, where a task is a means to some end (most tasks are means to ends) then the concern and effort put into seeking the end goal can either improve or harm performance on the task.

The message of traditional motivation theory as well as that from Humphreys and Revelle (1984) is that 'trying hard' improves performance. According to control theory, however, trying hard is not enough. It is necessary to try hard in the right way. Performance is enhanced only when people try hard to complete the task itself, and trying hard to achieve the end goal for which the task is a means can under some circumstances reduce the effort put into the task itself.

I said at the beginning of this chapter that performance is a function of ability and motivation. The relationship can now be made more precise. Tests of ability reflect processing capacity. The motivational characteristics of the person (as expressed by error sensitivity within the hierarchy) can affect on-task processing capacity and thereby affect that person's <u>measured</u> ability. Thus, whatever the person's "true" ability, motivational characteristics contaminate measures of ability by altering performance on these measures in ways which are situation specific.

REFERENCES

Ashby, W. R. (1952). <u>Design for a brain</u>. New York: Wiley.

Atkinson, J. W. (1957). Motivational determinants of risk-taking behavior. <u>Psychological Review</u>, <u>64</u>, 359-372.

Atkinson, J. W. (1981). Studying personality in the context of an advanced motivational psychology. <u>American Psychologist</u>, <u>36</u>, 117-128.

Atkinson J. W., & Birch, D. (1978). <u>An introduction to motivation</u>. Princeton: Van Nostrand.

Boden, M. A. (1972) <u>Purposive explanation in psychology</u>. Cambridge, MS: Harvard University Press.

Carver, C. S., & Scheier, M. F. (1981). <u>Attention and self-regulation: A control-theory approach to human behavior</u>. New York: Springer Verlag.

Carver, C. S., & Scheier, M. F. (1982). Control theory: A useful conceptual framework for personality-social, clinical, and health psychology. <u>Psychological Bulletin</u>, <u>92</u>, 111-135.

Humphreys, M. S., & Revelle, W. (1984). Personality, motivation, and performance: A theory of the relationship between individual differences and information processing. <u>Psychological Review</u>, <u>91</u>, 153-184.

Hyland, M. E. (in press). A control theory interpretation of psychological mechanisms of depression: Comparison and integration of several theories. <u>Psychological Bulletin</u>.

Hyland, M. E., Coates D. S., Curtis. C., Hancocks, M., Mean, L., & Ogden, C. (1986). <u>Control theory of motivation: Theory and some data</u>. Unpublished manuscript. Plymouth Polytechnic,

Plymouth, UK.

Murray, H. A. (1938). Explorations in personality. New York: Oxford University Press.

Navon, D., & Gopher, D. (1979). On the economy of the human processing system. Psychological Review, 86, 214-255.

Ogata, K. (1970). Modern control engineering. Englewood Cliffs, NJ: Prentice Hall.

Porter, A. (1969). Cybernetics simplified. London: English Universities Press.

Powers, W. T. (1973). Behavior: The control of perception. Chicago: Aldine.

Powers, W. T. (1978). Quantitative analysis of purposive systems. Psychological Review, 85, 417-435.

Vroom, V. H. (1964). Work and motivation. New York: Wiley.

Weiner, B. (1980). Human motivation. New York: Holt.

Weiner, B. (1983). Some methodological pitfalls in attributional research. Journal of Educational Psychology, 75, 530-543.

Weiner, B., & Kukla, A. (1970) An attributional analysis of achievement motivation. Journal of Personality and Social Psychology, 15, 1-20.

Wiener, N. (1948). Cybernetics: Control and communication in the animal and the machine. Cambridge, MS: M.I.T. Press.

AUTHORS INDEX